ENGLISH PRISON LAW

Sally Ramage

iUniverse, Inc.
New York   Bloomington

ENGLISH PRISON LAW

Copyright © 2009 by Sally Ramage.

*All rights reserved. No part of this book may be used
or reproduced by any means, graphic, electronic, or
mechanical, including photocopying, recording, taping or
by any information storage retrieval system without the
written permission of the publisher except in the case of brief
quotations embodied in critical articles and reviews.*

*The information, ideas, and suggestions in this book are not intended
to render legal advice. Before following any suggestions contained
in this book, you should consult your personal attorney. Neither
the author nor the publisher shall be liable or responsible for any
loss or damage allegedly arising as a consequence of your use
or application of any information or suggestions in this book.*

iUniverse books may be ordered through booksellers or by contacting:

*iUniverse
1663 Liberty Drive
Bloomington, IN 47403
www.iuniverse.com
1-800-Authors (1-800-288-4677)*

*Because of the dynamic nature of the Internet, any Web addresses or
links contained in this book may have changed since publication and may
no longer be valid. The views expressed in this work are solely those of
the author and do not necessarily reflect the views of the publisher, and
the publisher hereby disclaims any responsibility for them.*

*ISBN: 978-1-4401-4917-7 (sc)
ISBN: 978-1-4401-4918-4 (ebk)*

Printed in the United States of America

iUniverse rev. date: 6/5/2009

Contents

CHAPTER 1 - LEGISLATION 1
CHAPTER 2 - STATUTORY AGENCIES AND NON-
             GOVERNMENTAL ORGANISATIONS...43
CHAPTER 3 - PUBLIC FUNDING 63
CHAPTER 4 - THE ADULT PRISON SYSTEM 73
CHAPTER 5 - JUVENILES IN PRISON 95
CHAPTER 6 - CATEGORISATION, ALLOCATION AND
             SENTENCE PLANNING...............123
CHAPTER 7 - RIGHTS AND PRIVILEGES 157
CHAPTER 8 - REQUESTS AND COMPLAINTS........223
CHAPTER 9 - PRISON DISCIPLINE 241
CHAPTER 10 - CRIMINAL OFFENCES COMMITTED IN
              PRISON 279
BIBLIOGRAPHY 299
APPENDIX 1 - THE PRISON (AMENDMENT) RULES
              2008.............................301
APPENDIX 2 - CONSOLIDATED PRISON RULES 1999 305
APPENDIX 3 - PRISON ACT 1952 367
APPENDIX 4 - THE PRISON (AMENDMENT) RULES
              2005 421
APPENDIX 5 – PRISON DISCIPLINE MANUAL
              1995.............................427
APPENDIX 6 - LIST OF UNITED KINGDOM PRISONS 587
INDEX –ENGLISH PRISON LAW....................599

ENGLISH PRISON LAW
TABLE OF STATUTES, CONVENTIONS AND REGULATIONS

Table of Statutes	
Access to Justice Act 1999	63, 67, 381
Asylum Act 2008	1
Criminal Justice Acts	1, 14
Children and Young Persons Act 1933	66, 109, 503
Crime and Disorder Act 1998	14, 46, 152, 263, 340, 402, 408, 409, 559, 572
Crime (Sentences) Act 1997	1, 14, 46, 66, 67, 144, 218, 284, 311
Criminal Justice Act 1988	100, 110, 389, 390, 399, 402, 403, 405
Criminal Justice Act 1991	36, 37, 67, 246, 306, 307, 311, 245, 346, 360 - 362, 372, 373, 375 - 381, 388, 403, 564, 566 - 567, 580 - 581
Criminal Justice Act 2003	1, 29 - 31, 110, 148 - 149, 151, 153, 195, 306, 382, 408 - 409, 412,
Criminal Justice and Court Services Act 2000	154, 376 - 377, 390, 402 - 403, 405
Criminal Justice and Immigration Act 2008	119, 402
Criminal Justice and Public Order Act 1994	37, 254, 284, 379, 387 - 388, 390, 402 - 403, 405
Extradition Act 2003	154
Human Rights Act 1998	1, 34, 39, 161, 169, 196, 208, 323
Knives Act 1997	100
Police Act 1997	27, 28

Police and Criminal Evidence Act 1984	15, 23, 284, 379, 391, 535
Police and Criminal Evidence (Northern Ireland) Order 1989	27
Powers of Criminal Courts (Sentencing) Act 2000	14, 30 -31, 139,155, 231, 346, 376 - 377, 400 - 403, 408 - 410, 513, 564, 574
Prevention of Crime Act 1953	100
Prison Act 1952	1 - 2, 16, 21, 37, 43, 133, 141, 154, 157, 160, 241, 254, 293, 295, 301, 303, 306, 313, 318, 321, 335 - 337, 351, 354, 367, 387, 399, 407, 410, 421 - 422, 557
Public Order Act 1994	37, 100, 254, 284, 373, 377, 379, 387 - 388, 390, 402 - 403, 405
Regulation of Investigatory Powers Act 2000	1, 26
Repatriation of Prisoners Act 1984	145
Terrorism Acts	21, 25
Violent Crime Reduction Act 2006	100 - 101
Regulations, etc.	
Civil Legal Aid (Assessment of Resources) Regulations 1989	69
Contracted Out Prisons) Order 1992	37
Criminal Defence Service (General) (No 2) Regulations 2001	66 - 67
Prison (Amendment) (No.2) Rules 2000	26, 305
Prison Rules 1964	2, 16, 274, 362 - 365

Prison Rules 1999	1-2, 10, 26, 44, 123, 141, 157, 160, 166, 176 - 177, 179 - 180, 185, 187 - 188, 192, 194, 208, 210 -211, 214, 242, 244, 246, 255, 262, 265, 268 - 269, 301 - 302, 305, 406, 422, 427, 557
Prison Service Orders and Instructions	2, 10, 15
Remand in Custody (Effect of Concurrent and Consecutive Sentences of Imprisonment) Rules 2005	153
Security Manual, Prison Service Order 1000	25
Conventions	
Convention on the Rights of the Child	53, 60 - 62, 111, 115, 171
European Convention on Human Rights	8, 34, 84, 137, 158 - 159, 162 - 163, 165, 171, 195, 197, 202, 217, 220, 287, 544

Table of Cases

A-G Reference (No 71 of 2002) [2002] EWCA Crim 2217, [2003] 1 Cr App Rep (S) 99
108

Becker v Home Office [1972] 2 QB 407
9, 218

Brooks v Home Office, Times, 17 Feb 1999
36

Campbell v United Kingdom [1992] 15 EHRR 137, Series A no 48
16, 186

Campbell and Fell v United Kingdom [1985] 7 EHRR 165
44

Cannan v Secretary of State for the Home Department [2003] (unreported)
25

Claire F v Secretary of State for the Home Department [2004] EWHC 111 (Fam)
143

Council of Civil Service Unions v Minister for the Civil Service [1985] AC 374
44

Ferguson v Home Office [1977] Times, 8 October
45

H v Home Office [1992] Independent, 6 May
45

Henson and Magraw [2007] EWCA Crim 1308
33

Hogg [2007] EWCA Crim 1357
31

Hollies [1995] 16 Cr App R (S) 463
32

Ibrahim Karagozlu v Commissioner of Police of the Metropolis [2006] EWCA Civ 1691
91

Knight v Home Office [1990] 3 All ER 237
45

Konrad Pilecki v Poland [2008] UKHL 7
154

Leech v Deputy Governor of Parkhurst Prison [1988] AC 533
3, 5, 44, 546

Levin (on appeal from a Divisional Court of the Queen's Bench Division), 19 June 1997
14

McCotter v UK, (EC Commission decision 18632/21), 15 EHRR CD 98
129

National Westminster Plc v Rabobank Nederland [2006] EWHC 2332 (Comm)
22

O'Reilly v Mackman [1982] 3 All ER 1124
44

R (on the application of K) v Parole Board [2006] EWHC 2413 (Admin), CO/6826/2006
109

R v Accrington Youth Court, ex p Flood [1998] 1 WLR 156
112

R v Allery [1993] 14 Cr App Rep (S) 699
103

R v Appleton [1999] 2 Cr App Rep (S) 289
106

R v Asquith Youth [1994] 16 Cr App Rep (S) 453
104

R v Broom [1993] 14 Cr App Rep (S) 677
103

R v Bull [2000] 2 Cr App Rep (S) 195
106

R v Burton [1993] 14 Cr App Rep(S) 716
103

R v Busby [2000] 1 Cr App Rep (S) 279
107

R v Bryne [1995] 2 Cr App Rep (S) 34
104

R v Catterall [1993] 14 Cr App Rep (S) 724
103

R v Chesterton [1997] 2 Cr App Rep (S) 297
105

R v Central Criminal Court, ex p. Francis & Francis (a firm) [1989] A.C. 346, HL
23

R v Cowap [2000] 1 Cr App Rep (S) 284
107

R v Cunningham [2006] EWCA Crim 1092, (2007) 1 Cr App R(S) 14
30

R v David Francis Beiber, CA (Crim Div) 23 July 2008
120

R v Deputy Governor of Parkhurst Prison, ex p Hague, Weldon v Home Office [1992] 1 AC 58
9, 17, 45

R v Derby Magistrates' Court, ex p. B [1996] A.C. 487, HL
24

R v Donovan [2004] EWCA Crim 1327, [2005] 1 Cr App R(S) 16
108

R v E [2004] EXCA Crim. 1243
26

R v Edwards [2006] EWCA Crim 3362, (2007) 1 Cr App R(S) 106
30

R v Ellingham [1999] 2 Cr App Rep (S) 243
106

R v Fairburn [1998] 2 Cr App Rep (S) 4
106

R v Farrar [2006] EWCA Crim 3261, [2007] Crim LR 308
30

R v Governor of HM Prison Latchmere House, ex p Jarvis (20 July 1999, unreported)
132, 134

R v Governor of HM Prison Maidstone, ex p Peries [1997], Times, 30 July
132

R v Governor of Whitemoor Prison ex parte Main [1998] 2 All ER 491, [1998] EMLR 431
21

R v Gregory and Mills [1969] 2 All ER 174, [1969] 1 WLR 455, 133 JP 731
152

R v Hamilton [2000] 1 Cr App Rep (S) 91
107

R v Harvey [1997] 2 Cr App Rep (S) 306
105

R v Home Secretary ex parte Doody [1994] 1 AC 531 at p 561A, [1993] 3 All ER 92, [1993] 3 WLR 154
17, 110, 137

R v Howe [2006] EWCA Crim 3147, [2007] 2 Cr App Rep (S) 47, [2007] Crim LR 395.
149

R v Johnson [2006] EWCA Crim 2486
30

R v Jones [1994] 15 Cr App Rep (S) 856
104

R v Kamber Azam [2007] EWCA Crim 3376
149

R v Kingham [1994] 16 Cr App Rep (S) 399
104

R v Kitching [2000] 2 Cr App Rep (S) 194
107

R v Lang [2005] EWCA Crim 2864, [2006] 2 Cr App R (S) 3, [2006] 1 WLR 2509, [2006] 2 All ER 410
30

R v Mapp [2002] EWCA Crim 3182; [2003] 2 Cr App Rep (S)
108

R v McLaughlin [1994] 16 Cr App Rep (S) 357
104

R v McLellan [1993] 15 Cr App Rep (S) 351
103

R v Netts [1997] 2 Cr App Rep (S) 117
105

R v Nolan [1992] 13 Cr App Rep (S) 144
103

R v Prince [1996] 1 Cr App Rep (S) 335
105

R v R [1994] 4 All ER 260
23

R v Remi Akinyeme [2007] EWCA Crim 3290
149

R v S, 30 August 2007
30

R v Secretary of State for the Home Department, ex p Briggs, Green and Hargreaves [1996]
COD 168, upheld by the CA [1991] 1 All ER 397
18

R v Skidmore [1996] 1 Cr App Rep (S) 15
104

R v Secretary of State for the Home Department, ex p A [2000] 1 All ER 651
548

R v Secretary of State for the Home Department, ex p Daly [2001] UKHL 26
136, 161, 175, 178, 207

R v Secretary of State for the Home Department, ex p Doody [1994] 1 AC 531
17, 110, 137

R v Secretary of State for the Home Department, ex p Leech [1994] QB 198
17, 161

R v Secretary of State for the Home Department, ex p Simms and O'Brien [1999] 3 All ER 400
17, 161, 174, 178

R v Secretary of State for the Home Department, ex p Duggan [1994] 3 All ER 277
44, 137

R v Secretary of State for the Home Department, ex p O'Dhuibhir [1997] COD 315 CA
178

R v Secretary of State for the Home Department, ex p Quaquah [2000] 03 LS Gaz R 36
40

R v Secretary of State for the Home Office, ex parte Mellor [2001] 3 WLR 533
35, 175, 194, 232

R v Secretary of State, ex p Quinn [1999] LS Gaz, 26 May
134

R v Slater [1998] 2 Cr App Rep (S) 415
106

R v Spalding [1995] 16 Cr App Rep (S) 803
104

R v Steven John Hostettler [2008] EWCA Crim 292
151

R v Steventon [1992] 13 Cr App Rep (S) 127
103

R v Thomas [2004] EWCA Crim 3092; [2005] 2 Cr App Rep (S) 10
108

R v Thompson [1997] 2 Cr App Rep (S) 223
105

R v Wakeman [1999] 1 Cr App Rep (S) 222
105

R v Yildrim Balci and Dakarayi Mtifi [2008]
189

R v Young [2000] 2 Cr App Rep (S) 248
108

R (Bloggs) v Home Secretary [2003] EWCA 686
89

R (Burgess) v Secretary of State for the Home Department [2001] 1 WLR 93
128

R (DT) v Home Secretary [2004] EWHC 13 Admin
112

R (Howard League) v Home Secretary [2002] EWHC 2497 (Admin)
117

R (Lord) v Secretary of State for the Home Department [2003] EWHC 2073 (Admin)
138

R (McLeod) v HM Prison Service [2002] EWHC 290 (Admin)
290

R (Morgan Grenfell & Co. Ltd) v Special Comm. of Income Tax [2003] 1 A.C. 563, HL
25

R (P and Q) v Secretary of State for the Home Department [2001] 1 WLR 2002
87, 142

R (SP) v Home Secretary [2004] EWHC 1418 Admin
110, 118

R (Sunder) v Home Secretary [2001] EWCA Civ 1157
138

R (Williams) v Secretary of State for the Home Department [2002] EWCA Civ 498
138

Raymond v Honey [1983] 1 AC 1
9, 16

Rebecca Noone v Governor of HMP Drake Hall and Secretary of State for Justice [2008] EWHC 207 (Admin)
153

Roelofs v Netherlands, 1 July 1992, No 1943592
137

Ross [1994], Times, 9 June, CA
136

Stone v Clerk to the Justices Plymouth Magistrates' Court [2006] EWCA Civ 1691
34

Three Rivers D.C. v. Governor and Company of the Bank of England (No.5) [2003] Q.B. 1556, CA (Civ. Div.)
22-23

Van der Ven v The Netherlands, Case No. 50901/99, 4 February 2003
137

Watkins v Secretary of State for the Home Department [2006] UKHL 17, (2006) 2 AC 395
92

CHAPTER 1- LEGISLATION

1.1. STATUTES

There is little primary legislation that is directly concerned with prisons and imprisonment. Although various Acts of Parliament do, from time to time, contain important provisions for prisoners (e.g. the Criminal Justice Acts and the Crime (Sentences) Act 1997, the Human Rights Act 1998, Regulation of Investigatory Powers Act 2000, the Criminal Justice Act 2003, Asylum Act 2008), the only piece of legislation that deals solely with the prison estate is the Prison Act 1952. Thus, there is no primary source that contains an exhaustive explanation of the rights to which those in custody are entitled and the facilities and privileges, which they can expect. In order to gain an understanding of prison law and to be able to provide effective advice to prisoners, it is necessary to refer to the three different levels of source materials. The starting point is necessarily the Prison Act 1952 as, whilst it does not actually contain detailed information on the day-to-day life of prisoners, it is the primary source of decision-making power and sets the context for the management of the prison estate. There follows a discussion of the Prison Rules 1999 and 2005, the relevance of changes introduced by the Criminal Justice Act 2003 and then the status of policy documents and their impact on case-law. Finally, the legal status of 'contracted out' prisons is explored.

1.2. THE PRISON RULES

Much of the Prison Act 1952 is concerned with establishing very basic principles, such as who has legal responsibility for managing prisons and implementing appropriate rules, rather than with the actual rules and regulations themselves. More detail is supplied in the Prison Rules 1999 (which consolidated and updated the Prison Rules 1964) issued pursuant to the Act. In many instances, these Rules will refer to discretionary powers, which are to be exercised by either a prison governor or the Secretary of State. It is the discretionary powers that often get to the root of prison life and will in many cases be the matters on which prisoners will need advice and representation. The manner in which these powers are to be exercised and the details of how the Rules are to be implemented are contained in a series of policy documents issued by Prison Service Headquarters. These are currently in the form of Prison Service Orders and Instructions ('PSOs' and 'PSIs') and have previously been issued as Standing Orders, Circular Instructions, and Advice and Instructions to Governors.

1.3.1. OVERVIEW OF THE PRISON ACT 1952

The main purpose of the Prison Act ('The Act') is not to make detailed provision for the running and management of prisons but to vest authority in those who do hold this power. The corollary of this is that the Act actually says very little about prisoners' rights and the obligations of the state to those in their custody.

The Home Secretary is charged with the duty of '*general superintendence*' over prisons and is empowered to 'make contracts and do acts necessary for the maintenance of prisons and the maintenance of prisoners' (s 4(1)). Section 4(2) goes on to require the Home Secretary to ensure compliance with the Act and the Prison Rules. There is no explanation as to the manner in which compliance should be guaranteed. The section does, however, establish that the Home Secretary is the person ultimately responsible for the manner in which prisons are run and for ensuring that the duties and obligations of the state towards those in custody are properly fulfilled.

1.3.2. ROLE OF THE SECRETARY OF STATE

Section 4(2) is important in that it places clear responsibility on the Secretary of State, and it is the Secretary of State who is accountable for any failure to properly comply with this duty. Conversely, this power was often invoked when defending actions brought by prisoners against prison governors' administrative and disciplinary decisions. The argument advanced was that s 4 amounted to an ouster clause whereby the power to ensure compliance with the Prison Act and Rules was vested solely in the Secretary of State and it was only if he failed to fulfil this obligation that judicial review could be sought. It was not until 1988 that this interpretation was finally laid to rest following the decision of the House of Lords in *Leech v Deputy Governor of Parkhurst Prison* [1988] AC 533, a challenge to a governor's use of formal disciplinary powers. Lord Bridge perceived this argument as an attempt to undermine the jurisdiction of the court in a manner, which was incompatible with the principles of administrative law.

1.3.3. ROLE OF THE CHIEF INSPECTOR AND INDEPENDENT MONITORING BOARDS

The Act goes on to make provision for two '*watchdog*' bodies: the Chief Inspector of Prisons (s.5A) and the Independent Monitoring Boards (formerly Boards of Visitors) (ss.6 to 9). The Chief Inspector is under a duty to inspect prisons with particular regard to conditions and the treatment of prisoners, to report to the Home Secretary and to submit an annual report that must be laid before Parliament.

The Chief Inspector's powers are limited to reporting and it is not possible for binding recommendations to be made. The Chief Inspector will prepare reports on individual prisons throughout each year and will provide a general commentary on prison conditions in the Annual Report. The individual inspections are often highly critical and, despite the fact that they have no formal legal status, they can provide important evidence of particular conditions and policies in a given prison at a particular time.

1.3.4. ROLE OF THE HOME SECRETARY

The Home Secretary is also required to appoint an Independent Monitoring Board for each prison and for these Boards to be allowed to visit the prison and to hear complaints. The rights of free access to any part of the prison at any time, and to see any prisoner at any time are protected by the Act (s. 6(3)). Originally, Boards also had a disciplinary function in that they acted as adjudicators for disciplinary charges that were considered too serious to be heard by the governor. This power was abolished in 1992 following the Woolf Report, when it was considered that their watchdog role was incompatible with that of upholding prison discipline. The confidence of prisoners in the Boards to hear and act upon their complaints was seriously undermined by the fact that the same Boards would also be hearing charges against them and awarding punishments of forfeiture of remission. There was a general assumption amongst prisoners that the Boards were too willing to accept the authority of prison staff without question and that it was not possible to have a fair hearing at adjudications. This situation was exacerbated by the fact that the Boards would be hearing the more serious charges and awarding significant punishments. Following the removal of this power, all adjudications are now carried out by prison governors or independent adjudicators.

1.3.5. ROLE OF THE BOARDS

The Boards do still have one key role to play in the maintenance of discipline in prisons. When a governor authorises the segregation of a prisoner, this can only be done for a period of up to three days in the first instance. Following that three-day period, any decisions to continue segregation must be authorised by the IMB (Prison Rule 45). The fact that there is a direct supervisory body for decisions of this nature is important in principle, but in practice, there will be very few occasions when the Board will not accept the governor's decision in such cases.

1.3.6. ROLE OF PRISON OFFICERS

Prisons are required to have a governor, a chaplain, a medical officer and such other officers as 'may be necessary' (s.7). The statutory obligation for prisons to have a governor is of importance in assessing the nature of the governor's duties. These powers are distinguishable from those exercised by the Home Secretary and are defined in detail in the Prison Rules. Whilst it is true that the extent of the governor's powers is decided by the Home Secretary, the fact remains that it is the governor who is obliged to carry them out. The governor is empowered, with leave of the Secretary of State, to delegate the powers conferred directly on him/her to another officer at the prison (Prison Rule 81).

1.3.7. ROLE OF THE GOVERNORS

It was this point that was considered fundamental in *Leech v Deputy Governor of Parkhurst Prison* [1988] AC 533, when Lord Bridge held that governors' powers were amenable to judicial review in their own right. The court observed that whilst the Prison Rules established the offences against discipline and the punitive powers available, there was no provision for the Home Secretary to direct the governor on how to adjudicate a particular charge, or as to what punishment should be awarded.

1.4. Prisoners' location and accommodation

Section 12(1) states that prisoners may lawfully be confined in any prison, whether on remand or convicted and s.12(2) states that prisoners may be transferred from one prison to another. This power is expressed to rest with the Home Secretary but can be delegated to the governor. For practical purposes, the importance of s.12(1) is that it establishes that a prisoner has no right to be held in any particular prison. It is a common misunderstanding of prisoners and their families that there is a duty for them to be located in a prison convenient for visits. No such right exists and whilst a whole range of factors are to be taken into account when determining location, any challenges to the allocation decisions can only be made within the confines of administrative law

1.5. Governor's liability

Whilst in custody, the governor has responsibility (and liability) to each prisoner in his/her prison. This stems from the fact that the governor of the prison is deemed the legal custodian (s.13).

1.6. Prison Fit for purpose

The accommodation available must be certified as being fit for its purpose by the Home Secretary (s.14). The certificate requires inspection of size, heating, lighting, ventilation and fittings. Certification is carried out by officers appointed by the Home Secretary and there is no independent system of certification. The requirements and standards that are to be met are not specified and consequently may be changed depending upon prevailing conditions and the changing requirements of each prison. The Chief Inspector of Prisons will frequently express opinions as to the living conditions in particular prisons and, if standards were to fall below a certain level, the conditions of detention may give rise to a cause of action in domestic law or under the European Convention on Human Rights. In general, however, the section is only important in terms of litigation if a prisoner is detained in accommodation that has not been certified.

1.7.1. DISCIPLINARY AND MISCELLANEOUS PROVISIONS FOR PRISONERS

The Act contains a number of further provisions that are of some importance to prisoners, although the powers created are expanded in far detail in the Prison Rules and policy documents. These sections are as follows:

(1) Section 16A provides the authority for mandatory drugs testing and gives all prison officers the power, on the authority of the governor, to require prisoners to provide a sample of urine (or other non-intimate sample) for the purposes of testing for the presence of controlled drugs.

(2) Section 25 creates the power to authorise the early release of prisoners. The actual schemes that are put into place for remission of sentence is made under the powers created by s.47.

(3) Section 28 creates the power to discharge prisoners temporarily on the grounds of ill health.

(4) Section 30 allows discharge payments to be made to prisoners.

(5) Sections 39 to 42 create offences of assisting prisoners to escape from a prison, bringing alcohol, tobacco or other unauthorised articles into a prison and require notices to be displayed outside of prisons recording these provisions.

(6) Section 49 states that any time spent unlawfully at large during the currency of a sentence does not count towards that sentence.

1.7.2. SECRETARY OF STATE'S POWER TO MAKE PRISON RULES

Perhaps the most important section of the Act is s.47, which allows the Secretary of State:

'to make rules and regulations for the management of prisons, remand centres, detention centres and youth custody centres, and for the classification, treatment, employment, discipline and control of persons required to be detained therein.'

These rules must be made by statutory instrument, as in Statutory Instrument 2005, No.869. At s.47(2), there is an important safeguard to any rules that are made:

'Rules made under this section shall make provision for ensuring that a person who is charged with any offence under the rules shall be given a proper opportunity of presenting his case.'

This section emphasises the duty that exists in common law and under the European Convention on Human Rights to ensure that the rules must follow the principles of natural justice in the administration of prison discipline.

1.7.3. THE LEGAL STATUS OF PRISON RULES

The Prison Rules were most recently fully updated in April 1999 when they were redrafted to take account of the 25 amendments that had been introduced since 1964. Further ad hoc amendments have occurred in August 2002 (to take account of the new disciplinary regime) and in April 2005. They contain a mixture of provisions and refer to both general policies, such as the purpose of imprisonment (Prison Rule 3), and to more specific obligations and duties that are imposed upon the Prison Service. A large number of the Rules confer discretionary powers which are supplemented by documents issued explaining how discretion should be exercised. The remaining rules of importance to prisoners are concerned with the formal disciplinary system that must be adopted. The Prison Rules are not, in themselves, justiciable and were not intended to be so.

In 1972, Lord Denning commented that:

'If the courts were to entertain actions by disgruntled prisoners, the governor's life would be made intolerable. The discipline of the prison would be undermined. The Prison Rules are regulatory

directions only. Even if they are not observed, they do not give rise to a cause of action.' (Becker v Home Office [1972] 2 QB 407).
Lord Wilberforce clarified the situation slightly ten years later when he stated that prisoners retain all civil rights that are not taken away, either expressly or by the fact of their imprisonment. However, he went on to say that, as there is no contractual relationship between prisoners and the prison authorities, there must be reliance on the normal laws of tort in order for an action to be brought (*Raymond v Honey* [1983] 1 AC1). It was not for another ten years that the present position was fully established by the courts. In *R v Deputy Governor of Parkhurst Prison, ex p Hague, Weldon v Home Office* [1992] 1 AC 58, the House of Lords examined the public and private law rights of prisoners. Although the decision contains dissenting opinion, the Lords agreed that the Prison Rules do not give rise to any specific private law rights. As a result, it is apparent that the Rules are in fact justiciable to the extent that they are amenable to judicial supervision through judicial review. In the private law sphere, whilst prisoners retain the right to bring ordinary private law actions in cases of negligence, there is no right to bring an action for breach of statutory duty in respect of non-compliance with the Rules. Thus, the manner in which the Rules are implemented is amenable to judicial review, and breaches of them may be evidence in support of negligence actions, but the Rules do not confer any additional right to litigate. However, practitioners do need to be familiar with the Rules in their context as the source of authority from which more detailed regulations are made.

1.7.4. CONSISTENCY THROUGH RULES

The varying nature of the Rules and the fact that they contain a mixture of policy statements, obligations to prisoners and discretionary powers leads to much confusion as to their status. Broadly speaking, the Rules will set out general powers and duties, which are to be implemented in the running of prisons. In order to ensure consistency and fairness throughout the system, a series of documents are issued described as Prison Service Orders and Instructions. These documents are designed to fill in the details of the everyday management of prisons and will deal with everything from the fees to be paid to visiting dentists to the facilities that are to be allowed to prisoners, and to the arrangements for mandatory drugs testing.

1.7.5. THE KEY PROVISIONS OF PRISON RULES 1999, AS AMENDED

The Prison Rules 1999 are reproduced in the appendices and each Rule is discussed in the following individual chapters in context. Broadly, they are divided in the following manner:

Part I

Rules 1–11	Statement of intent, maintaining good order and discipline, classification of prisoners, privileges, temporary release, women prisoners and requests and complaints. Rule 2 amended in 2005 to provide for adjudication before a District or Deputy District Judge.
Rules 13–19	Religion
Rules 20–22	Medical attention
Rules 23–31	Physical welfare and work
Rules 32–33	Education and library
Rules 34–39	Prisoner communications (letters and visits)
Rules 40–44	Property, removal and records. Rule 42 amended in 2005 to prohibit a copy of any personal record being given to a person not authorised to receive it.
Rules 45–50	Special control, supervision, restraints (including segregation) and drug taking. New Rules 50B inserted in 2005 regarding provision of urine sample for drug testing.

Rules 51–61	Offences against discipline. Rule 51 amended in 2005. New Rule 52A inserted in 2005 to provide defence to intoxication. New Rule 55B inserted in 2005 to provide for review of punishment.
Part II	
Rules 62–69	Officers of prisons. Amendment to Rule 61 in 2005.
Part III	
Rules 70–73	Persons having access to prisons. Amendment to Rule 71 in 2005.
Part IV	
Rules 74–80	Boards of Visitors
Rules 81–85	Supplemental

The Rules have been described as falling into five distinct categories. These consist of general policy objectives, rules of a discretionary nature (normally concerned with privileges that may be afforded), rules concerning administration and rules of specific individual protection. Whilst those Rules concerned with discretionary rights such as temporary release (Prison Rule 6), or correspondence (Prison Rule 34) are of importance, the classes of prisoners who are allowed to benefit from these privileges and the manner in which that discretion should be exercised are set out in the policy documents issued by Prison Service Headquarters. Many of the Rules therefore do little other than to give a general power or create a general right that is then subject to policy and interpretation as to how it should be implemented.

1.7.6. KEY RULES OF THE DISCIPLINARY PRISON SYSTEM

The key Rules are those that are concerned with the formal and informal disciplinary system. In effect, this means Prison Rules 45 to 61, which are concerned with maintaining good order and discipline and the formal disciplinary code that is applied to prisoners. These provide a list of the offences against prison discipline (Prison Rule 51), the procedure to be followed when laying a charge (Prison Rules 53 to 54) and the punishments that can be awarded to prisoners once a charge has been proven (Rules 55 to 60). Where new offences are to be created or the powers of punishment are to be extended, these must be incorporated into the Prison Rules by statutory instrument. There have been many calls for a revision of the Prison Rules and for a national set of minimum standards to be approved and incorporated. In the Woolf Report, it was suggested that a set of accredited standards should be prepared and that prisons should be certified once they had reached these standards. Despite support for a minimum set of standards from many diverse bodies and individuals, the official approach to the Prison Rules remains one of minor revision when considered necessary, rather than a complete overhaul.

1.7.7. THE NOMS OFFENDER MANAGEMENT MODEL 2006

The Carter Review of the prison system in 2003 was undertaken within the context of dramatic increases in the use of prison and probation. Carter identified three key reasons for this:
An increase in the number of offenders caught and sentenced;
An increase in the overall seriousness of the crimes brought together; and
An increase in the overall seriousness of the sentence severity for specific offences.

However, the increase in prison sentences may relate to the fact that the UK has had 30 criminal justice statutes created since 1997, with 3,000 new criminal offences. Carter's Report recommended the creation of a national offender management service (NOMS) to separate the case management of offenders from the provision of prison places, treatment services or community programmes. Carter said that there needs to be a clearly defined and simplified hierarchy of command. After the 2003 Carter Report, there was the 2004 government report titled *'Reducing Crime- Changing Lives.'* Thereafter the government published eleven documents relating to prisoners between 2004 and 2006.

The National Offender Management Service (NOMS) was introduced in 2004 with the former Director General of the Prison Service, Martin Narey appointed as Chief Executive. The concept behind NOMS was to ensure a greater degree of co-ordination between the agencies responsible for people convicted of crime, both in terms of the practical aspects of managing the prisons and probation services and in terms of integrating policy work, sentencing policy and financial considerations.

In 2005, NOMS model stated that offender management should span the whole of any single period of engagement, including periods of remand. The model describes an evidence-based, offender-focussed approach to work with individual offenders. Arrangements are also being made to allow sharing of information between Prisons and Probation Areas through a new mechanism *'Data share'* which will give *"read only"* access to core case information to support offender management. *Delius*, a case management system in use by some Probation Areas, was implemented where existing case management systems are in urgent need of replacement. This was hoped to improve the OASys (the offender assessment system) which became a single national system across probation and prisons.

1.8.1. THE CRIMINAL JUSTICE ACTS AND OTHER LEGISLATION

Other legislation which is of direct relevance to prison issues are the various Criminal Justice Acts issued since 1967, the Crime (Sentences) Act 1997, the Crime and Disorder Act 1998 and the Powers of Criminal Courts (Sentencing) Act 2000. These Acts contain major legislative provisions for parole, early and compassionate release, recall of prisoners on licence and computation of sentences (e.g.: CJA 1991, ss 34 to 48; C(S) A 1997, ss 28 to32). The Criminal Justice Acts continue to introduce changes in the regulations affecting sentence calculation and licence conditions on a regular basis. The legislation amends and updates old legislation.

1.8.2. HEARSAY EVIDENCE FROM OTHER PRISONERS

Hearsay evidence is allowed against prisoners extradited to other countries as in the case *In Re Levin, (on appeal from a Divisional Court of the Queen's Bench Division)* on 19 June 1997, when the House of Lords said that the accomplice's evidence is a matter, which can be raised at trial, when the facts about his position can be fully ascertained. Computer printout evidence is admissible at common law and its weight is a matter for the tribunal of fact. Today, section 114 of the CJA 2003 is now available to both parties and it can provide the defence with opportunities to admit evidence that would previously have been inadmissible.

In *R v McLean,* the court was concerned with a fatal stabbing alleged to have been committed by McLean and three others as part of a joint enterprise. One of the co-accused made a statement to a prison officer that one of the other accused had stabbed the victim and put the blame for the offence on him. The Crown did not seek to adduce this evidence as it was informally obtained and would have been excluded. However, McLean and the defendant who had made the statement applied to have it admitted. The trial judge refused to admit it. In the Court of Appeal it was conceded that the statement was not a confession and could not be adduced under s 76A of the Police and Criminal Evidence Act 1984. What McLean wanted in evidence was not a confession by a co-accused but an out-of-court accusation by one of the co-accused against another. The decision of the trial judge was challenged on the basis that he had approached the question on a false basis. This position had now been changed by the CJA 2003. If such evidence is admitted in the interests of justice, the jury is by law entitled to consider it, to determine its weight and to make up its mind whether it can, or cannot, rely on it. It becomes evidence in the case generally and not just against one defendant. In the event, the Court of Appeal ordered a retrial.

1.8.3. CHANGED CRIMINAL PROCEDURE RULES

The fifth amendment of the Criminal Procedure Rules came into force in April 2008. This introduced new rules about case management, anti-social behaviour orders ('ASBO') and serious crime prevention orders ('SCPO'). To complete the committee's comprehensive revision and simplification of the procedure rules for the Court of Appeal, there are new rules about appeals from that court to the House of Lords. All of these changes came into force on 7 April 2008.

1.9.1. PRISON SERVICE ORDERS AND OTHER POLICY GUIDANCE

The mechanics of the everyday running of prisons are largely determined by the guidance documents issued by the Prison Service referred to as Prison Service Orders and Instructions (PSOs and PSIs- formerly Standing Orders, Advice and Instructions to Governors and, before then, Circular Instructions). PSOs are a statement of policy and the exercise of discretion in a particular area. They have been issued to cover topics such as reception to prison, discharge, temporary release, communications and calculation of sentences. Prison Service Instructions and Orders are also issued on an ad hoc basis to amend or update information in the older Standing Orders or Instructions. They are also the mechanism by which changes to policy, such as the revisions to home leave criteria or new Prison Rules are communicated to prison governors. These directives, although often made under powers contained in the Prison Rules, do not have any statutory authority. An example of the relationship between statute, statutory instrument and these directives may be found by examining the changes made to Standing Order 5B which deals with prisoners' correspondence.

1.9.2. STANDING ORDER 5 B: PRISONERS' CORRESPONDENCE

Standing Order 5B has been subject to a number of challenges both domestically and in international law. In *Raymond v Honey* [1983] 1 AC 1, it was found that prisoners were being denied the right to have unfettered access to a court, as letters being sent by a prisoner were being stopped in accordance with Standing Order 5B. Standing Order 5B had been issued, *inter alia*, to provide a code of working practice that complied with Prison Rule 37 and allowed privileged communications to be sent to certain classes of people in certain circumstances. It was held that neither the Prison Act 1952 nor the Prison Rules 1964 contained any provisions that would allow correspondence of this nature to be impeded. The result was that the Standing Order had to be amended to ensure that this right was protected.

In *Campbell v United Kingdom* [1992] 15 EHRR 137, Series A no 48, the European Court of Human Rights held that the right afforded to prisoners to privileged correspondence with lawyers was insufficient to comply with the Convention. This decision was then followed by *R v Secretary of State for the Home Department, ex p Leech* [1994] QB 198, which held that the right to unimpeded legal correspondence with solicitors was an integral component of the fundamental right of a prisoner's access to the courts. As a result, Prison Rule 37 (now Rule 39) was amended to allow privileged correspondence in a far wider variety of cases and an Instruction to Governors ('IG') was issued to remedy the defect. The Instruction to Governors declared the new policy and procedures that were to be adopted and these were eventually incorporated into Standing Order 5B.

In *R v Secretary of State for the Home Department, ex p Simms and O'Brien* [1999] 3 All ER 400, the House of Lords found that the application of a policy in Standing Order 5 banning all visits by journalists to prisoners was unlawful, even though the statutory provision under which the policy was formulated was lawful. Whilst it is established that these official prison documents are amenable to judicial review when they lead to unlawful administration, it is also arguable that they can establish explicit rights for, and obligations to, those in custody. This arises because they set out particular obligations that the Prison Service undertakes to prisoners. Therefore, if the Prison Service decides to adopt a particular procedure or policy in one of these documents and subsequently fails to follow its own procedures, these actions may be reviewable (see e.g. *R v Deputy Governor of Parkhurst Prison, ex p Hague, Weldon v Home Office* [1992] 1 AC 58).

It is lawful for the prison authorities to alter the nature of the rights and privileges that prisoners are entitled to during the currency of a prison sentence, providing that the correct procedures are followed. Since the decision of the House of Lords in *R v Secretary of State for the Home Department, ex p Doody* [1994] 1 AC 531, the Prison Service has been forced to adopt good administrative practice. An attempt to challenge changes in the policy to home leave based on legitimate expectation was dismissed by Kennedy LJ in the court's decision:

'So, Mr Beloff submits, that upon analysis, all that the applicants could legitimately expect was to have their application for home leave decided by reference to the criteria current at the time of the application. We think this is right. (see *R v Secretary of State for the Home Department, ex p Briggs, Green and Hargreaves* [1996] COD 168, a decision which upheld that in the case [1991] 1 All ER 397). The compromise of these two positions appears to be that 'rights' which do not appear in statute or the Prison Rules can be afforded to a prisoner by the Home Secretary voluntarily adopting a particular policy or procedure. If these rights concern the adoption of good administrative practice, then they acquire an independent status, which makes it more difficult for them to be subsequently removed. However, if they are concerned with expectations as to discretionary decisions or privileges, it is possible for them to be changed, providing that the proper procedures are followed and primary legislation is not infringed.

1.9.3. PRISON RULE 2: PRISONER COMMUNICATION

Prison Rule 2 of the 1999 Prison Rules defines "*communication*" as:

"*communication includes any written or drawn communication from a prisoner to any other person, whether intended to be transmitted by means of a postal service or not, and any communication from a prisoner to any other person transmitted by means of a telecommunications system*"

1.9.4.1. PRISON RULES 34 AND 35: PRISONER COMMUNICATION AND INTERCEPTION

Prison Rule 34 deals with communications generally and Prison Rule 35 deals with personal letters and visits. Prison Rules 35A and 35B deal with the bugbear of interception of communication of prisoners. Rules 35A and 35B are as follows:

"35A Interception of communications

(1) The Secretary of State may give directions to any governor concerning the interception in a prison of any communication by any prisoner or class of prisoners if the Secretary of State considers that the directions are

(a) necessary on grounds specified in paragraph (4) below; and

(b) proportionate to what is sought to be achieved.

(2) Subject to any directions given by the Secretary of State, the governor may make arrangements for any communication by a prisoner or class of prisoners to be intercepted in a prison by an officer or an employee of the prison authorised by the governor for the purposes of this rule (referred to in this rule as an "authorised employee") if he considers that the arrangements are—

(a) necessary on grounds specified in paragraph (4) below; and

(b) proportionate to what is sought to be achieved.

(3) Any communication by a prisoner may, during the course of its transmission in a prison, be terminated by an officer or an authorised employee if he considers that to terminate the communication is—

(a) necessary on grounds specified in paragraph (4) below; and

(b) proportionate to what is sought to be achieved by the termination.

(4) The grounds referred to in paragraphs (1) (a), (2) (a) and (3) (a) above are—

(a) the interests of national security;

(b) the prevention, detection, investigation or prosecution of crime;

(c) the interests of public safety;

(d) securing or maintaining prison security or good order and discipline in prison;

(e) the protection of health or morals; or

(f) the protection of the rights and freedoms of any person.

(5) Any reference to the grounds specified in paragraph *(4)* above in relation to the interception of a communication by means of a telecommunications system in a prison, or the disclosure or retention of intercepted material from such a communication, shall be taken to be a reference to those grounds with the omission of sub-paragraph *(f)*.

(6) For the purposes of this rule "interception"—

(a) in relation to a communication by means of a telecommunications system, means any action taken in relation to the system or its operation so as to make some or all of the contents of the communications available, while being transmitted, to a person other than the sender or intended recipient of the communication; and the contents of a communication are to be taken to be made available to a person while being transmitted where the contents of the communication, while being transmitted, are diverted or recorded so as to be available to a person subsequently; and

(b) in relation to any written or drawn communication, includes opening, reading, examining and copying the communication.

35B Permanent log of communications

(1) The governor may arrange for a permanent log to be kept of all communications by or to a prisoner.

(2) The log referred to in paragraph *(1)* above may include, in relation to a communication by means of a telecommunications system in a prison, a record of the destination, duration and cost of the communication and, in relation to any written or drawn communication, a record of the sender and addressee of the communication".

1.9.4.2. COMMUNICATION PRIVILEGES

There are several kinds of communication privileges, namely:
legal professional privilege;
journalist-source privilege;
marital privilege (which governs confidential communications between spouses);
doctor-patient privilege;
psychiatrist-patient privilege and

priest-penitent privilege.

Of these, only legal professional privilege is recognised in prison and even this has been constrained by the Terrorism Acts 2000 and 2006.

1.9.4.3. LEGAL PRIVILEGE

The hotly debated issue of legal professional privilege and hues of its interpretation began with the judgment in *R v Governor of Whitemoor Prison ex parte Main* [1998] 2 All ER 491, [1998] EMLR 431, when Kennedy LJ at page 505E, said:

"In my judgment legal professional privilege does attach to correspondence with legal advisers which is stored by a prisoner in his cell, and accordingly such correspondence is to be protected from any unnecessary interference by prison staff. Even if the correspondence is only inspected to see that it is what it purports to be that is likely to impair the free flow of communication between a convicted or remand prisoner on the other hand and his legal adviser on the other, and therefore it constitutes an impairment of the privilege. However, as Whitemoor and Parkhurst escapes demonstrated, it is essential to maintain security in closed prisons, and to that end s 47(1) of the Prison Act 1952 permits rules requiring that periodically, and without prior notice, cells, and everything therein be thoroughly searched. That necessarily involves examining correspondence so far as necessary to ensure that it is in truth bona fide correspondence between the prisoner and a legal adviser and does not conceal anything else."

Legal privilege should therefore be applied to Regulation 155, which states:

"Legal adviser of prisoner. A legal practitioner, or his clerk if duly authorised in writing to act for him, shall be allowed to communicate with a prisoner in custody at a station. Such communication shall take place within sight of but out of hearing of a member of the Force."

1.9.4.4. LEGAL PRIVILEGE APPLIES TO DOCUMENTS

In 2006, the English High Court decided that legal advice privilege protects confidential communications passing between lawyers and clients, but does not protect preparatory materials, even if they are created for the purpose of enabling lawyers to advise. Such preparatory materials are protected only if they are subject to litigation privilege. This means that if the preparatory documents were created for the dominant purpose of gathering evidence to use in pending or contemplated legal proceedings or for giving legal advice in relation to such proceedings, they might enjoy legal privilege. If litigation is not pending or contemplated, preparatory materials will not be privileged.

In the case of *National Westminster Plc v Rabobank Nederland* [2006] EWHC 2332 (Comm), the court was asked to consider whether the defendant could claim privilege over two categories of documents. The documents in question were: (i) two documents which were communications through the defendant's audit department, which had been disclosed in error and which the defendant sought to recover; and (ii) documents produced during the defendant's initial investigation into the events which are at the centre of the litigation. The court confirmed the state of the law following *Three Rivers District Council v Bank of England* (No 5) [2003] QB 1556 and (No 6) [2005] 1 AC 610, and decided that legal advice privilege could be claimed only for confidential documents passing between the client and its legal advisers for the purpose of giving or obtaining legal advice or assistance. The Court decided that such privilege does not apply to the "*sort of preparatory work which does not constitute communications between lawyer and client*".

1.9.4.5. LEGAL PRIVILEGE APPLIES TO REPORTS FROM URINE AND BLOOD TESTS

In *R v R* [1994] 4 All ER 260, the statutory definition of 'subject to legal privilege' in s 10 of the PACE 1984 Act applied to enable the defendant to object to the blood sample being produced in evidence or to oral evidence of opinion based on it, since the sample constituted an item 'made' in the general sense of 'brought into existence' for the purposes of legal proceedings. It followed that the appellant's sample of blood was an item 'subject to legal privilege' within s 10(1)(c) of the Act and that the appellant was entitled to object to its production or to opinion evidence based on it. This case would have bearing on Prison Rule 50B and tests for drugs in prisoners would not be subject to privilege in a case of criminal offence in a prison.

1.9.4.6. LEGAL PRIVILEGE APPLIES TO ORAL COMMUNICATIONS

Legal privilege applies to confidential written or oral communications between a professional legal adviser and his client, or any person representing the client, in connection with and in contemplation of, and for the purpose of legal proceedings (litigation privilege) or in connection with the giving of legal advice to the client (legal advice privilege). This formulation of legal privilege is based on section 10(1)(a) and(b) of the Police and Criminal Evidence Act 1984 which was intended to express the common law rule in *R v Central Criminal Court, ex p. Francis & Francis (a firm)*[1989] A.C. 346, HL (per Lord Goff at p. 396).

It is not necessary for a communication to have been received before privilege can be claimed. A document intended to be a communication between solicitor and client is privileged even it if is never communicated as in *Three Rivers D.C. v Governor and Company of the Bank of England (No.5)*[2003] Q.B. 1556, CA (Civ. Div.). This common law right to consult legal advisers without fear of the communication being revealed is a fundamental condition on which the administration of justice rests. Once established, no exception should be allowed to its absolute nature (see *R. v. Derby Magistrates' Court, ex p. B* [1996] A.C. 487, HL). Consultations with lawyers should take place in a manner which favours full and uninhibited disclosure (see *Campbell v. UK*, 15 E.H.R.R. 137, ECtHR).

1.9.4.7. OTHER COMMUNICATION PRIVILEGES NOT RECOGNISED IN PRISON

Most of the rules of evidence are designed to get at the truth. The rules of evidence exclude unreliable information from the consideration of the trier of fact. Privileges, however, are an exception. Privileges generally exclude reliable information in order to further a competing social policy.

This most well entrenched evidentiary privilege, which is applicable in every English jurisdiction, protects confidential communications between a lawyer and a client for the purpose of legal advice. The rationale of the lawyer-client privilege is that clients will not be candid with their lawyers if everything clients disclose to their lawyers can be used against them in court, and lawyers cannot give sound legal advice to their clients if clients are less than candid in their disclosures to their lawyers. Because this privilege facilitates full and candid discussion between the lawyer and the client, the privilege enhances the overall reliability of the legal process, even though it renders inadmissible some evidence that might be both relevant and reliable.

1.9.4.8. DEROGATION OF LEGAL PRIVILEGE BY TERRORISM ACTS

The right to legal privilege cannot be overridden by general or ambiguous statutory words. An intention to override must be expressly stated or appear by necessary implication (see *R (Morgan Grenfell & Co. Ltd) v Special Commissioner of Income Tax* [2003] 1 A.C. 563, HL). The Terrorism Acts are temporary provisions which over-ride but do not derogate the rights of a fair trial (which underpin the concept of legal professional privilege) in alleging a temporary state of emergency in the United Kingdom, which excuses such derogation.

1.9.4.9. PRISONERS MANUSCRIPTS

In *Cannan v Secretary of State for the Home Department and another* [2003], the decision at para 23, states:

"It is well established that the right of access to a court, the right of access to legal advice and the right to communicate confidentially with a legal adviser under the seal of legal professional privilege are three important rights which a prisoner continues to enjoy. To the extent to which procedures curtail or interfere with or fetter these rights then they can only do so if the procedures are appropriate, lawful and proportionate in the context of the need to maintain the security and safety of the prison and within the context of the need to maintain good and efficient management".

In *Cannan,* the issue was one of prisoner's communication via his notebook, which was regulated under Standing Order 4 of which, paragraph 40 states:

"*Disposal of completed notebooks etc.*

Prisoners may send out completed books, diaries or personal organisers, or any other art or written material that is not correspondence, unless they contain any material of the kind prohibited in general correspondence under Standing Order 5B."

In relation to the powers of the prison authorities, Security Manual, Prison Service Order 1000, paragraph 36.14 states:

"*In relation to Category A prisoners all correspondence, both incoming and outgoing (expect between a prisoner and his or her legal advisers . . .) must be read as a matter of routine in the following cases . . .".*

The decision in *Cannan* was that the Prison authorities have a right to read a manuscript of a prisoner.

1.10.1. COVERT INTERCEPTION OF PRISONERS' COMMUNICATIONS

Section 4 (4) of the Regulation of Investigatory Powers Act 2000 ('RIPA') provides that prisoners' communication can be intercepted under Prison Rules. The Prison Rules 1999, Rules 35A to 35D, inserted by the Prison (Amendment) (No.2) Rules 2000, apply. Similar provisions exist for Young Offender Institutions. A Protocol of the National Offenders Management Service (NOMS) details the procedure:

"Police investigators must contact the Prison Liaison Officer who will assess the feasibility of any planned operation. Written application must be made via the Police Advisors Section at NOMS Head Quarters and upon approval, police investigators will be given access to intercept products obtained under Prison Rules."

1.10.2. INTERCEPT IN PRISON PROCEDURE INSIDE PRISONS

Interception in prison is lawful under section4 (4) Regulation of Investigatory Powers Act ('RIPA'). Intercept products will be for police intelligence purposes. The subject of the interception must be the principal subject of the investigation. Prison Rules cannot override the RIPA. *Interception must not take place if the subject of interest is outside the prison and communicating with a prisoner.* However, if the speech of the party outside prison is not recorded, it does not amount to an interception as in the case of *R v E* [2004] EXCA Crim. 1243. Also, the action must be proportionate to what is sought to be achieved and must be in the interest of national security or public safety; or the prevention, investigation or prosecution of serious crime as defined in s. 81(3) of the Regulation of Investigatory Powers Act or for securing or maintaining prison security or good order and discipline in prison.

A warrant is needed to intercept the communication of a prisoner who is not the principal subject of the investigation

(s.5, RIPA) as for the interception of communication of a person outside prison with a prisoner.

In high security prisons, telephone calls of all prisoners are stored in the prison. Police investigators can apply for Production Orders under the Police and Criminal Evidence Act for the stored communications to be produced.

1.10.3. INTERCEPTION OF LEGALLY PRIVILEGED INFORMATION

The Police Act 1997 section 98 defines what is legally privileged information as does Article 12 Police and Criminal Evidence (Northern Ireland) Order 1989. Legal privilege is attached to the provision of professional legal advice by persons or organisations qualified to do so, but if such communication is made with the intent to furthering a criminal purpose, it is not protected by privilege.

RIPA does not prohibit such interception but it provides that additional criteria must be met, as per Paragraph 3.6 of the Interception of Communication Code of Practice, and RIPA provides that all Codes of Practice relating to RIPA are admissible in evidence in criminal and civil proceedings.

Paragraph 3.6 of this Code states:

"In general, any application for a warrant which is likely to result in the interception of legally privileged communications should include, in addition to the reasons why it is considered necessary for the interception to take place, an assessment of how likely it is that communications which are subject to legal privilege will be intercepted. In addition, it should state whether the purpose (or one of the purposes) of the interception is to obtain privileged communications. This assessment will be taken into account by the Secretary of State in deciding whether an interception is necessary under section 5(3) of the Act (RIPA) and whether it is proportionate. In such circumstances, the Secretary of State will be able to impose additional conditions such as regular reporting arrangements to be able to exercise his discretion on whether a

warrant should continue to be authorised. In those cases where communications which include legally privileged communications have been intercepted and retained, the matter should be reported to the Interception of Communications Commissioner during his inspections and the material be made available to him if requested".

1.10.4. INTERCEPTION OF INFORMATION CONTAINING CONFIDENTIAL PERSONAL INFORMATION

Confidential personal information is defined in section 99 of the Police Act 1997. Also, the RIPA does not prohibit such interception. Examples of such information are documents containing information about one's personal health, mental health, and counselling sessions undergone. A warrant is necessary to intercept such information and paragraph 3.9 of the Code outlines the steps to be taken:

Interception of Communications Code of Practice paras 3.9 to 3.11 state:

"*Similar consideration to that given to legally privileged communications must also be given to the interception of communications that involve confidential, personal information and confidential journalistic material. Confidential personal information is information held in confidence concerning an individual (whether living or dead) who can be identified from it and the material in question relates to his physical or mental health or spiritual counselling. Such information can include both oral and written communications. Such information as described above is held in confidence, if it is held subject to an express or implied undertaking to hold it in confidence, or it is subject to a restriction on disclosure or an obligation of confidentiality contained in existing legislation. For example, confidential, personal information might include consultations between a health professional and a patient, or information from a patient's medical records.*

Spiritual counselling is defined as conversations between an individual and a Minister of Religion acting in his official capacity, and where the individual being counselled is seeking or the Minister is imparting forgiveness, absolution or the resolution of conscience with the authority of the Devine Being(s) of their faith. Confidential journalistic material includes material acquired or created for the purposes of journalism and held subject to an undertaking to hold in confidence, as well as communications resulting in information being acquired for the purposes of journalism and held subject to an undertaking."

1.11.1. CRIMINAL JUSTICE ACT 2003- SERIOUS OFFENDERS

As regards sentencing and release, for serious offences Parliament decided on life imprisonment for public protection, subject to the possibility of release, or the indeterminate sentence, the IPP,(Imprisonment for Public Protection) with minimum term, and subject to release only when assessed to be no longer dangerous Criminal Justice Act 2003 ss 224 to 226 and 229 to 230.

Imprisonment for Public Protection ('IPP') has replaced the traditional discretionary life sentence. The IPP sentence is a sentence of imprisonment for an indeterminate period. The pre-conditions are that:

- the offender is aged 18 or over;
- he is convicted of a serious offence;
- the serious offence took place after 4 April 2005;
- the court is of the opinion that there is a significant risk to members of the public of serious harm of further violent or sex offences.

The IPP sentence must be life where so justified. The basis of the view need not necessarily be a previous conviction, although allegations of earlier reprehensible conduct should be established to the satisfaction of the judge (*R v Farrar* [2006] EWCA Crim 3261, [2007] Crim LR 308). Any disputed issue on fact should be resolved in the normal way(see the case of *R v Johnson* [2006] EWCA Crim 2486; *R v Cunningham* [2006] EWCA Crim 1092, [2007] 1 Cr App R(S) 14. The leading case is *R v Lang* [2005] EWCA Crim 2864, [2006] 2 Cr App R (S) 3, [2006] 1 WLR 2509, [2006] 2 All ER 410).

A serious offence is a specified violent offence or sex offence which carries a sentence of life or a determinate period of 10 years or more (see the case of *R v Edwards* [2006] EWCA Crim 3362, [2007] 1 Cr App R(S) 106). Evidence of a medical condition, e.g. in sexual assault and indecency, must be considered (see the case of *R v S*, 30 August 2007).

1.11.2. CRIMINAL JUSTICE ACT 2003 AND WHOLE-LIFE ORDERS

The Criminal Justice Act 2003, s.269, deals with mandatory life sentences for murder and provides:

"If the offender was 21 or over when he committed the offence and the court is of the opinion that, because of the seriousness of the offence, or of the combination of the offence and one or more offences associated with it, no order should be made under subsection (2), the court must order that the early release provisions are not to apply to the offender".

Schedule 21 of the Criminal Justice Act 2003 sets out examples of cases of murder in which a *"whole life order"* may be the appropriate starting point. The Powers of Criminal Courts (Sentencing) Act 2000, s.82A(4), includes a parallel provision in connection with life imprisonment for offences other than murder, whether imposed as discretionary life sentences or automatic life sentences for offences committed before April 4, 2005, or with statutory life sentences imposed under the Criminal Justice Act 2003, s.225, for *"serious specified offences"* punishable with life imprisonment committed on or after April 4, 2005. Section 82A states:

"If the offender was aged 21 or over when he committed the offence and the court is of the opinion that, because of the seriousness of the

offence or of the combination of the offence and one or more offences associated with it, no order should be made under subsection (2) above, the court shall order that, subject to subsection (5) below, the early release provisions shall not apply to the offender."

A whole life order may not be made in conjunction with a sentence of imprisonment for public protection: see s.82A (4A). The application of s.82A (4) to a pre-Criminal Justice Act 2003 life sentence imposed for rape and other sexual offences was considered in R v *Hogg* [2007] EWCA Crim 1357). The 64-year-old appellant was convicted of two offences of rape and one of indecency with a child; he pleaded guilty to other offences of indecency. The appellant was a frequent visitor to the house of an accomplice. The house had a large garden equipped with toys and other items which were used for the purpose of grooming young boys for sexual abuse. Video cameras were fitted inside the house to record the sexual activity. The appellant, who had 14 previous convictions for sexual offences and had been sentenced to terms of up to 10 years' imprisonment, admitted various offences in relation to two seven-year-old boys. He was sentenced to life imprisonment for rape and various concurrent sentences for the other offences, with no minimum period specified for the purposes of the Powers of Criminal Courts (Sentencing) Act 2000, s.82A. The sentencing judge observed that the appellant qualified for an automatic life sentence under the Powers of Criminal Courts (Sentencing) Act 2000, s.109, by virtue of a previous conviction for attempted rape, and in any event, he satisfied the criteria for a discretionary life sentence. The judge indicated that the appellant's long history of the child abuse was such that it was inconceivable that he would have ever be released into the community.

The appellant submitted that the factor which determined whether or not a minimum term should be set was the seriousness of the offence or offences, not the risk posed by the offender. The issues of risk were addressed by the Parole Board when it came to consider whether or not to release the offender at the expiration of the minimum term. This distinction had been made clear in R v *Hollies* [1995] 16 Cr.App.R. (S.) 463. It was submitted that, though the appellant's offences were serious, they did not come within that rare and exceptional category of seriousness justifying a whole life sentence. The Court accepted the appellant's submissions. The imposition of a life sentence was designed to protect the public from the offender, whereas the period specified under s.82A was meant to reflect the degree of punishment, retribution and deterrence appropriate for the offences. In determining whether or not to impose a minimum term, the court was required by s.82A to consider the seriousness of the offence or the combination of offences. Only in rare and exceptional cases would it be appropriate to impose no minimum term. Although the offences committed by the appellant were very grave, the Court agreed that they did not come within that rare and exceptional category. It seemed from the judge's remarks that in deciding not to impose a minimum term he had in mind primarily the need to protect other young boys from the appellant in the future. That was not the appropriate criterion to apply. The Court was satisfied that a minimum term should have been specified on the facts of the particular case. The appropriate notional determinate sentence was 20 years, with the result that the minimum term would be fixed at half of that period, 10 years, less 465 days spent in custody on remand.

A similar approach to the making of a whole life order in a murder case was adopted in *Henson and Magraw* [2007] EWCA Crim 1308. The second appellant was convicted of two counts of murder, both committed before December 18, 2003, and therefore subject to the transitional provisions of Sch.22 of the 2003 Act. The second appellant discovered that the victim of the first murder was a police informant who had provided the police with information about the appellant's activities. The victim was lured to Scotland and probably killed in 2001. His body had never been found. The victim of the second murder was an associate. He was lured from his home on the pretence of participating in a burglary, and abducted in a car. His body was found some weeks later buried in a shallow grave. The second appellant, who had numerous previous convictions for offences including armed robberies, was sentenced to life imprisonment with a whole life order. The sentencing judge observed that under the previous regime in cases of exceptional gravity the sentencing judge was entitled to say that the offence was so serious that no minimum term could be fixed. He commented that both murders had been planned, and in the case of the second victim, there was evidence of extreme and gratuitous violence. It was submitted in respect of the second appellant that it was wrong to say that a recommendation of *"no minimum period"* would have been justified under the earlier system. Rix L.J. said that in the case of the second appellant, a starting point of 30 years had been reached and exceeded. The Court accepted that it was not necessary on the grounds of seriousness to sentence the second appellant to a whole life order. The Court accepted that there were still worse crimes involving attacks on sections of the public at large, or crimes which would create a great and long lasting revulsion for members of the public. The sentencing judge erred in sentencing the second appellant on the basis that no minimum period could properly be set. The Court considered that such a recommendation would not have been made under the earlier regime. A minimum term of 35 years was substituted.

1.12.1. THE HUMAN RIGHTS ACT 1998

The Human Rights Act ('HRA') was enacted to give effect to the European Convention on Human Rights. The right to liberty is temporarily lost when a person is indicted and convicted and sent to prison. The natural consequence of being sent to prison is the diminishing of rights and freedoms with loss of benefits that are enjoyed outside prison. Freedom of movement and enjoyment of privacy are severely restricted and health and safety, as a consequence, are placed at risk due to the large numbers of prisoners in proximity, as a consequence of which, it is more likely that a communicable disease may be contracted. Stress and mental illness are more likely to occur due to the regimentation and depersonalisation of prison life. In *Turner v Safety* [1987], the court decided that prison regulation which impinges on the civil rights of a prisoner is nonetheless valid if it is reasonably related to *'legitimate penological interests.'*

1.12.2. RIGHT TO A FAIR TRIAL- ARTICLE 6 HRA

In the case *R (on the application of Stone) v Clerk to the Justices at Plymouth Magistrates' Court* [2007], a committal order was made in respect of a convicted drug trafficker's failure to comply with a confiscation order that had been made 13 years previously. The claimant (S) applied for judicial review of a decision of the defendant magistrates to make a committal order. S had been convicted of drug trafficking offences, sentenced to imprisonment and made the subject of a confiscation order. After S's release from prison, the prosecuting authorities sought to obtain the sums of money that remained payable under the confiscation order. The proceedings culminated in the court deciding to make the committal order, a decision that was taken 13 years after the confiscation order was originally made. This was a breach of her human right to a fair trial.

1.12.3. THE RIGHT TO FOUND A FAMILY- ARTICLE 8 HRA

In the case *R v Secretary of State for the Home Office, ex parte Mellor* [2001] 3 WLR 533, Gavin Mellor sought the court's permission to artificially inseminate his wife whilst he was still in prison. His submission was that prison restriction on conjugal rights was pragmatic. He submitted that giving a sample of his semen could not be seen as endangering the security of the prison and that artificial insemination provided a means of enforcing his right to found a family which was compatible with his imprisonment. His case was unsuccessful. Lord Phillips said:

"It is an explicit consequence of imprisonment that prisoners should not have the opportunity to beget children whilst serving their sentences until they come to a stage where they are allowed to take leave on temporary licence; serious and unjustified public concern would be likely if prisoners continued to have the opportunity to conceive children while serving sentences, that whilst many children are brought up by single parents, the evidence suggests that children do better when they have close contact with both parents...".

The denial of artificial insemination in this case did not prohibit this prisoner forever from founding a family, but only delayed him from doing so and such interference is permitted by Article 8(2) (dealing with proportionality) of the Convention.

Although this prisoner was unsuccessful in his application for artificial insemination, he was allowed to marry his wife in prison, in accordance with Article 12 of the Convention. However, conjugal visits are not permitted in English prisons and such denial constitutes an interference with his Article 8 rights of respect for one's family life.

In *X v Switzerland*, a case about the prohibition of conjugal visits in Switzerland's prisons, it was held that the prisoner's breach of his Article 8 rights was justified for the prevention of disorder or crime and would endanger the security of the prison.

1.12.4. RIGHT TO UPHOLD FREEDOM OF THOUGHT, CONSCIENCE AND RELIGION- ARTICLE 9 HRA

Article 9 includes the freedom to change one's religion or belief in public or in private. The right to uphold religious belief, whether in prison or not, is absolute.

1.12.5. RIGHT TO LIFE- ARTICLE 2 HRA

If a prisoner is ill, be it physically or mentally ill, he should always have the right to be treated immediately and appropriately. In a case *Brooks v Home Office*, Times Law Report, 17 Feb 1999, a pregnant woman prisoner was deprived of immediate medical treatment and lost one of her baby twins. Hers had been a known high-risk pregnancy and it was known by the Prison officers that she was expecting twins. The prisoner sued the Home Office for medical negligence after one of her babies was still-born. Her case was successful in that it was decided that the female prisoner was entitled to expect the same high care standard as of those free and pregnant women in the United Kingdom. However it was decided that a delay of five days in obtaining specialist advice was not a breach of duty!

1.13.1. CONTRACTED OUT PRISONS: THE STATUTORY BASIS

A contentious statutory change is contracted-out prisons. These effectively privatised prisons operate within the framework of the rest of the Prison Service. The first provision for contracted out prisons was made in the Criminal Justice Act 1991, ss 84 to 88. These were accompanied by provisions to allow private escorts to be introduced (ss 80 to 83). The Secretary of State is permitted by the Act to introduce contracted out prisons for sentenced prisoners. Statutory instruments were passed in 1992 (Criminal Justice Act 1991 (Contracted Out Prisons) Order 1992 and Criminal Justice Act 1991 (Contracted Out Prisons Order) No 2 1992) and permitted all prisons to be contracted out. The provisions extend to Scotland through the Criminal Justice and Public Order Act 1994, which also contained various minor modifications to the 1991 Act. The provisions for '*private*' prisons in the 1991 Act were then rewritten by the Criminal Justice and Public Order Act 1994, which empower the Secretary of State to enter into contracts for the running of a prison or any part of a prison.

1.13.2. THE PRISON ACT 1952 APPLIES

The Prison Act 1952 applies to all contracted out prisons save to the extent that a different set of officers are put in place to run the prisons (CJA 1991, s 84(1)). In place of governors, directors are appointed to run the prison. Directors have the same powers as governors except that they are not allowed to conduct adjudications or to segregate prisoners, apply restraints or to order confinement in a special cell, except in cases of extreme emergency. Controllers are appointed by the Secretary of State to oversee the running of the prison by the director. The disciplinary powers removed from the director are now vested in the controller, who is also charged with the responsibility for reviewing the running of the prison and reporting to the Secretary of State. Area managers are now the direct line mangers for private prisons as they are for state prisons (AG 21/95). Therefore, appeals against operational and disciplinary decisions are directed to the area manager.

1.13.3. PRISON CUSTODY OFFICERS

The officers employed to run prisons are known as '*prison custody officers*'. The duties of these officers are to prevent escapes from custody, to detect and prevent the commission of unlawful acts, to ensure good order and discipline and to attend to the well-being of prisoners. Reasonable force may be used in pursuance of these duties. These officers have the power to search inmates in accordance with the Prison Rules and to conduct searches of visitors. Searches of visitors do not extend to full body searches but only to outer layers of clothing which may be removed. Prison Custody Officers can work in directly managed prisons, those that are not contracted out and vice versa (CJPOA 1994, s. 97). The purpose of these provisions is to enable services at directly managed prisons to be contracted out if so desired.

The Secretary of State is empowered to intervene in the running of the prison in cases where the controller appears to have lost control or where it is necessary to preserve the safety of any person or to prevent serious damage to property. In such cases, a Crown servant can be appointed to act as governor of the prison and this person then assumes the powers of both the director and the controller.

1.13.4. PRISON ESCORT OFFICERS

The contracting out of prisons was accompanied by a contracting out of the prisoner escort system. This covers the delivery of prisoners to court, to and from police stations and other prisons and for the custody of prisoners outside of prison for temporary purposes (CJA 1991, s. 80). Disciplinary breaches by prisoners under such escort are treated as if they had been committed in the custody of the governor or controller of the prison and a charge may be laid by the prison custody officer (CJPOA 1994, s. 95).

1.13.5. THE CONTRACT DOCUMENT

The standards to be utilised in the running of the prison will be set out in the contract between the contractor and the Secretary of State. The actual contracts for private prisons are not public documents. The Prison Rules do apply, but policy documents such as Standing Orders may not apply. The Secretary of State can oblige the contractor to comply with any policy and procedural decisions that are deemed necessary. The contract for a private prison sets out the regime standards that are to be applied in the prison, including such matters as time out of cells, association, medical care and suicide prevention. The numerous problems that have been experienced in the running of private prisons, in terms of contract compliance, assaults on staff, poor medical care, escapes from custody and suicides were documented by the Prison Reform Trust in a special section on private prisons in their quarterly publication, *Prison Report*.

1.13.6. THE LEGAL IMPLICATIONS

The privatisation of prisons was a rapid process and by 2002, seven contracted out prisons had already been built and put into operation, with a further two original state prisons having been contracted to private management. The majority of escort services have also been contracted out. The legal status of private prisons does make legal action more complex. Actions for ill-treatment and the the causes of action remain the same as for people in state prisons, the defendant being the company which holds the contract for the prison. When considering claims in which a breach of the Human Rights Act 1998 is alleged, private prisons do exercise the State's power to imprison. The contractor is carrying out a public function (HRA 1998, s. 6(3) (b)). The defendant in judicial review applications concerning administrative decisions made in the contracted out prison which do not raise HRA issues are the private contractors (see Livingstone, Owen & Macdonald *Prison Law* (2002) OUP, pp 35–6). However, it is still possible to commence public law challenges against the Secretary of State for failing to enforce a contract relating to a private prison.

1.13.7. LIABILITY

The legal situation is complicated by agencylaw. In the case of immigration detention centres, where the statutory authority for contracting out came into force at the end of 1999, the extent to which the Secretary of State can abrogate responsibility for the custodial function of immigration detention is questionable (see e.g. the obiter comments of Turner. J in *R v Secretary of State for the Home Department, ex p Quaquah* [2000], 03 LS Gaz R 36). There is direct statutory authority for contracting out and so the issue of whether the Home Office remains liable for the acts or omissions of independent contractors remains open to debate. The issue for practitioners to identify in advising clients wishing to take private law claims in respect of events in contracted out prisons is whether there is any purpose or advantage to be gained in seeking to hold the Home Office responsible. Given the size and resources of the private companies running such prisons, it is difficult to identify any such advantage as a general matter of principle.

1.13.8. THE MANAGEMENT STRUCTURE OF THE PRISON SYSTEM

The management of the prison system has been in a state of constant change for the past decades, and in May 2004 the National Offender Management Service was introduced by the Home Office. The Secretary of State for the Home Department retains personal accountability to Parliament for the administration of the prison estate. However, the responsibility for the day-to-day management of prisons and prison policy rests with the Prison Service, an executive agency since 1993. The Prison Service is run by a Director General. The country is divided into 13 geographical areas with each area having its own Area Manager. In addition, there is a Manager for Women's Prisons, Young Offender Institutions and Juveniles.

The Prison Service retains certain operational functions at its headquarters rather than at local prisons, the most notable being responsibility for the classification and movement of category A prisoners, who fall under the remit of the Directorate of High Security Prisons. The responsibility for the review of life-sentenced prisoners rests with the Lifer Review and Recall Section. ('LRRS'), integrated into the Prison Service in 1993 then back to the Home Office department in 2003 under the control of the Department of Correctional Services. The LRRS is housed within the prison service's headquarters building.

1.14. CONCLUSION

How society treats those in Prison is a measure of society's civilisation because the removal of a person's liberty is a very serious matter. Prison law is a hybrid of criminal law, civil law and public law and an increasing amount of case-law is being produced. The 1998 Human Rights Act has dramatically affected the prison service, prisons and prisoners. There has been a tightening of the guidance on recall of prisoners released on licence at the latter part of their sentence and also a transfer of the decision making to civil servants.

When a defendant in a criminal case pleads or is found guilty, there is often a risk of a custodial sentence for the purposes of punishment, deterrence and rehabilitation. Prison has a strict disciplinary system which can result in a host of consequences, two of which are a reduction in status / privileges and additional days added to the custodial portion of their sentence.

CHAPTER 2 - STATUTORY AGENCIES AND NON-GOVERNMENTAL ORGANISATIONS

2.1. Introduction

The major piece of legislation that addresses the prison system is the Prison Act 1952 and although it has been subject to amendments, the Act has not substantially changed in the past 57 years. The statutory framework appears to be static because the Prison Act 1952 is primarily an enabling legislation. The power to make rules for the running of prisons is devolved to the Home Secretary, who exercises this power by way of statutory instrument. These rules provide for further devolution of a wide range of discretionary decisions to civil servants and prison governors. The policies and decisions that result are subject to the authority of common law and judicial interpretation.

2.2. Prisoners' Issues

Prisoners will generally resort to the law in two situations: when seeking to enforce public law rights by way of judicial review and when pursuing private law remedies for damages. From the time that a person is sentenced to imprisonment until the date of release, a series of administrative decisions will be made. These will encompass issues ranging from the length of time to be served in custody and the prisons in which the sentence will be served and the procedures and policies that are adopted for release. The decision maker derives the power to decide upon these matters from public law sources rather than from an agreement or action between private parties (see *O'Reilly v Mackman* [1982] 3 All ER 1124 and *Council of Civil Service Unions v Minister for the Civil Service* [1985] AC 374).

2.3. PUBLIC LAW -NO DISCRETIONARY DECISIONS

Public law decisions can be divided into two separate areas. One area of public law relates to rights which accrue to people in custody over which there is no discretion by the decision maker. One example is the minimum number of visits a prisoner can receive (Prison Rules 1999, Rules 33 to 39) . Another example is the right to be considered for parole at a certain stage of one's sentence. The second area of public law relates to situations where a decision maker is obliged to make a decision, but retains an element of discretion. One example of this second area of public law include substantive parole decisions and security categorisation (see the case of *R v Secretary of State for the Home Department, exp Duggan* [1994] 3 All ER 277). Another example is the exercise of disciplinary and quasi-disciplinary powers (as in Prison Rules 1999, Rules 51 to 61, illustrated in two cases :

Campbell and Fell v United Kingdom [1985)]7 EHRR 165;and *Leech v Deputy Governor of Parkhurst Prison* [1988] .

2.4. PRIVATE LAW REMEDIES OF FINANCIAL COMPENSATION

The private law remedies that are relevant to prisoners concern the circumstances in which the right to financial compensation will arise. This may be in respect of injuries suffered at work or through dangerous premises (see *Ferguson v Home Office* [1977] Times, 8 October); negligent medical treatment (see *Knight v Home Office* [1990] 3 All ER 237); assaults by other prisoners or members of staff (see *H v Home Office* [1992] Independent, 6 May; loss of and damage to property and intolerable conditions of detention (*R v Deputy Governor of Parkhurst, ex p Hague* [1992] 1 AC 58). The general principles of tort apply to such claims. The main problems that arise when advising prisoners on matters of both public and private law is of identifying the provisions and regulations that guide decision makers and establishing the duty of care that is owed to a prisoner.

2.5. STATUTORY INSTRUMENTS BY EXECUTIVE DECISION

One of the key difficulties with the law as it is applied to prisoners is that it is susceptible to change at very short notice. Many of the statutory provisions provide authority for decisions to be made or policies to be put in place. As a consequence, there is enormous scope for practices and policies to be altered at very short notice. For example, policies for parole eligibility and temporary release have been altered by the executive. Judicial authority mostly states that prisoners only have a legitimate expectation that they will be treated in accordance with whatever policy is in force at a given time (*see Green & Hargreaves* [1997] 1 All ER 397).

2.6. Laws which gain Royal assent but are not enforced immediately
A further problem can arise when new legislation is passed but is not implemented immediately or is implemented in stages. The Crime (Sentences) Act 1997 completely re-wrote the legislation for release on parole licence. The parole provisions for prisoners serving determinate sentences were never implemented and were repealed by the Crime and Disorder Act 1998.

2.7.1. Government Agencies
The relevant agencies are:
the Chief Inspector of Prisons,
the Prisons and Probation Ombudsman and
the Parole Board

2.7.2. Penal Reform Agencies
Examples of various penal reform agencies are:
the Prison Reform Trust;
the Howard League for Penal Reform;
the Penal Affairs Panel of the Unitarians General Assembly of Free Christian Churches; and
The Children's Rights Alliance.

2.8. Statistics of Adults in Custody in the UK in August 2008

Prison population on Friday August 15, 2008	83, 783
Number of women prisoners	4,419
Number of persons in police cells	52

2.9. The state of UK Prisons
Lord Ramsbotton made a speech about the state of UK prisons. He said:

"My Lords, our prison system is in crisis. It is not the fault of the Prison Service that prisons are overcrowded, underresourced and subjected to a non-stop barrage of criticism in Parliament, the media and by the public as well as an absolute torrent of legislation, initiatives and conflicting instructions from Government, much of which appears to be motivated by knee-jerk reaction to events rather than considered strategic direction. Nor is it the prison system's fault that over the past 15 years the penal system has become increasingly politicised, with political parties vying with each other, in what is described as penal populism, to appear toughest on crime. This obscene competition has been described as an arms race in which neither is prepared to give way in case it results in electoral catastrophe. Thanks to media attention, law and order assumes a high profile with floating voters, which is another reason it demands political attention.

The aim given to the Prison Service stems from that given to the criminal justice system as a whole, namely to protect the public by the prevention of crime, by preventing reoffending. Yet with the reconviction rate running at 64.7 per cent for all adult males within two years of being released—10 per cent higher than in 1997, when this Government took office—the prison system is clearly failing to achieve that aim. No amount of sweet talk or selective use of other statistics can alter this inalienable fact. The reconviction rate, which can be broken down into different categories, but above all can be measured, remains the only one by which success or failure can be judged. Should we accept this situation as being inevitable with a prison system or should we try to do something about it?

When I was appointed Chief Inspector of Prisons in 1995 I was told that a good day for the Prison Service was one on which no one escaped and no one was locked out and held in a police cell for which it had to pay, the current rate being £459 per night or £28 million per year. I was also told that improvements were only made by implementing recommendations made by outsiders following disasters. It was interesting that outsiders saw instantly what was wrong, which insiders—who presumably must have known that all was not well—obdurately refused to publicly acknowledge or do anything about until pushed. This might seem cynical, but within a week of being appointed I realised that there was more than a grain of truth in it. Already I could see serious flaws in the structure of both prison system and prison management that were, and remain, considerable impediments to good practice.

I am second to no one in my admiration for the wonderful and dedicated work that countless people, official and volunteer, carry out with and for prisoners throughout the prison system. I also recognise that there have been a considerable number of improvements affecting treatment and conditions, but I am concerned about how many of them die when the governor of the prison concerned changes. I am also aware of the frustration and anger of those who know how much more could be done with and for prisoners if only the system allowed it.

Those of us in a position to put forward positive proposals, as we in this House are privileged to be able to do, should make every effort to persuade both the Government and the Prison Service that, by changing their attitude to facts that they may not like, as well as laying themselves open to helpful and well intentioned outside advice, they are far more likely to bring about the improvements that they say they desire.

The Prison Service is run quite unlike a business, school, hospital or armed service in that, with a single exception, no one is responsible or accountable for any functional area, and budget conformity and process are the determining factors. Of course, these are important, but they are not wholly appropriate when dealing with people. People must be treated like people, the best weapon in that treatment being other people. If you manage people like commodities, you may get some paper answers, but they will be totally meaningless as far as the development of a person is concerned.

Unfortunately, no one from outside looks at the way in which the Prison Service is managed. When Mr Justice May reinstigated *independent inspection in 1979, one of the reasons being to satisfy public disquiet over solely in-house inspection, he instigated it only for prisons and not for the Prison Service as is the case for the police service, the Probation Service and the Courts Service. Neither Michael Howard nor Jack Straw would agree to initiate the necessary primary legislation to allow me to do this when I asked to inspect Prison Service headquarters.*

The current situation has not been dreamed up or imposed by either the Ministry of Justice or the Prison Service, but inherited from a decision in 1962 to make prisons a department of the Home Office, with a senior civil servant as director-general. All those brought in to examine and report on subsequent disasters have commented in one form or another about the implications of asking civil servants to perform operational tasks for which they are not qualified. Lord Mountbatten in 1963, my noble and learned friend Lord Woolf and Sir Raymond Lygo in 1990, and Sir John Woodcock and Sir John Learmont in 1995 all drew attention to such issues as:

"The number of decisions being taken by people without relevant experience",

and the importance of Ministers' advice coming from a wider range of professional, academic and lay sources than that provided by the Prison Service".

They also reached the following conclusions:

"Better prisons cannot be achieved by a piecemeal approach ... Unless there was a preparedness on the part of the Home Office to take its hands off the management of the Prison Service in its day-to-day business, and allow itself to be constrained by matters of policy only, then it would not be possible to effect the changes deemed desirable and which have become very clear to me as being necessary"

It was further stated:

"Vesting all the authority in an accounting officer is a device which is understood and readily accepted by the Civil Service but I do not believe that it is an apt model for the complex task of

managing the Prison Service ... The high security estate should be managed as a whole rather than piecemeal. An Operational Director should be appointed".

Those are just six out of a whole volume of recommendations. However, the final recommendation was implemented for high-security prisons, an escape from which was held to be particularly damaging for the Home Secretary. It was instigated with considerable success, as I saw for myself. Consistently directed high-security prisons stand out as a coherent group, with huge advantages such as the ability to turn good practice somewhere into common practice everywhere. I have never been able to fathom why this success was not at once copied in other failing parts of the system.

Unfortunately, the same did not happen to one of the recommendations made by my noble and learned friend Lord Woolf, although it was turned into a priority in the White Paper Custody, care and justice: The way ahead for the Prison Service in England and Wales. This was published in 1991 and endorsed by all political parties, but it still rests on the shelf. It included a commitment to develop community prisons which will involve the gradual realignment of the prison estate into geographically coherent groups serving most prisoners within that area."

If only this had happened. Organisations such as the CBI, chambers of commerce and Remploy tell me that employers would much more readily look for solutions to skills shortages among prisoners held locally. Mental health and drug treatment practitioners tell me how much easier it would be if prisoners remained in the same region. Millions of pounds would no longer be wasted on moving prisoners all over the United Kingdom to fill empty cells, sometimes in the middle of courses, or to prisons in which identified needs cannot be met, and so on.

Why, if all this is known about some of the avoidable contributors to the crisis in our prisons, on top of all the reports of inspectors, penal reformers, academics and other interested organisations, is no notice taken of recommendations designed to help resolve a *crisis, unless they are initiated in-house or in-political party? The Government will say that much is being done, pointing to the volume of work to which I have already made reference. They will point to two management inquiries that recommended the retention of the status quo. Indeed they did, but one was entirely in-Prison Service, and the other could by no means be called independent because one of its members was the deputy director-general of the Prison Service and another was one of its non-executive directors.*

The noble Lord, Lord Carter of Coles, has written two reports, each accepted without discussion and before consultation, both bearing on my case. Neither addressed the management or structure of the prison system but rather the management of the management and the building of more prisons. Indeed, his last report prompted the chief inspector to comment that building seemed to determine policy, rather than policy determine building. Professor Nicola Lacey, in one of her Hamlyn lectures for 2007, entitled "Escaping the Prisoners' Dilemma", said:

"If the dynamics of penal populism are a structural feature of 'late modern' society, all avenues for institutional reform, designed to counter the culture of control, seem blocked".

Are they? She goes on to say:

"An escape from the cell of penal populism . . . will be possible only if the two main political parties can reach a framework agreement about the removal of criminal justice policy—or at least key aspects of policy such as the size of the prison system—from party political debate. This might be done by setting up an initial Royal Commission or something of yet wider scope . . . a further important condition would be the reconstitution of some respect for expertise in the field".

Her statement interested me because I first thought about a royal commission some 10 years ago. I am by no means alone in that.

I am interested to see that, recently, more and more people are coming to a similar conclusion. royal commissions have fallen out of favour in recent years, allegedly in favour of Select Committees.

I now submit that in the case of the prison system, urgent consideration should be given to their reintroduction. I would go further. Royal commissions are ad hoc advisory committees, formally appointed by the Crown, by virtue of its prerogative powers. The last one, under the noble Lord, Lord Runciman, was appointed to examine criminal justice in 1992, reporting in 1993. The risk of appointing a one-shot commission is that its report will, like so many others, merely gather dust on a shelf, having been studiously ignored by those it attempts to help but who do not want to listen.

There is a precedent for a better alternative. In 1970 a Royal Commission on Environmental Pollution was established to be an independent standing body to advise the Queen, the Government and the public on environmental issues. Its remit is to advise on matters concerning pollution, on the adequacy of research and the possibilities of danger. Within this it has freedom to consider and advise on any matter it chooses and the Government may also request consideration of particular topics. But the primary role of the commission is to contribute to policy development in the longer term by providing an authoritative factual basis for policy-making debate and setting new policy agendas and priorities. In reaching its conclusions, the commission seeks to make a balanced assessment, taking account of the wider implications for society of any measures proposed.

It seems to me that that is precisely what is needed in the case of our prisons. An expert outside body, taking a balanced look at current dangers and future trends, making balanced assessments and giving advice on the wider implications for society of any measures proposed, is what the prison system lacks. Imprisonment is a very complex matter and I know that other noble Lords intend to bring out many more aspects that would also benefit from such outside scrutiny than I am able to cover in the time available.

I realise that it is easy for me from these Benches to bemoan how party politics appear to have distorted penal policy, but I believe that both the Government and the Prison Service would benefit from regular examination by independent experts rather than rely on current practices, which have produced so many flawed outcomes. Governments come and go, but prisoners will be in prison no matter which party is in power, and continuity of direction is of supreme importance to them and the public. I therefore hope that the Minister and his colleagues will not dismiss this proposal as just another debate. I feel that I am on the tip of an iceberg, the rest of which consists of many others inside and outside this House who feel and say the same thing. We all stand ready to help move the proposal forward in any way we can, and look forward to being invited to do so. I beg to move for Papers".

2.10. 1. CHILDREN'S RIGHTS ALLIANCE

The Children's Rights Legal Advocacy Network was first established by CRAE in February 2005. The new Legal Advocacy for the Rights of Children (LARC) network was launched in May 2008, with a seminar on strategic litigation and the rights of children in custody. The network aims to foster and promote the use of legal advocacy to improve respect for children's human rights and equality in England. Any non-governmental organisation with an interest in children's human rights can join. The CRAE is a founding member of Participation Works, a consortium of six leading children and young people's organisations that provides expert advice to anyone wanting to increase the participation in decision-making of children and young people. Other consortium members include the British Youth Council; the National Children's Bureau; the National Council for Voluntary Youth Services; the National Youth Agency and the organisation called Save the Children - England.

2.10.2. CRAE'S SUMMARY OF THE CONVENTION ON THE RIGHTS OF THE CHILD

Article 1
This Convention applies to everyone aged 17 or under.

Article 2
All the rights in this Convention apply to all children and young people without any discrimination.
Article 3
Adults should always try to do what is best for children and young people.
Governments must do everything to make sure children and young people are safe and well looked after.
Article 4
Governments must do all they can to make sure children's and young people human rights are upheld.
Article 5
Parents can give children and young people advice and help about children's rights. The more a young person knows and understands, the less advice and help a parent needs to give.
Article 6
Every child and young person has the right to life
Governments must do all they can to make sure every child and young person has the best possible life.
Article 7
Children and young people have the right to a name and a nationality.
Children and young people have the right to be cared for by both parents.
Article 8
Governments should do everything possible to protect the right of every child and young person to a name and nationality and to family life.
Article 9
If a court is thinking about who a child or young person should live with, everyone affected by the decision should get the chance to be heard - including the child.
Every child and young person has the right to keep in regular contact with both parents, so long as this is the best thing for the young person.

Article 10

If a child or a parent wants to live in another country, the decision about this should be made quickly and fairly.

A child or young person whose parents live in another country has the right to keep in touch with them.

Article 11

Governments must work together to stop children and young people being taken illegally to another country.

Article 12

Every child and young person has the right to express his or her views freely – about everything that affects him or her.

The child's or young person's views must be given 'due weight' depending on his or her age and maturity.

The child or young person has the right to be heard in all decision-making processes, including in court hearings. The child or young person can speak for him or herself, or someone else can speak for him or her.

Article 13

Every child and young person has the right to freedom of expression, including the right to all kinds of information and ideas (unless there are legal restrictions).

Article 14

Every child and young person has the right to freedom of thought, conscience and religion (unless there are legal restrictions).

Governments must respect the right of parents and guardians to give advice to the child and young person about this right. The more a child or young person knows and understands, the less advice parents need to give.

Article 15

Every child and young person has the right to meet people and to gather in public (unless there are legal restrictions).

Article 16

The law must protect every child's and young person's right to privacy.

Article 17
Governments must make sure children and young people have access to lots of different information.
Governments must encourage the media to give information to children and young people and protect them from harmful information and materials.
Article 18
Governments must do all they can to help parents look after children well.
Parents are the most important people in children's and young people's lives. Parents must always do what is best for children and young people.
Article 19
Governments must do everything to protect children and young people from all forms of violence, abuse, neglect and mistreatment.
Help must be available for children and young people who are hurt by violence, abuse, neglect and mistreatment.
Article 20
Children who are separated from their parents have the right to special protection and help.
Article 21
The child's best interests must be the top priority in adoption.
Governments can support adoption between countries.
Children and young people who are adopted by people in another country must have the same protections as children adopted by people in their own country.
Article 22
Governments must give protection and humanitarian help to children and young people who are refugees, or who are trying to be accepted as refugees.
Governments must give protection and humanitarian help to children who are trying to be accepted as refugees.
Article 23

Every disabled child and young person has the right to a full life and to active participation in the community.
Article 24
Every child and young person has the right to the best possible health and health services.
Article 25
Children and young people who are in care or live away from home for health reasons have the right to have their care reviewed regularly.
Article 26
Governments must support every child's and young person's right to have enough money.
Article 27
Children and young people have the right to a standard of living that helps them develop fully.
Parents have the main responsibility for making sure children and young people get this right.
Governments must support parents. The amount of help the Government gives depends on how rich the country is.
Article 28
Every child has the right to free primary education.
Governments must encourage secondary education, making it available and accessible to every child and young person
Access to higher education must be based on the ability to benefit from it.
Governments must make sure children and young people get information about education.
Governments must encourage regular school attendance.
Governments must make sure that school discipline protects the dignity of children and young people, and is in line with their rights in this Convention – so no hitting or humiliation.
Article 29
Governments agree that the aim of education is to help the fullest possible growth of the child's or young person's personality, talents and mental and physical abilities.

Education must help children and young people:
respect human rights
respect their parents
respect their and others' culture, language and values
have self-respect
respect the environment.

Article 30
Children and young people from minority communities must not be stopped from enjoying their own culture, religion and language.

Article 31
Every child and young person has the right to rest, play and leisure.
Governments must promote children's and young people's involvement in the arts.

Article 32
Every young person has the right to be protected from harmful work and economic exploitation.
Governments must do everything to protect this right.
Governments must set a minimum age at which young people can work, and they must introduce rules to protect young people in work.

Article 33
Governments must do everything to protect children and young people from illegal drugs.

Article 34
Governments must do everything to protect children and young people from sexual exploitation (including prostitution) and sexual abuse.

Article 35
Governments must do everything to protect children and young people from being taken away, sold or trafficked.

Article 36
Governments must protect children and young people from all other exploitation.

Article 37
Governments must do everything to protect children and young people from torture or other cruel, inhuman or degrading treatment or punishment. This is an absolute right, with no excuses for any breach of it.

Children and young people must not be given a death sentence or life imprisonment without the possibility of release.

Children and young people who are locked up should be able to challenge this quickly in court.

Children and young people must only be arrested or locked up as a last resort and for the shortest possible time.

Every child or young person who is locked up must be treated with respect.

Every child or young person who is locked up must be separated from adults, unless it is better for him or her to be with adults.

Every child or young person who is locked up has the right to keep in contact with his or her family, through letters and visits.

Article 38
Governments agree to abide by international human rights law in relation to wars.

Governments must do everything to stop children under 15 from being involved directly in a war.

Governments must do everything to protect and care for children who are affected by war.

Article 39
Governments must give good support to children and young people who have been hurt, abused or exploited.

This support must promote children's and young people's health, self-respect and dignity.

Article 40
Every child or young person accused, or convicted, of committing a crime must be treated with respect. Every child or young person accused, or convicted, of committing

a crime must be treated in a way that helps them to respect the human rights of others. Every child or young person must be treated as innocent until found guilty. Every child or young person should be told as soon as possible why they have been arrested and charged with a crime. Every child or young person accused of a crime must be given immediate access to a lawyer. No child or young person can be forced to give evidence in a court. Every child and young person has the right to an interpreter if they do not understand the country's main language. The child's and young person's right to privacy must be fully respected at all times. Governments must set up a separate criminal justice system for children and young people. Governments should promote a minimum age of criminal responsibility.

Wherever possible, children and young people in trouble should not have to go to court. Courts should always try to avoid sending children and young people to institutions. There must be many ways to help children and young people in trouble with the law, including care, guidance and counselling.

Article 42

Governments must make sure everyone gets information about this Convention – that includes you and all the people you know!

Articles 41 and 43 to 54 state that adults and governments must work together to promote and protect all the rights in this Convention.

2.10.3. THE EUROPEAN CONVENTION ON THE RIGHTS OF THE CHILD VERSUS THE UN CONVENTION

There are many rights in the Convention on the Rights of the Child that are not in the European Convention on the Rights of the Child, and therefore not protected by UK law. These include, for example, the right to an adequate standard

ENGLISH PRISON LAW

of living and the right to the best possible health care, the right to play, children's right to have their views given due weight in all matters affecting them, the right to protection from all forms of violence and the right to maintain contact with both parents (unless this is not in the child's best interests). The UN Convention on the Rights of the Child requires that children must only ever be brought to court or given a custodial sentence as a very last resort and these essential rights are not protected by the Human Rights Act.

In October 2002, the UN Committee on the Rights of the Child recommended that the UK *'incorporate into domestic law the rights, principles and provisions of the Convention to ensure compliance of all legislation with the Convention'.*

The Joint Committee on Human Rights and the All-Party Parliamentary Group for Primary Care and Public Health support making the Convention on the Rights of the Child part of UK law, as do the major children's charities in England.

2.10.4. CHILDREN IN CUSTODY- THE PROTECTION OF THEIR RIGHTS

CRAE's aim is for all children to be removed from penal custody. Prison is no place for a child. The small number of children that must be locked up in order to protect the public should be held in local child-centred facilities with highly skilled staff that can meet their needs and enable rehabilitation, the CRAE argue. The UK imprisons more children than most other industrialised countries. There have been 30 child deaths in custody since 1990, but none of these deaths has warranted a public inquiry.

In 2005 and 2007, CRAE wrote to the European Committee for the Prevention of Torture to inform it of *the use of deliberately painful restraint in child custody*. The Committee visited the UK in December 2007, and Ministers subsequently suspended the 'nose distractio' restraint. In July 2008 the government confirmed that the 'nose distraction' restraint has been prohibited.

On October 4 2002, the UN Committee on the Rights of the Child issued a comprehensive report on the UK's implementation of the Convention on the Rights of the Child. The UN Committee's concluding observations set out the actions required by government to make a reality of children's human rights in the UK.

2.11. REPORTING TO THE UNITED NATIONS

When UN member states ratify the Convention on the Rights of the Child, they must report to the UN initially after two years, then every five years. The UN Committee on the Rights of the Child examines written evidence and meets with Government representatives. Before it meets with Government, it holds private discussions with non-governmental organisations (NGOs) and with children and young people.

NGOs are invited by the UN Committee to submit a written report highlighting areas of concern, as well as significant progress in implementing the Convention on the Rights of the Child. The CRAE co-ordinates the NGO England alternative report to the UN Committee. The CRAE's submission in March 2008 was endorsed by more than 100 NGOs in England. It made 152 recommendations, of which at least 100 are urgent.

CHAPTER 3 - PUBLIC FUNDING

3.1. INTRODUCTION

The Access to Justice Act 1999 established a framework for the public funding of legal representation in the criminal courts. It created the Legal Services Commission to replace the Legal Aid Board. It created the Criminal Defence Service which secures access to legal advice, assistance and representation in criminal matters. It also created the Community Legal Service (CLS) which deals with the public funding of civil matters.

Legal aid funding helps people to protect their basic rights and get a fair hearing; to access the court process to sort out disputes and to solve problems that contribute to social exclusion. One of the major historical problems that prisoners have faced when seeking legal representation was that lawyers found it difficult to obtain payment for work undertaken, or were unaware of what the proper source of legal aid income is for prisoners' cases. The confusion was compounded by franchising and contracting, introduced by the Legal Services Commission ('LSC'), with prison work moving between civil and criminal legal services provision.

Work relating to prisoners' rights initially fell between these two services. Although prisoners' rights work is primarily civil in scope, it is very often dealt with by criminal practitioners.

The LSC developed a discrete prison law contract which is available to firms which do not apply for the general criminal contract. The general criminal contract authorises all work falling within the prison law area in any event.

There remains some cross-over with the CLS and civil work. Actions for damages for prisoners, arising from personal injury or death, intentional torts (e.g. assault, misfeasance in public office) or neglect of duty will still fall within the civil contracting scheme and are dealt with under the Actions Against the Police Contract (which incorporates all actions against detaining authorities).

Funding for judicial review remains part of the civil funding scheme. Firms with a criminal (or prison law) contract can apply for certificated funding for judicial reviews on a case-by-case basis. Firms with a contract for public law can advise on any public law matters affecting prisoners, including judicial review proceedings. This ensures that practitioners who have expertise in public law can deal with judicial review cases for prisoners.

The legal aid scheme makes provision for lawyers to receive payment when acting for prisoners in three ways: for general advice and assistance (previously known as the Green Form or the Claim 10 scheme); for advocacy assistance at oral parole hearings and for prison disciplinary proceedings (previously known as ABWOR); and for full public funding certificates to be issued for representation in litigation. The vast majority of work that is undertaken on behalf of prisoners will be carried out under the advice and assistance scheme (previously known as the Claim 10 or Green Form scheme). In general, physical representation for prisoners is either not permitted (e.g. when the Parole Board considers determinate prisoners' cases and conducts paper reviews of those of mandatory lifers), or is completely discretionary and very rarely permitted (e.g. governors' adjudications or internal decision-making boards in the prison itself). The only exceptions to this general rule are in the case of oral parole hearings and disciplinary hearings heard by independent adjudicators, where legal representation is generally permitted as of right (subject to financial eligibility).

By far the majority of cases in which prisoners will seek legal advice will first involve representations being made on their behalf. These representations may be made with the intention of changing an adverse decision, such as re-categorisation or temporary release, or may be made with a view to securing a favourable outcome to a decision yet to be made, such as release on parole licence. In either situation, litigation cannot normally be contemplated until initial representations have been made and it is not possible to assess in advance whether there will be grounds to apply for a full legal aid certificate to commence litigation. As a consequence, by far the majority of work undertaken for prisoners will only be covered by the advice and assistance scheme, and this may never progress further.

The particular problem with prisoners seeking to receive advice has been the manner in which they come to instruct solicitors. As the normal route of booking an appointment and attending the solicitor's office is not possible, prisoners will generally seek to obtain advice either by telephoning a solicitor or writing to him/her. The problem the solicitor and prisoner will then face is how the solicitor will come to be paid for this work. This will be equally as true for existing clients who raise new issues relating to their imprisonment as it is for new, possibly unsolicited enquiries. The contracting scheme resolved many of these problems by enabling devolved powers to be exercised to accept postal applications from persons in custody and to provide advice in urgent cases prior to the signing of the CDS forms.

3.2. SCOPE OF PRISON LAW

Paragraph 4 of The Criminal Defence Service (General) (No 2) Regulations 2001 confirms that the LSC funds Advice and Advocacy Assistance to anyone who:

"* *requires advice and assistance regarding his treatment or discipline in prison (other than in respect of actual or contemplated proceedings regarding personal injury, death or damage to property);*

* is the subject of proceedings before the Parole Board;

*requires advice and assistance regarding representations to the Home Office in relation to a mandatory life sentence or other parole review."

The General Criminal Contract determines the circumstances in which Advice and Assistance and Advocacy Assistance can be given of the General Criminal Contract). These are:

* Advice and Assistance on legal issues arising from his or her treatment or discipline within the prison system other than in respect of actual or contemplated legal proceedings in which there is a claim for damages for personal injury, death or damage to property (which fall within the scope of the Community Legal Service);

*Advice and Assistance on legal issues arising from his or her sentence;

*Advocacy Assistance in proceedings before a Governor or other prison authority;

*Advocacy Assistance to a Client who is a discretionary life prisoner whose case has been referred to the Parole Board under sections 28(6) and (7) or 32(4) of the Crime (Sentences) Act 1997; an automatic life prisoner under section 2 of the Crime (Sentences) Act 1997 whose case has been referred to the Parole Board under sections 28(6) and (7) or 32(4) of the Crime (Sentences) Act 1997; serving a sentence of detention during her majesty's pleasure under section 53 of the Children and Young Persons Act 1933 whose case is referred to the Parole Board under sections 28(6) and (7) or 32(4) of the

Crime (Sentences) Act 1997; or serving any other sentence where the Parole Board decides to convene an oral hearing under section 32(3) of the Criminal Justice Act 1991.

3.3. JUDICIAL REVIEW APPLICATIONS

Public funding for judicial review applications is possible under crime contracts. Work that can be carried out under the Crime category is generally excluded from the CLS with some exceptions and these include

"Advice and Assistance to prisoners concerning their treatment by the prison authorities or those arrested concerning their treatment by the police' which can be carried out under the Actions against the Police etc category, and advice and assistance to prisoners who may be the subject of directions made or to be made by the Home Secretary under the Mental Health Act 1983 which can be carried out under the Mental Health category.

These overlaps allow those with crime or prison law contracts to advise on Prison Service complaints procedures and Ombudsman complaints (eg in relation to injuries), and for those with claims against the police and for contracts to advise on the same matters in relation to claims for compensation in the courts. Personal injuries that do not come within the "Actions against the Police" category are excluded by the Access to Justice Act 1999, Schedule 2 , unless they can be brought back in as cases of serious abuse of power, significant breach of human rights, liberty at issue, or significant wider public interest. Clinical negligence cases are also be funded under this category.

3.4. FINANCIAL ELIGIBILITY

The Criminal Defence Service (General) (No 2) Regulations 2001 determine financial eligibility for Advice and Assistance and Advocacy Assistance and are updated annually. Para. 5 states that Advocacy Assistance is available where weekly disposable income does not exceed £87 and disposable capital does not exceed £1,000. Eligibility for Advice and Assistance is less generous than for Legal Help since December 2001, even though advice may be given under both schemes in relation to the same set of facts.

3.5. WORK LIMITATIONS AND PAYMENT RATES

The upper limits of work that can be carried out before applying for an extension on CDS5 are £300 for Advice and Assistance and £1,500 for Advocacy Assistance. Claims must be submitted within three months of the matter concluding. If a matter commences as Advice and Assistance but develops into Advocacy Assistance (e.g. a mandatory lifer parole review which starts on the papers but is eventually concluded at an oral hearing), payment can be claimed at the Advocacy Assistance rate for all work conducted on the file.

It is within the discretion of the conducting solicitor as to whether to instruct counsel on any given case. The principle applied is that the instruction of counsel must not lead to any increase in costs, and so any duplication of time resulting from the decision cannot be claimed. Counsels' fees must be claimed as part of the profit costs on the case and not disbursements and so it is important to agree with counsel in advance that payment will be made at the prescribed rates. Funding for prison law matters is subject to an assessment of the merits of the case. In deciding whether to authorise funding, it is therefore necessary to make a file note of the reasons why the case is considered to justify the expenditure of public funds, usually by reference to the importance of the matter to the client.

3.6.1. LEGAL AID CERTIFICATES

When prisoners make an application for a legal aid certificate for the purposes of litigation, the appropriate form for assessment of their finances relates to people not in receipt of state benefits (currently CLSMEANS 1). Whilst this may seem unusual for people with little or no income (as income support is not available to those serving custodial sentences), a full financial assessment is required. Prisoners should be advised to include details of their prison wages in the section headed 'Other Relevant Information' and not in the section that deals with employment. *This is because prison employment is not contractual but is part of the disciplinary code and so these 'wages' are not paid in the course of employment.*

If prison wages are entered in the 'employment' section of the form, it will delay the application, as the LSC will ask for a form confirming the amount of wages received to be submitted even though prison wages can never bring an individual above the financial eligibility. The one exception will be for those prisoners located in resettlement units and prisoners who are employed outside of the prison and receive a wage.

The major problem that will arise with the financial side of the application is the question of whether the finances of a prisoner's partner should also be assessed. The regulations provide that the income and capital of spouses shall be treated as the resources of the applicant, unless they are living apart, or the spouse has a contrary interest in the subject matter of the application. Opposite sex couples who live in the same household as if married are also covered by this provision (Civil Legal Aid (Assessment of Resources) Regulations 1989, Regulation 7).

In the past, the LSC have widely interpreted this to include couples who *normally* live together as if they are married, and this wording appears on the top of the assessment form. Area offices have sent forms to the spouses and partners of prisoners to declare details of their finances. This can create problems, either if the partner does not comply with the completion of the forms or if they are above the financial limit. It is arguable that, in the majority of cases, prisoners' partners should not be included in the financial assessment. Many relationships will not survive the stress of imprisonment and it is not really practical for a long-term prisoner to be classed as normally living with a person outside of prison. Financially, prisoners can only receive a set amount of income each year and their partner will not usually have any direct interest in the outcome of an application. Whilst this argument may be less valid for very short-term prisoners who have a firm intention to return to a matrimonial home at the end of the sentence, refusals to grant legal aid based on the financial situation of a partner may be vulnerable to challenge.

3.6.2. JUDICIAL REVIEW AND THE FUNDING CODE

The LSC issue detailed guidance on funding codes for judicial review. Funding will only be granted if all other administrative appeals and other procedures have been exhausted and where appropriate notification has been given to the proposed defendant. Representation will then only be authorised if the prospects of success are good, or if there is a wider public interest in the proposed challenge, the case has overwhelming importance to the client, or it raises significant human rights issues. All cases where permission has been granted will normally meet the criteria. Section 16 of the LSC Manual provides a more detailed analysis of the considerations pertaining to the grant of funding for judicial review. It identified the tendency for the courts to expect claimants to make full use of Ombudsman schemes prior to issuing proceedings .

3.6.3. CRIMINAL LEGAL AID SCHEMES - GRADUATED FEE SCHEME

Police Stations fixed fees were introduced in October2007. Best value competitive tendering was introduced in October 2008 and best value competition was introduced in 2009.

3.6.4. MAGISTRATES' COURTS

Revised standard fees, which include an element of travel and waiting, was introduced in main urban areas since April2007.

Best value competitive tendering was introduced in October 2008.

3.6.5. CROWN COURT
Revised graduated fees scheme for advocates was introduced in April 2007.
Litigators graduated fees was introduced in October 2007.
A single graduated fees scheme was introduced in October 2008.
Minimum Contract Size for Criminal Work - the decision on where to set the minimum contract size for criminal work was made in 2007.
Very High Cost Cases in the Crown Court-(VHCCC) - a panel of Very High Cost Criminal Cases (VHCCCs) suppliers was introduced in October 2007.

3.6.6. CIVIL LEGAL AID SCHEMES
Standard terms for a unified contract were introduced in April 2007. Standard terms allow for a minimum income level. Unified contract with a fixed minimum income level of £25,000 or £50,000 was introduced in April 2007.

3.6.7. LEGAL AID RATES -FAMILY PROCEEDINGS COURTS
Rates were harmonised in April 2007. TFF Replacement Scheme was implemented in October 2007 for both solicitors and for the not-for-profit sector. NfP's are paid the same fees as solicitors since October 2007.

3.6.8. CARE PROCEEDINGS GRADUATED FEE SCHEME
Revised Care Proceedings Graduated Fees– apart from advocacy –were implemented since October 2007. Single standard rates for advocacy work (covering both solicitors and barristers), were implemented since April 2008.

3.6.9. FAMILY LAW– PRIVATE
Revised graduated fees were implemented since October2007

3.6.10. IMMIGRATION & ASYLUM
Graduated Fee Scheme and proposals for services were implemented since October2007.

3.6.11. MENTAL HEALTH
Graduated Fee Scheme were implemented since October 2007.

CHAPTER 4 - THE ADULT PRISON SYSTEM

4.1. INTRODUCTION

It has been argued that changes in life circumstances, such as being employed, living with a wife or girlfriend, or modifying alcohol or drug use, alter the crime patterns of convicted men in the United Kingdom. It is widely believed that criminal behaviour is the result of a basic propensity that is established early on and persists throughout life, and that changing life circumstances in adulthood are unlikely to alter this criminal propensity. Others have theorized that short-term factors such as being dismissed from a job, quarrelling with a wife or girlfriend, or abusing alcohol or drugs may be important catalysts in adult patterns of criminal behaviour. However, recent research results strongly demonstrate that social events during adulthood *are* related to crime. In such research results, increases or decreases in specific criminal behaviours vary, depending on which life circumstance was undergoing change. Some life circumstances affected all types of offending; others affected only one type of crime. Use of illegal drugs was related to all four measures of offending. For example, during months of drug use, the odds of committing a property crime increased by 54 percent; the odds of committing an assault increased by over 100 percent. Overall, illegal drug use increased the odds of committing any crime sixfold. Living with a wife was associated with lower levels of offending, specifically assault; however, living with a girlfriend was associated with higher levels of any crime, especially drug crimes. These findings support results of other research showing that lack of marital attachment is a strong predictor of adult criminality. Attending school reduced the likelihood of committing any crime by 52 percent and involvement in drug crimes by 61 percent. Surprisingly, working was only weakly related to adult criminal behaviour.

The only variable that was not related significantly to any measure of crime was justice supervision in the form of probation or parole. Justice supervision did lower rates of offending modestly, but it did not produce substantial reductions in crime among these serious offenders. The criminal careers of adult offenders do not necessarily follow a predetermined course. Short-term life circumstances may sharply increase or decrease criminal activity among serious offenders. Inmate pre-release and transition programs need to focus on helping these offenders avoid life circumstances that may lead to increased criminal activity and adopt activities that will reduce their involvement in crime. It is possible that the combined effects of several crime-inhibiting life circumstances will bring about substantial long-term change in patterns of criminal behaviour among previously incarcerated adults.

Black people may be more aware of racial discrimination in law-enforcement and other domains, leading to higher levels of disaffection. Consistent with this expectation, recent analyses of public opinion suggests that the " Black-White difference" in support for the criminal justice system actually increases with income (Bobo et al., 1992; Cose, 1993; Hochschild, 1995).

4.2.1. MEN'S PRISONS

Despite official recognition that the maintenance of family relationships can contribute to a reduced risk of re-offending by ex-prisoners , the literature documenting the multiple difficulties experienced by the female partners of imprisoned men is extensive (Morris, 1965: Caddle & Crisp, 1996: Davies, 1980: Davis, 1992: Hardwick, 1986: Light, 1989: Light, 1992: Light, 1995: McDermott & King, 1992: Neate, 1990: Noble, 1996: Paylor & Smith, 1994: Peelo, M. et al, 1991: Shaw, 1987 Shaw, 1992). Throughout the literature, there are accounts of problems with visiting; supplying clothes and personal or educational items; capricious and inconsistent application of institutional rules and a lack of privacy or opportunities for intimacy. In contrast with many other jurisdictions, the United Kingdom has *no* provision for private or conjugal visits, although some inmates many be allowed brief periods of home leave.

Women visiting offenders may face abuse and hostility from prison officers or be subject to intimate searches, contrary to the Prison Rules. Poor public transport can make visiting difficult, and lack of provision for visitors can make it especially hard for women visiting with children. Families also pay a price for their ties to incarcerated relatives. Family members must overcome the obstacles to communicating with relatives in prisons, for example, using public transport to reach far-away prisons; the necessity to accepting expensive collect calls from prison, and exchanging letters which have been screened by prison authorities (Braman 2003; Travis 2004). Like the prison inmates, visitors are exposed to the many small routines and humiliations of institutional life, such as waiting to be called, passing through metal detectors, surrendering identification, and submitting to searches.

4.2.2. LOCAL PRISONS

Local prisons are so called because they tend to be located in towns or cities. They are where prisoners are held on remand and when first convicted. Local prisons are almost always old buildings and due to their age and general state are more likely to be infested with vermin and cockroaches than the other, newer prisons. Prisoners are generally held on remand in the local prison nearest to the court where their case will eventually be heard, and so there is a constant turnover of prisoners as newly arrested prisoners are remanded into custody, and others are released or transferred following trial. Local prisons are the first point of entry into the prison system and, because receptions of new prisoners are initiated by the courts rather than managed by the Prison Service, they are all overcrowded.

4.2.3. SHORT-TERM CONVICTED PRISONERS
In addition to remand prisoners, local prisons contain short-term convicted prisoners and newly convicted long-term prisoners awaiting initial allocation. Some long-term prisoners will return to local conditions from time to time for re-allocation or when they are transferred in the interests of good order and discipline.

4.3. 1. CONDITIONS AT HMP WANDSWORTH
Regimes at local prisons are the most deprived in the system. Prisoners often complain that they are denied access to work, association and education. A report into HMP Wandsworth published by the Chief Inspector of Prisons on 3 June 2003 found that 53% of prisoners said that they had never had any association and only 14% of the population had six hours or more out of their cells on a daily bais, a breach of Prison Rules. Prisoners report difficulties in gaining access to telephones in the short time allowed out of cell and only 12% said that they could shower more than five times a week. Most prisoners were without any purposeful activity at all and many told the Inspectorate Team that they spent 23 hours a day locked in their cells.

4.3.2. CONDITIONS AT HMP LIVERPOOL
Conditions at HMP Liverpool are even worse than at Wandsworth, according to the Chief Inspector's report published on 28 May 2008, which described an *'unacceptable regime'*. There were 1443 prisoners there in August 2008. The report found that 'the availability of showers, association and exercise was far below the average for other local prisons. Some prisoners were reduced to one shower and one change of clothing per week .Association was limited, and liable to cancellation. Most prisoners had association on only one day during the week, and there was a 25% chance on one of the eight prison building wings that even this would be cancelled.. The report stated that the induction wing at Liverpool is *'some of the worst accommodation we have seen, with cockroach infestation, broken windows and unclean toilet facilities'.*

4.4. CATEGORISATION, ALLOCATION
Following their conviction, prisoners are categorised and allocated to other types of establishment The exceptions to this are where someone is serving such a short sentence that there is not enough time to allocate them elsewhere, or, occasionally, they may agree to stay behind as labour at the local prison.

4.5.1. TYPES OF HIGH SECURITY PRISONS
At the present time, there are nine high security prisons in the UK. Five high security prisons hold long-term convicted adult male prisoners. These are Sutton, Frankland, Long Lartin, Whitemoor, and Wakefield Four high security prisons, Durham, Woodhill, Belmarsh and Doncaster, are local prisons of which two, Woodhill and Durham, also contain close supervision centres. Doncaster, Woodhill and Belmarsh provide maximum security remand facilities. All of the high security prisons take standard and high risk category A prisoners. Exceptional risk category A prisoners are held in special security units within the confines of the high security prisons. Each high security prison will only take a specific

quota of category A prisoners, and the rest of their population is largely made up of category B prisoners and the occasional category C prisoner whom the prison has not been able to transfer to conditions of lesser security.

4.5.2. FACILITIES IN HIGH SECURITY PRISONS

Because of the length of time that the majority of prisoners in high security conditions are serving, they are likely to receive a much better regime than that offered in other prisons. There are more educational facilities. High security prisons for convicted prisoners have facilities for prisoners to purchase and cook their own food. It is also common practice for prisoners to be able to wear their own clothing and to have the facilities to wash and dry their clothes. The list of items that high security prisoners are allowed to keep in their possession is extensive and covers far more items than those allowed for prisoners in other parts of the system. However, prisoners' ability to hold property has been affected by the system of volumetric control which was introduced following the Woodcock and Learmont Inquiries into security in the high security prison system. The Inquiries recommended that prisoners' property allowances should be severely restricted, as excessive amounts of property hindered effective searching. The introduction of the Incentives and Earned Privileges ('IEP')scheme in the mid-1990s has also adversely affected prisoners' ability to purchase items, or have property sent into prison.

4.5.3.1.SPECIAL SECURITY UNITS AND HIGH SECURITY UNITS

Special Security Units ('SSU') were conceived in the 1960s in recognition of the fact that there was a group of prisoners for whom escape should be made impossible. SSUs are effectively prisons within a prison. They are fully self-contained, and facilities include an exercise yard (which is fully enclosed), a gym, facilities for association including television, hobbies room etc, and their own visits room and segregation cells. They have their own perimeter security overlooked by closed circuit television cameras and the perimeter security of the dispersal prison where the SSU is housed surrounds both the prison itself and the walls of the SSU. Until 1994 when six prisoners escaped from Whitemoor SSU, it was thought that escape from an SSU would be impossible. There are two SSU/HSUs in operation at present .Whitemoor SSU holds convicted exceptional risk category A prisoners, and Belmarsh High Security Unit holds remand prisoners provisionally categorised as high or exceptional risk category A, similarly categorised convicted prisoners who are on temporary transfer, and detainees who have been arrested under the Prevention of Terrorism legislation but have not been charged or convicted of any offence.

4.5.3.2. SSU PROCEDURES

Security procedures dominate the SSUs, which are physically claustrophobic and which have been thought to have a detrimental effect on prisoners' health and well-being. Judicial review proceedings caused the government to ask its Chief Medical Officer, Sir Donald Acheson, to conduct research as to the long-term health of SSU prisoners (*Review on the Effects on Health in the Special Secure Units at Full Sutton, Whitemoor, and Belmarsh Prisons* (unpublished)).

4.5.4.1. CLOSE SUPERVISION CENTRES (CSC)

From 1969 to 1983 there were ten major disturbances and riots in the prison estate. In response to this, a Home Office working party was established to 'review the maintenance of control in the prison system including the implications for physical security, with particular reference to the dispersal system, and to make recommendations. This working party became known as the Control Review Committee (CRC), and published its report '*Managing the Long-Term Prison System*' in 1984. The CRC said that the existing facilities of transfers in the interest of good order and discipline, and segregation are not suitable long-term solutions. It recommended that: *'a number of small units should be established for prisoners in this group (ie prisoners presenting control problems which cannot be dealt with in normal prison conditions).'*

This provided the basis of the Close Supervision Centre (CSC) estate.

Close Supervision Centres operate as part of a national management strategy which aims to enable dangerous, disturbed, and disruptive prisoners to develop a settled and acceptable pattern of behaviour. The functions of the CSCs are to:

"(a) to remove the most seriously disruptive prisoners from main location prisons and contain them instead in small, highly supervised units;

(b) to provide the opportunity for individuals to address their disruptive behaviour, aiming to stabilise prisoners and prepare them for a return to main location prisons;

(c) to provide long term containment of those who continue to pose a serious threat."

4.5.5. Dangerous and Severe Personality Disorder Units(DPSD)

Dangerous and Severe Personality Disorder (DPSD) Units are for prisoners whose level of dangerousness is linked to a personality disorder and where risk can be reduced by addressing the underlying personality disorder prior to, or alongside, offending behaviour. Prisoners suitable for allocation to DPSD units are those who are high risk, and have a clinically significant PCL-R score (a psychological risk assessment tool also known as *'the psychopathy checklist'*). There is no requirement that they portray poor institutional behaviour but the CSC Referral Manual states that such prisoners are likely to have required a lot of management support that may have resulted in a lengthy adjudication history, that they may have spent time transferring between segregation and health care units, and that they may have had several disciplinary transfers. Prisoners need not consent to referral for a DSPD unit.

4.6. CATEGORY B TRAINING PRISONS

There are ten category B training prisons, at Albany, Dovegate, Garth, Gartree, Grendon, Kingston, Lowdham Grange, Parkhurst, Rye Hill and Swaleside.

Category B training prisons have a secure perimeter and relatively high levels of staffing. They offer prisoners a more relaxed regime than in high security prisons and there is less internal security. Opportunities for work and education should be available. Each category B training prison has different allocation criteria, and these inevitably affect the type of regime offered and the type of prisoners received. All of these prisons take life sentence prisoners

Gartree is a main lifer centre, taking prisoners who are in the first three years of their sentence, and Kingston only takes life sentence prisoners. Albany is particularly noted for assessing prisoners for, and running, sex offender treatment programmes Levels of physical security at category B prisons differ dramatically. Swaleside's security is not dissimilar to a high security prison and it is generally considered to be the highest security category B training prison. Albany, Parkhurst and Gartree are former dispersal prisons. Category B, C and D prisoners may be held in category B training prisons, although those of lower security categories will almost certainly apply for transfers elsewhere.

4.7. CATEGORY C PRISONS

Category C prisons make up one of the largest parts of the prison estate, and there are 33 such establishments. Like category B training prisons, they vary enormously from prison to prison. In general, category C prisons have lower levels of staff supervision and less perimeter security. Many category

C prisons have dormitory accommodation rather than, or as well as, cellular accommodation, and many long-term prisoners find this difficult to cope with. Because there is less staff supervision, there will often be more rules in operation. Prisoners found to be in breach of the rules will be more likely to be charged with breaches of Rule 51 of the Prison Rules than they would be in conditions of higher security. In general, prisoners are expected to be more accountable for their actions and to take more responsibility for their behaviour. Category C and D prisoners are held in these prisons.

4.8. CATEGORY D/OPEN PRISONS

There is very little security in category D prisons, and prisoners tend not to be locked up, and often retain their own keys to their rooms. Perimeter security often consists of little more than a fenc. Prisoners are only transferred to open conditions if the Prison Service is satisfied that they can be trusted not to abscond. Because of the ease with which prisoners could abscond, and in response to local feeling in the community, some open prisons will not take prisoners convicted of sexual offences.

Prisoners in open conditions are likely to be released from prison regularly in order to work, make town visits and temporary releases on resettlement or facility licence. Open prisons do not usually have full-time medical staff, and so prisoners will be released to attend local hospitals, dentists and opticians rather than being treated by Prison Health Care staff. Prisoners with serious medical problems which require constant attention or monitoring will often not be allocated to open conditions and will remain in prisons where there is full-time medical care.

4.9. RESETTLEMENT PRISONS

The first resettlement prison to open was at HMP Latchmere House in 1991. Since then, several smaller units have opened at local and category C and D prisons. Long-term prisoners are transferred to resettlement prisons towards the end of their sentences in order that they might re-establish their links with their families and the wider community and obtain paid employment. It is hoped that this will significantly diminish rates of recidivism. Because much of prisoners' time will be spent outside the prison, the facilities at resettlement prisons are generally poorer than at other prisons. Prisoners found guilty of breaches of prison discipline will generally be transferred out to higher security establishments, as are those who are suspected of being involved in any subversive behaviour.

4.10. Vulnerable Prisoners' Units (VPU)

Prisoners convicted of sexual offences and others are, historically, not acceptable to the mainstream prison population (because they are informers, in debt to other prisoners, or former police or prison officers) and they might have asked to be segregated for their own protection under the provisions of Rule 45 of the Prison Rules. Whilst this removed the immediate threat of violence from other prisoners, it meant that the most vulnerable prisoners in the system were often held in the very worst conditions in the prison system.

In response to an increase in the number of prisoners segregated for their own protection, the Prison Service set up a number of Vulnerable Prisoners' Units ('VPU')which were intended for:*'... a relatively small number of medium and long sentence prisoners – mainly sex offenders and child abusers , who will fail all attempts to survive on normal location and who will need to remain in a protected environment until their discharge, whilst having the benefit of the facilities available to other medium and long term prisoners.'* (Report of the Prison Department Working Group on the Management of Vulnerable Prisoners (1989)).

Sex offenders and other vulnerable prisoners may be held in the whole range of prison conditions during their sentences. Some prisons hold them on normal location, others have specific wings where they are segregated from mainstream prisoners, and there are a number of prisons that specialise in the containment and treatment of sex offenders, e.g. HMP Whatton, which only holds categoryC sex offenders.

4.11.1. WOMEN'S PRISONS

There are 19 prisons in the female prison system. Unlike men's prisons, women's prisons are simply categorised as either open, closed or local prisons. Female youth offenders are held with adult prisoners in prisons which will have certain areas designated as young offender institutions. In March 2005, 35% of women were held for drug offences and only 10% of adult women sentenced to prison are convicted of offences involving violence. The majority of women serve short sentences in comparison to male prisoners. Women prisoners held for drug offences must be medically treated if they are addicts and witholding of such medical treatment can be viewed as torture and a breach of their human rights as occurred in the case of *McGlinchey and others v. The United Kingdom* [1999]. Judith McGlincheydied in hospital on 3 January 1999, aged 31. Ms McGlinchey, who had a long history of heroin addiction and was asthmatic, was convicted of theft and sentenced to four months' imprisonment on 7 December 1998. While in prison (between 7 and 14 December 1998) she manifested heroin-withdrawal symptoms, had frequent vomiting fits and lost a lot of weight. The day after her admission she was seen by a doctor who prescribed treatment for her various problems, including medication for her heroin-withdrawal symptoms. The nursing notes showed that one dose of the prescribed drug was omitted at midday on 8 December 1998 . The doctor saw her again on 10 December 1998, prescribed an injection for the continuing withdrawal symptoms and gave instructions for her weight to be monitored. The next day she was moved to intensive care where she was kept on a life-support machine and heavily sedated. She died on 3 January 1999. The applicants, her relatives, complained, under Article 3 of the European Convention on Human Rights, that Ms McGlinchey had suffered inhuman and degrading treatment in prison prior to her death and that there had been no effective remedy available to them to bring a complaint. They alleged, among other things, that the prison authorities had deliberately withheld her medication and locked her in her cell as a punishment for her difficult behaviour; that they had administered her medication irregularly; and that she had been left ti lie in her own vomit. The Court said that ill-treatment had to attain a minimum level of severity to fall within the scope of Article 3. The State had a duty to ensure that a person was detained in conditions which were compatible with respect for human dignity, including proper provision for their health and well-being in the form of the requisite medical assistance. No compensation was available under English law for the suffering and distress that the Court had found to amount to a violation of Article 3. The Court concluded that Ms McGlinchey, or the applicants acting on her behalf, should have been able to apply for compensation for the non-pecuniary damage she had suffered. As there had been no remedy by which to examine the standard of care given to her in prison and the possibility of obtaining damages, there had been a breach of Article 13.

4.11.2. CLOSED LOCAL WOMEN'S PRISONS

Seven prisons operate as closed local prisons (Brockhill, Edmunds Hill, Eastwood Park, Low Newton, Holloway, Styal and New Hall) and women will be held in one of these prisons whilst they are on remand, until they are allocated to another establishment after conviction, or where they are serving short sentences. Female category A remand prisoners are held at Holloway prison, as are women who are in need of psychiatric care. The remaining closed women's prisons are Bronzefield, Buckley Hall, Bullwood Hall, Cookham Wood, Durham, Downview, Foston Hall, and Send. These operate similar regimes to category B and C prisons in the men's prison estate. Holloway is a reman prison for women but keeps some long-term prisoners for significant parts of their sentences.

4.11.3. CONVICTED CATEGORY A WOMEN PRISONERS

The main reasons for their current category 'A' status are convictions for a terrorist offence; the likelihood of attempted escape, of reoffending, and public reactions. Category A prisoners are automatically subjected to strip-search before and after all legal and social visits. Lights may be kept on at night. Visitors have to be cleared by police and the Home Office, a process that takes weeks. Durham Prison is one of the most famous in the country. It has been the home of some of Britain's most infamous criminals over the years, including serial murderers Mary Ann Cotton, Rose West and Myra Hindley and terrorist bomber Judith Ward; convicted category A prisoners. Durham prison also held drug smuggler Sandra Gregory. A women are held in a discrete wing at Durham (whose other functions are a local prison for male prisoners, and a close supervision centre). This is the highest security prison in the women's prison estate In 2003 it was revealed that Durham had the highest suicide rate of all prisons in England. An extremely critical report was published in 2004 by the Chief Inspector of Prisons which found that conditions in the female wing of Durham prison were restricted, oppressive and claustrophobic. Since then, all female prisoners were moved out of Durham prison which now holds Category B local male prisoners. Bronzefield Prison is a privately managed prison, opened since June 2004 for the UK's category A women prisoners. It is currently the only prison to house Category A prisoners in the female estate

4.11.4. OPEN WOMEN' PRISONS

There are three open women's prisons – Askham Grange, Drake Hall Morton Hall and East Sutton Park.

4.11.5. 1.WOMEN'S PRISONS WITH MOTHER AND BABY UNITS

In addition to the above, there are five mother and baby units in the women's prison estate. These are found at HMPs Bronzefield, Askham Grange, Styal, Holloway, New Hall. The purpose of mother and baby units is to: *'allow the mother/baby relationship to develop whilst safeguarding the child's welfare.'* (PSO 4801, 2nd edn). The 'culture and ethos' of the units is described as follows: *'It is policy that babies are not locked in rooms. When mothers on the units are required to remain in their rooms, room doors will not be locked. The ethos of mother and baby units is that they are fair and open ... all documents relating to babies will be disclosed to the mother. The whole application process must be conducted openly, with the mother involved at all stages.'* (PSO 4801, p 4). Figures from the Ministry of Justice show that 283 children were born in prisons in England and Wales between April 2005 and July 2008. The latest sentencing guidelines stress that in cases where jail is not regarded as essential courts may regard pregnancy as a mitigating factor. There are seven specialised mother and baby units in prisons across England. New babies can stay with their mothers for between nine and 18 months, and often leave when their mothers finish their sentences. Older children of women serving longer sentences are taken either to live with relatives outside prison or are put into care.

Holloway and New Hall have facilities for women to keep their babies with them up until they are nine months old; Style and Askham Grange will allow mothers to keep their babies until they are 18 months old. No information is yet available about age limits applying in Bronzefield. Female prisoners have taken litigation to keep their babies with them longer than the prescribed age limits, and some cases have been successful (see, for example, *R (P & Q) v Home Secretary* [2001] 1 WLR 2002, where the Court of Appeal found that a blanket policy to remove a child at 18 months was unlawful, and that each case should be considered on its own particular facts).

4.11.5.2. Criteria for acceptance in Women's Prisons Mother and Baby Unit

In considering women's applications to go to a mother and baby unit, the following criteria are considered by the Admissions Board:

'It is in the best interests of the child/children to be placed in a mother and baby unit.
The mother is able to demonstrate behaviour and attitude which is not detrimental to the safety and well-being of other unit residents (or the good order and discipline of the unit).
The mother has provided a urine sample which tests negative for drugs.
The mother is willing to remain drug free.
The mother is willing to sign a standard compact, which may be tailored to her identified individual needs.
The mother's ability and eligibility to care for a child is not impaired by health or legal reasons.. The Admissions Board is normally made up of an independent chairperson, the mother, an operational officer of the mother and baby unit, a probation officer, a social services representative, a nursery nurse, a health visitor and any other appropriate professionals.

The Board will have access to a dossier of information from Social Services, security reports, medical reports, a wing conduct report, and information from the Probation Service. Where a woman is refused a place on the mother and baby unit, arrangements will be made for her to be separated from her child. The mother must be involved in planning the separation, where appropriate. If there is a care order or supervision order in force, or if the child's safety is at risk, then Social Services will take the lead in arranging the separation. There is a right of appeal against the refusal to offer a place and 'no impediment must be placed in the way of the prisoner who wishes to express her grievance outside the system, eg by taking legal advice.

4.12. PROTECTED WITNESS UNITS

The Prison Service does maintain special units to house protected witnesses. Guidance on admission criteria is contained in PSI 71/2000. Allocation is highly exceptional, and made only if supported by the CPS and a police officer of at least the rank of assistant chief constable. Those housed in PWUs are all referred to as 'Bloggs' with a number. As the allocation of prisoners to such units is because of threats to their safety or their life, ECHR, article 2 (the right to life) is engaged in the decision making process (see *R(Bloggs 61) v Home Secretary* [2003] EWCA 686). In *Bloggs61* the Court of Appeal confirmed that when looking at such decisions it was inappropriate to apply a formula of general application, but to consider whether, in light of all the relevant facts, a prisoner's right to life might be infringed by a refusal to locate in a PWU. Despite the unqualified nature of the article, given the context of such decisions, the court will show some deference to the decision maker and will not therefore conduct a full merits review.

4.13. ISSUES IN ADULT PRISONS

There are many issues relating to adult prisons, violence in adult prisons and even violence in women prisons. Prisons housing men have long been regarded as very dangerous places and a review of the literature reveals that inmate on inmate violence in men's prisons is a wide-spread and well-documented phenomenon (see e.g., Robertson, 2003; Toch, 1998; Walters, 1998). Preliminary efforts to explore violence among female inmates suggest that violence and aggression among female inmates is a substantial problem and is more prevalent than previously suspected (Campbell, 1986; McGuire, 2005). Even sexual violence, once believed to be a problem only among male inmates, appears to be an issue for female inmates as well (Easteal, 2001). More research is necessary to establish what infections there are among prison population, and other health issues. Another issue is the impact of imprisonment on family life. Studies of the effects of crime and the economy on marriage supports a skeptical view of imprisonment's corrosive effect on family life. Criminal offenders are often found to have weak family attachments. For example, the young delinquents studied by Robert Sampson and John Laub (1993, 132) were 2 to 4 times more likely to get divorced than their nondelinquent counterparts. While married, men with criminal backgrounds were 2 to 3 times more likely to be only weakly attached to their wives. Fathers with criminal records are also less likely to be closely involved with their children, and their families are more unstable (e.g., Farrington 1989; Baker and Mednick 1984). Consequently, low rates of family attachment among exprisoners may be due to a selection effect and not imprisonment. Criminal offenders—the men selected to go to prison—are less likely to develop strong ties to wives and children regardless of whether they are incarcerated. Weak marital and family connections have long predated the prison boom in the poor black neighbourhoods that supply the penal system with inmates. The term incapacitation usually describes how incarceration reduces crime by restraining prisoners from committing crime in society (Zimring and Hawkins 1995). Just as the penal system restrains prisoners from crime, it may also restrain them from performing the prosocial roles of suitor, spouse, and parent. While incarcerated, prisoners of course have little opportunitiy to meet partners and get married.

Married men are prevented from contributing emotionally and financially to their primary relationships.

For incarceration to matter, prisoners must have family and friends to be incapacitated from. Kathryn Edin and her colleagues (2004) interviewed a large number of incarcerated fathers and their children in Charleston, South Carolina, and argued that the effects of father absence are farreaching:

Incarceration often means that fathers miss out on those key events that serve to build parental bonds and to signal to the community that they intend to support their children both financially and emotionally. These key events include attending the child's birth or observing developmental milestones such as walking and talking. The father's absence at these crucial moments, we argue, can weaken his commitment to the child and, years later, the child's own commitment to his or her father (Edin et al. 2004, 57).

4.14. DAMAGES FOR MISFEASANCE IN MOVING PRISONERS FROM ONE PRISON TO ANOTHER

An important issue is that of moving prisoners about from one category of prison to another and in *Ibrahim Karagozlu v Commissioner of Police of the Metropolis*

[2006] EWCA Civ 1691, in which was found that loss of liberty was a form of special or material damage sufficient to support a claim for misfeasance in public office if the other ingredients of the tort were made out, and loss of residual liberty, such as a further restriction on a claimant's liberty caused by movement from open to closed prison conditions, was also actionable in misfeasance. The facts were that in March 2002, following the receipt of information from the police that K's life might be in danger if he remained in open conditions, he was moved to a closed Category B prison. K complained about his transfer, contending that he was not in any danger, and asked that his case be investigated. In October 2002 K was returned to the open prison and re-categorised as a Category D prisoner. K subsequently sought damages, including aggravated and exemplary damages, against C in misfeasance and the second defendant Home Office in both misfeasance and negligence. As against C, K alleged that the information leading to his transfer was false and was known to be false, and had been passed to the prison service maliciously with the intention of causing him damage.

The Home Office applied to strike out K's claim against it and succeeded. K then appealed and it was held that loss or damage was an essential ingredient of the tort of misfeasance, (*Watkins v Secretary of State for the Home Department* (2006) UKHL 17 , (2006) 2 AC 395applied). A person who was unlawfully detained and lost his freedom as a result of false imprisonment was entitled to general damages. It was not correct in principle to distinguish between what was injury or damage for the purposes of false imprisonment on the one hand and for the purposes of the tort of misfeasance on the other. In the absence of a claim for identifiable loss, a successful claimant should be entitled to recover general damages for loss of liberty in the case of either tort, assessed in accordance with the guidelines laid down in Thompson. Thus, loss of liberty was a form of special or material damage sufficient to support a claim for misfeasance in public office if the other ingredients of the tort were made out.

4.15. PSYCHIATRY REPORT OF ADULT PRISONS

Responsibility for the provision of health care moved from the Home Office to the Department of Health during a transitional period from April 2003 to 2006. The Report in 2006, titled '*Prison Psychiatry:Adult Prisons in England and Wales*' concerned itself with the development of psychiatric services in prisons in England and Wales. Prison healthcare is provided within a larger institution with a radically different philosophy and culture to health, being primarily centred upon security and control. Resources are likely to be limited both in quantity and diversity. The epidemiology of mental disorder and the nature of prison environment result in the role of the psychiatrist in prison being a particularly challenging one. As to drug addiction in prisons, the Report recommends that addiction specialists increase their input into prison healthcare. *'Those developments include a greater awareness of the extent of substance misuse in prison; its association with ill health, overdose, suicide and criminal recidivism; and the introduction of maintenance treatment for opiate addiction. We therefore recommend that there should be sessional input from addiction specialists, who will establish protocols of care; advice on complex case; initiate research; provide an input into training; help develop drug strategies and liaise with other professionals, for example forensic psychiatrists and hepatologists'.*

The Report highlights important differences between male and female prison establishments and male and female prisoners, including differences in the epidemiology of mental disorder and particular issues around childcare and separation from children. In 2003 one in four of the prison population came from a minority ethnic group compared to one in eleven of the general population.

4.16. YOUTH IN ADULT PRISONS

There have been many reports of young people held in adult prisons where they will experience an acute lack of purposeful activity. The Prison Service was holding young offenders in adult prisons by reclassifying individual cells as young offenders' institutions. The practice emerged during investigations by the inquiry into the murder of Zahid Mubarek, who was beaten to death in Feltham young offenders' institution in 2001. The inquiry visited eight prisons and found that in at least one privately run adult prison, HMP Altcourse in Fazakerley, near Liverpool, young offenders were being held in cells on the same wing as adult offenders. There are about 2,900 children in penal custody, of whom about 230 are in secure children's homes, 270 in secure training centres and the remainder in young offender institutions

4.17. CONCLUSION

Recent reports show that the United Kingdom prison system is in great danger of collapse from overcrowding. There is much amiss in UK prisons including suicides, psychiatric illnesses and drug addictions. Other health issues are in need of reporting and it is not known how many prisoners are suffering from HIV infection and other infections from cross-contamination due to overcrowding. The situation is dire.

CHAPTER 5 - JUVENILES IN PRISON

5.1.1. INTRODUCTION

The word juvenile is defined differently by varying terms including youthful, immature, childish etc., and the juvenile delinquent may be defined as a young person who habitually breaks the law, especially somebody repeatedly charged with vandalism or other anti-social behaviour. Thus those offences committed by adults and punishable, which when committed by children or youth under the age of eighteen are denoted as juvenile crimes and the juvenile courts deal with such cases.

5.1.2. UNACCEPTABLE JUVENILE BEHAVIOUR

Youth crime and anti-social behaviour are often fuelled by alcohol and peer pressure. In addition to the powers recently introduced by the Government surrounding anti-social behaviour, the introduction of Anti Social Behaviour Orders (ASBOs) and Acceptable Behaviour Contracts (ABCs), figures indicate that 65% of those who received an intervention, such as a warning letter or ABC, did not re-offend, with the figure rising to 93% after three interventions had occurred.

5.1.3. KNIFE-CARRYING YOUTH WILL BE CHARGED

A greater number of searches on young people are to be conducted and more search equipment is to be provided, to help take weapons off the streets. The consequences will also be graver, with those over 16 facing prosecution for the first time if found carrying a knife. Furthermore, those under the age of 16 will face prosecution on their second offence. Due to the success of the neighbourhood policing initiative there are over 3,600 neighbourhood policing teams consisting of nearly 30,000 officers and PCSOs to work with the community to identify young offenders and prevent their offending or anti-social behaviour from escalating. Building on this community plan, young people who are involved in crime will be made to engage with youth workers and ex gang members, working in partnership with the police, in an attempt to combat the negative influence that delinquent peer groups can have. There are also proposals to expand Operation Staysafe, where police use existing child protection legislation to remove children and young people from the street late at night to a place of safety. Current trials have suggested that this is an effective approach in preventing crime, with each operation removing an average of twenty children from the streets each night.

Upon arrest, an assessment by a Youth Offending Team worker is currently dependant on a referral by the police and will typically occur several days after the young offender has been in police contact. Under new proposals a Youth Offending Team worker will be based at the police station, or will be available on call, which will allow for an assessment immediately after arrest and the opportunity, if appropriate, to divert young people from the Youth Justice System. In addition, the number of after school police patrols will be increased to tackle anti-social behaviour and disorder at school closing time and transport interchanges. Local intelligence from schools, parents and the local community will assist the police patrols in targeting problem areas. Research from young people in particular suggested that an increased presence of police and PCSOs in between young people and the police promote school safety and reduce the risks of crime and anti social behaviour. To build on this further, it is planned that every school will have a named police contact.

5.1.4. SUPPORTING YOUNG VICTIMS

In recent years the Government has significantly improved the services for victims of crime, particularly through the introduction of the Code of Practice for Victims of Crime. Extra protection is available for young witnesses, with those under the age of seventeen, automatically considered vulnerable, and as a result, entitled to an enhanced service and special measures in court. Despite this, however, young people are less likely to report crimes to the police, even though they are more likely to be victims of crime than adults are. Research shows that this is often because young people are afraid to come forward. To tackle this, innovative ways of supporting young victims will be tested and good practice guidance will be issued on how best to support young witnesses before they attend court.

5.1.5. FAMILY INTERVENTION PROJECTS

Due to poor and indifferent parenting, some children are particularly vulnerable and as a result are at a greater risk of offending. The action plan introduces measures which will provide support, both to young people and their families, as a means of preventing future offending. Family Intervention Projects were introduced in 2006 and have proved successful. As a result the Government wants to build on this success by extending the reach of intensive family intervention to every local authority within the next three years. The focus is to ensure that existing services, such as Sure Start, are better targeted to the 110,000 families with children who are most likely to become prolific offenders. Surestart is a government programme designed to ensure that every child receives the best possible start in life (please see http://www.surestart.gov.uk/). By 2010 the aim is to reach 20,000 families across the country. There will be additional support for parents of young offenders, or those at risk of offending, provided through existing Youth Offending Team measures. The Government is also exploring ways to better engage parents in the Youth Justice System, including a requirement for them to take a greater responsibility for their children's behaviour. This could include giving parents a legal responsibility to ensure that their child completes a sentence, not dissimilar from their current duty to ensure their child attends school. There will be an expansion of Safer School Partnerships ('SSP') which can significantly improve the relationships.

On a wider scale, there is a need for the Government to be responsive and accountable to young people and the rest of the community. This will be achieved by ensuring that they are involved in tackling youth crime and in the decisions that affect them. Information will be provided to young people and their parents about the dangers and risks involved so they can protect themselves; building on the advertising campaign recently launched by the Government and further helping to tackle knife crime by setting up youth forums to engage young people with the police and policy makers. The detention of people under 18 years of age, especially in Prison Service establishments, is a contemporary topic in the wake of many assaults by youths on youths at the present time.

Anti-social behaviour among British youth today is a phenomenon never seen before. Instances of gangs of young people attaching and murdering other young people, rioting, attacking the police, attacking anyone who admonishes them, are rife. Law-abiding citizens are living in the United Kingdom in terror of youths.

5.2. CHILDREN NOT PLANNED FOR IN UK PRISONS

The prison industry is a very profitable privatised industry in the UK. For these reasons:-

(i) In September 2003, Serco estimated that its existing UK prisons and correctional services contracts were valued at £2 billion.

(ii) They are run by multinational companies such as Group 4, Premier, Serco, Sodexho and Securicor. All the Immigration Detention Centres are privately operated.

(iii) These and other companies also design and build prisons, transport prisoners, run holding cells in courts, supply food, supply the police with equipment and so on. There are now ten private prisons in the United Kingdom. These prisons hold 9 per cent of the prison population.

That young people commit crime at a high rate is no revelation. Age is so fundamental to crime rates that its relationship to offending is usually designated as the "age-crime curve." This curve, which for individuals typically peaks in the late teen years, highlights the tendency for crime to be committed during an offender's younger years and to decline as age advances. For example, figures on rates of robbery and burglary, broken down by age, indicate that for both these crimes, the peak age of offending has been about age seventeen, after which there is a rapid decline as the offender gets older. For burglary, the rate falls to half the peak by age , rate moving to a sharp peak at age eighteen instead of the more traditional flat peak covering the entire eighteen to twenty-four age group, whereas the fall-off for robbery is somewhat slower, reaching half the peak rate by age twenty five.

5.3.1. KNIFE CRIMES AND RELEVANT LEGISLATION

Levels of knife crime are around 6-7% of all violent crime. A 2003 Home Office report noted that out of a total of 18,900 people stopped and searched in 2001–2002 under s60 of the Public Order Act 1994 (i.e. in 'anticipation of violence'), 7% were found to be carrying an offensive or dangerous instrument, and 1% ended up being arrested for possession Laws restricting the sale, carrying, use and production of knives are contained in a number of pieces of legislation: the Prevention of Crime Act 1953; the Restriction of Offensive Weapons Act 1959; the Criminal Justice Act 1988; the Public Order Act 1994; the Offensive Weapons Act 1996; the Knives Act 1997; the Criminal Justice Act 1988; and the Violent Crime Reduction Act 2006.

The minimum age at which one can buy a knife is eighteen. However, having a knife in a public place (including schools) without a 'lawful reason' is a criminal offence, which carries a penalty of up to four years' imprisonment. A knife carried in a public place without a lawful reason is likely constitute an 'offensive weapon', which is defined by the Prevention of Crime Act 1953 as '*any article made or adapted for use for causing injury to the person, or intended by the person having it with him for such use by him or by some other person*'. The carrying of a knife while committing another crime (such as burglary or theft) is likely to result in a harsher sentence. It is also an offence to use another person to mind a weapon. If the person is a child, this is considered to be an 'aggravating' factor when sentencing the perpetrator. Although it is an offence (under the Violent Crime Reduction Act 2006) to have an article with a blade or point in a school or public place without good reason, this does not apply to folding pocket knives with a blade of less than three inches. On the other hand, certain types, such as flick knives, gravity knives and replica samurai swords are banned altogether. The police have the power to stop and search individuals within a given area for offensive weapons, including knives.

5.3.2. KNIFE CRIMES IN SCHOOLS
Under the Violent Crime Reduction Act 2006 school, staff are entitled to search pupils for knives. Police constables also have the right to enter a school and search the premises and/or people if there are 'reasonable grounds for suspecting' that weapons are held there.

5.3.3. KNIFE CRIME STATISTICS
Up to 2007, knives have been included in the category of 'sharp instrument', which includes bottles, glass, screwdrivers etc. According to the Homicide Index (a record of all suspected homicides occurring in England and Wales), 35 per cent of victims were killed using a 'sharp instrument' in 2005/06 – by far the single largest category of method of homicide. Official figures for homicides caused solely by the use of knives are being collected by police forces from 2007/08.

5.4. MURDER BY YOUTHS
The increase in murder by very young people in recent years has not at all been matched by increases among the older groups (aged 24 and over). Among young people over age 24, murder rates have even declined. Thus, much of the general increase in the aggregate homicide rate (accounting for all ages) in the late today is attributable to the spurt in the murder rate by young people.

5.5. GUN CRIME BY YOUTHS
Also intensifying the fear of crime is the increasing involvement of guns in homicides committed by young people. This factor generates fear because of the recognition that young people are less likely to exercise the restraint necessary to handle dangerous weapons, particularly rapid-fire assault weapons. As to the immediacy of the gun violence problem, prevention needs to be accompanied by stronger enforcement. The rate of homicides committed by young people, the number of

homicides they committed with guns, and the arrest rate of non-white juveniles for drug offenses has risen sharply.

The age cohort responsible for much of the recent youth violence is the smallest it has been in recent years. By contrast, the cohort of children ages 5 to 15, who will be moving into the crime-prone ages in the near future, is larger. This suggests that if current age-specific rates do not decline, Prison planning needs to begin now to address the increase in crime likely to occur as this group grows older.

5.6.1. DRUGS AND YOUTH CRIME

The public has a vague sense of a link between the growth in juvenile violence and drugs. In part, this derives from recognition that, especially in the past decade, a major factor affecting many aspects of criminal behaviour has been the illicit drug industry and its consequences. The acceleration in drug arrests of young men reflects a major recruitment of sellers to market "crack. The process starts with the illicit drug industry, which recruits juveniles partly because they work more cheaply than adults, partly because the sanctions they face are less severe than those imposed by the adult criminal justice system, and partly because they tend to be daring and willing to take risks that more mature adults would eschew. The plight of many urban juveniles, many of whom see no other comparably satisfactory route to economic sustenance, makes them particularly vulnerable to the lure of the profits of the drug industry. The growth in the drug arrest rate of juveniles is evidence of this recruitment. Ecstasy is a drug in the same category as heroin and cocaine and the normal starting point for possession of such a drug with intent to supply is 5 years. The following table is an indication of sentencing for ecstasy- with no rational rhyme of reason to sentences.

5.6.2. Sentences for Drug Crimes

Case	Citation	Sentence	Facts
R v Steventon	[1992] 13 Cr App Rep (S) 127	2 years	Possession of 730 grammes of cannabis resin, with unexplained financial transactions over 2½ years
R v Nolan	[1992] 13 Cr App Rep (S) 144	2 ½ years	Supplying half an ounce of cannabis to boys aged 15 and 16
R v Allery	[1993] 14 Cr App Rep (S) 699	5 years	Possession of 19 Ecstasy tablets
R v Broom	[1993] 14 Cr App Rep (S) 677	3 years	Possession of 190 Ecstasy tablets with intent to supply
R v Burton	[1993] 14 Cr App Rep(S) 716	5 years	Possession of 1,470 Ecstasy tablets with intent to supply
R v Catterall (20-year-old)	[1993] 14 Cr App Rep (S) 724	2 years	Possession with intent to supply and supplying Ecstasy and LSD
R v McLellan	[1993] 15 Cr App Rep (S) 351	2 years	Supplying ONE tablet of Ecstasy

Case	Citation	Sentence	Facts
R v Jones	[1994] 15 Cr App Rep (S) 856	4 years	Possession of 27 Ecstasy tablets with intent to supply
R v McLaughlin	[1994] 16 Cr App Rep (S) 357	4 years	Possession of 1,000 Ecstasy tablets with intent to supply
R v Kingham	[1994] 16 Cr App Rep (S) 399	3 years	Possession of 199 Ecstasy tablets and 79 LSD tablets
R v Asquith Youth	[1994] 16 Cr App Rep (S) 453	3 years	Possession of 48 Ecstasy tablets with intent to supply
R v Spalding	[1995] 16 Cr App Rep (S) 803	18 months	Possession of 54 Ecstasy tablets minding them
R v Bryne	[1995] 2 Cr App Rep (S) 34	12 months	Possession of 18 Ecstasy tablets to share with friends
R v Skidmore	[1996] 1 Cr App Rep (S) 15	2 years	Offering to sell fake Ecstasy tablets in nightclub

ENGLISH PRISON LAW

Case	Citation	Sentence	Facts
R v Prince	1996] 1 Cr App Rep (S) 335	5 years	Possession of 10 wraps of heroin at 27% purity weighing a total of 491 milligrammes and admitted supplying the heroin to his son who was serving a sentence of imprisonment
R v Chesterton 16-year-old	[1997] 2 Cr App Rep (S) 297	3 years	Supplying LSD to schoolboys at school of which one defendant was an ex-pupil
R v Harvey	[1997] 2 Cr App Rep (S) 306	3 ½ years	Possession of 900 Ecstasy tablets with intent to supply but acting as warehouseman
R v Netts	[1997] 2 Cr App Rep (S) 117	5 years	Possessing 94 kilograms of cannabis resin
R v Thompson Youth	[1997] 2 Cr App Rep (S) 223	4 years	Supplying Ecstasy at a nightclub
R v Wakeman	[1999] 1 Cr App Rep (S) 222	18 months	Offering to supply Ecstasy tablets to friend

Case	Citation	Sentence	Facts
R v Fairburn	[1998] 2 Cr App Rep (S) 4	3 ½ years	Possessing 92.8 kilogrammes of herbal cannabis
R v Slater Youth	[1998] 2 Cr App Rep (S) 415	3 years	Attempting to smuggle 198 mg of heroin into a prison where the defendant's brother was serving a sentence
R v Ellingham 20-year-old	[1999] 2 Cr App Rep (S) 243	3 years	Attempted to take 0.1 grammes of heroin into prison to supply to her boyfriend
R v Appleton	[1999] 2 Cr App Rep (S) 289	5 years	Serving prisoner -for possession of small quantities of heroin, cannabis resin, herbal cannabis and amphetamine with intent to supply
R v Bull 21-year-old	[2000] 2 Cr App Rep (S) 195	9 months	Supplied 2 Ecstasy tablets to friend who later died from heart failure

Case	Citation	Sentence	Facts
R v Busby	[2000] 1 Cr App Rep (S) 279	6 months	Possession of 14 Esctasy tablets with intent to share with friends
R v Cowap	[2000] 1 Cr App Rep (S) 284	4 years	Possessing a wrap containing half of one gramme of cocaine of 96% purity with intent to supply to her boyfriend who was a serving prisoner
R v Kitching	[2000] 2 Cr App Rep (S) 194	18 months	Supplied small quantities of cannabis to pupils aged between 15 and 17
R v Hamilton	[2000] 1 Cr App Rep (S) 91	2 years	Attempted to smuggle 6.02 grammes of heroin into a prison for use by a prisoner

Case	Citation	Sentence	Facts
R v Young	[2000] 2 Cr App Rep (S) 248	2 ½ years	Possessing 10.7 grammes of heroin and 25.9 grammes of cannabis with intent to supply - defendant attempted to smuggle the drugs into a prison for her boyfriend who was serving a life sentence
A-G Reference (No 71 of 2002)	[2002] EWCA Crim 2217, [2003] 1 Cr App Rep (S) 99	18 months	Sale of 17 Ecstasy tablets and possession of another 32 tablets
R v Mapp	[2002] EWCA Crim 3182; [2003] 2 Cr App Rep (S)	8 months	Supplying 2 tablets at cost price
R v Thomas	[2004] EWCA Crim 3092; [2005] 2 Cr App Rep (S) 10	2 years	Possession of 5,000 mushrooms with intent to supply
R v Donovan	[2004] EWCA Crim 1327, [2005] 1 Cr App R(S) 16	6 months	Possession of 409.9g cannabis with intent to supply

(Table produced by Sally Ramage. Sources: English caselaw)

With the above table in mind, a look at prison sentences suitable for juveniles is needed. The position is that person under 18 year old can be given the following determinate custodial sentences (see Chapter 12 for life sentences for children):

A Detention and Training Order (DTO, is now imposed under s 100 of the Powers of the Criminal Courts (Sentencing) Act 2000). The DTO was introduced to rationalise the pre-existing sentencing arrangements for children, and so replaced the sentence of detention in a Young Offender Institution for 15 to 17 year olds and the secure training order for 12 to 14 year olds. The maximum sentence is 24 months, and generally, half is served in custody and half in the community. Youth Offending Teams (YOTs) are responsible for Sentence planning during the custodial and community parts of the sentence. It can be imposed on offenders who commit offences before their 18th birthday.

A sentence under PCC(S) A 2000, s. 91 (which replaced Children and Young Persons Act 1933, s. 53) is imposed for serious offences for which adults could receive a sentence of 14 years or more. The sentence is for a fixed term and calculated in the same manner as Sentences of imprisonment for adults. It can be imposed on 10 to 17 year olds. The sentence of detention in a Young Offender Institution is only available for those aged 18 and above (PCC(S) A 2000, s. 96).

5.7. GUNS ARE LETHAL IN IMMATURE HANDS

Life sentences are given to juveniles who kill, as in *R (on the application of K) v Parole Board* [2006] EWHC 2413 (Admin), CO/6826/2006, in an application for permission to apply for judicial review brought on behalf of a 15 year old young man, 'K'. K challenged a decision of the Defendant Board made on 5 June 2006 that he was not suitable for early release. K was sentenced to 4 years imprisonment for three offences of robbery, one offence of possession of an imitation firearm at the time of commission of an offence and one offence of handling stolen goods. He also asked for other robberies and an offence of attempted robbery to be taken into consideration. The Reports on K said that he was highly likely to return to being involved in anti-social and offending behaviour at this time, despite the progress he had made at Sutton Place. The Board refused K's application for parole.

According to the Criminal Justice Act 2003, section 227 or 228 as soon as a prisoner, to whom this section applies, has served one-half of the appropriate custodial term, and the Parole Board has directed his release under this section, it is the duty of the Secretary of State to release him on licence. The judicial review bore in mind the words of Lord Mustill in *R v Home Secretary ex parte Doody* [1994] 1 AC 531 at p 561A, [1993] 3 All ER 92, [1993] 3 WLR 154:

'*The court must constantly bear in mind that it is to the decision maker, not the court, that Parliament has entrusted not only the making of the decision but also the choice as to how the decision is made.*'

The Judicial Review considered the human rights of the child and said that the law may frequently require more exacting standards of fairness on the part of authorities dealing with children than would be necessary or appropriate in the case of an adult. *(R (SP) v Home Secretary* [2004] EWHC 1418 Admin,) and quashed the Board's decision not to release the young man.

5.8. YOUTH PRISON STATISTICS

There are currently just fewer than 11,000 under 21's in prison in the United Kingdom. Approximately 3000 of these youth are held in the 15 dedicated Young Offender Institutions (YOIs). Young Offender Institutions were introduced under the Criminal Justice Act 1988, but special centres for housing young offenders have existed since the beginning of the 20th Century. Prisoners serving sentences at young offenders institutions are expected to take part in at least 25 hours of education per week, to improve their behaviour, to develop practical skills for use in the outside world and to prepare them for lawful employment following their release. There are also opportunities for prisoners to undertake work in Community Service Volunteer programmes. The number of juveniles in prison in the United Kingdom has more than doubled since 1993 despite a decline in the number of children convicted or cautioned for offences. The U.K. has the greatest number of imprisoned juveniles of all of the European Member States.

5.9.1. UNITED NATIONS CONVENTION ON THE RIGHTS OF THE CHILD (UNCRC)

The UNCRC is the most successful U.N. human rights treaty with regard to the number of nations that have signed and ratified the treaty. The UNCRC states, *"Neither capital punishment nor life imprisonment without possibility of release shall be imposed for offences committed by persons below eighteen years of age."*

Article 3.1 of UNCRC provides that:

'In all actions concerning children, whether undertaken by public or private social welfare institutions, courts of law, administrative authorities or legislative bodies, the best interests of the child shall be a primary consideration.'

Article 37(c) provides that:

'States parties shall ensure that ... Every child deprived of liberty shall be treated with humanity and respect for the inherent dignity of the human person, and in a manner which takes into account the needs of persons of his or her age. In particular, every child deprived of liberty shall be separated from adults unless it is considered in the child's best interests not to do so'.

5.9.2. UK RESERVATION OF ARTICLE 37(C) UNCRC

The UK government has entered a reservation to the UNCRC in respect of art 37(c) in relation to the separate accommodation of children from adults *'where at any time there is a lack of suitable accommodation or adequate facilities for a particular individual in any institution in which young offenders are detained, or where the mixing of adults and children is deemed to be mutually beneficial'*.

5.10. CASE-LAW ON PRISON ACCOMMODATION OF JUVENILES

There is no dedicated female YOI. This means that girls have routinely ended up being held in adult prisons. A policy of allocating girls to adult prisons without consideration of their individual circumstances under the previous legislative framework was held to be unlawful in *R v Accrington Youth Court, ex p Flood* [1998] 1 WLR 156. A further challenge to the legality of holding under 18 year old girls in Prison Service accommodation was made by a girl who at the age of 16 was transferred into HMP Eastwood Park from a LASCH because of the pressure on places caused by the introduction of secure remands for some 12–14 year olds (see the case of *R(DT) v Home Secretary* [2004] EWHC 13 Admin). The challenge failed, and the court held that the current legislative framework allowed 16 year old girls to be sent to prison and therefore such allocations were not unlawful.

5.11.1. JUVENILE PRISON CONDITIONS

A 2004 report revealed that of the juveniles in prison, 83% of boys and 65% of girls had been previously excluded from school. 41% of boys were aged 14 or younger when last in school; 37% of boys and 43% of girls had previously spent time either in a care or foster home or both; as many girls as boys (1 in 6) reported having an alcohol problem on arrival in prison, and significantly more (40%) admitted to a drugs problem. Around one third said they received help with these problems in prison; 12% of boys reported having children of their own. 5% of girls had their own children, and 3% were pregnant;

and almost half of boys and a quarter of girls had previously been held in a YOI or STC on a different sentence.

The Report revealed the following findings about prison conditions:

*About one in four of the boys and girls were from black or minority ethnic groups.

*One in five boys said staff had physically restrained them.

*24% of boys and 12% of girls said they were hit, kicked, or assaulted by young people while in prison.

*Less than half of the boys were allowed to shower daily and only 18% could go outside for exercise each day.

*A quarter of all young people said they had not received a visit from anyone.

*Only about one in five boys had spoken to an advocate since being imprisoned.

5.11.2. SOLITARY CONFINEMENT OF JUVENILE PRISONERS

In March 2008, former Jersey care home manager, Simon Bellwood, told a tribunal how he stopped a policy of locking children in solitary confinement, solitary confinement being the tool used by the prison for dealing with everyday behaviour problems. There is currently an independent inquiry into the use of strip-searching, physical restraint and solitary confinement of juveniles in penal custody in the UK.

5.11.3. PLACES OF DETENTION

Persons under age 18 can be detained in either:

Local Authority Secure Children Homes (LASCHs); or

Secure Training Centres (STCs); or

Young Offender Institutions (YOIs).

A detailed policy on where children should be detained is contained in the YJB's Secure Facilities Placement Guidance (issued in September 2001). Notwithstanding the Prison Service's creation of a discrete estate for the under 18s *'for children and young people judged to be too vulnerable to be detained in Prison Service accommodation, priorities have been set for their placement elsewhere'.*

5.12. YOUTH PROBATION

Traditionally, the juvenile justice system has employed sanctions, treatment, and rehabilitation to change problem behaviours after they have occurred. Advocates of a prevention-based approach to crime control invite the scorn of critics who believe prevention amounts to little more than feel-good activities. Yet the practitioner—the probation officer , confronted daily with young people in trouble, is often aware of the need for effective prevention. Once they have experienced the reinforcing properties of drugs and are convinced of crime's profitability, young people are difficult to turn around. Once invested in the culture of crime, they reject the virtues attributed to school and family. For them, school is not a place of attachment and learning, but of alienation and failure; family is not a source of love and support, but of unremitting conflict.

5.13. CUSTODY FOR MALE JUVENILES

Prison or, more properly, 'custody' can mean several different things if you are a young person, and means different things depending on whether you are a girl or a boy.

There are three types of 'secure accommodation' in which a juvenile male can be placed:

(i) Secure Training Centres (STC)- there are 4 STCs in England, run by private operators, housing children aged seventeen or younger.

(ii) Local Authority Secure Children's Homes (LASCH): -generally used to house children aged 12 to 14 and 'vulnerable' boys aged 15 and 16.

(iii) Young Offender Institutions (YOI): Run by the Prison Service for 15 to 21 year old boys.

5.14. CUSTODY FOR JUVENILE FEMALES

Girls aged 16 or younger may be held in LASCHs, but the United Kingdom has no YOIs for girls. As a result, if you are a girl and you receive a custodial sentence you will be sent to a juvenile wing of an adult female prison. There are currently around 70 girls under the age of 18 years old in adult prisons and they are held there in breach of the United Nations Convention on the Rights of the Child. The Youth Justice Board, which is responsible for the administration of the juvenile justice system, and Her Majesty's Prison Service consider the removal of 15 and 16 year old girls from adult prison a priority. However, prisons ill-equipped to deal with the unique problems of young people (such as Holloway in London) continue to hold 17 year olds while the government cements plans to build separate prisons for them.

Local Authority Secure Children's Homes aim to provide young people with support tailored to their individual needs. To achieve this, they have a high ratio of staff to young people and are generally small facilities, ranging from 5 to 38 beds. LASCHs Homes are generally used to accommodate young offenders aged 12–14, girls up to the age of 16 and 15 to 16 year old boys who are assessed as vulnerable. The YJB contracts individually with local authorities for the accommodation within them, or can 'spot purchase' as and when required. They are inspected by the Commission for Social Care Inspection.

5.15. SECURE TRAINING CENTRES (STCs)

Secure Training Centres are purpose-built centres for young offenders up to the age of 17. They are run by private operators according to Home Office contracts, which set out detailed operational requirements. The YJB manages these contracts. There are now four STCs in England, with the opening of Oakhill in August 2004:

Oakhill in Milton Keynes;
Hassockfield in County Durham;
Rainsbrook in Rugby;

Medway in Kent.

They house vulnerable young people who are sentenced to custody in a secure environment where they should have access to education and rehabilitative regimes. They differ from YOIs in that they have a higher staff to young offender ratio (minimum of three staff members to eight detainees) and are smaller in size, which means that in principle the individual's needs can be met more easily. They are inspected by the Commission for Social Care Inspection.

5.16. Young Offender Institutions (YOIs)

Young Offender Institutions are facilities run by the Prison Service (with the exception of Ashfield YOI and Parc YOI which are run by private contractors). They accommodate 15 to 21 year olds, although 18 to 21 year olds are generally kept separated from those under 18 years. The Youth Justice Board is only responsible for placing young people under 18 years of age in secure accommodation. The YJB is generally less able to address the individual needs of young people. YOIs are usually considered to be inappropriate accommodation for more vulnerable young offenders. YOIs are inspected by the Chief Inspector of Prisons.

5.17. Serving the sentence

In relation to sentences imposed under PCC(S) A 2000, s 92 states that detention may be in such place and under such conditions as the Secretary of State may direct. In practice, the placement of these children is the responsibility of the 'section 53/92 Unit' within the Juvenile Group at Prison Service Headquarters, who will arrange the appropriate secure accommodation through the YJB.

Secure accommodation is defined as that available in YOIs, STCs, LASCHs or such other accommodation as the Secretary of State may direct. (s 107(1)). The guidance also states that it is not possible to make an absolute statement about which factors will have priority in all cases. Different factors may be more or less important, depending on the circumstances of each young person. The main factors that will affect the placement decision are vulnerability; the need to make local placements; matching regimes to need; needs arising from gender and other factors (S3.01).

In relation to those serving DTOs the policy envisages that: under 15 year olds will go to an STC or LASCH depending on individual circumstances; bed availability and closeness to home; girls over 15, whether deemed vulnerable or not, will be placed in non-Prison Service ; accommodation if available; otherwise, they will be placed in designated Prison Service ;facilities for juvenile girls; boys aged 15 or over and deemed not vulnerable by the relevant YOT will normally go to the local YOI; whenever a young person deemed vulnerable is placed in a YOI, the Placement

5.18. THE ALLOCATION OF CHILDREN TO PRISON SERVICE ESTABLISHMENTS

The policies on allocation recognise that resource implications and the availability of places will often affect where children are detained. The very limited number of places in LASCHs means that vulnerable children will often end up in Prison Service accommodation. The unsuitability of YOIs for children, and especially those considered vulnerable, was highlighted in evidence considered by the court in
R (Howard League) v Home Secretary [2002] EWHC 2497 (Admin)).

5.19.1. REGIMES APPLICABLE TO CHILDREN IN YOIS

With the introduction of the DTO, the Prison Service introduced a distinct estate for under 18s so that they would only be detained in YOIs reserved for this group, or those containing special units for them. Also introduced was specific policy guidance as to the regimes that should be available to those serving DTOs in YOIs. The Children Act does not impose any duties onto the Prison Service itself. This does mean social services departments may be under a duty to assess the needs of children held by the Prison Service. PSO 4950 now confirms that 'the Children Act 1989 relates to all young people under the age 18. Prison Service juvenile regimes must reflect the principles and the spirit of the Act'. PSO 4950 requires YOIs holding children to create Child Protection Committees (CPC) which should include a representative of the local Area Child Protection Committee, a representative of the local YOT and a representative from the Social Services Department for the area in which the establishment is situated. The YOI's child protection procedures must be based on an outline included at Annex B1 to PSO 4950. The courts have decided that unless there are reasons of good order, discipline or urgency, an opportunity to make representations should be given before detained children are put into segregation (*R (SP) v Home Secretary* [2004] EWHC 1418 Admin). There is need to protect vulnerable children from the risk of self-harm and the NAO report stated that there were 460 incidents of self-harm in 2002. In 2008 there were a total of 2,040 incidents of self-inflicted injury reported at young offender institutions. This is compared with 1,835 incidents in 2007. Some of the worst-performing institutions have witnessed increases in self-harm figures of 50 per cent or more since 2006. These include Feltham, Glen Parva, Rochester, Stoke Heath and Warren Hill.

The death of Joseph Scholes, a highly vulnerable 16 year old boy in HMYOI Stoke Heath on 24 March 2002 demonstrates the inadequacy of the Prison Service estate in providing care for vulnerable children, and highlights concerns about YJB allocations. He had a history of depression, self-harm and suicide attempts. He was sentenced to a DTO of 24 months for involvement in the theft of mobile phones and despite his vulnerability was allocated by the YJB to a YOI.

He killed himself nine days into his sentence. Evidence before the Coroner who investigated his death showed that Prison Service accommodation was wholly inadequate for him as it had neither the resources or facilities to deal with someone so vulnerable. In an unprecedented move, the Coroner wrote to the Home Secretary in support of a public inquiry into the death, so that these issues can be properly investigated, although this was rejected by the Home Secretary.

5.19.2. Sentencing and Custody

A key principle of sentencing is that no young person should be sent into custody unless a court is able to specify why dealing within him or her in the community is not appropriate. In applying this however, perceptions that the Youth justice system is too lenient must also be addressed. Measures previously introduced to address reoffending include an increased use of curfews and electronic tagging and an extended use of restorative justice, which aims to bring together victims and offenders. The Government aims to tackle youth crime by strengthening the involvement of the community in the delivery of justice to young offenders. This includes giving the public the chance to identify what reparation work they would like young people on community sentences to carry out, and telling them when this has taken place.

There is to be a greater use of the referral order, which requires young offenders to attend a youth offender panel of community volunteers to answer for their actions and make amends to victims, will be introduced thorough measures in the Criminal Justice and Immigration Act 2008.

A new Youth Rehabilitation Order (YRO) will be implemented from autumn 2009. It will replace nine existing sentences, building on their best elements and making the sentencing framework clearer and more coherent. Courts will be able to tailor the Order to meet the assessed needs of each offender, adding different requirements including undertaking treatment for drug or substance abuse or subjecting them to a curfew which is electronically monitored. In addition, the new Youth Conditional Caution (YCC) will be piloted from April 2009 for 16-17 year olds in a bid to reduce the number of young people who are taken to court for relatively low-level offences. Conditions include requiring the young offender to make amends to their victims and taking an active role in the local community.

5.20. CONCLUSION

A reduction in youth crime can only be achieved if all services and local agencies work together. In support of this the Government will strengthen its response at local level by enhancing the role of Children's Trusts. These will include setting specific responsibilities for improving outcomes, in particular on the prevention of youth crime and re-offending. The duty to co-operate with Children's Trusts will be extended to schools and Sixth Form Colleges. Such involvement will help in early identification and referral of vulnerable young people at a greater risk of crime. Local partners, including the police, will have a leading responsibility for reducing youth crime and the Government will support them in the challenge the Youth Crime Action Plan presents; to focus their efforts on the major priority to make communities safer and improve the lives of children.

The prison system for juveniles is evolving and better prisons are being planned. Cases and decisions challenging the Parole Board's decisions show that when they relate to juveniles, the courts try hard to give leniency, as seen if the decision in *R (on the application of K) v Parole Board [2006]* is compared with the case *R v David Francis Beiber [AKA oleman], CA (Crim Div)23 July 2008,* when the former tried hard to make allowances for the juvenile whilst the latter complied with ruling that the imposition of a sentence of life imprisonment would not invoke a violation of Article 3, Human Rights Act. Although youth crime is increasing and the annual rate of youth crime dealt with through the criminal justice system deals with about 70,000 youths, only 12,000 are sentenced to a penal institution.

CHAPTER 6 - CATEGORISATION, ALLOCATION AND SENTENCE PLANNING

6.1. SECURITY CATEGORISATION

Rule 7 of the Prison Rules 1999 requires the Secretary of State to classify prisoners. The power is expressed broadly to take account of:

'age, temperament and record and with a view to maintaining good order and facilitating training and, in the case of convicted prisoners of furthering the purpose of their training and treatment ...' (Rule 7(1))

The arrangements for the separation of inmates should not *'unduly deprive a prisoner of the society of other persons'* (Rule 7(4)). Rule 4 of the YOI Rules provides that inmates may be classified, in accordance with any directions of the Secretary of State, taking into account their ages, characters and circumstances. For the allocation of under 18 year olds serving custodial. Rule 7 goes on to state that unconvicted prisoners should be kept out of contact with convicted prisoners to the extent that the governor considers that this can reasonably be done. An unconvicted prisoner may never be required to share a cell with a convicted prisoner. This relaxes the previous provisions that forbade mixing in living areas under any circumstances. Adult male prisoners are subject to a more comprehensive system of categorisation than women prisoners and young offenders.

6.2. THE CATEGORISATION OF ADULT MALES

The broad power contained in the Rules once again leaves a great deal of detail to be filled in by the policy documents issued by the Prison Service. The present categories for adult males were first established following a report of the Inquiry into Prison Escapes and Security by Lord Mountbatten in 1977. This established four security categories ranging from A, reserved for the most dangerous prisoners, to D, the lowest category. The procedures for determining a prisoner's category are now set out in PSO 0900, although there is specific guidance on category A procedures contained in PSO 1010.

All prisoners can be made category A, whether unconvicted, female or young offenders. The remaining three categories of B, C and D are reserved for convicted, adult male prisoners. Chapter 1 of PSO 0900 deals with the categorisation and allocation of this group of prisoners. The primary criteria for categorisation are:

'*Category A*: Prisoners whose escape would be highly dangerous to the public, the police or the security of the state and for whom the aim must be to make escape impossible.

Category B: Prisoners for whom the very highest conditions of security are not necessary but for whom escape must be made very difficult.

Category C: Prisoners who cannot be trusted in open conditions but who do not have the resources or will to make a determined escape attempt.

Category D: Prisoners who can be reasonably trusted in open conditions.' (PSO 0900)

Unsentenced prisoners are placed in category U (unclassified) and are normally assumed to require accommodation appropriate to category B. However, PSO 0900 does state that in principle unconvicted prisoners could be considered for category C conditions if there is enough information available to show that category B conditions are not necessary and the decision is approved by the area manager.

6.3. ESCAPE LIST PRISONERS

Prisoners who have successfully escaped or who have attempted escape or for whom there is intelligence that they may try to escape are formally listed as 'E-list' (escape list) prisoners. They are subject to tighter monitoring and, in prisons, will be denied access to activities and locations from where it is considered they may be successful in escaping. Escape list prisoners are subject to stringent security measures set out in an appendix to the Security Manual that require them to be located in the same cells as category A prisoners, with a low-wattage night light for observation at night. They will be subject to are hourly checks of their cells and changing of cells at least once a month without notice. In addition, E List prisoners must wear distinctive E List clothing, normally jackets and trousers with distinctive yellow markings, known to prisoners as patches..

The decision to allocate a prisoner to a security category, save for category A prisoners, rests with the governor of the prison. This will normally be the local prison where the prisoner has been on remand. Perhaps the most important part of this guidance in relation to the initial decision is:

'Prisoners must be categorised objectively according to the likelihood that they will seek to escape and the risk that they would pose should they do so.'

The PSO states that all male prisoners 'must be placed in the lowest category consistent with the needs of security and control'. This is an ongoing duty, as every prisoner, at each stage of their sentence, should be in the lowest category that meets the security risk. These guidelines are of great importance because the security category determines the type of prison to which prisoners are allocated, and also affects other decisions such as entitlement to temporary release on licence. Parole decisions are also affected by the security category of the applicant.

PSO 0900 also provides further detailed guidance on the initial categorisation decision. The starting point is that:

"All prisoners must be regarded as probably suitable for Category D on first categorisation unless they:
- *are sentenced to over 12 months for any offence of violence;*
- *are convicted of any but the most minor sex offence;*
- *have a previous sentence of over 12 months for any violent or sexual offence and did not serve part of that sentence in an open prison;*
- *have current or previous convictions for arson or any drugs offence involving importation or dealing; or*
- *have a recent history of escapes or absconds.'*

After applying these criteria, prisoners should be regarded as 'probably suitable' for category C unless they:
- *are sentenced to over 7 years for any violent or sexual offence;*
- *have a previous sentence of over 7 years for any violent or sexual offence and did not successfully serve part of that sentence in a Category C prison;*
- *have a current sentence exceeding 10 years; or*
- *have a recent history of escape from closed conditions, or have significant external resources which they might use to assist an escape attempt."*

The Order makes it clear that the above criteria must not be seen as either exhaustive or inflexible and a refusal to consider departing from them in the appropriate case would accordingly render a decision unlawful. The application of these criteria should provide a provisional categorisation which can be overridden on control grounds only 'where there is clear evidence that the prisoner will require higher levels of supervision than available in prisons for which the initial criteria have indicated he is suitable'

The Order anticipates that those convicted of non-violent offences or serving short to medium sentences will normally be category C, whilst those convicted of a serious, violent, sexual or drug related offence will normally be category B. However, the Security Manual states that *'no prisoner should be in category B unless he really needs to be held in highly secure conditions'*. Civil prisoners and fine defaulters will normally be category D, as will those who have successfully served a previous sentence in an open prison, unless the new offence is clearly more serious.

The two stage process of initial categorisation will be carried out by the 'Observation, Allocation and Classification' (OCA) unit in the prison . The first stage is a provisional assessment on paper using form ICA1 which directs the documents that should be collected to inform the decision, and contains an algorithm to determine the provisional categorisation. This is followed by consideration of any issues that may override the provisional category as suggested by the algorithm . Any such reasons should be recorded on the form.

The ICA 1 (Initial Categorisation and Allocation) form that records the initial categorisation decision is an open document and can be disclosed to the prisoner, although PSO 0900 confirms that details of allegations against the prisoner may be withheld temporarily from the prisoner on the authority of a governor grade where, for example, disclosure of such details may compromise ongoing investigations.

Although initial and subsequent categorisation decisions will have a significant impact on the conditions of imprisonment, and also the progress the prisoner may make towards release, the courts have held that neither ECHR, art 5 nor 6 is engaged in the decision making process. This is so even when considering whether a prisoner is so dangerous as to warrant category A (see the *Sunder* case below, and in relation to article 5,ECHR, in the case of *R (Burgess) v Secretary of State for the Home Department* [2001] 1 WLR 93).

6.4. THE INITIAL ALLOCATION OF ADULT MALE PRISONERS

Once it is decided which category is appropriate to the prisoner, the decision is made as to where he should be transferred. In the minds of prisoners, security categorisation and allocation are often inextricably linked. However, PSO 0900 warns that while the two procedures will be completed by the same OCA unit, allocation 'must form a process distinct from categorisation.' The Order confirms that an interview with the prisoner should form part of the allocation process unless the sentence is for less than six months . Allocation should take place as soon as practicable after sentence.

The Order also sets out the criteria and priorities used in the allocation process. The three priorities, which are not always compatible are:

"•*the needs of security, including control;*
•*the need to make the maximum use of available spaces in training prisons; and*
•*the needs of the individual prisoner.'*
Staff who work in OCA units are advised that while the main factor in considering where a prisoner should be transferred to after conviction is the security category, account must also be taken of:
•*his suitability for particular types of accommodation (factors such as vulnerability, age, etc);*
•*his medical and/or psychiatric needs that may require a particular type or level of care;*
•*need for identified offence-related behavioural programmes to confront assessed risk;*
•*his home area, or that of his likely visitors;*
•*his educational or training needs or potential;*

•*the published allocation criteria for individual establishments resettlement needs [in line with procedures set out in PSO 2300]".*

PSO 2300 on Resettlement confirms that 'family ties and resettlement needs may therefore be outweighed by other considerations. But, to the extent permitted by operational requirements and a balanced assessment of the prisoner's overall needs, allocation decisions must seek to reinforce the resettlement process'. Whilst the impact on a prisoner's family life of his/her location will engage ECHR, article 8, it will only be in extreme cases that the allocation decision will not be justified under art 8(2) (see EC Commission decision 18632/21 *McCotter v UK*).

Whilst a prisoner should be given the lowest possible security categorisation at all stages in his sentence, other factors may come into play and cause a prisoner to be allocated to a prison which is of a higher security category than his categorisation would appear to merit. This may be because of the type of offence that he has been found guilty of – certain open prisons may not accept prisoners convicted of certain offences, for example. However the Order makes it clear that prisons should never modify the categorisation process in order to match prisoners to available places .

Where a prisoner is allocated to a prison of a higher security rating than his category is, this should be confirmed by a senior officer and the reasons recorded on the ICA1 Form. A prisoner should only be allocated to a prison of a *higher* rating than his category 'on the grounds that no available space is available in prisons of the correct category'.

The procedure for initial allocation is for the OCA department to complete form ICA1, which indicates the sources of information that may be necessary. For prisoners serving over six months, and in other cases, where necessary, the prisoner should be interviewed and any comments he wishes to make should be recorded on the form. On completion of the process, which will also take into account any healthcare needs, the officer making the decision will decide which kind of establishment is suitable for the prisoner, giving reasons, and the prisoner is entitled to a copy of the ICA form if this is requested . The prisoner can complain about the allocation decision through the normal complaints procedure.

Category C prisons are divided into four groups depending upon whether their control capability is deemed very good, good, medium or poor. The aim was to regulate the number of prisoners meeting the high risk criteria outlined above by awarding one point for being under 25 at the date of conviction, one point for serving less than four years, and one point for serving a sentence for burglary or robbery. A category C prisoner who meets all three of the above is defined as a 'score 3' inmate. Each group of prisons is allowed to take a certain percentage of score 3 prisoners. Where control is deemed to be 'very good' the population may comprise 18% score3 inmates, where control is 'poor' a maximum of 8% of the population may be score 3.

6.5. SUBSEQUENT CATEGORISATION DECISIONS

As prisoners have to be in the lowest appropriate category at any given stage in their sentence, prisons must have procedures for reviewing security category as prisoners may become less likely to escape or re-offend. Similarly, it is possible for prisoners to be moved to a higher security category. Chapter 2 of PSO 0900 contains the policy on recategorisation. It is anticipated that further guidance will be published late in 2004 in relation to the recategorisation of D of prisoners serving very long sentences.

In relation to the timing of reviews all prisoners other than those serving less than 12 months must have their security category reviewed at regular intervals, or whenever there is a significant change in their circumstances. Those serving between one and four years should have reviews every six months, and those serving four or more years annual reviews. PSO 0900 states that the key issue is whether there has been any change in the risk the prisoner poses. Re-categorisation is again a two stage process. The decision maker must first balance the risk of the prisoner escaping against the risk to the public should such an escape or abscond succeed. The provisional decision on whether the prisoner should remain in the same category or be upgraded or downgraded that results is then subject to consideration of whether any control factors point to a different categorisation.

The Order states that prisons can delegate the authority to categorise either to a recategorisation board or to a single manager, although the final decision has to be approved by a Governor 4 grade or above. The decision making process and final decision is recorded on a form RC1, which again is open to the prisoner. The form breaks down the key matters to be taken into account, namely:

(i) An assessment of escape or abscond risk – this will record any escape history and any factors since initial categorisation that point to a higher or lower risk of escape/abscond (such as working in positions of trust, or the length of sentence having been reduced on appeal). Details of allegations the disclosure of which may prejudice ongoing investigations may be withheld temporarily on the authority of a governor grade .

(ii) An assessment of risk to the public – this will record the current and any previous offences and the degree to which risk to the public can be assessed as having changed, through attending offending behaviour programmes, for example.

(iii) The provisional decision – taking into account the information above, the governor or recategorisation board must make a provisional decision on whether the security category should be changed.

(iv) The governor or recategorisation board making the final decision must consider whether there are any other factors that might indicate that the prisoner still needs the supervision of a higher category (eg a low risk prisoner suspected of bullying may be considered unsuitable for open conditions).

The prisoner should be informed of the decision and the reasons for it and, as the RC1 form is an open document, this can be requested so the decision making process can be examined in detail.

The courts have also held that the categorisation process does require reasons (*R v Governor of HM Prison Maidstone, ex p Peries* (1997) Times, 30 July). Given the sources of information used in these decisions, it is difficult to ensure that considerations which are not strictly relevant to category do not inform the decision. For example, a prisoner who is considered to be 'difficult' may not in fact present an escape risk or a danger to the public. The extent to which a decision may be challenged will depend on the precise reasons given. It is in the nature of administrative decisions such as these that if carefully worded reasons are given for a decision, a challenge can be extremely difficult to mount. Complaints about categorisation decisions can be made though the normal complaints procedure, and can be made to the Prisons and Probation Ombudsman once that procedure has been exhausted.

The Order does make clear that there may be a need for reviews outside the normal time frames where there has been a change of circumstances relevant to escape risk or risk to the public. Such circumstances could trigger either upgrading or downgrading . Even where there is an urgent need to place a prisoner in a higher security prison because of an incident giving rise to concern, the prison must complete the RC1 form to explain why the existing category is no longer appropriate. If the transfer needs to occur at extremely short notice the form should still be completed and forwarded to the new prison as soon as possible. This provision of the Order was introduced following a successful claim for judicial review (*R v Governor of HM Prison Latchmere House, ex p Jarvis* (20 July

1999, unreported), where the court held that a transfer from an open to a category B prison for reasons of good order and discipline was unlawful for failure to follow the recategorisation procedures contained in former policy, especially as there did not appear to be any urgent circumstances warranting a by-pass of normal procedures.

The courts have made a distinction between the procedural safeguards applicable to the recategorisation of prisoners serving determinate sentences, and those serving life sentences. As categorisation decisions for lifers can have a more direct impact on liberty, the requirements of fairness are more stringent. In *R(McLeod) v HM Prison Service* [2002] EWHC 290 (Admin) the court accepted that the new policy in PSO 0900 on urgent recategorisation was lawful even though it did not provide for an opportunity for the prisoner to have disclosure of relevant material and an opportunity to make representations prior to the recategorisation decision (as would be the case for lifers).

Prisons may have their own local criteria for recategorisation. These should not be too rigidly applied. A common example of this is a requirement that a prisoner serve a certain proportion of their sentence before being eligible for recategorisation. Whilst prisons may have their own criteria, these must not be inflexible, as otherwise they will be vulnerable to challenge on the basis that the criteria defeat the requirement that every prisoner is required to be in the lowest category possible at each stage of their sentence and that this will depend upon a proper assessment of risk, not length of time served.

6.6. REALLOCATION

Many prisoners will serve their sentences in a number of different prisons. For example, a prisoner serving more than ten years could be initially allocated to a category B high security prison, and then 'progress' through to a category B training prison, category C conditions and finally an open prison. Given the terms of Prison Act 1952, s 12(1), that prisoners 'may lawfully be confined in any prison', it is clear that prisoners do not have a right to be in any particular prison. As mentioned above, it will only be in extreme cases that a move will breach a prisoner's ECHR, article 8 rights.

A decision to move a prisoner where to do so would pose a real danger that he would be prejudiced in the conduct of his defence may breach the fundamental right of access to courts and/or the right to a fair trial contained in ECHR, article 6 (see *R v Secretary of State, ex p Quinn* [1999] LS Gaz, 26 May).

The previous Prison Service guidance on categorisation and allocation did contain specific guidance on reallocation, which is not now contained in the new policy. The previous policy noted that reallocation:

(i) Precedes the transfer of a prisoner to another establishment of the same category, as a result of an assessment that he is unsuitable to remain at his present establishment, or could appropriately be moved to another of a different type to fulfil needs identified during the sentence planning process, *or*

(ii) Follows the process of recategorisation.. The Order stated that a prisoner considered for reallocation should be treated in virtually the same way as one being allocated for the first time with reference to ICA 1. If the change in category is due to a review and this has resulted in a lowering of category, the prison will make arrangements with a prison of a lower security category for the prisoner's transfer there. It must be assumed that the continuation of this process is implicit in the terms of the new policy in PSO 0900.

The requirement to follow such procedures even where a governor wishes to transfer a prisoner for reasons of good order and discipline would appear to make a transfer consequent to a failure to do so unlawful (see *R v Governor of HM Prison Latchmere House, ex p Jarvis*)).

Standing Order 1H, which deals with some of the administrative matters surrounding transfers, anticipates that transfers may need to be made to relieve overcrowding, although prisoners whose 'domestic circumstances would be gravely prejudiced' should not be transferred for this reason . Standing Order 1H also states that prisoners other than those in category A should be able to inform their family or other intending visitors of an impending transfer, and should be provided with a letter with first class postage for this purpose. The medical officer should certify that prisoners are fit for travel before transfer.

Life sentence prisoners between categories B and C are now allocated by the individual prisons under separate arrangements . They are only moved to open conditions after the acceptance of a Parole Board recommendation. Category A lifers are managed, like all category A prisoners, centrally by the Directorate of High Security Prisons. For the most part they will be held in high security prisons unless they are 'exceptional' or 'high' risk in which case they will be held in Special Secure Units.

6.7. CATEGORY A STATUS

This is the only category that can apply to all prisoners, whether male, female, and juvenile or remand. The decision to so classify a prisoner is made by the category A Panel which is comprised of various senior Prison Service officials at Prison Service Headquarters. Governors of individual prisons do not make the decision. The Panel can order that remand prisoners are 'provisionally' category A until the time of their trial and, if convicted, categorisation is reviewed at that time.

There are subdivisions within category A, relating to the escape risk of an individual. The subdivisions of escape risk are exceptional, high or standard escape risk. For those with a high or exceptional escape risk, even more restrictions will be placed upon them whilst in custody. Guidance on escape risk category is contained in the Security Manual. Standard risk prisoners 'are not considered to have the determination and skill to overcome the range of security measures which apply to the custody and movement of Category A prisoners.

High risk are those prisoners 'that have a history and background which suggest that they have the ability and determination' to overcome the same range of security measures and where there may be current information to suggest that they have associates or resources to carry out an escape attempt.

Exceptional risk prisoners are those that have the same features as high risk, but where the nature and extent of the external resources which could be called upon to mount an escape attempt are such that the level of threat posed requires that the prisoner be held in the most secure accommodation and conditions available to the Prison Service. The implications for a prisoner classified as category A are far-reaching. Only a small number of prisons are designated to hold prisoners of this category on a permanent basis, by and large the high security prisons. However, even within the high security system, some prisons are not deemed secure enough to hold high or exceptional escape risk prisoners. Only certain of the high security prisons are deemed secure enough for high and exceptional risk categoryA prisoners, who are kept in Special Secure Units (SSUs).

A failed challenge arguing for the removal of the strict category A restrictions for legal visits on the basis that the right to confidential was the case *R v Secretary of State for the Home Department, ex p Daly* [2001] UKHL 26.

Another level of restrictions relates to the regimes which are in operation within the prison itself. A summary of the special procedures applicable to category A prisoners is contained in an appendix to the Security Manual. Category A prisoners are liable to be moved more often than other prisoners, both from cell to cell within a prison and between prisons. No notification is given before moves are made, to ensure that security is not compromised. Challenges can be very difficult to sustain. In the case of *Ex p Ross* [1994] Times, 9 June, CA, Waite LJ considered that the governor of a prison was best placed to decide whether a category A prisoner posed a threat to discipline and, providing general reasons were given, the court would not interfere.

Attempts to challenge the random movement of high security prisoners in other countries through the European Convention on Human Rights also proved difficult as in the case *Roelofs v Netherlands* (1July 1992, No 1943592) In this case a Dutch prisoner had been held in isolation and moved continually following allegations from an informer that he was to escape from custody. The Commission found the case to be inadmissible on the grounds that administrative decisions such as these were imposed for security reasons and not as a sanction and could not therefore be regarded as a determination of the person's rights.

The European Court of Human Rights has considered the issue of when a high security regimes breaches the prohibition on inhuman or degrading treatment in article 3 of the Convention in the case of *Van der Ven v The Netherlands,* 50901/99, 4 February 2003. The prisoner complained that his visits were restricted to once a month and were held behind glass partitions, telephone calls were limited to two 10-minute calls a week, there was very limited association with other prisoners and no work or education, and he was subject to routine strip searches. The court was concerned about the severity of the conditions and held that the systematic use of strip searches required more justification than the state had provided, in light of all the other security measures in place and the fact that no unauthorised articles had been found on the prisoner, and article 3 was breached. This was against the background of psychological reports showing that the prisoner was experiencing difficulties in coping with the regime.

6.8. CATEGORY A PRISONER PAROLE

The case of *R v Secretary of State for the Home Department, ex p Duggan* [1994] 3 All ER 277 ousted the former premise that category A prisoners were not entitled to know of the reasons for their categorisation . The House of Lords case of *R v Secretary of State for the Home Department, ex p Doody* [1994] 1 AC 531 forced the authorities to set out principles of good administrative practice that included the right to know of the reasons why a decision has been made. It was accepted by the court that the criteria for placing a prisoner on category A meant that release on parole became practically an impossibility. Therefore, as the decision had a direct impact on the liberty of the subject, it was held that procedural fairness entitles prisoners to know of the gist of the reports that have been prepared, to make representations and to be informed of the reasons to maintain them as category A. An attempt to argue that there was a right to see the police information failed in the case of *R v Secretary of State for the Home Department, ex p Arif* (29 November 1996, unreported), HC).

The determination of a prisoner's security category does not engage ECHR, articles 5 or 6 was the decision in the case of *R(Sunder) v Home Secretary* [2001] EWCA Civ 1157 but in the case of *R (Lord) v Secretary of State for the Home Department* [2003] EWHC 2073 (Admin), the prisoner argued sussessfully that he was entitled to further disclosure in the individual circumstances of his case and to disclosure of On the DPA 1998 point the court held that the category A reports .The judge accepted the prisoner's argument that s 29 Data Protection Act could not justify a blanket policy of non-disclosure, and that material could only be withheld where there was a genuine concern that disclosure would be likely to prejudice either the prevention or detection of crime, or the apprehension or prosecution of offenders. Following this judgment, the Prison Service immediately changed the categoryA procedures to provide for full disclosure of the category A reports, subject to limited exceptions..

Although the courts have held that ECHR, article 5 does not apply directly to the categorisation process, it has been held that a prisoner should be entitled to an oral hearing to determine category A status as in the case of *n (Williams) v Secretary of State for the Home Department* [2002] EWCA Civ 498 when the prisoner challenged the fairness of the category

ENGLISH PRISON LAW

A procedures in his case and the court decided that the only way to ensure a fair hearing in the case was to order disclosure of the category A reports, together with an oral hearing at which the prisoner could be represented.

6.9. CATEGORISATION AND ALLOCATION OF MALE YOUNG OFFENDERS

Offenders aged 18 or over serving determinate sentences will now either be serving a sentence of detention in a young offender institution, or a sentence imposed under s 91 of the Powers of Criminal Courts (Sentencing) Act 2000 (detention for a fixed period for offences that attract sentences of 14 or more years for adults). Under 18 year olds will be serving a Detention and Training Order (DTO) or a s 91 term (see Chapter 6 for when under 18s are liable to end up in Prison Service establishments).

Unlike with adults, control issues are not taken into account in the categorisation decision. The decision is documented on Form ICA 2 which contains a formula for determining the provisional security category. The criteria in the algorithm are not to be treated inflexibly as there may be individual circumstances that justify a higher or lower category than provisionally indicated . Where the provisional category is overridden, the reasons must be recorded and the decision countersigned by a senior officer grade .

The process is carried out in two stages: first, completion of the form and, second, an interview with the prisoner . The form sets out the information that should be collated and taken into account, including escort records, and the OCA department should consider in individual cases whether any further reports are necessary such as probation or psychology reports .

Again, allocation should be treated as distinct from categorisation. The PSO states that there are two priorities governing the allocation of young offenders-the needs of security; and the needs of individual young offender..

In particular the OCA department should take into account his suitability for particular types of accommodation , factors such as vulnerability, immaturity etc,

his medical and/or psychiatric needs that may require a particular level of care; the need for identified offence related behavioural programmes to confront assessed risk;

his home area, or that of his visitors, maintenance of family ties; his educational or training needs; and any restrictions on allocation criteria agreed with local authorities, governors, Area Managers or the Estate Planning Section in Headquarters.

6.10. CATEGORISATION AND ALLOCATION OF FEMALE PRISONERS

Women prisoners and young offenders can be assigned one of four security categories: category A; closed conditions for whom the very highest conditions of security are not necessary but who present too high a risk for open conditions; cannot be trusted in open conditions or for whom open conditions are not appropriate; semi-open conditions who present a low risk to the public but who require a level of physical perimeter security to deter abscond; or open conditions who present a low risk; can reasonably be trusted in open conditions and for whom open conditions are appropriate. There have been particular problems with the allocation of under 18 year olds as there are no dedicated female YOIs .

As with young offenders, prisoners 'must be categorised objectively according to the likelihood that they will abscond and the risk that they would pose should they abscond'. The categorisation process is documented on Form ICA 3. Women should be initially considered for open conditions unless the current sentence is 3 years or more; the current offence is a serious offence of: actual or threatened violence or harm; a sexual nature; drug dealing or importation; the prisoner has previously received a sentence of 3 years or more within the past 5 years for a serious offence of: actual or threatened violence or harm, a sexual nature, drug dealing or importation; or the pattern of previous offending gives cause for concern; and the nature of the Schedule 1 status (conviction against a child) gives cause for concern.

Once the initial categorisation assessment has been made, the OCA department must carry out, on those prisoners assessed as not needing closed conditions, an assessment of suitability for open or semi-open conditions, on the basis that open or semi-open conditions may not be either suitable or appropriate.. Therefore, to be allocated to a semi-open or open prison the prisoner must be assessed as appropriate both on the risk and the suitability criteria. However, the policy confirms that category must be kept under regular review and that women prisoners are not retained in conditions of higher security longer than is necessary or appropriate. In particular, significant allocation issues which may need to be considered include:to facilitate visits from children, or other family members; to enable child-care arrangements to be sorted out; to complete any necessary offending behaviour work; and to facilitate any resettlement needs

6.11. MOTHER AND BABY UNITS

The Prison Rules 1999 make specific provision for the Home Secretary to allow women prisoners to keep their baby with them in prison 'subject to any conditions he thinks fit' (Rule 12(2)). The Prison Service amended allocation procedures to mother and baby units following a Review into Mothers and Babies/Children in Prison in 1999. The current guidance on applications to enter mother and baby units ('MBU') is contained in PSO 4801. The Order, whilst stating that the Children Act 1989 does not directly apply to Prison Service decisions made under the Prison Act 1952 states that the underlying principle of giving primacy to the welfare and best interests of the child should be followed where possible .

The admissions board must be a multi-disciplinary group and may include representatives from probation, social services, a health visitor, a nursery nurse and an independent chairperson. The mother should attend, unless unable to do so because of a medical condition or due to being located in a prison without a unit. If not able to attend, she must be invited to make a full written submission. If she can attend, she can invite a friend, who may be another prisoner or member of staff, to provide support. Each case must be considered on an individual basis and the criteria considered by the board will be as follows:-

*whether it is in the best interest of the child/children to be placed in a mother and baby unit;

*whether the mother is able to demonstrate behaviour and attitude which is not detrimental to the safety and well-being of other unit residents (or the good order and discipline of the unit);

*whether the mother has provided a urine sample which tests negative for drugs;

*whether the mother is willing to remain drug-free;

*whether the mother is willing to sign a standard compact, which may be tailored to her identified individual needs; and

*whether the mother's ability and eligibility to care for a child is not impaired by health or legal reasons.

An applicant will be refused if she fails to meet any of the criteria and reasons must be given for the decision.

In an extremely important decision the Court of Appeal in *R (Pand Q) v Secretary of State for the Home Department* [2001] 1 WLR 2002, decided that the Prison Service would be in breach to apply this policy in an inflexible manner. Clearly, if the welfare of the child was to be promoted then the policy would be self-defeating if separation at 18 months had a catastrophic effect on that welfare. Similarly, under article 8 there could be situations where the interests of the child outweighed other considerations arising from the mother's imprisonment.

The case is now the leading authority on how the courts will apply ECHR, art 8 in the prison context. Lord Phillips, in his summary of the Strasbourg case decision, stated the main findings as being:-

"i) The right to respect for family life is not a right which a prisoner necessarily loses by reason of his/her incarceration;

ii) On the other hand, when a court considers whether the state's reasons for interfering with that right are relevant and sufficient, it is entitled to take into account:

a) The reasonable requirements of prison organisation and security; and

b) The desirability of maintaining a uniform regime in prison which avoids any appearance of arbitrariness or discrimination;

iii) Whatever the justification for a general rule, ECHR law requires the court to consider the application of that rule to the particular case, and to determine whether in that case the interference is proportionate to the particular legitimate aim being pursued;

iv) The more serious the intervention in any given case (and interventions cannot come very much more serious than the act of separating a mother from a very young child), the more compelling must be the justification."

It has also been held that if a decision is made that a child should be removed from the MBU, its interests should be properly represented at the meeting making the decision. This requirement was not met by the attendance of a local authority representative who had only become involved in the case on the day of the meeting and was unaware of relevant facts in *Claire F v Secretary of State for the Home Department* [2004] EWHC 111 (Fam).

6.12. SENTENCE PLANNING

Sentence planning is contained in PSO 2200, the manual on sentence management and planning. Sentence planning assists in staff allocation. PSO 2200 introduced a national scheme for sentence management and planning with standard documents. It made sentence planning a requirement for all young offenders with at least 4 weeks to serve.

6.13. TRANSFERS BETWEEN JURISDICTIONS

Transfer between the different UK jurisdictions is dealt with in the Crime (Sentences) Act 1997, Schedule 1, brought into force on 1 October 1997.

Transfers will continue to require the consent of the Secretary of State of both the sending and receiving jurisdictions. Normally, transfer requests will be approved only where the prisoner has at least six months left to serve in the receiving jurisdiction before his or her release date at the time of making the request, and where the prisoner has no outstanding appeal against conviction or sentence, is not charged with further criminal proceedings, and is not liable to any further period of imprisonment in lieu of payment of any outstanding monetary orders made by a court.

Each application will be assessed on its individual merits, taking into consideration: the purpose for which the transfer is requested; whether the prisoner was ordinarily resident in the jurisdiction to which transfer is sought prior to the imposition of the current sentence; or whether members of the prisoner's close family are resident in that jurisdiction and there are reasonable grounds for believing that the prisoner will receive regular visits from them; or whether the prisoner has demonstrated through preparations that he has made for his life following release from prison that he intends to reside in the receiving jurisdiction upon release and he is in the later stages of his sentence; whether there are grounds for believing that the prisoner may disrupt or attempt to disrupt any prison establishment, or pose an unacceptable risk to security; and any compelling or compassionate circumstances.

When considering whether to make an unrestricted or a restricted transfer, the Secretary of State of the sending jurisdiction will take into account the period and terms of transfer requested by the prisoner, and whether, as a consequence of an unrestricted transfer, there would be likely to be any effect on the length of time which the prisoner would be required to serve, or on any post release supervision requirement.

Where an unrestricted transfer is granted, the prisoner will serve the remainder of his or her sentence in the receiving jurisdiction as if that sentence had been passed there, and will be subject for all purposes to the statutory and other provisions applying to prisoners within the receiving jurisdiction. A prisoner granted a restricted transfer will automatically remain, for the duration of his or her transfer, subject to the law governing release on licence, automatic release, post release supervision and recall applicable in the sending jurisdiction. In addition, any other condition relating to the terms of a prisoner's detention as the Secretary of State of the sending jurisdiction may deem appropriate in any particular case or class of case may be attached to the transfer. A prisoner transferred on a restricted basis will normally become subject for all purposes, other than those specified in any conditions attached to the transfer, to the statutory and other provisions applying to prisoners in the receiving jurisdiction , including, for example, such matters as categorisation.

Whether the provisions on temporary release of the sending or receiving jurisdiction apply to those granted restricted transfers depends on whether or not the transfer is time limited (eg for accumulated visits). If so, the temporary release provisions of the sending jurisdiction will apply: otherwise it will be those of the receiving jurisdiction.

6.14. REPATRIATION OF PRISONERS ACT 1984

The Repatriation of Prisoners Act 1984 came into effect on 15 April 1985, and facilitated ratification of the Council of Europe Convention on the Transfer of Sentenced Persons.

The Convention enables foreign nationals convicted and sentenced to terms of imprisonment to be transferred back to the country of which they are a national and to serve their sentence there (so long as the crime of which they are convicted also constitutes a criminal offence in their country of origin). Sentenced prisoners from countries which are signatories to the Convention are eligible to apply for repatriation so long as they have at least six months of their sentence left to serve until their earliest date of release and are not appealing against their sentence or conviction.

When the governor has received the prisoner's request, this should be forwarded to the Prisoner Administration Group at Prison Service Headquarters, and the following documents should be attached by the prison:

(1) copies of the indictment, warrants and court orders relating to the period of imprisonment;
(2) notice of recommendation for deportation (if relevant);
(3) an assessment of the security and control risks which the prisoner is thought to pose;
(4) the prisoner's disciplinary record;
(5) an assessment of the prisoner's medical condition, including any recommendations for future treatment;
(6) copies of social inquiry reports and probation reports;
(7) details of previous convictions;
(8) two recent photographs of the prisoner;
(9) police and/or customs and excise reports on the offence.

After receipt of the application, Prison Service Headquarters consults with the Secretary of State and the government of the country of which the prisoner is a national to decide whether repatriation is considered appropriate by all parties. The main bone of contention at this stage is the length of sentence which the prisoner will have to serve if s/he is repatriated.

The 1984 Act specifies two separate procedures under which sentences to be served after repatriation may be calculated –

the continued enforcement procedure, and the conversion of sentence procedure.

When the application for transfer is being considered the prisoner can only be given rough details of how long a sentence such an offence would be likely to attract. Again, the sentence cannot be longer than the original sentence and will take into account the period of time that the prisoner has already spent in custody, and the prisoner will be asked to consent to repatriation in view of the information given by the government of their home country.

The main problem that prisoners experience in applying for repatriation appears to be where the sentence that they would have to serve in their home country is significantly shorter than the sentence that they are serving in this country. In these circumstances the British government is likely to refuse to repatriate on the basis that for the sentence to be so reduced would undermine the British criminal justice system and reduce the deterrent effect to other foreign nationals.

If a prisoner is repatriated, his/her sentence will be enforced according to the law of the country in which they are then serving their sentence. However, if the prisoner subsequently decides to appeal against sentence or conviction, they would have to do so through the courts in this country, and their home country would have no jurisdiction.

A prisoner who is accepted for repatriation may be required to pay his/her own fare home at the discretion of the other country concerned. At 22 August 2004, the following countries other than the UK had ratified and brought into force agreements under the Convention: Albania, Andorra, Armenia, Australia, Austria, Azerbaijan, Bahamas, Belgium, Bolivia, Bulgaria, Canada, Chile, Costa Rica, Croatia, Cyprus, Czech Republic, Denmark, Estonia, Finland, France, Georgia, Germany, Greece, Hungary, Iceland, Ireland, Israel, Italy, Japan, Latvia, Liechtenstein, Lithuania, Luxembourg, Former Yugoslav Republic of Macedonia, Malawi, Malta, Mauritius,

Moldova, Netherlands, Nigeria, Norway, Panama, Poland, Portugal, Romania, San Marino, Serbia and Montenegro, Slovakia, Slovenia, Spain, Sweden, Switzerland, Tonga, Trinidad and Tobago, Turkey, Ukraine, United States of America, Venezuela.

UK also has some bi-lateral transfer agreements outside the Convention as well as being a member of a Commonwealth Scheme.

6.15. Sentence calculation using Sentencing Guidelines

Sentencing Guidelines by the Sentencing Guidelines Council form the most important source material for those who need to know the likely sentence which a court will impose in respect of a particular offence. Draft Guidelines are regarded by the court as persuasive. The eleven Sentence Guidelines documents to date are as follows:

'Overarching Principles: Seriousness'
'New Sentences: Criminal Justice Act 2003'
'Reduction in Sentence for a Guilty Plea'
'Breach of a Protective Order'
'Overarching Principles: Domestic Violence'
'Failure to Surrender to Bail'
' Manslaughter by Reason of Provocation'
'Robbery'
'Sexual Offences'
'Assault and other Offences Against the Person'
'Assaults on children and cruelty to a child'

A twelfth guideline titled 'Revised Magistrates' Court Guidelines' was implemented in August 2008.

A sentence of IPP was held to be justified where the offences consisted of downloading indecent images of children, the defendant had previous convictions for sexual offences, the defendant presented a low risk to children in his area and in his family, but the risk of him returning to the Internet was high and this case was *R v Howe* [2006] EWCA Crim 3147. In *R v Remi Akinyeme* [2007] EWCA Crim 3290, a sentence of imprisonment for public protection was however found to be inappropriate for causing death by dangerous driving and in *R v Kamber Azam* [2007] EWCA Crim 3376, a sentence of imprisonment for public protection, imposed following a guilty plea to causing a person to engage in sexual activity without consent, was found to be unlawful as it was unclear whether any of the counts in the indictment had occurred after the coming into effect of the dangerousness provisions of the Criminal Justice Act 2003.

6.16. Maximum Sentences for Statutory Offences

The table below illustrates the maximum prison terms that can be given by the court for some offences:

Imprisonable offence	MAXIMUM Sentence
Abortion	Life
aggravated burglary	Life
assaulting a policeman in the execution of his duty	6 months
assault occasioning actual bodily harm	5 years
Bigamy	7 years
Blackmail	14 years
burglary of a dwelling	14 years
burglary other than of a dwelling	10 years

Imprisonable offence	MAXIMUM Sentence
causing death by dangerous driving	14 years
causing grievous bodily harm with intent	Life
criminal damage committed with the intent to endanger life or by the use of fire	Life
criminal damage- non aggravated	10 years
dangerous driving	2 years
driving whilst disqualified	6 months
drunk, being in charge of a motor vehicle	3 months
forgery and counterfeiting offences	10 years
going equipped for burglary	3 years
handling stolen goods	14 years
having possession of a class A controlled drug	7 years
having possession of a class B controlled drug	5 years
having possession of a class C controlled drug	2 years
importing or supplying class A controlled drugs	Life
importing or supplying class B controlled drugs	14 years
importing or supplying class C controlled drugs	14 years
inflicting grievous bodily harm	5 years
interfering with a motor vehicle	3 months
obtaining and communicating information useful to an enemy contrary to s1 Official Secrets Act 1911	14 years
obtaining property by deception	10 years
obstructing a police officer the execution of his duty	1 month
Perjury	7 years
possession of firearm with intent to endanger life or carrying one with intent to commit an indictable offence	life

Imprisonable offence	MAXIMUM Sentence
Rape	Life
Robbery	Life
sexual activity with a child	14 years
sexual assault	10 years
taking a motor vehicle without the owner's consent	6 months
Theft	7 years
using threatening behaviour with intent to put a person in fear of violence	6 months
Wounding	5 years

The maximum sentence reflects the relative gravity of the various offences.

If a statute exists which creates an indictable offence punishable by imprisonment but does not state the maximum sentence, section 77 PCC(SA) 2000 applies and the offence will be punishable with up to two years imprisonment upon conviction on indictment. In the case, R v Steven John Hostettler [2008] EWCA Crim 292, the court said that criminal sentencing lawyers and the sentencing courts needed to be aware of the provisions of the Criminal Justice Act 2003 s.247 when considering the expected period to be served by prisoners subject to an extended sentence. In the instant case, there had been ignorance of that provision so that, even though the sentencing judge had accurately exercised his sentencing powers, the prisoner was potentially subject to a custodial sentence that exceeded the statutory maximum for the offence involved.

6.17. THE CALCULATION OF MULTIPLE SENTENCES

Where an offender is convicted of several similar offences committed at different times, he could be sentenced to consecutive terms of imprisonment. This means that one sentence runs from the end of the other. Consecutive terms can be imposed in respect of 2 or more offences with an aggregate maximum of 12 months where the court is dealing with 2 or more either way offences, or 6 months in any other case. . If the offender is already subject to two or more consecutive terms of imprisonment, any new consecutive sentence should be announced as consecutive to the total period of imprisonment to which he is already subject. One prison term cannot be made partly consecutive to another as in *R v Gregory and Mills* [1969] 2 All ER 174.

One of the main factors used to determine the type of sentencing served is past criminal history. An individual who is committing his or her first offence is more likely to inspire leniency and compassion in the judge and to receive a concurrent sentence.

THE SINGLE TERM SENTENCE

The Crime and Disorder Act 1998 introduced changes as to when multiple sentences form a single term which were aimed at simplifying the system. It amended CJA 1991, s 51(2), which determines when multiple sentences will be treated as forming a single term, where they were imposed on or after 30 September 1998. The position now is that sentences will only be treated as a single term where they are passed on the same occasion, or where they were imposed on different occasions and the prisoner has not been released under any of the early release provisions contained in CJA 1991, including HDC.

6.18. CONSECUTIVE SENTENCES
The Statutory Instrument 2005 No. -Remand in Custody (Effect of Concurrent and Consecutive Sentences of Imprisonment) Rules 2005, by section 240(4)(a) of the Criminal Justice Act 2003, makes the following Rules: Section 240(3) of the 2003 Act does not apply in relation to a day for which an offender was remanded in custody - if on that day he was serving a sentence of imprisonment (and it was not a day on which he was on licence under Chapter 6 of Part 12 of the 2003. The recent case of *R on the application of Rebecca Noone v Governor of HMP Drake Hall* [2008] EWHC 207 (Admin), illustrated that offenders sentenced to consecutive terms of imprisonment for offences committed after April 4, 2005, were unlawfully remanded because of a Home Office policy of treating the first sentence pronounced by the court as the lead sentence for calculating release dates was unlawful.

6.19. REMAND TIME
The Criminal Justice Act 2003, Part 12 substantially revises the law on sentencing.

The Act makes provision for a sentencer to give credit for time spent on remand in custody where a custodial sentence is passed. (CJA 2003 s 240. Where the court decides that a custodial sentence is justified some sentencers may decide to pass a community sentence instead, on the basis that the offender has already completed the equivalent of a punitive element in a sentence. Whereas the Act clearly states that time spent on remand is to be regarded as part of a custodial sentence unless the Court considers it unjust, it also states that sentencers passing a community sentence may have regard to time spent on remand, but no further information is given on how this discretion should be exercised.

Recommendations made by the court at the point of sentence will be of particular importance in influencing the content of the licence. This Sentencing Guidelines Panel recommendation only applies to sentences of 12 months and above pending the implementation of 'custody plus'.

6.20. YOUTH REMAND
Under 18 year olds will often be remanded into the care of the local authority prior to conviction. Remands to secure accommodation which is certified as being provided for the purpose of restricting liberty will always count to reduce sentences. A list of such accommodation is included at Annex E to PSO 6650.

6.21. CRIMINAL JUSTICE AND COURT SERVICES ACT 2000
When s61 of the Criminal Justice and Court Services Act 2000(PCC(SA)) comes into force,, all offenders ages 18 to 20 will be sentenced to imprisonment.

6.22. TIME SPENT UNLAWFULLY AT LARGE
Any time that a prisoner spends unlawfully at large (UAL) does not count towards the length of the sentence to be served (Prison Act 1952, s 49(2)). Prisoners will be UAL where they have absconded from prison, or where their licence has been revoked for the period until they return to custody. The effect for prisoners who spend time UAL is that their release dates are simply delayed by the relevant period of time by adding this period to the sentence

6.23. TIME SPENT AWAITING EXTRADITION
Time spent in a foreign jurisdiction awaiting extradition does not automatically count to reduce sentence (CJA 1991, s 47). Case law on the subject indicates that this time should be considered by the sentencing judge when passing sentence, and it should be stated whether any allowance is being made for this time. The criteria for deciding to extradite a prisoner is spelt out in the case *Konrad Pilecki v Poland* [2008] UKHL 7. In a conviction case to which the Extradition Act 2003

s.65(3) applied, s.10(2), as modified for multiple offences, did not require the judge to ask whether the sentence that was passed for each offence in the warrant satisfied the test in s.65(3)(c). If the other requirements of s.65(3) were satisfied, all he needed to do was determine whether the sentence for the conduct taken as a whole met the requirement that it was for a term of at least four months. If it did, he must answer the question in s.10(2) in the affirmative.

6.24. RETURNS TO CUSTODY

One area of sentence calculation that has been the subject of a great deal of litigation has been the meaning and effect of the power to return prisoners to prison under s 116 of the Powers of Criminal Courts (Sentencing) Act 2000 (originally contained in CJA 1991, s 40). This section makes provision for prisoners who are released from custody and then commit a further offence before the sentence expiry date to receive a further custodial sentence. The sentencing court can impose a term under PCC(S)A 2000, s 116 even where the prisoner has also had their licence revoked and been recalled to prison although if a prisoner's licence has been revoked the sentencing court should take this into account when deciding whether to impose a s 116 order and its length. Any time in custody following revocation of the licence will not count as remand time in relation to the new sentence.

6.25. DEFAULT AND CIVIL SENTENCES

Sentences imposed under civil powers or confiscation orders imposed to run consecutively to the criminal penalty must not be calculated into the single term.

6.26. CIVIL SENTENCES SERVED IN FULL

Certain civil sentences do not attract early release and must be served in full, ie imprisonment for breaches of/related to:
(i) an affiliation order;
(ii) a maintenance order;

(iii) national insurance contributions;
(iv) income tax;
(v) any other duty or tax collected by the Inland Revenue or Customs and Excise;
(vi) a legal aid contribution;
(vii) council tax.

In addition, prisoners remanded under the Family Law Act provisions cannot have this period reflected in their release date.

Chapter 7 - Rights and Privileges

7.1.1. Absolute Rights

Prisoners retain certain basic rights which survive despite imprisonment. The Prison Act 1952 is very brief in content. The Prison Rules are also very brief in content. Prisoners do however have a few 'absolute' rights. Prisoners lose only those civil rights that are taken away either expressly by an Act of Parliament or by necessary implication. For example, one right taken away by statute is that prisoners detained following conviction do not have a right to vote. The test in every case is whether the right is fundamental and whether there is anything in the Prison Act 1952, the Prison Rules 1999 or elsewhere which authorises the prison authorities to limit such a right. The test now applied is that the State can only place limits on prisoners' rights if they are necessary for the prevention of crime or for prison security. Any limitations placed upon such rights must also be proportionate to the aim which the authorities are seeking to achieve. There are a large number of cases which have been heard by the European Court of Human Rights which help clarify the extent to which limitations can be imposed. Prisoners have an absolute right to have visits from and to correspond with their solicitor. They do not have to tell the prison authorities why they wish to contact a solicitor, nor make any complaint about prison treatment to the authorities before contacting a solicitor for legal advice. This right was first recognised by the European Court of Human Rights and any attempts to interfere with such access are closely scrutinised by the courts. This right also includes preserving the confidentiality of any legally privileged material held by prisoners in their possession in prison.

7.1.2. REQUESTS AND COMPLAINTS

Should the prisoner wish to make a request a 'general application' form is usually submitted. If this does not prove successful or the prisoner wishes to make a complaint then PSO 2510 must be followed. Basically this provides a three stage appeal process starting with the prisoner submitting a Form Comp1. If this need should arise the prisoner should make contact with his / her legal advisor. Prisoners can access the prison ombudsman to make complaints about the prison. Prisoners have rights to visits, education, exercise and work as well as rights to send out letters and to get married.

7.2.1. RIGHT TO APPLY TO THE PAROLE BOARD FOR EARLY RELEASE

Many convicted prisoners must apply to the Parole Board for early release. The provisions differ for the various sentences. In a recent case, the prisoner wanted early release to Scotland. In *R (on the application of Graham Primrose) v Secretary of State for Justice* [2008] EWHC 1625 (Admin), a Scottish national serving a sentence in an English prison was unsuccessful in claiming discrimination under the European Convention on Human Rights 1950 Art.14 and the Race Relations Act 1976 after his application for early release from prison to a Scottish address on the Home Detention Curfew scheme had been refused by the secretary of state. There was no disproportionately prejudicial effect on Scottish nationals in the way that the scheme operated so as to amount to indirect discrimination and there was no direct discrimination based upon place of residence. The Parole Board must be demonstrably independent of the Secretary of State. See *R (on the application of (1) Michael Brooke (2) Gagik ter-Ogannisyan) v (1) Parole Board (2) Lord Chancellor & Secretary of State for*

Justice : R (on the application of David O'Connell) v (1) Parole Board (2) Lord Chancellor & Secretary of State for Justice : R (on the application of Michael Murphy) v (1) Parole Board (2) Lord Chancellor & Secretary of State for Justice, [2007] EWHC 2036 (Admin), in which the court decided that the arrangements for the Parole Board did not sufficiently demonstrate its objective independence of the secretary of state, as required by both English common law and the European Convention on Human Rights 1950 Art.5(4).

7.2.2. THE RIGHT TO APPEAL AGAINST THE CONVICTION.

It is possible to appeal a conviction if it can be shown that it is 'unsafe'. A conviction may be unsafe if, for example, the judge applied the law incorrectly or new evidence / facts have come to light after the trial. An appeal against sentence can be made if there are grounds that suggest the sentence imposed was 'manifestly excessive'. An appeal against conviction or sentence can be made at any time. However, time limits do apply and any significant delay can cause problems. As a result contact the prisoner should contact his solicitor as soon as possible. The case may involve the Crown Court, the Court of Appeal or the Criminal Cases Review Commission (CCRC). The right to challenge a prison governor's decision. Any decision made by a prison governor, probation officer or the Parole Board can be challenged by application for a judicial review. Judicial review is a civil law application to the High Court and there is a strict three month time limit with such cases. In *R v David Francis Bieber (aka Coleman)* [2008] EWCA Crim 1601, a whole life term was decided not be considered as a sentence that was irreducible. Any European Convention on Human Rights 1950 Article.3 challenge where a whole life term had been imposed should be made, not at the time of the imposition of the sentence, but at the stage when the prisoner contended that, having regard to all the material circumstances, any further detention would constitute degrading or inhuman treatment, again, enforcing the importance of following the time limitation rules in prison cases.

7.3. PRISONER POSSESSIONS

The question of what prisoners are entitled to in terms of contact with the outside world, with each other, their possessions and other facilities is a complicated one. The Prison Act 1952 and Prison Rules 1999 do contain minimum entitlements in some areas (e.g. the Prison Rules,R35 provides for a minimum number of social visits), but what prisoners should expect on top of these, or where the statutory framework is silent, has been a matter of debate. Despite the effect of the Woolf report in other areas, no such amendments were made.

7.4. PRISON RULES 1999, R8- INCENTIVES AND EARNED PRIVILEGES

The Prison Rules were amended (see now the Prison Rules 1999,R8) to allow for the introduction of 'Incentives and Earned Privileges' (IEP) schemes following the publication of the Woodcock Report, after which, each prison has their own scheme (as long as it meets the requirements of a national framework),

7.5.1. POLICY CHANGES AND STATUTES

Those areas of prison living not governed by statute are subject to policy changes throughout a prisoner's sentence, an instance of which is Secretary of State's significant reduction of prisoner entitlement to temporary release in respect of both newly sentenced and existing prisoners (in IG 36/1995). S a result of this policy change, prisoners who had signed compacts on the basis that they would benefit from the old entitlements argued that they had a legitimate expectation not to be affected by the changes. The Court of Appeal rejected this argument, holding that the only legitimate expectation the prisoners had was to the benefit of any lawful policy promulgated by the

Secretary of State from time to time (*R v Home Secretary, ex p Hargreaves* [1997] 1 All ER 397). The result is that prisoners are vulnerable to rapid changes relating to the quality of their living conditions, and contact with the outside world.

7.5.2. POLICY CHANGES IN BREACH OF FUNDAMENTAL RIGHTS

There are many areas where decisions or policies involve potential interferences with prisoners' fundamental rights, or rights under the UK Human Rights Act 1998. The degree to which interferences with these can be justified will depend upon the right in question. Even before the coming into force of the Human Rights Act 1998, the courts held that fundamental rights recognised in common law, such as that of access to a court or privileged legal advice, could only be restricted by clear statutory authority, or on the basis of a 'pressing social need' (the 'principle of legality': see e.g. R *v Home Secretary, ex p Leech* [1994] QB 198;R*v Home Secretary, ex p Simms and O'Brien* [1999] 3 WLR 328).

7.5.3. HUMAN RIGHTS ACT 1998

The Human Rights Act 1998, s 6 has made it unlawful for public bodies to act incompatibly with Convention rights. It was a case involving cell searches that confirmed that when examining whether a decision or policy is incompatible with Convention rights, the court has to decide whether the interference is proportionate, (*R v Home Secretary, ex p Daly* [2001] UKHL 26).

Other such challenges in the courts include issues of 'qualified' rights such as ECHR, Art 8, the right to respect for private and family life. Challenges can also be made as a request for a judicial review to have a public inquiry under the Inquiry Act 2006, as in the case of (on the application of *(1) K (2) AM (3) HM (4) LM) v (1) Secretary of State for the Home DepArtment (2) Kalyx* [2008] EWHC 1598 (Admin), although in this pArticular case the decision was not what the prisoner wanted.

The case does show the importance of heeding time limits for application and complaints. Secretary of State for the Home DepArtment did not breach his procedural obligation to investigate under the European Convention on Human Rights 1950 Art.3 by refusing to set up a public inquiry into disturbances at an immigration detention centre. The detainees had not made any complaint of Article 3 human rights breaches to the authorities at the time and an inquiry was no longer practicable. The claimant detainees (K) applied for a declaration that the first defendant secretary of state had breached his procedural obligation to investigate under the European Convention on Human Rights 1950 Art.3. K had been detainees at an immigration removal centre. K claimed that their Art.3 rights had been infringed before, during and after major disturbances at the centre as they had allegedly been assaulted by prison officers, kept locked-up in smoke-filled and flooded cells after a fire, kept outside in the cold for long periods and not given food or water or access to a toilet. In response to a request made by K through a human rights organisation the secretary of state had refused to set up a public inquiry under the Inquiries Act 2005 s.10. K applied for judicial review of that refusal. K had not made any complaint at the relevant time to the detention centre managers, police or Prisons and Probation Service Ombudsman. Further, what have been called 'the ordinary and reasonable requirements of imprisonment' (*Golder v UK* (1975) 1 EHRR 524) mean that the degree of enjoyment of some rights ,such as family contact, are affected. The courts are more likely to defer to the decision/policy maker as in R *(Samaroo) v Home Secretary* [2001] EWCA Civ 1139).

7.5.4.1. CORPORATE MANSLAUGHTER AND CORPORATE HOMICIDE ACT 2007 AND PRISONERS' CARE

As to the many suicides in prison as per Home Office statistics, there is still a culture of blame avoidance as in the case *R (on the application of Selina Warren) (Claimant) v HM Assistant Coroner for Northamptonshire (Defendant) & (1) GLS UK Ltd (2) Nestor Primecare Services Ltd (3) Syed Ahmed (4) Colin West (interested parties)* [2008] EWHC 966 (Admin), in which the decision was that whilst a coroner had been entitled, in respect of an inquest into a suicide in prison, to decline to call the evidence of a consultant psychiatrist instructed by the family of the deceased, were the inquest to have gone ahead without any evidence from an independent consultant psychiatrist, it would not have been compliant with the European Convention on Human Rights 1950 Article 2.

This case is particularly important in light of the Corporate Manslaughter Act 2007, in force since April 2008. Prisons can, in principle, be held responsible in criminal law for causing the death of prisoners who occupy their premises. The common law has long since recognised the offence of manslaughter where there is no intention to kill, and private companies which run some prisons as well as government owned prisons are liable. On 6 April 2008, the provisions of the new Corporate Manslaughter and Corporate Homicide Act 2007 came into force. It reforms the basis on which a prison can be found criminally liable for the death of a person to whom it owed a duty of care. The Act applies where the harm resulting in death occurred in the United Kingdom – it does it apply extraterritorially, nor does it apply retrospectively. Private prisons especially,(whether English or foreign registered) can be made a defendant in a prosecution, provided that the company operates in the United Kingdom.

Under this Act a prison will be guilty of an offence if it causes a fatal accident through the way in which it manages its business or activities. A prison is a public body incorporated by statute. The prison's failure in this regard must, however, amount to a grossly negligent breach of a duty of care to the victim. The victim must die as a result of harm that occurred within the United Kingdom.

7.5.4.2. FOREIGN PRISONERS

A foreign prisoner injured in a United Kingdom prison, who dies after he has been deported directly from a UK prison will be a victim within the meaning of the Act. A recent case which is a prime example of this occurring is when a foreign prison is caused harm by the decision of the senior prison officer to release the prisoner back to his home country, knowing that he is likely to be killed there. The word 'harm' is not defined in the Act and the emphasis in the Act is that as a consequence, the prisoner dies. A likely scenario portrays itself in the case on 14 January 2008, *GN (Iran) v Secretary of State for the Home Deartment* [2008] EWCA Civ 112, when the court decided that the Asylum and Immigration Tribunal had not erred in law in holding that an asylum seeker, who had been tortured and beaten by Iranian religious police after being accused of having adulterous affairs with female members of a gym that he managed, faced no risk if returned to Iran. Whether the prison would be too remote in such a case as this remains to be proved, but certainly, the Court authority might be so prosecuted for corporate manslaughter by the family of the deceased.

However, an British prisoner who is injured abroad but dies is a United Kingdom prison to which he is extradited is not, however (assuming it is clear-cut when the harm occurred and what the operative cause of death is). Individual prison officers cannot be charged with this offence because the Act does not apply to individuals because they cannot be accessories to an offence committed by an organisation. Before a prison can be convicted, it must be shown that a substantial part of the failure occurred at a senior level, i.e. failure of those prison officers who make significant decisions about the prison as a whole, or about substantial parts of the business, or who actually manage the prison (or a substantial part of it). The guide to the Act published by the Ministry of Justice confirms that senior management will include "both centralised, headquarters functions as well as those in operational management roles." Directors and those holding positions similar to a directorship will be senior management unless something unusual excludes them. Regional managers, or heads of different operational divisions, will be treated as senior management. senior management will not be able to plead delegation in its defence. Inappropriate delegation, or turning a blind eye by senior management can constitute a management failure for the purpose of the Corporate Manslaughter and Corporate Homicide Act 2007.

7.5.4.3. GROSS NEGLIGENCE

The corporate manslaughter offence is based on gross negligence. This means that the prison's conduct must have seriously fallen short of what the law expects. Notwithstanding the Corporate Manslaughter and Corporate Homicide Act 2007, in some cases before the Act was in force, proving just negligence and not gross negligence was enough to be found guilty of causing death by suicide as in the case *Anna Savage (Appellant) v South Essex Partnership NHS Foundation Trust (Respondent) & MIND (Intervener)* [2007] EWCA Civ 1375, In order to establish a breach of the European Convention on Human Rights 1950 Art.2, where it was alleged that there had been a failure to take reasonable measures to prevent the risk of suicide of a patient held under the Mental Health Act 1983 s.3, it was only necessary to show negligence rather than gross negligence.

7.5.4.4. PENALTY

A prison convicted of the corporate manslaughter offence can be fined with no upper limit to the fine, or the prison may receive a publicity order which will require that the prison publicise the fact of its conviction and certain details of the offence, in a way specified by the court. Publicity orders are not yet in force. The court may also set a remedial order, requiring the prison to address the cause of the fatal injury. However the Act does not set out any damages for the deceased prisoner's family, although, after such a corporate manslaughter conviction, the family of the deceased prisoner may then be advised by their solicitor to pursue damages in a civil case .

7.6. 1. PRISON VISITS

Rule 35(2)(b) of the Prison Rules 1999 provides that prisoners are entitled to receive two visits in every four-week period, but this may be reduced to one visit in each four-week period if so directed by the Secretary of State. These are known as 'statutory visits'. The Rules make allowance for the right to a visit to be deferred by the governor while a prisoner is subject to cellular confinement (r 35(5)). The courts have refused to hold that the basic level of visits allowable under the Rules represents an unjustifiable interference with the right to family life under ECHR, Art 8 (see for example, *R (K) v Home Secretary* [2003] EWCA Civ 744).

7.6.2. PRIVILEGE VISITS

In addition to statutory visits, the Rules make provision for 'privilege visits'. These may be conferred by the governor (Rule 35(3)) or the Independent Monitoring Board (Rule 35(6)). The Secretary of State also has the power to authorise additional visits for individual or particular classes of prisoners (Rule 35(7)). The Rules specify that Governor's privilege visits are to be allowed where necessary for the welfare of the prisoner or his family or as part of IEP schemes but there is no express guidance as to when the Independent Monitoring Board should use its power to authorise extra visits or to allow a statutory visit to last for longer than normal. Prisoners are also entitled to special visits from legal advisers and other people visiting in a professional capacity, such as probation staff, priests and consular officials. Privilege and special visits do not count against the number of statutory visits to which a prisoner is entitled.

7.7. REMAND OF UN-CONVICTED PRISONERS

Un-convicted prisoners may send as many letters as they wish at their own expense and will be allowed two second-class letters a week on which the postage will be paid by the prison authorities. Un-convicted prisoners are entitled to receive as many visits as they wish 'within such limits and subject to such conditions as the Secretary of State may direct, either generally or in a particular case' (r 35(1)). At the present time, the entitlement is to at least 90 minutes per week but it is up to the governor of each prison as to how these visits will be structured (Standing Order 5A(4)). Visitors do not need a visiting order to enter the prison, although it may be necessary for visitors to telephone in advance in an attempt to make visiting arrangements better structured. Once on a visit, the same rules apply as for convicted inmates. Un-convicted prisoners are also subject to IEP schemes although these will have to take account of their particular status. This means that certain behavioural indicators such as work performance should not be used, as remand prisoners cannot be required to work. Private cash limits are set out above. Un-convicted prisoners retain the right to wear their own clothes at all levels, and at basic level are entitled to a one-and-a-half hour visit each week. Entry will be to the standard regime in the first instance. In *R(Potter) v Home Secretary* [2001] EWHC Admin 1041, the court accepted that the fact a prisoner was on enhanced status whilst on remand did not necessarily mean that he should remain enhanced once convicted.

7.8. VISITS

Convicted prisoners are entitled to a minimum of 2 visit's every four weeks (policy allowing each to last 30 minutes) or a longer visit if directed by the Secretary of State. All visitors must be sent, by the prisoner, a V.O. (Visiting Order) prior to travelling or arranging the visit. It is also crucial to take acceptable identification. All visitors must be in possession of a valid visiting order to gain admittance to the prison. Visiting orders are issued to the individual prisoner, who then sends them out to the proposed visitor. They should be issued in sufficient time or as soon as it becomes due. The conditions for social visits are loosely defined so as to take place in 'the most humane conditions possible'. They are to be taken in the sight of a prison officer and are liable to take place within hearing of an officer if it is deemed necessary. In general, up to three visitors (not including children under 10) are permitted at any one time and they should take place in a visiting room with a table. Prisoners and visitors should be allowed to embrace each other. No tape recordings or photographs may be taken and if cameras or tape recorders are found, visitors will be asked to surrender them for return at the end of the visit. The film or tape is liable to confiscation and the contents may be checked. Any recording or photographs taken within the prison will be wiped and the film or tape returned to the visitor. Visits may be conducted in any language, but there are provisions for visits to be conducted in English, or monitored by a person who speaks the language used or tape recorded for later translation, if it is felt necessary in the interests of prison or national security or the prevention of crime.

7.9. SPECIAL ALLOWANCES

Special allowances are made for prisoners to accumulate visits and to visit other prisoners. If a prisoner is located in a prison where s/he is unable to receive visits, it is possible to accumulate between three and 26 visiting orders. The prisoner can then apply for a temporary transfer to a prison where it is possible to receive these visits. Normally, such transfers are for one month and should not be allowed more frequently than every six months.

7.10.1. VISITS ALLOWED BETWEEN TWO RELATED PRISONERS

Visits are also allowed between two prisoners at different prisons who fit the definition of close relatives. Arrangements can be made, subject to security and the availability of transport and accommodation, for the prisoners to be transferred to a prison where they can have a visit with each other. This privilege is to be permitted once every three months and each prisoner must surrender one visiting order. Due to current overcrowding in prisons, arranging inter-prison visits can often take several months or even years. Complaints regarding such delays have frequently been upheld by the Ombudsman. Pending the visit, arrangements can be made for inter-prison telephone calls.

7.10.2. RESTRICTIONS ON SOCIAL VISITS

In October 2000, following the introduction of the Human Rights Act 1998, the Prison Rules were revised to make the provisions governing restrictions on visits less vulnerable to challenges under the Act, particularly in relation to Art 8 of the ECHR. Rule 34(2) was therefore amended to prohibit restrictions on visits which interfered with Convention rights unless such restrictions are proportionate. These grounds upon which restrictions may be imposed essentially reflect the qualifications set out in Art 8(2) of the Convention and are as follows:

(i)   the interests of national security;

(ii)   the prevention, detection, investigation or prosecution of crime;

(iii)   the interests of public safety;

(iv)   securing or maintaining prison security or good order and discipline in prison;

(v)   the protection of health or morals;

(vi) the protection of the reputation of others;
(vii) maintaining the authority and impartiality of the judiciary; or
(viii) the protection of the rights and freedoms of any person (r 34(3)).

Rule 34(2) further provides that reliance on the specified grounds must be compatible with the convention right that is subject to the interference and that the restriction imposed must be proportionate to the aim that is sought to be achieved. The power to exclude visitors should only be used in exceptional circumstances for close relatives but is more widely available for other classes of persons. In general, it is clearly more appropriate to consider the use of closed visits before a decision to exclude a visitor is made, as this will be likely to meet the security concerns and therefore be the proportionate response.

7.10.4..BANNING VISITORS

Rule 73 of the Prison Rules provides that the Secretary of State may prohibit visits by a person to a prison or a prisoner for such periods of time as he considers necessary. Such prohibition must be proportionate to the stated aim and necessary on the following specified grounds:

(i) the interests of national security;
(ii) the prevention, detection, investigation or prosecution of crime;
(iii) the interests of public safety;
(iv) securing or maintaining prison security or good order and discipline in prisons;
(v) the protection of health or morals; or
(vi) the protection of the rights and freedoms of any person (r 35A(4)).

This power is not to be used to prohibit visits from members of the Independent Monitoring Board or to stop legal visits. One of the aims of the rule was to facilitate the issuing of guidance to governors on measures to be taken against visitors found to be smuggling drugs into prisons. Such guidance is found in PSO 3610, which states that visitors, including family members, found to be smuggling drugs into prisons should normally be banned from visiting for at least three months, followed by a period of closed visits for three months. The Order states that visitors must only be banned for drug smuggling if they are 'found to be engaging in this activity' and not on the basis of intelligence alone, or on the indication of a drug dog.

7.10.5. EXCEPTIONAL REASONS

The Order states that a ban must be the normal response unless there are 'exceptional reasons' for not imposing one. Ban are not allowd:

'•If a ban would cause disproportionate harm to the prisoner's or visitor's right to a family life (protected by the European Convention on Human Rights, Art 8).

•If a ban would cause disproportionate harm to the rights of the prisoner's child or children to access to a parent (UN Convention on the Rights of the Child, Art 9(3)).

•If the prisoner is a juvenile and a ban would cause disproportionate harm to his or her right of access to a parent.

•For exceptional compassionate or other grounds.'

7.10.6. CLOSED VISITS

Closed visits may be ordered whereby prisoners and their visitors will be afforded no, or limited, contact. These can be imposed 'where security or control considerations so require' and are commonly used when prisoners are suspected of receiving unauthorised Articles during visits (although in cases where drugs are involved, see below) or where behaviour in the visits room has breached standards of good order and discipline.. To limit disruption to contact with the outside world, the prisoner must be placed on closed visits for a specific period of time rather than for a set number of visits. All prisoners on closed visits must be reviewed every month to assess whether there is a continuing need for the restriction .

7.10.7. VISITS FROM CHILDREN

Separate provisions exist regarding visits where the prisoner is assessed as posing an ongoing risk to children. The governor is empowered to exclude visits to or from persons under 18 years of age where it is felt that this would not be in the best interests of the visitor or the inmate. Until recently, the provisions detailing contact between prisoners and children were set out in PSO 4400 and PSI 41/1998. While these documents still provide a useful overview of policy on child protection measures, they have recently been replaced by the Prison Service Public Protection Manual, 'Safeguarding Children'. At the time of writing, a full copy of the document was not available; however, a summary of the provisions contained on a Prisoner Information Sheet suggest that the rules have become more stringent. Governors are required to identify prisoners who have been convicted of or charged with an offence against a child or have a previous conviction for such offences. For those prisoners, contact with children will be limited to contact with children in their immediate family, and the children of a partner, provided the couple were living together as a couple prior to imprisonment. The definition of children includes sons and daughters, brothers and sisters, stepchildren, and adopted and foster children.

A prisoner will not be able to have contact with any other child unless the governor agrees that such contact would be in the interests of the child and after a full risk assessment has been carried out. Grandchildren will be considered if there is a substantial case for contact and the contact is in the interests of the child. In addition to the risk assessment, certain procedures, including checking the suitability of contact with the person who has responsibility for the child and the local Social Services department, must be carried out. In all cases the welfare of the child will be paramount.

The decision regarding the level of contact to be permitted is made by the Operational Manager. Four levels are specified, ranging from level one, where no contact is allowed and all correspondence and telephone calls will be monitored, to level four, where no restrictions apply and only random checks will be carried out on letters and telephone calls. It is specified that blanket policies should be avoided and rather governors should identify and manage the risk that the individual presents. Decisions to prevent or restrict contact should balance the risk presented by the offender and the needs of the child. When circumstances change, e.g.if a prisoner no longer denies his guilt and attends an offending behaviour programme, the decision must be reviewed.

7.10.8 .CASE-LAW –REFUSAL OF PERMISSION TO VISIT

In *R (Banks) v The Governor of HMP Wakefield and the Home Secretary* [2001] EWHC (Admin) 917 the claimant challenged the governor's decision to refuse him visits from his six year old nephew. The court rejected the claimant's argument that the restriction was ultra viresR4(1) of the Prison Rules, which provides that such special attention be paid to the relationship between a prisoner and his family as is desirable in the best interests of both. On the facts, the claimant's ECHR, Art 8 rights were found not to be engaged; however, the court concluded that even if there were an interference with these rights, it would be justified under Art 8(2) of the Convention. The court held that the Prison Service policy (then contained in PSO 4400) was compliant with Art 8 in that the restrictions that it imposed were justified by the need for effective measures to protect children.

7.10.9. VISITS FROM JOURNALISTS

Visits by journalists are subject to special provisions. The general guidance is that if these are made in a professional capacity, they should not be allowed. The governor has authority to exclude these without reference to any higher authority. If the visit is in a personal capacity, the governor can require that an undertaking is given by the prospective visitor that any material obtained will not be used for publication or other professional purposes Governors are allowed exceptionally to allow journalists to visit in their professional capacity on giving a:

'written undertaking that no inmate will be interviewed except with the express permission in each case of the governor and the inmate concerned, that interviews will be conducted in accordance with such other conditions as the governor considers necessary, and that any material obtained at the interview will not be used for professional purposes except as permitted by the governor.'

The Prison Service's contention that these provisions did not permit interviews with journalists unless the prisoner was incapable of communicating in another way was the subject of *R v Home Secretary, ex p Simms and O'Brien* [1999] 3 All ER 400. The House of Lords held that although the provisions of the Standing Order itself were not *ultra vires* the Prison Act or the Rules, there was a fundamental right for prisoners to seek through oral interviews to persuade a journalist to investigate the safety of their conviction and to publicise the findings in an effort to gain access to justice for the prisoner. This right was not inconsistent with the need to maintain order and discipline in prisons. Therefore the Secretary of State's interpretation of the Standing Order was unlawful, as such a blanket ban as he contended for could not be justified. The case of *Simms* was further examined in *R (Hirst) v Home Secretary* [2002] EWHC (Admin) 602 which considered the policy on prisoners contacting the media by telephone.

7.10.10. CONJUGAL VISITS AND STARTING A FAMILY

Prisoners in custody retain their right to marry under ECHR, Art 12 (established in *Hamer v United Kingdom* (1979) 4

EHHR 139). Although conjugal visits are allowed in some European countries, attempts to challenge the refusal of the UK prison authorities to allow such visits in any circumstances on the basis that such a policy breaches the prisoner's right to family life have failed. The Commission in Strasbourg found one application inadmissible on the basis that it was still within the UK's margin of appreciation to maintain such a blanket ban (*ELH and PBH v United Kingdom* [1998] EHRLR 231). Although the Prison Service do have a policy to allow access to facilities for Artificial insemination in exceptional circumstances, a prisoner who challenged a refusal to allow such access, for reasons which went beyond those relating to the need to maintain good order and discipline in prison, failed to establish that the refusal breached his rights under either ECHR, Art 12 (right to marry and found a family) or Art 8 (*R v Home Secretary, ex p Mellor* [2001] EWCA Civ 472). The court summarised the aim of the policy as being:

'*to limit the grant of AI facilities to those who can reasonably be expected to be released into a stable family setting, and to play a parental role in bringing up any child conceived by AI. Account must also be taken of public interest considerations. It is also the intention of the policy that AI should only be granted where it is necessary to facilitate conception (for example, in circumstances where for medical reasons the couple could not conceive naturally or where the woman's medical condition indicates that there is only a small window of opportunity left to the couple in which to conceive, so that conception would be unlikely following release) in order to avoid AI being used simply to circumvent the normal consequences of imprisonment. Any prisoner seeking AI facilities is expected to finance the cost of treatment.*'

In this conservative judgment, which predated *R v Home Secretary, ex p Daly* [2001] UKHL 26, the Court of Appeal held that the Home Secretary was entitled to have a policy in this area which allowed access to such facilities only in exceptional circumstances, and which also took into account a wide range of considerations that went beyond the need to maintain good order and discipline, such as public perception.

7.10.11. SEARCHING PRISONERS AND THEIR VISITORS

Both prisoners and their visitors are liable to be searched. Governors have a general power to search prisoners in their custody as they deem necessary and it appears to be increasingly common for searches to take place both before and after visits (Prison Rules 1999,R41(1)). The power to search visitors must be exercised more circumspectly, and it is arguable that a greater level of suspicion is required (Rule71(1)). In general, visitors to prisons will be subject to perfunctory 'pat down' searches on arrival and will be screened by the use of metal detecting equipment. The visitor cannot be required to submit to such a search, but access to the prison may be denied in that situation. More stringent searches can only be carried out with the consent of the visitor or by calling the police to carry out such procedures in accordance with PACE. Visits may be terminated if an officer believes it is necessary to prevent violence, where an unauthorised Article has been passed, where it is suspected that the rules concerning correspondence are being contravened (eg by passing out a letter), or where a conversation is overheard that indicates an escape attempt, or a plan to commit criminal offences or pervert the course of justice.

7.10.12. VISITS TO CATEGORY A PRISONERS

Visitors to category A prisoners are subject to special provisions (Security Manual 1999, annex 23A). Save for certain specified individuals, including members of the IMB and legal advisers, all visitors to prisoners in this category must be authorised under the Approved Visitors Scheme. The procedure is for the prisoner to submit details of their proposed visitor to the prison concerned, who then make arrangements for them to be vetted by the police. It is only once this approval has been obtained that the visitor is authorised to visit the establishment. Visitors to category A prisoners are more likely to be asked to submit to a search and all category A prisoners will be strip searched after open visits. Exceptional risk category A prisoners must have closed visits unless the Director of High Security Prisons consents to open visits.

7.10.13.1. VISITS BY LEGAL ADVISERS
Rule 38(1) of the Prison Rules 1999 requires that facilities be made available to legal advisers who are acting for prisoners in connection with legal proceedings to which the prisoner is a party. These facilities should allow the prisoner to be interviewed in sight of, but out of the hearing of, a prison officer. Rule 38(2) authorises this facility to be extended for the purposes of any other legal business, but makes the authority subject to any further directions that the Secretary of State may issue. Rule 2 defines 'legal adviser' as a prisoner's counsel or solicitor, including a clerk acting on behalf of a solicitor.

The phrasing of R38 has been designed to take account of numerous problems that had arisen over the construction of 'being party to legal proceedings'. Many applications had been made, both to the domestic and European Courts (e.g. *Guilfoyle v Home Office* [1981] QB 309 and *R v Home Secretary, ex p Anderson* [1984] QB 778) in which the precise meaning of these words was debated.

7.10.13.2. SECURITY ARRANGEMENTS FOR LEGAL VISITS
Various new security arrangements for legal visits with high security category A prisoners, such as observation cameras mounted above the tables at Belmarsh and 'closed visits' at Whitemoor were brought in following the Woodcock report. The use of such security measures raises problems as to how confidential advice may be given and one solicitor described having to get on to her knees to shout through a glass partition whilst at Whitemoor. However, a challenge arguing for the

removal of these restrictions for legal visits on the basis that the right to confidential legal advice was breached failed (*R v Home Secretary, exp O'Dhuibhir* [1997] COD 315, CA). However, the legal analysis on which this finding was based cannot be seen to survive the *Simms and O'Brien* decision by the House of Lords and in any event, it predated the HRA 1998 and the decision in *R v Home Secretary, ex p Daly* [2001] UKHL 26 which confirmed that courts would now consider whether any such interference with prisoners' Convention rights was genuinely necessary to meet a legitimate security concern.

7.10.13.3. .RESTRICTED CONTACT WITH PRISONER'S LEGAL REPRESENTATIVE

An example of how the courts will look at these issues now, and how much a prisoner's contact with his/her lawyer can be restricted in the context of high security prisons was examined in *Cannan v Home Secretary and Governor of HMP Full Sutton* [2003] EWCA (Admin) 1480. In this case the prisoner challenged the procedures in place for passing out and receiving legal documentation during legal visits. The policy included provisions for obtaining prior authority from prison staff and for legal documents to be checked for illicit enclosures. The Court of Appeal held that a policy that only allowed documents to be passed between lawyer and client where prior notice had been given, except in exceptional circumstances, would breach a prisoner's ECHR, Art 6 rights. There would clearly be situations which were not exceptional, for example where a solicitor may want to hand over documents relevant to case where there had not been time to obtain prior approval, where it would not be justified to prevent the exchange of documents. The policy therefore did not strike the right balance between the right to free communication between lawyer and client and the legitimate security concerns in the high security estate. The case stressed that, in relation to the wording of Prison Service policy guidance, especially that issued at a local level, 'the flexibility which every lawyer knows is built into a policy should be spelt out so that officers and prisoners understand it, and should not be left to implication or mere ad hoc discretion'.

7.11. 1. CORRESPONDENCE

Convicted prisoners may send one letter a week on which the postage will be paid - the 'statutory' letter - and at least one privilege letter, the postage for which must be paid for out of the private cash allowance. The statutory letter must not be withdrawn or withheld as pArt of punishment for a disciplinary offence. In addition, prisoners may be granted special letters, which do not count against the statutory or privilege letters allowance. A special letter should be granted, for example, after conviction to allow a prisoner to settle his or her business affairs, when transferred to a different prison or to make arrangements regarding employment and accommodation on release. In practice, prisoners in many prisons may send and receive more letters than this minimum allowance. Prisoners in open prisons have no restriction on the volume of their correspondence. The provisions for correspondence are also contained in the Prison Rules 1999, Prison Rules 34 and 35, and are closely linked to visits. Rule 35(2)(a) allows convicted prisoners to send one letter a week at public expense. Provisions are also made for prisoners to receive privilege and special letters and to exchange visiting orders for letters, at the discretion of the governor or as a privilege under IEP schemes. It is necessary to look to the Standing Orders for a more detailed explanation of what is actually permitted in practice.

Standing Order 5B commences with the following statement of principle:

'The policy of the Prison Service is to encourage inmates to keep in touch with the outside world through regular letter-writing, to respect the privacy of correspondence to and from inmates as

far as possible and to ensure that it is transmitted as speedily as possible.'.

7.11.2. SPECIAL LETTERS

Special letters are issued according to prisoner's needs. The general guidance is that they should be issued in the following circumstances:

(i) when they are about to be transferred to another establishment; or, if the prisoner is not given a special letter before transfer, on reception at the new establishment. The number of letters should correspond to the number of visiting orders the inmate has outstanding;

(ii) immediately after conviction if he or she needs to settle business affairs;

(iii) where necessary for the welfare of the prisoner or his or her family;

(iv) in connection with legal proceedings to which the prisoner is a pArty (but see legal correspondence below);

(v) if necessary to enable a prisoner to write to a probation officer or to an agency arranging accommodation or employment on release;

(vi) to write to the Parliamentary Commissioner for Administration (or the Prisons and Probation Ombudsman);

(vii) at Christmas, subject to the discretion of the governor .

The cost of special letters will normally be met from prisoners' own funds, save in the case of transfers, when they should be sent at public expense.

7.11.3. RESTRICTIONS ON CORRESPONDENCE

The permitted restrictions on visits that are set out inR34 of the Prison Rules 1999, and (see above) apply equally to correspondence. Therefore restrictions or conditions can be placed upon correspondence so long as they do not interfere with Convention rights. If there is interference, then it must be necessary on the grounds specified inR34(3) listed above, compatible with the Convention right being interfered with and proportionate to what is sought to be achieved. Letters must be in a particular format that includes the name of the sender and the address of the prison. Anonymous letters are forbidden and the address of the prison can only be omitted on request to the governor. On the same basis, letters sent to the prison must normally show the sender's name and address. In general, letters may be sent to any person, though recipients can request that letters are not sent and restrictions are placed on the following classes of people:

(i) correspondence to minors may be stopped if the person having parental responsibility makes such a request. Similarly, the person with parental responsibility for a minor in custody can request the stopping of correspondence between that minor and any other person except the minor's spouse .

(ii) the governor may prevent correspondence between a minor in custody and any person with whom it is thought it would not be in that minor's interests to communicate. In reaching this decision, the views of the minor's parents or guardian should be sought;

(iii) convicted inmates may write to each other if they are close relatives, or if they were co-defendants and the correspondence relates to their conviction or sentence. In all other cases, the approval of both governors must be obtained ;

(iv) correspondence with ex-prisoners is permitted unless the governor considers that this would impede the rehabilitation of either party or that there would be a threat to good order or security ;

(v) if a prisoner wishes to write to the victim of their offences, or a victim's family, an application must be made to the governor, who will consider whether it would cause undue distress. This provision does not apply to un-convicted prisoners, or where the victim is a close family member or has already written to the prisoner ;

(vi) correspondence with any person or organisation can be stopped if the governor has reason to believe that the correspondent is engaged in activities or planning which present a genuine and serious threat to the security or good order of that prison or the prison estate;

(vii) prisoners are only able to advertise for pen-friends with approval of the governor and after submitting the text of the advertisement .

7.11.4. CONTENTS OF CORRESPONDENCE

Correspondence may also be prohibited on the grounds of its contents. The following is a list of prohibited material:

(i) material which is threatening, indecent or grossly offensive, or which is known or believed to be false;

(ii) plans or material which would tend to assist in the commission of a criminal or disciplinary offence;

(iii) escape plans or material which jeopardises the security of the prison;

(iv) material that would jeopardise national security;

(v) descriptions of the making or use of any weapon, explosive, poison or other destructive device;

(vi) obscure or coded messages which are not decipherable;

(vii) material which is indecent and obscene under the Post Office Act 1953;

(viii) material which, if sent to, or received from, a child might place his or her welfare at risk;

(ix) material which would create a clear threat or present danger of violence or physical harm to any person, including incitement to racial hatred;

(x) material intended for publication or broadcast which is in return for payment, and concerns the prisoner's own crime or criminal history (unless it forms pArt of serious representations about conviction, sentence or comment on the criminal justice system), or identifies individual members of staff or other prisoners, or which contravenes the other restrictions on correspondence. In the case of *Nilsen v (1) Governor of HM*

Prison Full Sutton (2) Home Secretary [2003] EWHC 3160 the prison refused to return the applicant's autobiography (he was convicted of six murders) to him on the basis that it would be contrary to this provision. The applicant challenged the decision by way of judicial review. The court held that the restrictions imposed by the prison were prescribed by law and necessary in a democratic society. The applicant's argument that the provisions of the Standing Order were inconsistent with his rights under Art 10 of the European Convention was also rejected by the court;

(xi) in the case of convicted prisoners, material constituting the conduct of business activity unless it relates to a power of attorney, the winding up of a business following conviction or the sale or transfer of personal funds, or other personal financial transactions within set limits.

7.11.5. INTERCEPTION OF CORRESPONDENCE

Mail is censored in dispersal prisons - those designed to accommodate high-risk prisoners - and for all Category A prisoners, but otherwise letters will not routinely be read. Additional powers exist to vet letters sent by prisoners convicted of sexual offences against children. There is power for the governor to return an 'excessive' number of letters from a correspondent, and if they are 'overlong' the governor may request letters be limited to four sides of A5 paper. Letters may be returned to the sender if these requests are ignored. Complaints about prison treatment are no longer prohibited and letters - whether to family, to MPs, the ECHR, and so on - may not be stopped on this ground.

Prison Rules 35A–D contain a number of provisions governing the interception and disclosure of prisoners' correspondence. Legal correspondence is subject to separate rules examined below. This section of the rules was drafted with a view to making provisions compliant with Arts 8 and 10 of the ECHR.

Rule 35A authorises the interception of communication relating to any prisoner or class of prisoner so long as the interception is necessary on the same grounds as for interference with visits and correspondence (rRule 35A(4)).

Such interception must be proportionate to what is sought to be achieved. 'Interception' in relation to written or drawn communication is defined as including 'opening, reading, examining and copying'. The governor may not disclose the intercepted material to anyone who is not an employee of the prison or the Prison Service unless he considers that the disclosure is necessary on the specified grounds and proportionate to what is sought to be achieved by the disclosure. Third parties to whom this material may be disclosed include the police, the Immigration Department, Customs and Excise, MI5 and the Serious Fraud Office. The governor shall not retain any intercepted material for longer than three months unless he is satisfied that the retention of the material is necessary on the specified grounds and proportionate to what is sought to be achieved. Where material is retained for longer than three months the decision must be reviewed at periodic intervals. Such reviews must not be more than three months apart . The revised chapter 36 of the Security Manual, as introduced by PSI 57/2001, sets out further details regarding the interception of correspondence and develops the provisions governing routine reading of prisoners' letters which is set out in Standing Order 5B, para 32. It is anticipated that the National Security Framework that was intended to replace the Security Manual in 2004 will reproduce this guidance. As with the amended Rules, this chapter of the Security Manual was introduced in an attempt to limit challenges to provisions governing correspondence under the Convention. It provides that routine reading is necessary in order to prevent escape, in the interests of public safety, the prevention of crime and in some cases in the interests of national security or the economic well-being of the country . It also provides that prisoners must be informed that their correspondence will be subject to routine reading and that the provisions must only continue for as long as the governor is satisfied that the procedure is necessary and proportionate. Routine reading is reserved effectively for all prisoners (of whatever security category) held in a unit which holds category A prisoners, all category A and potential category A prisoners, whether convicted or un-convicted, and all prisoners on the escape list . In addition, offence-related routine reading will be applied to those prisoners deemed as posing a threat to children (under the child protection measures referred to above) and for those remanded for or convicted of specified offences, including sending obscene mail and offences under the Protection from Harassment Act 1997.

7.11.6. ROUTINE READING OF CORRESPONDENCE

Other prisoners may also be subject to routine reading so long as it is necessary on the grounds set out inR35A(4) of the Prison Rules 1999 and where the information required cannot reasonably be obtained by less intrusive means. The impetus to institute routine reading may be a request from the police or other investigating or prosecuting body. Routine reading of the correspondence of named individuals may continue only for as long as is necessary and the case must be reviewed every three months. Chapter 36 of the Security Manual also outlines provisions for random reading, which can be implemented in prisons outside the category A estate provided that the governor is satisfied that it is necessary and proportionate to a legitimate aim.

7.11.7 . UNCONVICTED PRISONERS

Rule 35(1) of the Prison Rules 1999 allows un-convicted prisoners to send and receive as many letters as they wish, but within such limits and subject to such conditions as the Secretary of State may direct. It is unusual for any restrictions to be placed on the number of letters sent and received. Category A remand prisoners will find that their letters are read, as will prisoners awaiting trial for certain specified offences (see above). Letters between a prisoner and his or her legal advisor are protected from interference and may not be read nor stopped, whether or not legal proceedings have been issued. There may be examination of such correspondence only to the minimum extent necessary to check that it is bona fide legal correspondence. If a letter is to be inspected it must be done in the presence of the prisoner.

Prisoners have fought a series of cases challenging the extent to which the prison authorities can interfere with legal mail (see *Silver v United Kingdom* (1983) 5 EHRR 347 and *R v Home Secretary, ex p Leech* [1993] 4 All ER 539). The succession of such cases culminated with *Campbell v United Kingdom* (1992) 15 EHRR 137, in which the European Court of Human Rights decided that routine reading of a Scottish prisoner's correspondence with his lawyer breached Art 8. This led to a comprehensive revision of the Prison Rule governing legal correspondence.

7.11.8. TREATMENT OF LEGAL CORRESPONDENCE

Letters between prisoners and legal advisors, the Courts, Criminal Cases Review Commission (CCRC), Prisons and Probation Ombudsman and the Parliamentary Commission for Administration (PCA) are afforded legal privilege (with the envelope appropriately marked 'Prison Rule 39', 'Young Offenders Institute Rule 14', or 'SO 5B 32 (3)') and are not to be opened and/or read unless there is well grounded suspicion that there is illicit content and/or enclosure. The opening of correspondence is authorised by an operational manager, and always opened in the presence of the prisoner.

Rule 39 now provides that a prisoner may correspond with his/her legal adviser and the court (the definition of a court includes the European Commission and Court of Human Rights and the European Court of Justice). Prisoners must be provided with writing materials on request for the purpose of sending such correspondence. There is no restriction imposed on this right, such as being pArty to legal proceedings. The governor can only open, examine and read such correspondence if there is reasonable cause to believe that it contains an illicit enclosure or that there is reasonable cause to believe that its contents may endanger prison security, the safety of others or are otherwise of a criminal nature. A prisoner whose legal correspondence is to be dealt with under these provisions has the right to be present when it is opened and shall be informed if it or any enclosure is to be read or stopped.

The rule allows legal mail to be handed in sealed and provides that it should not be read or examined except in accordance with instructions to prisons. IG 113/95 provides comprehensive guidance to prisons on how to comply with R39 (which wasR37A before the Prison Rules 1999 came into force). Letters from prisoners to legal advisers should be marked 'Rule 39' (or 'Rule 14' for young offenders) and as long as the recipient is a legal adviser or court (and prisons are advised to check the adviser's status) then the letter will be protected by the rule. The position with incoming post is slightly different. As long as an incoming letter is marked 'Rule 39' and is identifiably from a legal adviser (eg by a stamp on the back) then similarly it should be covered by the rule. Unfortunately IG 113/95 also describes a procedure agreed with the Law Society and Bar Council whereby it is suggested that advisers should send the sealed letter inside a covering letter to the governor asking him/her to pass it unopened to the prisoner. If in doubt, this procedure should be used. Notwithstanding the clear guidance given in the rule, and in IG 113/1995, prisoners continually complain about breaches ofR39 procedures.

7.11.9. ENCLOSURES IN CORRESPONDENCE

The ambit of R39 of the Prison Rules 1999 has been challenged in relation to prisoners in the close supervision centre at HMP Woodhill. There a practice was introduced of checking all incoming and outgoing legal correspondence for illicit enclosures on a blanket basis without individual suspicion of illicit enclosures. The rationale appeared to be that the prisoners in the CSC were of such a class that routine checking was justified, although even accepting this rationale it is hard to see how it would apply to incoming letters from solicitors. The matter was conceded, with Woodhill agreeing to adhere to the provisions of Rule 39.

In R *(Szuluk) v Governor of HMP Full Sutton* ([2004] EWHC (Admin) 514) a prisoner established that correspondence with doctors outside the Prison Service could also be treated on a confidential basis and excluded from the routine reading provisions. The case was reliant on its facts, as the prisoner was suffering from a life-threatening condition and was in need of continual care.

7.12.1. TELEPHONE CALLS

Card-operated telephones for the use of prisoners are being installed in all prisons so that closer links with family and friends can be maintained by those in prison. For security reasons all calls will be recorded and all calls may be monitored and recorded, except those to legal advisers, the Samaritans and other reputable organisations. Use of the telephone may be limited by the governor, but should not be restricted as pArt of a disciplinary punishment unless the offence was directly related to the misuse of the card-phone or phone card. The Prison Rules do not provide any absolute right to use telephones and pilot schemes have been introduced in some prisons to impose restrictions on the use of telephones by having pre-recorded messages informing the recipient of the call that the person calling is in prison. Although these types of restrictions are not prohibited by the Prison Rules, they may, in some circumstances, breach Article 8 of the Convention. In *R v Yildrim Balci and Dakarayi Mtifi* [2008], Chelmsford Magistrates Court, 23 July 2008, the defendants were charged with smuggling a mobile phone and SIM card into Chelmsford Prison. Charges were brought under the Offender Management Act 2007, in force this April 2008.

Since 2000, the Prison Service has introduced a new system to replace existing cardphones. Each prisoner now has a telephone account which they access through their Personal Identification Number (PIN). A visual display on the telephone handset shows the prisoner's credit balance which reduces automatically as the prisoner makes calls. The regulations governing the new system are set out in Prison Service Order 4400, which at the time of writing is still in draft form. Under the new system, two types of telephone services are specified. The call barring system enables prisoners to call any number except those specifically barred by the prison, as was the case under the old cardphone system. Barred numbers include the emergency services and direct enquiries. The call enabling system is a more restrictive regime and provides that prisoners can only call those numbers they have submitted and that have been approved by the prison. Prisoners subject to this system can also call 'globally approved' numbers, such as the Samaritans and the Ombudsman. The amount of approved numbers that each prisoner is entitled to under the call enabling system is limited and, following legal challenges, is currently specified to be 20 domestic numbers and 15 legal numbers, with the possibility of applying for a further account of 15 numbers if the circumstances require. Provisions are made for appellants to purchase additional Pinphone credits from their private cash account to speak to their legal advisers.

7.12.2. CALL ENABLING REGIME

The draft PSO specifies which prisoners will be subject to the call enabling regime. The list includes category A and Escape list prisoners and those subject to child protection measures. In addition, governors may place their establishment on a call enabling regime with the agreement of their Area Manager, if there is an operational need to do so. Although the draft PSO provides that the type of service available is linked to the level of risk posed by the prisoner, in practice the more restrictive system is becoming standard, with all category B and the majority of category C establishments being subject to the call enabling telephone system.

7.12.3. EXCEPTIONAL CIRCUMSTANCES

Provisions are made for prisoners to use the telephone in exceptional circumstances. Where there are urgent legal or compassionate circumstances, such as imminent court proceedings or a domestic crisis, Operational Managers have a discretion to allow a prisoner to make calls at the public expense. Operational Managers can also authorise inter-prison telephone calls between close relatives who are detained at different establishments. Foreign national prisoners or those with close family abroad must be permitted a five-minute call once a month where the prisoner has had no domestic visits during the preceding month. Consideration must be given to allowing such prisoners to have access to telephones outside normal hours to make calls to their country of origin.

7.12.4. BAR FROM CONTACT

The draft Order provides that if a member of the public requests that a prisoner should not be allowed to contact him or her, the prisoner's telephone account must be amended to bar him from contacting that person. Prisoners will also be barred from telephoning a pArticular individual or organisation where there are grounds for believing that the person or organisation is planning activities which present a threat to the security or good order and discipline of the prison. In addition, prisoners are not allowed to telephone a victim of their offence unless he or she is a close relative, the victim has first approached the prisoner, or the governor considers that the call would not cause undue distress to the victim. Governors must consult with their area manager before ordering any prisoner not to telephone a close relative, notwithstanding that such a prohibition would also be a breach of the recipient relative's breach of human rights, as in *Potter v Scottish Ministers* [2007] CSIH 67, in which the court decided that the Lord Ordinary had erred in failing to take into account the potential for the infringement of Convention rights of third pArties, namely the recipients of phone calls from prisoners, each of whom had rights under Art.8.

7.12.5. RESTRICTIONS ON TELEPHONE CALLS

The restrictions on visits and correspondence which are set out in Rule 34 of the Prison Rules apply equally to telephone calls. The revised chapter 36 of the Security Manual provides that prisoners must be informed that telephone calls which include any of the following are prohibited:

(i) plans or material which would assist any disciplinary or criminal offence;

(ii) escape plans or material that might jeopardise the security of the prison;

(iii) material which might jeopardise national security;

(iv) material associated with the making of any weapon or explosive;

(v) obscure or coded messages;

(vi) material which would create a threat or present a danger of violence or harm to any person, including incitement to racial hatred, or which might place a child's welfare at risk.

7.12.6. MONITORING AND RECORDING CALLS

Chapter 36 of the Security Manual also sets out detailed provisions for monitoring and recording telephone calls. The general rule is that all telephone calls made by prisoners in closed conditions may be recorded other than calls made to legal advisers or the Samaritans. Telephone calls in open prisons can only be recorded if there is reason to suspect that the prisoner is using the telephone for an illicit.. Routine listening to the recordings of telephone conversations, other than those with legal advisers or the Samaritans, must be initiated for prisoners who pose a threat to children, who are remanded for or convicted of an offence under the Protection from Harassment Act 1997 or convicted of an offence listed in the Sex Offenders Act 1997 . The listening may continue only for as long as the governor is satisfied that it is proportionate to what is sought to be achieved and is necessary for one of the reasons set out inR35A of the Prison Rules 1999. The procedure must be discontinued if it is no longer necessary and must be reviewed every six months. Prisoners must be informed that they will be subject to such monitoring. Routine listening can also be instigated for individual prisoners outside of the specified categories if it is necessary for one of the reasons set out in Rule 35A of the Prison Rules and where the information required could not reasonably be obtained by a less intrusive means.. Routine listening in these circumstances must be reviewed every three months. As with routine reading of correspondence, the impetus to institute such listening may be a request from the police or other investigating authority. Chapter 36 also sets out provisions for random listening. Generally, the percentage of calls listened to should be no more than five per cent, but the proportion may be increased if it is considered necessary, for example if there is evidence of widespread abuse of telephones being used for illicit purposes. The exact percentage should be agreed with the area manager and reviewed at regular intervals. Prisoners should be notified if telephones in their establishment are subject to random listening. The provisions relating to retaining and disclosing information from prisoners' correspondence which are set out in the Prison Rules 35A–D also apply to telephone conversations.

7.12.7. CALLS TO LEGAL ADVISORS
The Security Manual provides that calls made to a legal adviser are excluded from the provisions on recording 'in those prisons where technology allows the distinction to be made'. The risk of privileged conversations being recorded is not therefore excluded. Separate provisions apply to category A prisoners .

7.12.8. CALLS TO CATEGORY A PRISONERS
Category A and E List prisoners must be subject to the call enabling telephone system. Requests to have people other than the prisoners' approved visitors or close relatives added to a telephone list must be submitted to the Area or Operational Manager or to the Director of High Security Prisons .For high and exceptional risk category A prisoners and E List prisoners legal telephone calls must be listened to only to the extent necessary to ensure that the call is genuinely to a legal adviser. Once this has been established, monitoring staff must stop listening and the centrally held recording must not be listened to. Again, therefore, there is a risk that privileged conversations will be monitored.

7.12.9 .CALLS TO THE MEDIA
The draft Order provides that prisoners must not make calls to the media if it is intended, or likely, that the call will be used for publication or broadcast. Written applications to make such calls will be considered, but permission will only be granted in exceptional circumstances. Before an interview by telephone is allowed, an Operational Manager must be satisfied that the call is for a legitimate purpose, for example

to bring to light a miscarriage of justice which could not be satisfied by written communications or a visit. The wording of the above policy obviously reflects the reasoning of the House of Lords in *R v Home Secretary, ex p Simms and O'Brien* [1999] 3 All ER 400, HL (see above). In *R(Hirst) v Home Secretary* [2002] EWHC 602 (Admin) the claimant, a serving prisoner who actively campaigned for prisoners' rights, argued that the policy breached his rights under Art 10 of the ECHR. While the court confirmed that the policy making telephone contact with the media exceptional was not in itself unlawful, it found that the policy was insufficiently flexible as there appeared to be an assumption that sending information by letter will virtually always meet the prisoner's objective. The court held that to impose what was effectively a blanket ban was unlawful. The decision to deny prisoners this right must be justified strictly by reference to one of the aims set out in Art 10(2) of the Convention. This decision contains a very purposive analysis of how qualified rights, such as Art 10, survive imprisonment compared with decisions such as in *R v Home Secretary, ex p Mellor* [2001] EWCA Civ 472.

7.13. EXERCISE
A prisoner must have the opportunity to spend time in the open air at least once every day, subject to weather conditions and good order and discipline. The minimum period being 1 (One) hour.

7.14. TEMPORARY RELEASE
Rule 9 of the Prison Rules 1999, which provides the authority for release on temporary licence ('ROTL'), was substantially redrafted in 1995. The purpose of this redrafting was to enable the Secretary of State to introduce more stringent measures in respect of temporary release and to provide punitive sanctions for those who failed to comply with the terms of their licence. The move was in response to a series of press stories about prisoners who had re-offended whilst on release, but has been

severely criticised for impeding the rehabilitative programmes that are available to prisoners. It appears that prisoners on licence cannot be allowed to travel abroad, as in the case of *R (on the application of Rifat Mehmet) v London Probation Board* [2007] EWHC 2223 (Admin), when the court decided that a decision by the Probation Service to refuse an offender's request to travel abroad whilst on licence was not irrational and did not breach the European Convention on Human Rights 1950 Art.8. This case illustrates that the Board did at least give the prisoner the opportunity to have his argument against the decision heard unlike the case of *R (on the application of Benson) v Secretary of State for Justice* [2007], when the court decided that the Criminal Justice Act 2003 s.255(2), which provided for a prisoner released on conditional licence may make representations to the Secretary of State for Justice concerning any decision of the Secretary of State to revoke his licence, was compatible with the European Convention on Human Rights 1950 Art.5(4). The secretary of state was under a common law duty to act reasonably and fairly in considering such representations and in the instant case he had failed to discharge that duty. Rule 9(3) provides authority for prisoners to be released temporarily from prison for the following reasons:

(i) on compassionate grounds or to receive medical treatment;

(ii) to engage in employment or voluntary work;

(iii) to receive instruction or training not generally available in prison;

(iv) to participate in proceedings before any court or tribunal;

(v) to consult with a legal adviser where the consultation cannot take place in the prison;

(vi) to assist the police in their enquiries;

(vii) to facilitate a transfer between prisons;

(viii) to assist in the maintenance of family ties or the transition from prison life to freedom;
(ix) to visit the locality of the prison as one of the privileges underR8.

The rule provides that before release can take place, the Secretary of State must be satisfied that the person will not present an unacceptable risk of committing further offences (Rule 9(4)), or that the length of sentence and the frequency of release will not undermine public confidence in the administration of justice (Rule 9(5)). This duty is expressed in more severe terms for prisoners who have committed further offences whilst released on licence (Rule 9(6)). Prisoners may be recalled to prison at any time during a period of temporary release, whether or not their licence conditions have been broken (Rule 9(8)). A prisoner who has been recalled to prison in breach of his/her licence may apply to appeal this decision. They must contact their solicitor immediately and he will obtain the decision papers and proceed from there. If such an appeal fails, the prisoner still has Should that fail the solicitor may appear on the prisoner's behalf at an oral hearing before the parole board.

7.15.1. RELEASE RELATED COURT CASES

In *Peter David Dunn v Parole Board* [2008] EWCA Civ 374, it was decided that, where there had been a delay of 10 months in the Parole Board's review of the recall of a prisoner, a judge had been entitled to strike out claims under the Human Rights Act 1998 and for false imprisonment brought more than four years later by the prisoner. This decision assumes that the Parole Board is a legal "person" with Human Rights and that it would breach the Parole Board's right to a fair trial, Article 6, if the case were tried. On difference grounds, in *R (on the application of John Massey) v (1) Parole Board For England & Wales (Defendant) (2) Secretary Of State For Justice (Interested PArty)* [2008] EWHC 997 (Admin), the court decided that although a delay of five months between a recalled prisoner's application to the Parole Board to consider his representations about his return to custody and the hearing of the application was undesirable, it had not, in the pArticular circumstances, breached the European Convention on Human Rights 1950 Art.5(4). On the other hand, in the case of a lifer, *R (on the application of Paul Conrad) v Secretary of State for the Home DepArtment* [2007] EWHC 1796 (Admin), the court decided that the Secretary of State's decision that a parole review for a life-term prisoner would not be concluded within two years was incompatible with the European Convention on Human Rights 1950 Art.5(4). The Parole Board must be impArtial and in *R (on the application of Gulliver) v Parole Board* [2007] EWCA Civ 1386, the court decided that in considering whether to re-release a prisoner following his recall to prison by the Secretary of State , the Parole Board was not limited to reviewing the Secretary of State's decision and had to take account of all the evidence available to it at the time of its decision and consider public safety.

7.15.2. RISK ASSESSMENT FOR TEMPORARY RELEASE

There are three forms of temporary release: compassionate licence, facility licence and resettlement licence. Although eligibility differs for each form of release, in all cases a risk assessment must be completed before the release can be authorised. The main factors to be considered in completing this assessment are the risk that is posed to the public, whether the licence will be adhered to, the availability of suitable accommodation and whether the purpose of release is likely to be acceptable to reasonable public opinion (IG 36/95, Part II). The assessment is carried out in the prison but is subject to approval by the Lifer Management Unit for life sentenced prisoners and the Home Office Controller for contracted out prisons. Instruction to Governors 36/95 contains an appendix setting out the main areas to be investigated. These include some obvious areas for assessment, such as a prisoner's previous response to temporary release, custodial behaviour and home circumstances. However, other considerations are less easy to assess, such as the views of known victims or an offence analysis to see whether a prisoner may be prone to recidivism. It is difficult to see how prison staff will have either the information or resources to accurately assess this aspect of offending. Prisoners serving less than 12 months are not subject to sentence planning and less information is therefore available on them. The prison must obtain details of the offence, sentence and previous record, probation reports (pre- or post-sentence) where prepared, any police post-sentence reports and records of any previous custodial sentences. Generally, the application will be considered by a board at the prison which can either make a recommendation or defer a decision for further information. Any decision to authorise temporary release must be made by a governor of Grade 4 or above and, if such a governor is not available, the application must be referred to the area manager for a decision. Prisoners serving 12 months or more have more stringent arrangements in place.

7.15.3. COMPASSIONATE LICENCE

This is reserved for prisoners with exceptional personal circumstances that may include visits to dying relatives or attendance at funerals, marriage or religious ceremonies, medical appointments or for primary carers to resolve problems with their children. The two most common applications are to see ill relatives/attend funerals or to attend medical appointments. In the case of prisoners who have terminally ill relatives or who wish to attend funerals, this will usually only be authorised for 'close relatives'. Medical evidence or proof of the funeral is required to allow an application to proceed. The definition of close relative does not normally include 'in-laws', but may be extended beyond immediate relatives in certain circumstances, usually on the advice of the chaplain or a minister of the prisoner's . Release is normally for a very short period of time, eg to attend a funeral and a brief period of family mourning, but not attendance at a wake. PSI 46/1998, annex A created two further provisions for compassionate licence – that young offenders can be released on temporary licence to visit parents where the parents are unable to visit due to disability or serious illness and that prisoners in open or resettlement prisons can apply for compassionate licence to attend a weekly religious service. Prisoners may be allowed licence to attend medical appointments only once the full risk assessment has been carried out. Given the cumbersome process, this will often mean that compassionate release is unavailable in these circumstances and is only appropriate for prisoners who have to attend a series of outside appointments. The governor will seek the advice of the medical officer on the nature of the treatment and whether the prisoner is fit enough to attend unaccompanied. Lifers must have spent a minimum of six months in open conditions and have the application approved by Lifer Section to be eligible .

7.15.4. FACILITY LICENCE

In addition to those prisoners not eligible for any form of temporary release, categoryB prisoners may not be considered for facility licence. The general principles of this licence are to allow prisoners to participate in regime related activities (such as community service projects, employment and educational courses), to enable them to fulfil official purposes such as attending civil court hearings and, in certain circumstances, to attend job interviews or secure accommodation (PSI 53/2000, annex A). In order to be eligible, prisoners must have served at least one-quarter of their sentence, including any time spent on remand. Facility licence cannot be granted for purposes which might be regarded as purely social or recreational (PSI 46/1998, annex A) but must have a 'clear and substantive purpose which will allow reparation or help prisoners to lead law abiding and useful lives'. The duration of such a licence must not be for more than five consecutive days unless the needs of their employment require longer, although this can be granted each week and the governor must be satisfied that excessive grants of such a licence do not undermine the punitive element of a sentence. PSI 46/1998 removed the restrictions on paid work in the community for prisoners under facility licence. In exceptional circumstances, meetings with legal advisers can fall within the scope of facility licence.

7.15.5. RESETTLEMENT LICENCE

Eligibility to apply for resettlement licence is determined by length of sentence, as follows:

(i) Adult prisoners serving less than 12 months are ineligible (IG 36/1995, para 5.3).

(ii) Young offenders serving less than 12 months may apply after three months from the date of sentence or four weeks before their release date, whichever is the earlier.

Prisoners serving four years or more who were sentenced on or after 1 October 1992 may apply for release on resettlement licence once they have received their parole decision. If the parole decision is unfavourable, then adult male prisoners not held in open conditions must wait for a period of six months from the refusal or the parole eligibility date, whichever is the earlier. Prisoners held in open conditions who have been refused parole for the first time will have to wait either three months from the refusal or the parole eligibility date, whichever is the earlier . At subsequent parole reviews, the delay is two months from the refusal. Prisoners notified that they are to be granted parole may apply for resettlement licence to be taken before their release date, subject to there being sufficient time to arrange it .

(iv) Prisoners serving 12 months or more but less than four years may apply after having served one-third of the sentence or four months after sentence, whichever is the longer period .

(v) Prisoners sentenced before 1 October 1992 to sentences of four years or more may apply after having served one-third of their sentence (ie the parole eligibility date). Adverse parole decisions defer the timing of the application as above.

Entitlement to enhanced periods of temporary release are also provided for in PSO 2300, the Prison Service policy on resettlement.

7.15.6. LIFERS

Life sentenced prisoners are entitled to apply for all forms of temporary release. Those with a provisional release date may apply for all types of temporary licence after a minimum of four months in open conditions. Those in open conditions without a provisional release date may apply for a facility licence or compassionate licence after six months and a resettlement licence after nine months (Lifer Manual, chapter 11). The decision regarding ROTL for life sentence prisoners is now made by the governing governor, although decisions in contentious and high profile cases are made by the Lifer Unit (PSI 57/2002). Life sentence prisoners must be given opportunities to educate themselves. In a recent case, *Secretary of State for Justice v David Walker : Secretary of State for Justice v Brett James* [2008] EWCA Civ 30, the Secretary of State for Justice was in breach of his public law duty by failing to provide relevant offending behaviour courses to allow prisoners serving indeterminate sentences for public protection to demonstrate to the Parole Board by the time of the expiry of their minimum terms that their detention was no longer necessary for the protection of the public.

7.15.7 . MAINTAINING FAMILY TIES

The purpose of release on resettlement licence is expressed to be to enable prisoners to maintain family ties and links with the community and to make suitable arrangements for accommodation, work and training on release. Licences may be granted for between one and five days at a time. Unless the prisoner is at a resettlement prison, there must be a gap of eight weeks between each grant of a licence. For prisoners at resettlement prisons, more frequent grants of resettlement licence can be made, providing they have worked outside of the prison for at least two weeks.

In addition to ROTL, life sentence prisoners can apply for escorted visits, which generally consist of visiting a local town with one or more members of prison staff. To be eligible, the prisoner must be in category C or second stage conditions, be within twelve months of their next Parole Board review and within four years of tariff expiry. Lifers should have been in their current establishment for at least six months before an escorted visit takes place. In all cases, a full risk assessment must be carried out by a risk assessment board comprising the Lifer Manager, seconded probation officer and the prisoner's personal officer. The decision as to whether the prisoner is suitable for escorted absences will be made by the governing governor (PSI 57/2002). In a recent case, *Peter Davies v Secretary of State for Justice* [2008] EWHC 397 (Admin), the court decided that a life-sentence prisoner who complained of being moved from open to closed conditions did not have a sustainable claim for damages for false imprisonment, negligence or a breach of the European Convention on Human Rights 1950 Art.5. As to the claim in negligence, the relevant statutory regime did not give rise to a cause of action for the negligent performance of the relevant statutory duty.

7.15.8. BREACH OF LICENCE CONDITIONS

Governors are required to make spot checks on prisoners on temporary release to ensure, for example, that the prisoner is at the correct address or has not gone to the pub. The most common breaches of such licences are failing to return to prison on time, failing to return at all, or the commission of further offences whilst on licence. In all cases, this constitutes an offence against prison discipline and, on return to prison, charges should be laid against the prisoner immediately. If any criminal charges have also been brought or if the police are mounting their own investigation, the disciplinary proceedings will be adjourned pending their outcome. The governor must notify the local police force in any case where a prisoner has failed to return and inform the supervising probation officer. Where a prisoner has received a further sentence of imprisonment for an offence committed while released on temporary licence, governors are instructed not to make any further grants of temporary licence, save for exceptional cases, until the prisoner has been granted parole or is four weeks from the non-parole release date.

The Prisoners (Return to Custody) Act 1995 makes it a criminal offence for prisoners to be unlawfully at large. The offence is committed either:

(i)   by failing to return from a period of temporary release from prison within the time specified on the licence, without reasonable excuse; or

(ii)   by knowing or believing that an order has been made recalling him/her to prison and failing to take all necessary steps to comply with this, without reasonable excuse.

Prisoners who are convicted of the offence will be tried in a magistrates' court, which may impose a sentence of up to six months' imprisonment, and/or a fine not exceeding level 5 on the standard scale.

Dealing with an appeal against recall must not take a long time and recently a prisoner brought such a case to court. In the case of *R (on the application of Michael Robson) (Claimant) v (1) Parole Board (2) Secretary of State for the Home DeaArtment (Defendants) & (1) Governor of HMP Hacklington (2) Lifer Review & Recall section (3) National Probation Service (4) Governor of HMP Durham (interested parties)* [2008] EWHC 248 (Admin), the court decided that, in determining whether the Parole Board had dealt speedily with the lawfulness of a prisoner's continuing detention, the circumstances to be considered included the diligence shown by the authorities, the complexity of the issues, other factors bearing on when release from custody could properly be considered and the time periods involved.

7.16.1. POSSESSIONS

Standing Order 4 on 'Facilities' was issued to provide a framework for prisoners' possessions and other facilities under the version of the prison rule that was in force prior to the introduction of the Incentives and Earned Privileges ('IEP') schemes. It is due to be replaced by a new chapter of PSO 4000. Many of its provisions have been replaced with IEP schemes and other measures. Standing Order 4 requires prisons to publish a 'statement of their facilities (including a list of items that prisoners may normally retain in their possession)'. This will now cross over with entitlements under IEP schemes. PSO 4000, chapter 1, appendix 3 sets out acceptable privileges that prisons may include in schemes, and includes 'Possessions (including all previously in Standing Order 4 and establishment facility list items)'.

7.16.2. RETAINING PERSONAL POSSESSIONS

The general principle is for prisoners to be allowed to retain sufficient property to enable them to live as normal and individual an existence as possible within the constraints of custody. Property held by a prisoner in possession is for the use of that prisoner alone. It is only possible to lend, sell or give property to another prisoner with the permission of the governor, a measure designed to prevent racketeering. Although the Convention contains a right to peaceful enjoyment of property, this is subject to restrictions in the 'public interest' (Protocol 1, Art 1), which is widely interpreted and will include restrictions imposed to maintain orderly regimes in prisons. Standing Order 4 lists those possessions that prisoners are generally entitled to retain as:
(i)   a minimum of six newspapers or periodicals;
(ii)   a minimum of three books;

(iii) a combined music system, or a radio and either a record, cassette or compact disc player;
(iv) records/cassettes/compact discs in an amount that is reasonable;
(v) smoking material (convicted prisoners may have 80 cigarettes or 62.5 grams of tobacco, unconvicted prisoners 180 cigarettes or 137.5 grams of tobacco);
(vi) writing and drawing materials;
(vii) a watch;
(viii) a manual typewriter;
(ix) a battery shaver;
(x) batteries for personal possessions;
(xi) personal toiletries;
(xii) one plain ring;
(xiii) a medallion or locket;
(xiv) a calendar;
(xv) religious Articles at the discretion of the governor;
(xvii) a diary, an address book, postage stamps and phonecards

7.16.3. POSSESSION OF RELIGIOUS ARTIFACTS

The Prison Service Order on Religion (PSO 4550) provides that prisoners must be allowed to have possession or access to such Artefacts and texts as are required by their religion . The approved Artefacts and texts for each faith are detailed in the Order. Prisoners may have additional religious Artefacts or texts, so long as they are not deemed by the governor or relevant minister to be a threat to security or good order.

7.16.4. VOLUMETRIC CONTROL OF POSSESSIONS

The Woodcock Report into the Whitemoor escapes made a recommendation, in the light of security concerns about the amount of property prisoners in the dispersal prisons could accumulate, that:

'A volumetric control of all prisoners' possessions should be introduced forthwith to reduce dramatically the amount of property in possession/storage and facilitate effective searching.' (recommendation 6)

It was also a recommendation that this should apply to all prisoners notwithstanding their category. In response to this recommendation the Prison Service introduced volumetric control of property for all prisoners in IG 104/1995. This states that 'the standard limit for all prisoners is that property held in possession will be limited to that which fits into 2 of the new volumetric control boxes'. The boxes measure 0.7m x 0.55m x 0.25m. In addition, prisoners may have in possession 'one sound system *or* one outsize item' (ie one that will not fit into the boxes) and 'one birdcage' where birds are permitted. Exemptions in respect of all prisoners are made for legal papers, bedding and one set of clothes. Further exceptions are made for unconvicted prisoners in respect of property. Governors must consider whether in individual cases exceptions should be made. Property in excess of the limits can be handed out to relatives or friends and in exceptional circumstances property will be kept by the Prison Service at the central store in Branston.. Prison Service Instruction 05/2002 sets out guidance about applications made by prisoners who request access to a computer to assist with the preparation of their defence, appeal or related legal work. The PSI provides that 'any prisoner who requests access to IT facilities and demonstrates a real need for this ,i.e. refusing the request would raise a real risk of prejudicing the legal proceedings] must be granted access to the IT provided for this purpose for the period specified' . The particular circumstances that may lead to the provision of a computer are if the prisoner is conducting his own defence, if the prisoner is represented but has documents on disk that would make it unreasonable to disallow correspondence with their representative by disk, if the defence is complex, or if the prisoner has a disability . Generally, categoryA prisoners should not be allowed them in possession. If the governor makes an exception, or where prisoners of other categories are allowed computers, the Manual requires controls to be in place to monitor their use. These measures should ensure that:

(i) the computer does not have a modem whereby it can access systems outside the prison;

(ii) there is a competent member of staff who can check that only licensed copies of software are being used, and can check files to ensure that pornography, 'drug-related material', racist 'and other illegal or undesirable material is not present';

(iii) a careful watch is kept so that the computer is only used for the purpose for which it was allowed in possession;

(iv) during searches, floppy disks must be treated as documents and their contents scanned (although legally privileged material should by extension only be searched in accordance with the provisions in *R v Home Secretary, ex p Daly* [2001] UKHL 26 and the revised chapter 17 of the Security Manual); and

(v) floppy disks must be carefully controlled .

7.16.5. COMPUTERS AS POSSESSIONS

Prisoners have successfully challenged refusals to allow computers on an individual basis, and such challenges will be strongest where the need for a computer is tied to the fundamental right of access to the courts, or the Convention right to a fair hearing under Article 6. In R *(Ponting) v (1) Governor of HMP Whitemoor and (2) Home Secretary* [2002] EWHC (Admin) 215, the Appellant had been granted access to a computer, but challenged the restrictions set out in a compact which limited his use of the machine to certain times and conditions. The court accepted that Art 6 rights were engaged; however, no universal finding of principle was made on the particular issue. The court declined to substitute its own decision on the basis that it involved an assessment based on expertise of running prisons rather than a legal question. The court did, however, recognise the increasing requirement of the prison authorities to make technology available to prisoners to ensure proper access to the courts.

7.16.6. FORFEITURE OF PERSONAL POSSESSIONS

The governor has the power to remove possessions and to arrange for them to be placed in stored property or handed out to relatives if it is felt that the volume of personal possessions may be such as to make effective searching unduly difficult, or if there is a risk to health and safety or good order and discipline. Magazines, newspapers and books can also be withdrawn if it is felt that they constitute a threat to good order and discipline, national security or the interests of the prison . This power has sometimes been invoked by governors to prevent access to political publications, or gay publications, although when challenged such items are normally allowed. As the right to free expression in Art 10 of the ECHR includes the right to 'receive and impart information', specific instances of withholding such material are open to challenge under the Human Rights Act 1998. In addition to these discretionary powers, the governor has the power to order the forfeiture of items on disciplinary grounds. Rule 55(1)(b) of the Prison Rules 1999 empowers governors to order the forfeiture of privileges as part of a punishment at an adjudication for a period of up to 42 days (21 days for young offenders). Forfeiture of educational notebooks, radios, writing materials and postage stamps should not normally be ordered.

7.17.1. PRISONERS' MONEY

The majority of purchases a prisoner can make are from the prison shop, or 'canteen'. Following the introduction of IEP schemes, new guidance was given to governors on the amount of private cash prisoners could spend. The most recent guidance is contained in PSI 08/2003, which amends the private cash information given in Appendix 1 and 2 of PSO 4000. It confirms the position under the Prison Rules 1999, R43(3) that prisoners are not to be allowed to keep cash on them and that accounts are maintained for them whilst in prison (para8). In *Duggan v Governor of HMP Full Sutton and* [2004] EWCA Civ 78 the Court of Appeal upheld the decision that no intention to create a trust could be found in the language of Rule 43(3). The basic position is that prisoners are allowed to spend from their earnings and, to supplement this, from their private cash . Private cash is defined as money in the form of cash, cheques or postal orders that is in the prisoner's possession at reception or is subsequently received from outside sources. The weekly private cash allowance is capped at various levels according to the incentive scheme the prisoner is on. The three levels of basic, standard and enhanced have weekly private cash allowances of £3.00, £12.50 and £20.00 respectively (£18.00, £37.50 and £40.00 for unconvicted prisoners. The amount of private cash a prisoner may accumulate in his 'spend' account is set at a maximum of ten times the weekly private cash allowance and this is the maximum amount that he can spend at any one time. However, the governor does have a discretion to override these limits to cover individual or exceptional circumstances, eg for purchases of expensive items.

7.17.2. PURCHASES OTHER THEN CANTEEN PURCHASES

Although prisoners' purchases are mainly confined to the canteen, it is possible to buy items by mail order, but these must be purchased from companies belonging to the Mail Order Protection Scheme and must be sent to the prison direct. It is increasingly common for prisons to severely limit the number of suppliers that prisoners can obtain goods from and often this means that they have a restricted choice of goods at high prices.

7.17.3. INCENTIVES AND PRIVILEGES

The system of privileges and facilities afforded to prisoners has been the matter of some discussion within the Prison Service.

All prisons are now required to operate a local incentives scheme intended to motivate prisoners to good behaviour and performance. Accordingly Prison Rules 1999,R8 states that:
"Systems of privileges ... may include arrangements under which privileges may be granted to prisoners only in so far as they have met, and for so long as they continue to meet, specified standards in their behaviour and their performance in work or other activities."
Guidance on the scheme is set out in PSO 4000, which was introduced by PSI 90/19910. Chapter 1 includes the National Framework for Incentives and Earned Privileges (IEP). The schemes established in individual prisons must have aims that are consistent with those set out in the National Framework. Prisons' individual schemes and amendments to them must be approved by the appropriate area manager .The seven privileges that are identified as the 'key earnable privileges' are:
(i) access to private cash;
(ii) extra and improved visits;
(iii) eligibility to pArticipate in higher rates of pay schemes;
(iv) community visits for category D prisoners, adult females and young offenders (subject to normal risk assessment procedures);
(v) access to in-cell television for standard and enhanced prisoners (see PSI 58/1998 for further details);
(vi) the ability to wear own clothes;
(vii) time out of cells for association .

7.17.4. Key earnable privileges

Whilst individual prisons can consider which privileges to include in their schemes, where the key earnable privileges are available, they must be included. Chapter 1, appendix 3 of the Order sets out other acceptable privileges that may be included in schemes. The list includes the best jobs available, cooking facilities, additional access to the gym and library, mail order facilities, own bedding, extra cell furniture and possessions. In

R (Cooper) v (1) Governor of HMP Littlehey and (2) Director General, HM Prison Service [2002] EWCA Civ 632 the court, whilst refusing permission to appeal on the basis that the application was made out of time, expressed hope that in the future prisoners would not have their access to educational facilities removed as part of the basic regime.

The first point to note from this framework document is that it relates to privileges and cannot affect prisoners' rights to statutory entitlements such as the right to two visits every four weeks. Similarly, time out of cell is linked to this scheme but it is not possible to undermine the right of prisoners to time in the open air under the Prison Rules 1999, Rule 30. Convicted prisoners on basic are essentially restricted to minimum entitlements (two social visits a month, minimum association and no entitlement to in-cell television, ability to wear own clothes, or earned community visits). Subject to availability, standard prisoners are entitled to all the key earnable privileges, and the difference between standard and enhanced is one of degree. For example, the table recommends that standard prisoners should have at least three visits per 28 days and enhanced prisoners four or five one-hour visits every 28 days. Prisoners should be allowed some association time with other prisoners although there is no statutory minimum in the Rules and the amount will therefore be hugely variable between prisons. Prisoners can only be denied association if segregated for their own protection or for reasons of good order and discipline under Rule 45, or as a punishment of cellular confinement following a disciplinary finding of guilt. IEP schemes apply to women's prisons, although all women prisoners can wear their own clothes.

7.17.5. THREE-TIER SYSTEM OF PRIVILEGES REGIME

IEP schemes are operated on a three-tier system of basic, standard and enhanced regimes. This can either by based on location (entire wings of prisoners on the same level) or simply on individual prisoners . The crucial difference is between basic and standard regimes, whereas the enhanced regime may only be slightly more favourable than standard, depending on the nature of the prison and the privileges available. On entry to the system prisoners should be placed on standard level. On transfer from other prisons, prisoners should be placed at least on standard even if they were on basic at their previous prison .Prisons can allow enhanced prisoners from other prisons entry on the enhanced level, but if they do not do so there should be provision for 'quick reassessments on arrival' so that enhanced status can be achieved . In *R (Potter) v Home Secretary* [2001] EWHC Admin 1041 the court confirmed that where a prisoner was transferred from one prison to another he should remain on the same IEP level until that level could be properly assessed.

Guidance on how behaviour will be assessed appears in PSO 4000, chapter 1, appendix 5. This sets out the following principles:
'(a)   standards of behaviour and performance must clearly demonstrate the criteria for movements to higher or lower privilege levels;
(b)   the emphasis must be on *patterns* of behaviour and performance and not generally on individual incidents;
(c)   prisoners as well as staff must be aware of the expected standards, and prisoners' points of view about their own behaviour and performance must be taken into account when assessments are made.' .
The appendix then sets out the factors that should be taken into account. Firstly 'institutional behaviour', which incorporates compliance with rules, formal disciplinary offences (a single offence should only trigger a review of level if 'serious', and a prisoner found not guilty will not have the IEP assessment used against him and more subjective assessments as to how

a prisoner relates to other prisoners and staff. Secondly, 'attitudes to sentence planning', including the use made of the personal officer scheme, the approach to the sentence and the willingness to make effective use of time in custody. Finally, the 'attitudes to relationships outside prison', including family members and victims, must be assessed. The appendix also sets out suggested criteria as to how behaviour should be assessed, although if such criteria are to be included in schemes they should be expressed so that it is 'clear what prisoners have to do, or not do, to fulfil criteria for gaining and retaining each privilege level or pArticular privilege'. The criteria are non-violence, non-discrimination, civility, mutual respect, treating others with justice and fairness, respect for establishment rules and routines, due regard for personal hygiene and health, due regard for others' health and safety and effort and achievement in work and other constructive activities. Whilst prisons can introduce compacts setting out the facilities to be expected and the behaviour required for the various levels, prisoners cannot be required to sign them and refusal to do so should not in itself affect privilege level .

7.18 .1. DECISION MAKING AND REVIEWS

Each prison must set out a statement which includes details of the criteria for earning and retaining privileges. Such criteria should take into account the provisions set out in PSO 4000, chapter 1, appendix 5 discussed above. Whilst it is recognised that standards will vary between establishments, governors should be able to state that:

'prisoners here earn and retain privileges above the basic level through good and responsible behaviour and, where appropriate, through their performance in work and other constructive activities.' .

Accordingly, decisions must be taken on general, objective and specified grounds, and be seen to be following from a pArticular pattern of performance and behaviour. Perhaps the main criticism of schemes by prisoners since their introduction in 1995 has been that officers are able to make negative reports without the prisoner having any realistic method of challenging them, and without the procedural safeguards of the formal disciplinary system. In response to this the guidance in PSO 4000 stresses that systems are not to be designed as 'secondary disciplinary' systems and must be determined by 'an open and fair process'.

7.18.2. PRISON BOARD AND PANELS TO MAKE DECISIONS

The Order encourages prisons to use boards or panels to make decisions and, whether they do or not, more than one officer must be involved in the decision-making process, and decisions to place prisoners on basic must be endorsed by at least a Principal Officer grade (unless derogation is agreed by the area manager) . Decisions must be based on 'correct information' and take into account 'the prisoner's perspective' and so schemes 'must seek to build in verbal and/or written warnings, and reports to boards must seek to reflect prisoner responses to these and any other relevant comments'.Clearly, given the more serious impact of being placed on basic, the requirements of fairness will be more stringent. Rule 8(4) of the Prison Rules 1999 requires schemes to 'include a requirement that the prisoner be given reasons for any decision adverse to him together with a statement of the means by which he may appeal against it.' Reasons need not be lengthy but must be sufficient to enable the prisoner to understand which criteria s/he has failed to meet and on what grounds. Where the decision is counter to representations made by the prisoner, it must indicate why a different view has been taken. In giving decisions the avenues of appeal must be stated.

7.18.3. PRISON PRIVILEGE LEVELS

Schemes must have a mechanism for reviews of prisoners' privilege levels. Although the Order does not specify minimum review periods for prisoners except those on basic, reviews will pArtly be dependent on time left to serve and some schemes will depend on prisoner application. Downward reviews may be triggered by a single serious incident, such as a finding of guilt at an adjudication (see above). Automatic reviews of prisoners on the basic level must take place at least once a month, and at least every 14 days for young offenders. The courts have proved reluctant to intervene in IEP schemes. In R v Home Secretary, ex p Hepworth [1998] COD 146 a number of prisoners, serving sentences for sex offences that they denied, challenged the prisons' policy that barred them from the enhanced level as pArticipation in the Sex Offender Treatment Programme ('SOTP') was required before they were eligible. Though this was a blanket policy with no discretion for consideration of individual cases, the judge stated:

'there are plain dangers and disadvantages in the court's maintaining an intrusive supervision over the internal administrative arrangements by which the prisons are run, including any schemes to provide incentives for good behaviour, of which the system in question is plainly an example. I think that something of the nature of bad faith or what I may call crude irrationality would have to be shown, which is not suggested here.'

This apparent return to an approach of judicial non-intervention in prisoners' cases was justified by comparison with cases involving categorisation, where the 'prisoner's aspiration to liberty' was much more clearly in issue. More recently, in *R (Potter) v Home Secretary* [2001] EWHC Admin 1041, the court confirmed that the refusal of a prison to grant enhanced status on the grounds of ineligibility to attend the SOTP, by reason of denial of guilt, was neither unfair nor irrational. The court also rejected an argument that ECHR, Art 8 rights had been infringed by the IEP policy of increasing access to the family as a reward and reducing such access as a penalty.

7.19. MISBEHAVIOUR

In practice, alleged misbehaviour can result either in a formal disciplinary charge being laid, or impact on a prisoner's incentive level. Often the impact on a prisoner's quality of life will be greater and last for longer if action is taken within the IEP scheme, yet the procedural safeguards involved are much weaker. Another problem is that the linking of incentive level with sentence planning can impact unfairly on those challenging their convictions (as in *Hepworth* and *Potter*). Many prisoners continue to feel that IEP schemes constitute 'informal' disciplinary systems. Furthermore, the fact that the National Framework gives governors wide discretion as to what may be included in schemes means that the problems of inconsistency in what prisoners may expect, as identified in the Woolf Report, continues.

7.20. ELECTORAL RIGHTS

The restriction on prisoners voting contained in s 3 of the Representation of the People Act 1983 was successfully challenged in the European Court of Human Rights (*Hirst v United Kingdom* 74025/01) which held that the applicant, a post-tariff discretionary life sentenced prisoner, had suffered a breach of Art 3 of Protocol 1 of the Convention as a result of his disenfranchisement.

European court case law has established that Art 3 of Protocol 1 guarantees individual rights, including the right to vote and to stand for election. Although central to democracy and the rule of law, these rights are not absolute, and Contracting States are granted a wide margin of appreciation in relation to these rights. The court noted the divergences in law and practice within Contracting States. Recently in *Mustafa Kamel Mustafa (aka Abu Hamza) v (1) United S(2) Secretary of State for the Home DepArtment* [2008] EWHC 1357 (Admin) , it was decided that a judge had properly made an order sending a case to the Secretary of State for the Home DepArtment for her decision as to whether the appellant should be extradited to the United States in relation to terrorism-related charges, and the subsequent decision of the secretary of state to extradite him was unassailable. An allegation by the appellant that the evidence against him was tainted by torture, contrary to the European Convention on Human Rights 1950 Art.3, was unsupported by evidence. Another Art.3 case was *R (on the application of Vaclovas Faizovas) v Secretary of State for Justice* [2008] EWHC 1197 (Admin), in which it was decided that the handcuffing of a prisoner whilst he received chemotherapy treatment did not breach his rights under the European Convention on Human Rights 1950 Article 3 because he represented a risk to the public and there was a risk that he would escape.

7.21. DISENFRANCHISEMENT OF PRISONERS

The court questioned whether the disenfranchisement of prisoners pursued a legitimate aim, and doubted the validity of the aims put forward by the government: the prevention of crime and punishment of offenders and the enhancement of civil responsibility and respect for the rule of law. In any event, the court considered that the restriction imposed under RPA 1983, s 3 was disproportionate to any aim it sought to achieve. It noted that s 3 does not apply to prisoners on remand, those imprisoned for default in paying fines or those detained for contempt of court, and that the restriction is lifted as soon as a prisoner is released. However, s 3 does apply to a large category of prisoners irrespective of the length of their sentence, and the nature or gravity of their offence. It could not be argued that the applicant's disenfranchisement automatically formed part of his punishment, as he had served the tariff part of his life sentence. However, the court accepted that it was for a Contracting State to determine the parameters of any restrictions on prisoners' voting rights, and that it would not speculate whether the applicant would still have been deprived of the right to vote even if a more limited restriction had been applied in accordance with the requirements of Article 3 of ECHR, Protocol 1. Clearly the decision will require the government to legislate further in this area.

7.22.1. PRODUCTION AT COURT IN COURT

Prisoners who are engaged in civil litigation, be it against the Secretary of State, the Home Office, the Prison Service or any of its employees, or simply in other civil matters unrelated to their imprisonment such as child care, will often face difficulties when their action reaches the stage where their attendance at court is necessary. There has been a great deal of resistance to production in those circumstances and, where attendance is authorised, the prisoner has been asked to pay a contribution towards the costs of production. The principle that a prisoner may be taken to court for these purposes arises from the Crime (Sentences) Act 1997, Sch 1, para 3. This gives the Secretary of State power to authorise any person detained in the UK to attend any other place in the UK where it is desirable in the 'interests of justice or for the purposes of attending any public inquiry'. Any person who is produced under this section remains in custody throughout the time they are outside of prison (Sch 1, para 3(3)). This section does not actually create any rights, being merely an enabling section to permit attendance at court. The power granted to the Secretary of State is to decide whether it is 'desirable' in the interests of justice for a prisoner to be so produced. Current Prison Service policy is set out in PSO 4625, which is discussed further below. The judiciary has never developed a consistent approach to this matter (for earlier discussions on this point see *Becker v Home Office* [1972] 2 QB 407 and *R v Governor of Brixton Prison, ex p Walsh* [1985] AC 154) although detailed guidance can be obtained from *R v Home Secretary, ex p Wynne* [1992] QB 406, CA. The Court of Appeal looked at these provisions in some detail on behalf of a category A prisoner who was seeking to attend a judicial review hearing that he was conducting in person. The application was actually dismissed because the prisoner had failed to make a formal application to the prison governor to be produced and prisoners must be made aware that this is an essential step to take when attendance at court is necessary.

7.22.2. ECHR DIRECTLY ENFORCEABLE IN JUDICIAL REVIEW PROCEEDINGS

Now that ECHR, Art 6 is directly enforceable in judicial review proceedings, the position of applicants is even stronger. Prison Service Order 4625 was issued in 2002 in an attempt to limit challenges under the Human Rights Act. The PSO provides that the primary consideration when dealing with a request to produce a prisoner to attend a civil hearing must be whether it is in the interests of justice that he or she should attend. If it appears that the prisoner's case would suffer detriment if they did not attend, this would be a strong case for allowing the production . This must be balanced against the normal security considerations, including risk to the public . The prison must be able to demonstrate that a decision to refuse production on the basis of a prisoner's risk assessment is reasonable in all the circumstances. Decisions regarding production at court are made by the governor. All movement of category A prisoners outside the prison must be authorised by the Directorate of High Security Prisons.

Chapter 2 of the PSO sets out a checklist of points to be taken into account in relation to ECHR, Art 6, including whether the prisoner's personal attendance is necessary, whether he is legally represented and whether there are any alternatives to production at court. It goes on to state that Art 6 'is only engaged where the prisoner has an arguable claim. A refusal to produce a prisoner whose claim is frivolous would not impose Article 6 rights. One indication that a case is frivolous might be a refusal of legal services funding'. This represents the dissenting view in *R v Home Secretary, ex p Wynne* [1992] QB 406 outlined above and a decision not to produce a prisoner on this basis could be open to further challenge. A decision not to produce a witness, however, can breach Art 6 and in the recent case of *R (on the application of Terry Lake) v (1) Governor of Highdown Prison (2) Independent Adjudicator (3) Secretary of State for Justice* [2007] EWHC 3080 (Admin), the court decided that whilst an independent adjudicator had the power to require a witness to attend a disciplinary hearing involving a serving prisoner she had not been asked to exercise that power, and as a result the prisoner had not had his European Convention on Human Rights 1950 Article 6 rights infringed. This should have been a breach of Article 6, had it not been that the Adjudicator was not requested to do so and it is assumed that it could be proved that he was not requested to do so. Yet in *R (on the application of John Haase) v (1) Independent Adjudicator District Judge Nuttall (2) Secretary of State for Justice* [2007] EWHC 3079 (Admin), in relation to prison disciplinary proceedings against serving prisoners the system of hearings by independent adjudicators, in which the prosecution case was presented by a prison officer who might be a witness, was not incompatible with the European Convention on Human Rights 1950 Art.6. There was no other witness called but the prison officer.

7.23. THE COSTS OF PRODUCTION

The prisoner's ability or willingness to pay for production must not be a factor in deciding whether he or she is produced at court . The courts have accepted that it is not unlawful or unreasonable for a charge to be made to the prisoner and that the Secretary of State was under a duty to ensure that this charge was reasonable in light of the ability of the prisoner to pay. The standard fee is currently £40.00 for the escort day and a charge of £1.00 per mile in excess of nine miles .Provisions are also made for circumstances where alternative methods of transport to court, such as taxis, are employed.

7.24. Prisoner contribution

Once the governor has decided that production should go ahead, consideration will be given to whether it is reasonable to ask the prisoner to contribute towards the cost. The governor has a discretion to charge a lower sum within the prisoner's means .Sources of funding can include private cash or funds available from outside the prison, including from the Legal Services Commission. Lawyers should still argue for the costs in such cases to be set at the lowest possible level so as to discharge their duty to the Legal Services Commission. Should the prisoner refuse to contribute towards the cost of production even though they appear to have sufficient funds, then the governor must decide how to proceed. The decision must weigh the interests of justice against the refusal to pay. The PSO notes that this scenario has not yet been challenged in the courts and it is suggested that governors err on the side of caution and produce a prisoner in borderline.

Chapter 8 - Requests and Complaints

8.1. AN OVERVIEW OF THE PROCEDURE

The Prison Rules 1999 impose a duty to deal with prisoners' complaints. This duty is firstly placed upon the governor (r 11) – who may delegate it under r 81 – and secondly on the Independent Monitoring Board. Requests and complaints procedures were reviewed during 1999 and 2000, as a result of concerns that the old system was not working as intended. Consequently, Prison Service Order 2510, 'Prisoners' Request and Complaints Procedures' sets out a new system replacing that contained within the old Prisoners' Requests/Complaints Manual.

The main changes in the new system are that complaints are dealt with separately from requests and there is no generic form dealing with both; complaint forms are freely available to prisoners and no longer have to be applied for; completed forms are posted into a locked box on the prison wing; and there is no longer an appeal to Prison Service Headquarters (although Headquarters retains responsibility for dealing with 'reserved subjects'.. Ordinary complaints are divided into three stages, all of which are answered within the establishment.

Stage 1 is usually a response from a wing officer, stage 2 a response from a manager and stage 3 is a response from the governing governor. From there, the prisoner can appeal to the Prisons Ombudsman if s/he is still dissatisfied with the response.

8.2. THE ROLE OF INDEPENDENT MONITORING BOARDS

Independent Monitoring Boards retain their statutory duty to satisfy themselves that prisoners are being treated properly and to hear their requests and complaints. The IMBs at each prison are responsible for implementing their own procedures for hearing requests and complaints and should make these known to staff and prisoners within the establishment. Prison staff must ensure that any request to speak to a member of the IMB is passed to the Board 'promptly.' The IMB also has a responsibility to monitor the systems for dealing with requests and complaints and should examine applications books and complaints logs and the monthly complaints statistics. They should report to the governor any problems with the operation of the system or areas of management identified in prisoners' requests and complaints.

Prisoners may make an application to the chairman of the IMB under the confidential access arrangements.

8.3. REQUESTS

Requests are dealt with via a system of oral and written applications. Oral wing/landing applications must be held daily in a private room, if possible, and governor's applications must be held every day except Sundays and public holidays. In practice, governor's applications are not heard by the governing governor, but by a senior member of staff. Oral applications should 'provide an opportunity for staff to listen to a prisoner's problem, to give advice, and to deal with straightforward matters quickly' . Establishments may decide to run a system of written applications, although this is not compulsory. If such a system is operated, then it is up to the establishment itself to design appropriate forms and decide how many stages the applications procedures should follow. Where forms are used, prisoners must be able to pick up the forms freely and should be able to hand them in to an officer during oral applications .

The applications procedure is meant to provide an intermediate stage between informal conversation with a prison officer and making a formal complaint. Although the policy is that prisoners should be encouraged to use the applications procedure to resolve any issues, it is not compulsory for them to do so before they invoke the formal complaints procedures .

If prisoners do not wish to use the applications procedures, or if a problem is not dealt with to their satisfaction by the oral or written applications processes, then they should follow the complaints process.

8.4. COMPLAINTS

The complaints procedures are based upon ten principles outlined in PSO 2510, chapter 4:

1. Openness. The procedures must be well publicised and all prisoners must know how to make a complaint.
2. Simplicity. Procedures must be simple, easy to understand and free of unnecessary bureaucracy, subject to the need to incorporate safeguards and maintain proper records where necessary.
3. Ease of access. It must be easy to make a complaint and obstacles must not be put in the way of prisoners who wish to do so.
4. Timeliness. Complaints must be resolved within a reasonable time according to set deadlines wherever possible.
5. Fairness. Complaints must be considered fairly and properly.
6. Responding at an appropriate level. Complaints must be answered at the most appropriate level and by the most

appropriate member of staff. In most cases this will be at the lowest suitable level, subject to the condition that prisoners are able to appeal to a higher level if they are not satisfied.

7. Confidentiality. Confidentiality must be respected as far as is practicable within a prison environment. This is particularly important in respect of confidential access complaints.

8. Appropriate redress. Appropriate action must be taken when complaints are upheld.

9. Freedom from penalty. Prisoners must not be penalised for making a complaint.

10. Use of the system to provide management information. Management must make use of statistical and other information provided by the system.

There are four different complaints forms. Ordinary complaints are made on a white COMP 1 form, appeals against the reply to ordinary complaints are made on a white COMP 1A, confidential access complaints on a pink COMP 2, and appeals against adjudications on a blue ADJ 1. Envelopes should be provided with the confidential access forms. All forms should be freely available on prison wings, by or near a locked box for the postage of completed forms.

Complaint forms and guidance on the submission of complaints are printed in a range of 20 different languages, and prisoners whose first language is not English should be allowed to submit a complaint in their own language. However, the process will take longer, as the complaint and reply will need to be translated . Staff are instructed that they should assist prisoners who have difficulties in reading and writing in making their complaints and that staff should also consider the possibility of allowing prisoners who are visually impaired to complain on large print forms, braille, or on an audio cassette .

Prisoners must submit their complaints within three months from the date when the matter leading to their complaint arose, the date upon which they became aware of that matter, or the date upon which s/he was found guilty at adjudication. However, prison establishments and, in the case of adjudications, Headquarters staff, do retain discretion to consider complaints submitted outside the deadline where exceptional circumstances apply, where there are good reasons for the delay, or where the issues raised are so serious as to override the time factor . Initial complaints are known as stage 1 of the process and should be submitted on form COMP 1.

Staff responding to formal complaints are advised that their response must 'properly address the points made by the prisoner, irrespective of whether the complaint is upheld or rejected. The response must be based upon accurate and up to date information and must stick to the point. Decisions must not be taken arbitrarily or give the impression that they have been taken arbitrarily' Where a complaint is upheld, the reply should outline the action being taken to give redress .

Prisoners should receive a reply to their stage 1 complaints, submitted on COMP 1, within three week days of submission for an ordinary complaint, ten week days if they make allegations against a member of staff, ten week days if they involve another establishment, or five week days if they are . If the reply is delayed, then an interim response should be sent explaining to the prisoner the reason for the delay and giving an idea of when s/he might expect a substantive response .

If the prisoner is unhappy with the response provided, then s/he should move on to stage 2 of the procedures by appealing on form COMP 1A within seven days of receipt of the stage 1 reply.

This appeal should be answered by someone at a higher management level than the person who responded to the initial complaint . If, exceptionally, the initial complaint was dealt with at a managerial level, and there is not a further management level below the governing governor, then the complaint will be answered by the governing governor, who provides a response encompassing both stages 2 and 3 of the procedures . Prison Service Headquarters continue to deal with complaints made through solicitors and MPs, as well as with litigation. They will also advise establishments upon request.

8.5. CONFIDENTIAL ACCESS

Prisoners have a right to make a complaint on form COMP 2 in a sealed envelope to the governing governor, the area manager or the chair of the Independent Monitoring Board. The use of confidential access is appropriate where the complaint is 'about a particularly serious or sensitive matter, where it would be reasonable for the prisoner to feel reticent about discussing it with wing staff or having it become known to administrative and wing staff through the normal complaints procedure'. Examples are complaints about ill treatment, complaints about the conduct of wing staff and complaints touching on sensitive medical issues.

Following receipt of a confidential access complaint, the person to whom it is addressed should decide whether or not the form was properly submitted under the confidential access procedure. If not, s/he may choose whether to answer the complaint anyway, a governor may pass it on to a manager for reply, the IMB may pass it to the governor, and Headquarters may return it to the establishment. Alternatively, the form might be sent back to the prisoner with an explanation as to why confidential access is not appropriate, or passed to the complaints clerk so that it can be dealt with under the normal complaints procedures . In deciding how to treat the form, the recipient should consider the nature of the complaint, the reasons given by the prisoner as to why s/he is using confidential access, and the extent to which misuse of the system might be encouraged by providing a response even if a complaint is inappropriate for confidential access .

8.6. RESERVED SUBJECTS

Complaints about 'reserved subjects' should be sent to the relevant department at Prison Service Headquarters. Reserved subjects are those where the governor at the establishment has no power to make a decision. They include appeals against adjudications, category A status, category A transfers, complaints by lifers about matters that are the responsibility of Lifer Review and Recall Section, parole, deportation and early release on compassionate grounds. Although the response is made by staff at Headquarters, the views of staff at the prison will often be sought before any decision is made. For example, if a category A prisoner submits an application to be escorted to a funeral, staff at that prison will be asked to give their views as to whether the prisoner is suitable to be permitted an escorted absence and whether the reason for the application is valid. Therefore, although the final decision rests with Headquarters staff, prison staff will have a large input into the decision-making process. Prisoners are not expected to know that their complaint is about a reserved subject, and the complaints clerk at the establishment should sift out such complaints and forward them to the relevant Headquarters department for a response, together with any relevant documentation. .

8.7. CATEGORY A PRISONERS

Requests/complaints submitted by category A prisoners can be dealt with by the prison unless the prisoner's category A status is relevant to the issues raised in the request/complaint. Queries about their security categorisation, transfers and allocation, approved visitors, change of name, applications for marriage, telephone calls, and 'supergrass' casework will all need to be referred to the Directorate of High Security Prisons at Headquarters rather than at the establishment.

8.8. LIFE SENTENCE PRISONERS

Lifers' complaints will be reserved subjects if they relate to lifer review procedures, applications for release on temporary release for high profile prisoners, review dates and tariff, the Parole Board's decisions and recommendations, Ministerial responses to Parole Board recommendations, the revocation of a life licence, or a request to change their names. Such complaints will be conveyed either to the Lifer Review and Recall Section or the Parole Board.

8.9. PAROLE

Complaints relating to any aspect of the parole process for determinate sentenced prisoners will be dealt with by the Early Release and Recall Section at Headquarters. There is no formal right of appeal against a Parole Board refusal, and although prisoners may submit complaints, this will not lead to their papers being put back in front of the Parole Board unless there have been major changes in the prisoner's circumstances which were not considered when the parole decision was made, or where there has been procedural impropriety.

8.10. ADJUDICATIONS

If a prisoner complains about a finding of guilt at adjudication, the Briefing and Casework Unit or Directorate of High Security Prisons will conduct a full paper review. The transcript of the adjudication and any other documentation should be forwarded by the prison, and the adjudicator should also provide a memo containing their comments on the issues raised in the prisoner's complaint.

8.11. DEPORTATION

Prisoners who are illegal entrants or liable to deportation are able to submit complaints relating to their immigration status. These will be forwarded to the Immigration and Nationality Directorate. Prisoners who want to appeal against a decision to deport them or to make representations asking to be given further leave to remain in the UK should seek advice and representation from a solicitor or an organisation specialising in immigration issues, such as the Joint Council for the Welfare of Immigrants, Immigration Advisory Service or the Refugee Legal Centre.

8.12. RELEASE ON COMPASSIONATE GROUNDS

Complaints asking for compassionate release should be dealt with by the Early Release and Recall Section. The prison will be asked to give detailed supporting evidence or obtain this from other agencies (eg hospitals, social workers etc).

8.13. SPECIAL REMISSION

Prisoners may apply for early release from prison on the basis that they have rendered 'some commendable service to the prison authorities or to the community at large that merits some tangible recognition' (Request/Complaint Staff Manual, annex M, para 1) or where there has been a 'pledge of public faith' due to a miscalculation of sentence. In these circumstances it is possible to apply to have the sentence reduced by operation of the Royal Prerogative of Mercy. Such applications are made via the complaints system and the governor will need to provide supporting evidence.

8.14. ALLOCATION OF YOUNG OFFENDERS SENTENCED UNDER POWERS OF CRIMINAL COURTS (SENTENCING) ACT 2000, SS 90–91

Such young offenders are centrally managed at Prison Service Headquarters. Governors will be asked to give their views.

8.15. MOTHER AND BABY UNITS

Prisoners' complaints relating only to the refusal to admit them to a mother and baby unit, a decision to separate them from their child, or any aspect of their treatment whilst in a mother and baby unit are dealt with by the Operational Manager for Women's Prisons.

8.16. ARTIFICIAL INSEMINATION

Applications for artificial insemination are dealt with by the Family Ties Unit at Prisoner Administration Group. Guidance on this issue is found in the case of *R v Secretary of State for the Home Department, ex p Mellor* [2001] EWCA Civ 472.

8.17. TRANSFER TO SCOTLAND, NORTHERN IRELAND, ISLE OF MAN, JERSEY OR GUERNSEY, AND REPATRIATION TO OTHER JURISDICTIONS

for transfer to another jurisdiction are dealt with by the Cross Border Transfer Section, Prisoner Administration Group.

8.18. ALLEGATIONS AGAINST THE GOVERNING GOVERNOR

These are referred to the Briefing and Casework Unit or to the Directorate of High Security Prisons, depending on the type of prison involved.

Headquarters should provide substantive responses to complaints about reserved subjects within six weeks of the prisoner submitting them .If this is not possible, then an interim reply should be forwarded to the prisoner explaining the reasons for the delay and telling him/her when a full response is likely to be provided.

There is no internal appeal against a reply on a reserved subject, and so a prisoner who remains dissatisfied should contact the Prisons Ombudsman or seek legal advice.

8.19. COMPLAINTS ABOUT MEMBERS OF STAFF

If a prisoner complains about a member of staff 'imputing misconduct, which, if true, would constitute a disciplinary or criminal offence or would seriously detract from his or her reputation', then governors must follow the guidance set out at chapter 11 of PSO 2510. The management of the establishment itself should initiate and conduct the investigation of such complaints, and decide on the action needed and respond to the prisoner's complaint. The prison is also responsible for initiating any formal disciplinary proceedings mounted against the member of staff in question. Staff at the Briefing and Casework Unit or the Directorate of High Security Prisons will respond to confidential access complaints making serious allegations against prison staff and will also deal with correspondence from Ministers or other officials who make allegations against prison staff.

The Discipline Policy Team at Headquarters are able to provide advice as to whether allegations against staff should be referred to the police, whether staff should be suspended from duty and upon the appropriate action to take following either a police or internal investigation.

If it is decided that an internal investigation should be mounted, then this should be carried out in accordance with the provisions of PSO 1300 (Investigations). The level of the investigation will be decided by line management, the governing governor, or the area manager, depending on the seriousness of the allegation made. Responsibility for the investigation usually lies with the line management of the prison.

8.20. COMPLAINTS WITH A RACIAL ASPECT

All incidents with a racial aspect, however minor, must be recorded by the Race Relations Liaison Officer, and so the complaints system 'must ensure that a racial aspect to any complaint is recognised, recorded, and investigated'. Staff are advised that 'a racial incident is defined as any incident which is perceived to be racial by the victim or any other person'. Forms COMP 1, COMP 1A and COMP 2 all include a box which a prisoner should tick if the complaint has a racial aspect.

An ordinary complaint which has a racial aspect should be passed to the Race Relations Liaison Officer after it has been registered by the complaints clerk. The RRLO should then open a racist incident reporting form, make enquiries, and make a report to the chair of the Race Relations Monitoring Team at the prison. The RRLO should reply to the prisoner's complaint unless it is decided that 'the racial aspect is minor or tangential'. In such cases the RRLO should pass the complaint on to the appropriate member of staff for a reply, contributing a view on the racial aspect of the complaint.

If a complaint with a racial aspect is re-submitted as a stage 2 or 3 complaint, the member of staff considering the appeal must inform the RRLO and should normally liaise with him/her in providing a response.

Where a prisoner submits a confidential access form raising an issue with a racial aspect, the recipient of the form must inform the RRLO of the reference number, date of the complaint, nature of the complaint, and the action taken. However, the prisoner should not be identified.

If a prisoner complaining about a reserved subject has ticked the 'racial aspect box' on the form, the complaints clerk should provide a copy of the form to the RRLO before forwarding it on to Headquarters and forward a copy of the reply to the RRLO when received.

8.22. COMPLAINTS ABOUT BULLYING

Complaint forms include a box for the prisoner to tick where the complaint is about bullying, so that the anti-bullying procedures laid out in PSO 1702 can be implemented if necessary.

8.23. COMPLAINTS WHICH INVOLVE ANOTHER ESTABLISHMENT

Where a prisoner complains about events that occurred at another establishment or during transfer, the prison where the complaint is submitted is responsible for ensuring that s/he is provided with a response. The establishment where the prisoner was held at the relevant time is generally responsible for providing a draft response or the information upon which the response should be based .

.Prisons are advised that they are not expected to be responsible for investigating or overturning decisions made at other establishments. However, if it is apparent that an initial response provided by the previous establishment is factually incorrect, then they may overturn a response to a complaint. However, they 'should wherever possible agree the new response with the previous establishment' .

8.24. THE PRISONS AND PROBATION OMBUDSMAN

The office of Prisons Ombudsman – now the Prisons and Probation Ombudsman – was created in 1994 following recommendations in the Woolf Report. The post does not have a statutory basis, and if complaints are upheld the Ombudsman can only make recommendations to the Director General of the Prison Service or the Home Secretary. In the vast majority of cases recommendations are followed, although a significant minority are rejected (6.6% according to the Ombudsman's 1998–99 annual report).

The Ombudsman's remit has varied since the creation of the office. The current remit is covered in the Terms of Reference . The Ombudsman can investigate complaints about all decisions affecting prisoners made by Prison Service staff and those working in prisons if not employed by the Prison Service (eg prison probation officers, staff in privately run prisons, prison teachers, and members of Boards of Visitors) with the exception of decisions involving the clinical judgement of doctors.

If a complaint to the Prison Service remains unanswered after six.. However, in practice, if there has been a delay of more than six weeks the Ombudsman is likely to chase up the response rather than commence a full investigation at that stage.

A complaint to the Ombudsman does not have to be made on any specific form and can be made by letter. The current remit states that complaints must be submitted by 'individual prisoners' and so prisoners should either write themselves or, if a complaint is drafted on their behalf, sign the complaint before it is sent. In practice, however, the Ombudsman will accept complaints from legal representatives and MPs as long as they have permission to act from the prisoner.

Prisoners' letters to the Ombudsman may be sent at the prison's expense under confidential access although of course this does not mean that the nature of the complaint will not be disclosed to prison staff, as the Ombudsman may need to discuss the complaint with prison officials in the course of investigating it. Prison staff must not prevent the submission of complaints, nor judge their eligibility, eg on time grounds .

Letters sent to the Ombudsman can be handed in sealed, as long as they are marked 'confidential access' and the address is correct, and can only be opened if there is reasonable cause to believe they contain an illicit enclosure, and then only in front of the prisoner . Correspondence from the Ombudsman to prisoners should be clearly identified as such on the envelope and marked as confidential. They should not be opened by prison staff unless there is reason to believe that they did not originate from the Ombudsman's office and, in such a case, they should be passed to the governor who should check with the Ombudsman's office that an inquiry is ongoing. If there is any remaining doubt, a letter purporting to be from the Ombudsman should only be opened in the presence of the prisoner concerned .

The Director General of the Prison Service is to ensure that the Ombudsman has 'unfettered access to Prison Service documents', including classified material (Terms of Reference, and Prison Service staff 'must co-operate fully with all requests from the Prisons Ombudsman or his staff for information, material or access to establishments and prisoners' .

Prison Service staff should identify information they believe comes within the above grounds and also check the Ombudsman's draft reports .The Ombudsman's access to information normally withheld from prisoners is one of his most important powers for prisoners.

Staff from the Prison Ombudsman's office may visit any prison establishment in the course of an investigation and may interview prison staff (who can take a colleague or trade union representative with them or prisoners who consent to an interview. Visits with prisoners should be in the sight but out of the hearing of prison staff, and do not count against a prisoner's allowance of visiting orders.

The Ombudsman has the power to seek to 'resolve the matter by local settlement'.. This process of local resolution is designed to deal with matters which are not 'reserved subjects' under the requests/complaints procedure (see above) and where the Ombudsman anticipates that the complaint will be upheld. Both the prisoner and the governor of the relevant prison must consent to the procedure . The idea is that this procedure will provide a speedier resolution for relatively minor complaints that can be dealt with at a local level where the investigation.

On 6 January 2004 the Prisons Minister announced that from 1 April 2004 the Prisons and Probation Ombudsman's remit would extend to the investigation of all deaths of prisoners, residents of probation hostels and those in immigration detention. The report of the Joint Committee on Human Rights into deaths in custody which was published on 14 December 2004 recommended that the Ombudsman should be given a statutory basis in order to facilitate this role.

8.25. THE PARLIAMENTARY COMMISSIONER FOR ADMINISTRATION

Prisoners have the right to complain to the Parliamentary Commissioner for Administration and may do so at the same time as pursuing their complaint through the internal procedures or the Prisons Ombudsman. The PCA's role is described in PSO 2510 as 'to investigate complaints by persons who claim to have sustained injustice in consequence of maladministration in connection with the exercise of the administrative functions of a body within PCA's jurisdiction (which includes the prison service and anyone acting on its behalf)'. This may include matters such as avoidable delay, faulty procedures, misleading or inadequate advice and refusal of access to official information. The PCA normally requires that the body against whom the complaint is made has heard the complaint and had an opportunity to rectify the situation.

Complaints should be submitted through an MP, normally the prisoner's constituency MP, within 12 months of the date upon which the events giving rise to the complaint arose. The MP will then consider whether the complaint is worthy of submission to the PCA, although the PCA's office will make the final decision on this. If the PCA decides that an investigation is not justified, then he will inform the MP accordingly. It is up to the MP to inform the prisoner. Where the PCA decides that a complaint is worthy of investigation, he will normally contact the prison service to see whether the matter may be resolved informally.

If resolution is not possible at this stage, then the PCA may begin a statutory investigation. He will send a written statement of the complaint to the MP and the Permanent Secretary of the Home Office, who will forward this to the Director General of the Prison Service. The Director General should reply to this statement within three weeks, enclosing all relevant documentation. If the complaint is considered to be justified, the response should outline the action that it is proposed should be taken to remedy the situation. When the PCA receives the Director General's response and supporting documentation, his office will commence any further enquiries considered necessary to complete the inquiry and will write a report of the outcome. The PCA will send a draft report to the Director General for comments on matters of fact and presentation and responses to the recommendations made. A reply should usually be given within three weeks. On receipt of this reply, the PCA issues his final report to the Permanent Secretary of the Home Office and the MP. This will incorporate the action that the prison service has agreed to take in response to any recommendations made.

The PCA's recommendations should, so far as possible, put the prisoner back into the position that s/he would have been in if the maladministration' had not occurred. Although the PCA cannot order the prison service to provide a remedy, the government usually accepts the recommendations made. However, if his recommendations are not accepted, then the PCA may lay a special report before Parliament and may also recommend changes to procedures and instructions to prevent recurrence of the maladministration identified .

Chapter 9 - Prison discipline

The formal disciplinary system

9.1. Offences against prison discipline

The power to discipline prisoners for misconduct whilst they are in prison is contained in the Prison Act 1952, s 47(1). This provides for rules to be made for the discipline and control of prisoners, and gives prisoners the right to have a proper opportunity to present their case if charged with an offence. An offence against prison discipline may be treated as having been committed in the prison at which the prisoner is held (Criminal Justice Act 1961, s 23(1)), and thus a prisoner who commits an offence at one establishment may be charged and adjudicated upon at another prison. Unless a contrary indication is made, all references in this section relate to paragraphs of the 1995 edition of the Prison Discipline Manual ('PDM'), which has been updated by the Prison Service following the changes to the discipline system in 2002. The Manual is available on the prison service's web site.

The list of offences against prison discipline with which a prisoner may be charged are contained the Prison Rules 1999, Rule 51, the full text of which follows:

'51. A prisoner is guilty of an offence against discipline if he:
(1) commits any assault;
(1A) commits any racially aggravated assault;
(2) detains any person against his will;
(3) denies access to any part of the prison to any officer or any person (other than a prisoner) who is in the prison for the purpose of working there;
(4) fights with any person;
(5) intentionally endangers the health or personal safety of others or, by his conduct is reckless whether such health or personal safety is endangered;
(6) intentionally obstructs an officer in the execution of his duty, or any person (other than a prisoner) who is at the prison for the purpose of working there, in the performance of his work;
(7) escapes or absconds from prison or from legal custody;
(8) fails to comply with any condition upon which he is temporarily released under Rule 9;
(9) administers a controlled drug to himself or fails to prevent the administration of a controlled drug to him by another person (but subject to Rule 52);
(10) is intoxicated as a consequence of knowingly consuming any alcoholic beverage;
(11) knowingly consumes any alcoholic beverage other than that provided to him pursuant to a written order under Rule 25(1);
(12) has in his possession:
(a) any unauthorised article, or
(b) a greater quantity of any article than he is authorised to have;
(13) sells or delivers to any person any unauthorised article;

(14) sells or, without permission, delivers to any person any article which he is allowed to have only for his own use;
(15) takes improperly any article belonging to another person or to a prison;
(16) intentionally or recklessly sets fire to any part of a prison or any other property, whether or not his own;
(17) destroys or damages any part of a prison or any other property, other than his own;
(17A) causes racially aggravated damage to, or destruction of, any part of a prison, or any property, other than his own;
(18) absents himself from any place he is required to be or is present at any place where he is not authorised to be;
(19) is disrespectful to any officer, or any person (other than a prisoner) who is at the prison for the purpose of working there, or any person visiting a prison;
(20) uses threatening, abusive or insulting words or behaviour;
(20A) uses threatening, abusive or insulting racist words or behaviour;
(21) intentionally fails to work properly or, being required to work, refuses to do so;
(22) disobeys any lawful order;
(23) disobeys or fails to comply with any rule or regulation applying to him;
(24) receives any controlled drug, or, without the consent of an officer, any other article, during the course of a visit (not being an interview such as is mentioned in Rule 38);
(24A) displays, attaches or draws on any part of a prison, or on any other property, threatening abusive or insulting racist drawings, symbols or other material.
(25) (a) attempts to commit,
(b) incites another prisoner to commit, or
(c) assists another prisoner to commit or to attempt to commit, any of the foregoing offences.'

9.2. CHARGING

Prisoners are generally charged with a disciplinary offence by any officer who witnessed the breach of the Rules. Alternatively the charge can be laid by an officer who discovers that the offence has been committed. Rule 53(1) of the Prison Rules 1999 requires that a prisoner should be charged as soon as possible, and at the latest within 48 hours of the offence being discovered. If the charge is not laid within 48 hours then a finding of guilt at adjudication will be void unless there are 'exceptional circumstances'. A charge is laid when a form F1127 ('Notice of Report') is handed to the prisoner. F1127 contains details of the time, date and place of commission of the offence, the paragraph of r 51 under which the prisoner has been charged, details of the allegations made against the prisoner, and the date and time of the hearing. The charge must be laid out in sufficient detail for the prisoner to have a full understanding of the allegation made . Prisoners are advised that they may write out their defence to the charge on the back of the form, and state whether they wish to call any witnesses. At the same time as being handed the F1127, prisoners may also be given an information sheet, F1145 ('Explanation of Procedures at Disciplinary Charge Hearings') which provides a brief explanation of the stages that the adjudication will follow. Prisoners should be allowed time to prepare their defence, and thus they must be charged at least two hours before the adjudication takes place.

A charge cannot be reduced during the adjudication, and therefore if it is not clear which of two charges a prisoner may be guilty of, staff are advised to lay two separate charges, one or both of which may be dropped at adjudication if it transpires that there is not enough evidence against the prisoner to support it .

Although prisoners can be charged with several separate offences which arise from the same incident (eg a prisoner who breaks a window whilst fighting with another prisoner could be charged under Rule 51(4) for fighting and under Rule 51(17) for damaging prison property), they cannot be charged twice for what is essentially the same offence. Therefore a prisoner who refuses to go to work cannot be charged under Rule 47(18) for absenting himself from a place where he is required to be present and Rule 47(19) for disobeying an officer's order that he should go to work. Prisoners may not be charged with continuing offences, and so a prisoner who refuses an order to clean the toilets and is charged with that offence may not be charged again if he refuses the same order a couple of hours later .

If, in the course of an adjudication, the adjudicator considers that a prisoner is not guilty of the offence with which he has been charged, but may be guilty of a different offence, the original charge may be dropped and a new charge laid so long as this is still within 48 hours of the discovery of the alleged offence. In this case, the proceedings must be started afresh and a different governor should hear the newly laid charge .

9.3. THE IMPACT OF THE EZEH AND CONNORS DECISION

In *Ezeh and Connors v UK* [2004] 39 EHRR 1, the European Court of Human Rights found that where a prison disciplinary offence was serious enough to warrant the imposition of additional days of imprisonment as a punishment, ECHR, art 6 applied. The court considered a long line of previous decisions on prison and military discipline which has established the principle that the meaning of criminal charges is autonomous from domestic law and must ultimately be decided by reference to the nature of the charges themselves and the potential penalties (*Engel v Netherlands* [1976] 1 EHRR 706). In the prison context, the ECtHR had previously held that the old system of prison discipline where Boards of Visitors had virtually unrestricted powers to award the loss of remission did amount to criminal proceedings and this had resulted in the changes in the Criminal Justice Act 1991 which vested the power to award additional days to the governor and set more stringent limits on the number of days that could be awarded (*Campbell & Fell v UK* {1984] 7 EHRR 165).

In *Ezeh and Connors*, the court considered that the changes to the early release scheme brought in by the CJA 1991 made it clear that prisoners had a statutory right to be released at a certain point of their sentence and therefore the award of additional days delaying those release dates represented a genuine interference with liberty. Although the ECtHR generally gives greater leeway to matters which are disciplinary in nature and affected targeted groups of individuals as opposed to the public at large, it was considered that the potential interference with liberty was such that any prospect of additional days being awarded brought the matter within the criminal sphere. The consequence of this judgment was that additional days should only be awarded following a finding of guilt before an independent and impartial tribunal and that the guarantees of ECHR, article 6 in relation to criminal proceedings (such as the right to legal representation) applied. This decision was upheld by the Grand Chamber. However, the special needs of prison discipline, which have been explicitly recognised by the ECtHR in *Ezeh and Connors*, mean that it is still possible to distinguish certain aspects of prison disciplinary charges from criminal trials. For example, even at hearings before the independent adjudicator, there is no right to a public hearing of the charge (*R (Bannatyne) v Home Secretary and Independent Adjudicator* [2004] EWHC 1921 (Admin)).

Following the ECtHR's judgment the government introduced the Prison Amendment Rules 2002, amending the Prison Rules 1999. Prison Rule 53(2) provides that a disciplinary charge may be inquired into by a governor or an adjudicator and Rule 53A provides that upon a first hearing of a charge the adjudicating governor 'shall determine whether it is so serious that additional days should be awarded for the offence if the prisoner is found guilty'. If the governor decides that it is so serious, then the charge should be referred, together with any other charge arising out of the same incident, to an independent adjudicator. Otherwise, where additional days of imprisonment are thought not to be warranted, the governor will proceed to inquire into the charge himself. However, there remains a right for the governor to refer a case at any stage of the proceedings, including after a finding of guilt, to an independent adjudicator if the governor considers that an award of additional days might be merited (Rule 53A(3)(b).

This power to refer a charge, even after a finding of guilt, is potentially contentious. ECHR, art 6 generally requires that first instance criminal proceedings meet the safeguards of that article (*De Cubber v Belgium* [1984] 7 EHRR 236). If the prison governor enters a finding of guilt and then refers the case to an adjudicator for punishment, it is difficult to see how the 'trial' can have been conducted by an impartial tribunal as is required.

Independent adjudicators are local district judges who sit at their local prisons on a regular basis. Where a charge is referred to an independent adjudicator, then s/he should normally begin enquiries into it within 28 days of the referral (Prison Rule 53A(3)).

9.4. LIFERS' ADJUDICATIONS

As lifers cannot be granted additional days of imprisonment, the Prison Service's policy is that their cases should not be referred to the independent adjudicator unless they are charged along with determinate sentenced prisoners whose charges are so referred (Prison Rule 53A(2)(a)(ii), and see also Prison Discipline Manual, para 4.5)). In *R (Tangney) v Secretary of State for the Home Department* [2004] EWHC 2888 Admin

Moses J held that this does not breach ECHR, article 6 or the principles of good public administration, even though the consequences of a finding of guilt at an adjudication for a life-sentenced prisoner can be even more serious than for determinate prisoners, given the possible impact this can have on the prospects of release on parole licence. The court took the view that in order for art 6 to be engaged in the context of prison discipline, there had to be a power on the part of the tribunal to order a deprivation of liberty and that there was insufficient nexus between a governor's finding of guilt and a subsequent parole review.

9.5. LEGAL REPRESENTATION

Where a case has been referred to an independent adjudicator for investigation, legal representation will be allowed at the hearing (Prison Rule 54(3)).

All prisoners, including those who are to be tried by a governor, should be allowed to consult a solicitor for advice before their hearing if they so wish. Governors and independent adjudicators are advised that they must adjourn the hearing for this purpose if, after the charge has been read out, a prisoner who has not had reasonable time to contact a solicitor requests legal advice, or if the first time a prisoner asks to consult a solicitor is during the hearing . Further requests by a prisoner to consult a solicitor should be considered as they arise. In making decisions as to whether to grant the adjournment and the length of adjournment to grant, adjudicators should consider the nature of the charge and any impending release date.

At the beginning of an adjudication, the prisoner should be asked if s/he requires any assistance in putting forward a defence. This could be either a solicitor or a 'McKenzie friend'. A McKenzie friend only has a limited role in the proceedings, and may attend the hearing, take notes, and offer advice and support to the prisoner . Prisoners may choose their own McKenzie friend, but the adjudicator can remove the

McKenzie friend from the hearing if it is considered that s/he is interfering with the proceedings or participating without the adjudicator's permission.

Although, unlike in hearings referred under Rule 53A, there is no right to legal representation in hearings before governors, there remains a discretion to permit such representation, or the attendance of a McKenzie friend. In considering whether to grant a request for such assistance the adjudicating governor should comply with the judgment in *R v Secretary of State for the Home Department, ex p Tarrant* [1984] 1 All ER 799. This held that in deciding whether a request for representation should be granted, the governor should have regard to the following factors:

(a) the seriousness of the charge and the potential penalty;
(b) whether any points of law are likely to arise;
(c) the capacity of the prisoner to present his own case;
(d) whether or not there are likely to be any procedural difficulties;
(e) the need for reasonable speed in hearing the charge;
(f) the need for fairness as between prisoners and between prisoners and prison staff.

If legal representation is granted, then the hearing will be adjourned for the prisoner either to instruct a solicitor or find a McKenzie friend. If the request is denied, then the request will be noted on the record of the proceedings together with the reasons for refusal. The adjudication will then proceed.

Where, in the course of explaining why they need legal representation, the prisoner incriminates himself by disclosing something which would make it impossible for the adjudicator to be unprejudiced in hearing the charge, the adjudication should be adjourned and heard by another adjudicator at a later date.

A solicitor acting for a prisoner may ask for access to the prison or to prison staff prior to the hearing in order to interview potential witnesses or to look at the place where the incident took place. Such requests should be dealt with by a member of prison staff who is not involved in the adjudication process.

9.6. LEGAL AID

Solicitors may advise prisoners about adjudications under the CDS Advice & Assistance Scheme, and this would also cover appeals against findings of guilt. Legal representation at adjudications is funded by the CDS Advocacy Assistance Scheme.

9.7. AN IN-DEPTH LOOK AT THE CHARGES

The Prison Discipline Manual contains detailed guidance to adjudicators on the elements of each charge under r 51. In order to find a prisoner guilty of a charge, the governor must be satisfied beyond reasonable doubt that the prisoner is guilty, regardless of how the prisoner has pleaded .

(1) Commits any assault

A prisoner is guilty of assault if s/he intentionally or recklessly applies unlawful force to another person, or causes another person to fear the immediate application of unlawful force (although adjudicators are advised that a charge under para 17 is preferable in this instance). In order to find a prisoner guilty of assault, the adjudicator must be satisfied that:

(a) the prisoner applied force to another or committed an act which put the other person in fear of immediate application of force;

(b) the prisoner intended to do so or was reckless as to whether this would happen;

(c) the force was unlawful, ie was not applied in self-defence or in order to prevent the commission of a serious crime .

(2) Detains any person against his will

This relates to situations where a prisoner takes a hostage. Adjudicators are advised to consider whether the hostage and the hostage taker were acting together, and if so to consider whether a charge may more appropriately be brought if staff have been denied access to part of the prison where the incident took place.

In order to find a prisoner guilty of this offence, the adjudicator must be satisfied that:

(a) the hostage's freedom of movement was inhibited by force or by the threat of force;

(b) the hostage was detained against their will. If the accused can show that the victim collaborated, then this will be a complete defence, although the adjudicator should establish whether the incident started out as a joint venture, and then turned into a situation whereby the victim was prevented from withdrawing against their will. In such circumstances a prisoner may be found guilty;

(c) the prisoner intended the victim to be detained against their will, or was reckless as to whether this would happen.

(3) Denies access to any part of the prison to any officer or any person (other than a prisoner) who is at the prison for the purpose of working there

Prisoners who erect barricades or deny access to a part of the prison are liable to be found guilty of this offence. In order to find a prisoner guilty, the adjudicator must be satisfied that the following elements of the charge are present:

(a) someone working at the prison was denied access to any part of it;

(b) the prisoner intended that this should be so, or was reckless as to whether it would happen.

(4) Fights with any person

In order to find a prisoner guilty under this paragraph, the adjudicator must be satisfied that:

(a) the prisoner intentionally committed an assault by inflicting unlawful force on another prisoner in the context of a fight;

(b) the fight must involve at least one other person and constitute more than one blow. It should have continued for

'a sufficient time to amount to a fight in the ordinary sense of the word';
(c)   self defence is a complete defence, and so, where two prisoners are charged with fighting each other, one may be found guilty of fighting and the other found not guilty on the basis of self .

(5) Intentionally endangers the health or personal safety of others, or, by his conduct, is reckless as to whether such health or personal safety is endangered

The elements of this charge are that:
(a)   there was a 'definite and serious' risk of harm to the safety of at least one person other than the prisoner;
(b)   this danger was caused by the prisoner's behaviour;
(c)   the prisoner intended to cause the danger, or was reckless as to whether it would occur .
(

6) Intentionally obstructs an officer in the execution of his duty, or any person (other than a prisoner) who is at the prison for the purpose of working there, in the performance of his work

This charge covers both physical obstruction of an officer and situations whereby a prisoner might provide false information to an officer. The elements of the charge are as follows:
(a)   there was some sort of obstruction;
(b)   the person who was obstructed was working at the prison, and was attempting to perform his or her work;
(c)   the prisoner intended that the person should be obstructed .

(7) Escapes or absconds from prison or from legal custody
This charge is aimed at prisoners who actually get away from the prison and are not caught as they are attempting to escape or abscond. An adjudicator may only be satisfied as to the

guilt of a prisoner when the following elements of the charge are made out:

(a) the prisoner was held in legal custody, including on escort to or from a prison or whilst working outside the prison;

(b) the prisoner escaped or absconded;

(c) the prisoner had no authority to do so;

(d) the prisoner intended to escape or abscond (ie s/he knew that s/he was leaving lawful custody without authority);

(e) it is a complete defence for the prisoner to plead that s/he believed that s/he had authority to leave.

(8) Fails to comply with any condition upon which he is temporarily released under Rule 9

When a prisoner is temporarily released s/he will be issued with a licence which lists the conditions which should be complied with. An offence under this paragraph could range from failing to return to prison on time to drinking alcohol whilst temporarily released.

Many prisoners who fail to return to prison on time use the defence that they were too ill to travel and licences should include a statement which should be signed by a doctor if the prisoner is unfit to return. If this statement is signed by a doctor then the prisoner has a complete defence to the charge. If the prisoner produces any other medical evidence, the adjudicator should consider whether or not this amounts to certification that the prisoner was unable to travel back to the prison on time.

For a finding of guilt to be made, the adjudicator must be satisfied of the following:

(a) the prisoner was released on a temporary release licence containing clear conditions of which the prisoner was aware. The licence was signed by a governor with authority to do so;

(b) the prisoner intentionally or recklessly did not comply with one or more of the conditions;

(c) there was no justification for the prisoner's failure to comply with the conditions.

A prisoner who did not return on time will have a defence to the charge if they can show that they were genuinely unable to get back to the prison because of circumstances beyond their control. Prisoners who are charged with a criminal offence committed on temporary release may be charged with an offence against prison discipline if they have also breached their licence conditions.

The Prisoners (Return to Custody) Act 1995 makes it a criminal offence to be unlawfully at large without reasonable excuse following a period of temporary release on licence, or whilst knowing or believing that an order has been made for their recall to prison and failing to take all necessary steps to comply with it as soon as is reasonably practicable without reasonable excuse. Prisoners convicted of this criminal offence may be sentenced by a magistrates' court to up to six months' imprisonment and/or a fine not exceeding level 5 on the standard scale

(9) Administers a controlled drug to himself or fails to prevent the administration of a controlled drug to him by another person (but subject to Rule 52)

Prisoners may be required to give a urine sample that will be tested to check for the presence of controlled drugs (Prison Act 1952, s 16A as amended by the Criminal Justice and Public Order Act 1994, s 151). Samples of sweat and non-pubic hair may also be requested for this purpose; however, samples of blood and semen may not.

All categories of prisoner are liable to be tested for drugs, and will be selected on a random basis, although if officers have a reasonable suspicion that a particular prisoner is involved in misusing drugs, that person may be tested more frequently than others .

Governors may make their own provisions for the collection of urine samples within their establishments, although the following provisions should be a common feature in establishments:

(a) prisoners will not be given prior warning that they will be required to give a sample;

(b) prisoners should be given precise instructions, asked to remove bulky outer clothing, and be searched thoroughly;

(c) prisoners will be given 'as much privacy as is consistent with the need to prevent adulteration or substitution of false samples ... a greater invasion of privacy may be necessary of those individual prisoners caught cheating';

(d) samples will be divided, and one-half will be kept in case of appeal. Samples will be sealed and the seals signed by the prisoner.

Prisoners who refuse to provide a sample can be charged under the Prison Rules 1999, Rule 51(22), for disobeying a lawful order, and where prisoners cannot provide a sample they may be segregated for up to five hours and provided with controlled amounts of water (r 50(7)).

If the prisoner tests positive, then so long as the sample was taken under the provision of Rule 50, the prisoner may be charged with an offence under Rule 51(9). Rule 52 provides statutory defences, and these are:

(a) that the controlled drug was lawfully in the prisoner's possession for their own use;

(b) that the controlled drug was administered in the lawful supply of the drug by another person;

(c) the controlled drug was administered by or to him in circumstances which he did not know and had no reason to suspect that such a drug was being administered; or

(d) that the drug was administered under duress or without consent in circumstances where it was unreasonable to resist.

(10) Is intoxicated as a consequence of knowingly consuming any alcoholic beverage

This charge is meant to deal with prisoners who are clearly intoxicated rather than those who have taken a small amount of alcohol.

In order to find a prisoner guilty of this offence the adjudicator must be satisfied beyond reasonable doubt that:

(a) the accused was intoxicated. If a prisoner is found to have been 'elated beyond the point of self control' then it is said that this will 'satisfy the test of intoxication'. However, 'skylarking' or 'an excess of high spirits' are not sufficient;

(b) the intoxication was caused, either wholly or in part, by the consumption of alcohol. The adjudicator must enquire into the possible causes of reported behaviour such as slurred speech, instability, or the smell of alcohol on a prisoner's breath;

(c) the accused knowingly consumed the alcohol. Therefore, the prisoner may advance in his/her defence that they were given a spiked drink .

(11) Knowingly consumes any alcoholic beverage other than any prescribed to him pursuant to a written order of the medical officer under Rule 20

This offence is less serious than (10) above. It deals with situations where a prisoner is not intoxicated but has knowingly consumed alcohol which was not prescribed to him or her.

In order to find a prisoner guilty of the offence, the adjudicator must be satisfied beyond reasonable doubt that:

(a) the prisoner's behaviour was as a result of consuming alcohol. 'The evidence should be such as would lead a reasonable and right thinking person to conclude that the accused had consumed alcohol' .

(b) the accused knowingly consumed the alcohol (as for (10) above);

(c) it is a complete defence to the charge that the alcohol was prescribed by a medical officer.

(12) Has in his possession (a) any unauthorised article, or (b) a greater quantity of any article than he is authorised to have

Paragraph (a) of this charge covers situations where the prisoner had something in his possession which is unauthorised (eg drugs, firearms) or an article which is authorised in itself but is not authorised in this instance (eg because it was issued to another prisoner).

(13) Sells or delivers to any person any unauthorised article

This charge covers articles which are unauthorised in themselves or are not authorised to a particular prisoner. Before finding a prisoner guilty the adjudicator must be satisfied that the following are established:

(a) the article was sold or delivered by the accused to another person (who does not have to be a prisoner);
(b) the article was not authorised;
(c) the prisoner intended to sell or deliver the article or was reckless as to whether they were selling or delivering it. It would be a defence for the prisoner to plead that they believed they were authorised to pass on the article in that way.

(14) Sells, or without permission, delivers to any person any article which he is allowed to have only for his own use

In finding a prisoner guilty, the adjudicator does not have to establish whether the article was sold or delivered. However the following elements of the charge must be made out:

(a) the article was sold or delivered to someone;
(b) it was authorised only for the prisoner's own use;

(c) the prisoner did not have permission to pass the article to someone else .

(15) Takes improperly any article belonging to another person or to a prison (or young offender institution)

This is essentially theft, and in order for a prisoner to be found guilty at adjudication, the adjudicator must be satisfied of the presence of the following elements of the charge:
(a) there was an article which belonged to another person or to a prison;
(b) the prisoner took physical control of the article without permission;
(c) the prisoner intended to take the article without permission, or was reckless as to whether s/he did so .

(16) Intentionally or recklessly sets fire to any part of a prison (or young offender institution) or any other property whether or not his own

In order to be satisfied of the guilt of a prisoner charged with this offence, the adjudicator should establish the following:
(a) the prisoner set fire to part of the prison or some other property of a tangible nature;
(b) the prisoner acted with intent or was reckless as to whether they set fire to the property.

(17) Destroys or damages any part of a prison (or young offender institution) or any other property, other than his own

It is a defence for the prisoner to plead that they thought that the property belonged to them.

(18) Absents himself from any place where he is required to be or is present at any place where he is not authorised to be

This charge can apply to situations which occur both inside and outside a prison. For example, if a prisoner leaves an open prison to go and meet someone in the locality but has every intention of returning to the prison, then this would be appropriate rather than a charge of absconding.

A prisoner who pleads a genuine belief that they had permission to be somewhere, or was not required to be in a particular place will have a defence.

(19) Is disrespectful to any officer, or any person (other than a prisoner) who is at the prison for the purpose of working there, or any person visiting a prison

Disrespect can be shown by both verbal and physical behaviour. To be satisfied that the prisoner is guilty of the offence the adjudicator should ensure that the following elements are present:

(a)   there was an act which was directed towards a specific person or group of people;

(b)   the act was disrespectful in the ordinary meaning of the word and in the particular circumstances;

(c)   the person at which the act was aimed was either an officer, a visitor to the prison, or a person working at the prison;

(d)   the prisoner intended to be disrespectful or was reckless as to whether s/he was being so.

(20) Uses threatening, abusive or insulting words or behaviour

An adjudicator hearing a charge under this paragraph should be satisfied that the following elements are present before finding a prisoner guilty:

(a)   the prisoner did a specific act, adopted a general pattern of behaviour or said specific words;

(b) the above conduct was either threatening, abusive, or insulting (in the ordinary senses of these words) rather than annoying or rude;
(c) the prisoner intended to be threatening, abusive or insulting or was reckless as to whether he was so .

(21) Intentionally fails to work properly or, being required to work, refuses to do so

In laying a charge under this paragraph, an officer must specify which of the two separate offences it is alleged that the prisoner has committed. Where a prisoner is charged with intentionally failing to work properly, a finding of guilt can only be made if the adjudicator is satisfied that:
(a) the prisoner was lawfully required to work at the time and in the circumstances specified;
(b) the prisoner failed to work properly (this is measured against a standard of work expected);
(c) the prisoner intended not to work properly or was reckless as to whether s/he was doing so.
Thus, to be found guilty a prisoner must know that his work was not or may not be up to the required standard. A prisoner who pleads that s/he thought that s/he was working hard enough would have a defence to the charge.
Where a prisoner is charged with refusing to work, the adjudicator must establish that the following elements of the offence are made out before making a finding of guilt:
(a) the prisoner was lawfully required to work at the time and in the circumstances specified;
(b) the prisoner refused to work, either by act or omission;
(c) the prisoner intended to refuse to work or was reckless as to whether s/he was doing so.

(22) Disobeys any lawful order

A lawful order is defined as 'one which a member of staff has authority to give in the execution of his or her duties'. When hearing a charge under this paragraph the adjudicator must ensure that the following are established before finding the prisoner guilty:

(a) the action of the member of staff was an order. An order is 'a clear indication by word and/or action given in the course of his or her duties by a member of staff requiring a specific prisoner to do or refrain from doing something'
(b) the order was lawful;
(c) the prisoner did not obey the order within a reasonable period of time;
(d) the prisoner intended not to comply with the order or was reckless as to whether it was complied with.

(23) Disobeys or fails to comply with any rule or regulation applying to him

Many prisons have local rules which are not contained in the Prison Rules, and this charge aims to discipline prisoners who are alleged to have acted in breach of such rules.

Before a prisoner can be found guilty of this offence, the adjudicator must be satisfied that the following are established:

(a) the rule/regulation applied to the prisoner, who must have been aware of its existence, or reasonable steps must have been taken to draw it to his/her attention;
(b) the rule or regulation was lawful in respect of the particular prisoner concerned;
(c) the prisoner did not obey the rule/regulation, either intentionally or recklessly.

(24) Receives any controlled drug, or, without the consent of an officer, any other article, during the course of a visit (not being an interview such as is mentioned in Rule 38)

Before an adjudicator can be satisfied of guilt beyond reasonable doubt, it must be established that:

(a) the prisoner received a controlled drug or other article during the course of the visit;

(b) the prisoner knew the controlled drug or other article existed;

(c) the prisoner knew they did not have permission to have that article.

A genuine belief by a prisoner that permission had been granted to have that article would amount to a defence to the charge. However, if the prisoner were to argue that s/he was passed the controlled drug or article by another prisoner, the charge may still be proved providing the adjudicator can establish beyond reasonable doubt that the controlled drug or article was received during the course of the visit.

(25) (a) Attempts to commit, (b) incites other prisoners to commit, or (c) assists another prisoner to commit or attempt to commit any of the foregoing offences

This charge must specify whether (a), (b) or (c) above is relevant and must also specify the relevant paragraph of the Prison Rules 1999, Rule 51.

Where a prisoner is charged with an attempt, the adjudicator should be satisfied of the following:

(a) the prisoner did an act which was more than merely preparatory to the commission of the offence;

(b) the prisoner intended to commit the full offence.

Incitement is defined as 'seeking to persuade another prisoner to commit a disciplinary offence'. If the charge is one of inciting, the following elements should be made out before the prisoner is found guilty:

(a) the prisoner's action was communicated to other prisoners who were near enough to be able to respond to the incitement;

(b) the act was capable of inciting other prisoners to commit the full offence;

(c) the full offence was the consequence or the subject of the incitement;

(d) the prisoner intended or was reckless as to whether they incited other prisoners to commit the offence.

If a prisoner is charged with assisting the commission of an offence, the adjudicator must make out the following elements:

(a) another prisoner committed an offence (including an attempt);

(b) the prisoner on the current charge active.

Prison Rule 51A deals with the racially aggravated offences at Rule 51(1A), (17A), (20A) and (24A). This states that 'words, behaviour or material are racist if they demonstrate, or are motivated (wholly or partly) by, hostility to members of a racial group (whether identifiable or not) based on their membership (or presumed membership) of a racial group, and "membership", "presumed", "racial group" and "racially aggravated" shall have the meanings assigned to them by s 28 of the Crime and Disorder Act 1998'.

In ***R v Rogers*** House of Lords 28th February 2007, the statutory interpretation of the meaning of 'racial group' was confirmed as per section 28(4) Crime and Disorder Act 1988. The case concerned the use of the words "bloody foreigners" and "get back to your own country". Section 28, subsection 1, Subsection (1) provides that the offence is racially or religiously aggravated if either of two different circumstances exists:

"(a) at the time of committing the offence, or immediately before or after doing so, the offender demonstrates towards the victim hostility based on the victim's membership (or presumed membership) of a racial or religious group; or
(b) the offence is motivated (wholly or partly) by hostility towards members of a racial or religious group based on their membership of that group."

The court concerned itself with the outward manifestation of racial or religious hostility.

In *Attorney General's Reference No 4 of 2004* [2005] EWCA Crim 889, [2005] 1 WLR 2810 the Court of Appeal held that "someone who is an immigrant to this country and therefore non-British" could be a member of a racial group for this purpose. Whether the evidence in any particular case, taken as a whole, proves that the offender's conduct demonstrated hostility to such a group, or was motivated by such hostility, is a question of fact for the decision-makers in the case.

9.8. EVIDENTIAL MATTERS AND THE STANDARD OF PROOF

Adjudications operate to the same standard of proof as criminal proceedings. Before entering a finding of guilt, the adjudicator must be satisfied of guilt beyond reasonable doubt (*R v Secretary of State for the Home Department, ex p Tarrant* [1984] 1 All ER 799).

Although the standard of proof is beyond reasonable doubt, it was found in the *Tarrant* case that adjudicators are 'the masters of their own procedure' and therefore the strict rules of evidence do not automatically apply at such hearings. At para 5.7 of the Discipline Manual, there is a general prohibition against adjudicators relying on disputed hearsay evidence.

9.9. PUNISHMENTS

The range of punishments available is found in Prison Rules 1999, Rule 55 (for governors' punishments) and Rule 55A (for independent adjudicators' punishments) or the Young Offender Institution Rules 1988, Rule 60 (for governors' punishments) and Rule 60A (for independent adjudicators' punishments). The independent adjudicator's power to award additional days to a sentence of imprisonment derives from CJA 1991, ss 41–42. Punishments should take into account the circumstances and seriousness of the offence; the prisoner's custodial behaviour during the current sentence; the type of establishment; the circumstances of the prisoner; the effect of the offence on the regime; the general order and discipline of a closed establishment; and the need to discourage the prisoner and others from repeating the offence (Discipline Manual, para 7.6).

The Prison Service does not provide any central guidance to adjudicators on the appropriate punishments for particular offences. However, punishments handed down within any establishment should be consistent and, to achieve this, governors may set up a local tariff system.

The punishments contained in the Prison and Young Offender Institution Rules are listed below together with a brief explanation of what they entail:

(a) Caution – a warning not to repeat the offending behaviour.

(b) Forfeiture of facilities – the withdrawal of privileges listed in the Prison Rules 1999, Rule 8 for up to 42 days for adult prisoners and up to 21 days for young offenders.

(c) Exclusion from associated work or activities – this punishment is usually served on normal location in the prison and is for a maximum of 21 days for adult prisoners. The equivalent punishment for young offenders is that they may be excluded from any activity taking place in the YOI other than training courses, work, education or physical education for up to 21 days.

(d) Stoppage of earnings – all or part of a prisoner's pay may be stopped for up to the equivalent of 84 days' full pay for adults or 42 days' for young offenders. However, prisoners should normally be allowed to continue to purchase postage stamps and telephone credits.

(e) Cellular confinement – may be imposed for up to 21 days for adult prisoners and 10 days for young offenders aged 18 or over so long as the medical officer certifies that the prisoner is fit to undergo this punishment. Consecutive punishments of cellular confinement must not exceed 21 days in total for adults and 10 days for young offenders . Cells should be set aside in which prisoners serving a period of cellular confinement are located. These should contain a bed, bedding, table, chair and access to sanitary facilities. Otherwise, prisoners should be allowed all facilities other than those which are 'incompatible with cellular confinement' such as use of the canteen, use of private cash, and association with other prisoners.. Prisoners who are serving periods in cellular confinement should be checked on by an officer at least once every hour, and visited every day by the chaplain . Prisoners should be allowed to receive visits and have access to the telephone unless their 'behaviour and attitude made removal from cellular confinement impracticable or undesirable'.In practice it is rare for prisoners to be refused visits, and any visitor turned away from an establishment should make enquiries of the governor as to the reasons for the refusal and contact a legal adviser if they are worried.

(f) Additional days – may only be awarded by an independent adjudicator and so where a governor considers that a charge warrants a punishment of additional days, the charge must be referred to the independent adjudicator for hearing. Adult prisoners may be awarded up to 42 additional days of imprisonment in respect of any one offence (or offences arising from a single incident) if they are serving a determinate sentence. Additional days affect the prisoner's sentence by pushing back the parole eligibility date of prisoners sentenced before 1 October 1992 and the non-parole release date of prisoners serving sentences of four years and over. Remand and unsentenced prisoners may be given the prospective punishment of additional days and this will only take effect if they are sentenced to a period of imprisonment. The punishment cannot be awarded to lifers or to young prisoners serving a Detention and Training Order.

(g) Extra work – is only available as a punishment for young offenders, who may be required to work for up to two extra hours a day for up to 21 days.

(h) Removal from a wing or living unit – the maximum period for removal is 28 days for adults or 14 days for young offenders. The prisoner or young offender will continue to take part in the normal regime of the prison, but will be held in a cell or a room away from their normal wing or living unit for the rest of the time.

(i) Possessions of unconvicted or unsentenced prisoners – the right to have books, writing materials and 'other means of occupation' can be forfeited for any period. Prisoners found guilty of escaping or attempting to escape may forfeit their right to wear their own clothing .

9.10. CHALLENGING FINDINGS OF GUILT

Prisoners may apply for a finding of guilt at adjudication to be reviewed through the complaints procedure by submitting the complaint form ADJ 1 to the Prisoner Casework Unit or Directorate of High Security Prisons Support Unit at Prison

Service Headquarters. The prisoner or legal adviser may ask for the written record of the hearing in order to prepare their appeal, and they should not be charged any photocopying fees in connection with this. The appropriate team at Prison Service Headquarters will conduct a paper review of the case and will recommend to the area manager or the director of high security prisons whether to quash the finding of guilt and remit any punishments awarded.

The Prison Rules 1999, Rule 61(2) and YOI Rules 2000 allow prisoners who have been awarded additional days of imprisonment to apply to have them remitted. In order to be eligible to have an application considered, a prisoner must have been awarded no further additional days for a period of six months if an adult or four months if a young offender. The prisoner need not have been in prison custody throughout that period, and may have been in a special hospital, community home, in police custody, or temporarily released under the Prison Rules 1999, Rule 9 (para 8.6). The application process starts when a prisoner completes form F2129A and submits it for consideration. A prison officer will complete form F2129B which details the offences which led to the award of additional days, and also gives information about the prisoner's behaviour since. Where the prisoner has been held in another prison for at least half of the qualifying period, staff there should also be asked to submit a report. Reports from prison staff should be accurate and unbiased and should not include unsubstantiated information . The application is considered by a governor within one month of being submitted by the prisoner. Prisoners are allowed to appear before the governor and give information about the application orally if they wish to do so. In such cases, all reports considered by the governor should also be read to the prisoner so that s/he has an opportunity to comment on them. The report writers should also be present so that the prisoner may ask questions of them or they can give further information if necessary .

In making a decision as to whether to remit the additional days awarded, advises that the governor should take the following factors into account:

(a) whether the prisoner has a constructive approach to their imprisonment, makes the most of opportunities to participate in the regime and respects any trust placed in them;

(b) whether there has been any genuine change of attitude on the prisoner's part;

(c) the nature of the original breach of prison discipline for which the additional days were awarded and whether it is appropriate to remit days in recognition of a constructive approach and a change of attitude.

Prisoners are informed of the outcome of the application immediately and they should also be given a written decision on form F2129C within seven days of consideration of the application. This form should give details of the reasons for the decision, when they may apply again for the remission of additional days and, where appropriate, any amendments to their sentence dates.

9.11. THE INFORMAL DISCIPLINARY SYSTEM

The Prison Rules 1999, Rule 45 and YOI Rules 2000, Rule 49 provide for the removal of prisoners from normal location to the segregation block of an establishment. This may be for the prisoner's own protection (most commonly for sex offenders, prisoners who are in debt to other prisoners, or informants), or as a solution to the problem of managing prisoners whose presence on the wing is thought to pose a threat to the good order or discipline of the wing. In relation to those segregated for disciplinary reasons, PSO 1700 states that 'prisoners are only segregated for reasons of good order or discipline where there are reasonable grounds for believing that the prisoner's behaviour is likely to be so disruptive or cause disruption that keeping the prisoner on normal location is unsafe'.

Where a decision has been taken to segregate for reasons of GOoD, a Segregation Safety Algorithm must be completed by a registered nurse or doctor within two hours of the prisoner being placed in the segregation unit. This should determine whether there are any healthcare reasons why the prisoner should not be segregated. If no member of healthcare staff is on duty, then the prisoner should be observed every 30 minutes until the algorithm can be completed, unless he is on an F2052SH (suicide/self harm watch), in which case s/he should be observed at least five times an hour.

The final decision as to whether the prisoner should be segregated rests with the operational manager, who can authorise segregation for an initial period of up to 72 hours. Following the decision to segregate, the prisoner should be informed of the reasons for the decision, both orally and in writing and also told of the date when the first review of their segregation will take place.

The Segregation Review Board must take place within 72 hours of initial segregation and, if further segregation is authorised, at least every 14 days thereafter. The Chair of the Board must be an operational manager of Grade F or above, and it is mandatory that a representative of healthcare staff should also attend. Other staff who may be present are a segregation personal officer, a chaplain, and a psychologist. The prisoner should normally be present for at least part of the Board. A member of the IMB should also be present 'whenever possible', but in a purely observational role.

In deciding whether or not to authorise further segregation, the Board should have regard to the initial reasons for segregation, the behaviour and attitude of the prisoner since the last review, any concerns that may have come to light about how the prisoner is coping with segregation, and what the prisoner needs to demonstrate in order to be considered for a return to normal location or alternative accommodation. It is recommended that behavioural targets should be set, and that these should be reasonable, specific, relevant and time bound. Where segregation is to continue, the Board should consider whether there should be any improvements to the segregation regime currently offered. Prisoners may be given in-cell tv, radio/CD players, gym sessions, in-cell hobbies or mini-association periods as an incentive to improved behaviour.

The chair has the final decision on continued segregation and, if authorised, should sign the Governor's Continued Authority for Segregation. A member of the IMB present should also be asked to sign this to confirm that they are satisfied that the correct procedures have been followed and that a reasonable decision has been reached. If the IMB member does not agree with the decision reached, then s/he should attempt to resolve this informally with the Governor. If an agreement cannot be reached, then the IMB member may make a formal objection to segregation by lodging in writing the objections that they have. This document must be forwarded to the governing governor, who must make a written response to the Board member as soon as possible, and in any event within 48 hours. Both the governor and the IMB must make every possible effort to resolve the matter locally.

If the matter is not resolved at the establishment, then a copy of all the paperwork should be sent to the Area Manager. The Area Manager should arrange to meet with a member of the IMB or discuss the case over the telephone and determine what action should be taken as quickly as possible, or within five days at most. The Area Manager should then inform the IMB and the governor of his/her decision. If the IMB is still not satisfied, then they should bring the matter to the attention of the Operational Director or Deputy Director General of the Prison Service. If the disagreement persists, then a further appeal may be made to the Prisons Minister and Director General of the Prison Service.

Following a Review Board decision to continue a prisoner's segregation, the prisoner must be informed of the outcome of the review. If they are to remain in segregation, they should be given the reasons for that decision orally, and in writing on the form 'Segregation Privileges and Review Targets/Segregation Rewards and Behavioural Targets'. The reasons given to the prisoner on that form should reflect the discussions held during the Segregation Review Board and noted on the form 'Segregation Review Board – Governor's Continued Authority for Segregation'. The prisoner is advised of the behaviour and intervention targets set at the Board and advised of the date of the next review of their segregation.

So long as the above procedures are followed on each occasion, segregation can continue indefinitely. However, in practice a prisoner removed from normal location for a very lengthy period may well be considered for allocation to a Close Supervision Centre . Segregation unit regimes are generally impoverished. However, PSO 1700 states that governors should ensure that the restrictions placed on segregated prisoners are 'no more than necessary to protect the prisoner concerned or to maintain the good order or discipline of the establishment'. The regime should be 'as full as possible and only those activities that involve associating with mainstream prisoners should be curtailed'. Prisoners retain access to visits, use of the telephone, canteen, exercise and showers, but given that they usually have to make applications for access to these facilities and are generally only unlocked for short periods, it is often the case that access to telephones, exercise and showers is extremely limited.

Instruction to Governors 28/93 provides a 'Management Strategy for Disruptive Inmates' which gives staff at Prison Service Headquarters the power to compel prison governors to accept 'disruptive' prisoners at their establishments. Governors do have a right to appeal against the allocation of a prisoner whom they do not want to accept. All convicted prisoners held in category B prisons are liable to be dealt with under the strategy if they are deemed to pose '*serious* control problems'. The aim is to 'secure the return of a disruptive inmate to a settled pattern of behaviour on normal location'. The instruction introduced a five stage management strategy for dealing with disruptive prisoners. However, only the first three of those stages are still in use. The fourth stage has been overtaken by the introduction of the close supervision centre system, which replaced the special unit system (which was the fourth stage of the strategy).

9.12. THE MANAGEMENT PROGRAMME

Stage 1 – Internal action at the parent establishment
In the first instance, governors are advised that when a disruptive or subversive prisoner comes to their attention, they should consider whether there is cause to lay a disciplinary charge against that prisoner for breach of Rule 51, try to ascertain the reasons for disruptive behaviour, and try to persuade the prisoner to change that behaviour. Consideration should be given to moving the prisoner within the prison, either to another prison wing or to the segregation block under Rule 45. If this approach does not cause the prisoner to settle, or there are other 'exceptional' (undefined) circumstances, the prisoner will move on to stage 2.

Stage 2 – Temporary transfer from the parent establishment
If the governor considers that the temporary transfer of a 'seriously disruptive inmate is unavoidable', then transfer to a local prison may be arranged. This transfer is arranged in consultation with Prison Service Headquarters which advises as to the availability of vacant cells, which are always in the segregation blocks of local prisons. The prisoner is then transferred for a period of up to one month, and at this time the expectation will be that the prisoner will return to the parent establishment when the month expires. Prisoners and prison staff refer to this period as a 'lay down' and the idea is that it will provide a suitable cooling off period for the prisoner, who will then be prepared to settle.

If, however, the governor of the parent establishment does not want to take the prisoner back, then s/he may apply to the relevant department of Prison Service Headquarters explaining the reasons why a return to the establishment is thought to be unsuitable. If Headquarters accepts the governor's representations it will arrange for the prisoner to be allocated to another prison (stage 3). Alternatively it will reject the representations and order the governor to take the prisoner back.

Stage 3 – Centrally managed transfers to training and local establishments
If it is decided that the prisoner will not return to the parent establishment, then Prison Service Headquarters will arrange reallocation to either a high security prison, a local prison or a category B training prison. Governors are compelled to accept prisoners who are allocated to their establishments under stage 3, although they are able to 'appeal' to their area managers who liaise with Headquarters in an attempt to reach a solution.

9.13. TRANSFER TO A CLOSE SUPERVISION CENTRE

Close supervision centres ('CSCs') have replaced special units, transfer to which was stage four of the Management Strategy for Disruptive Inmates. The CSC system was first introduced in February 1998 following the insertion of a new Rule 43A into the Prison Rules 1964. The provision for CSCs is now contained in the Prison Rules 1999, r 46, which empowers the Secretary of State to direct a prisoner's removal from association and to confine him in a close supervision centre. The authority to remove a prisoner from normal location should not exceed one month, but this can be renewed at the end of each one-month period (Rule 46(2)).

Prisons wishing to refer a prisoner to a CSC are required to apply on a CSC Initial Referral Form to the CSC Management Team at Prison Service Headquarters. They must confirm that the prisoner has sufficiently exhausted all other options with regard to his management and control and that the CSC is the final remaining option; they must document, using recent evidence, the extent of his dangerous behaviour and risk towards himself/staff/other prisoners; and document, using recent evidence, how and why current management and control strategies are insufficient to protect the individual and others from harm .

The CSC Initial Referral Form must demonstrate that:

1   a prisoner has fulfilled the first three stages of the Management Strategy for Disruptive Inmates, and meet at least one of the following criteria:

(a)   s/he has been violent to staff and/or prisoners;

(b)   s/he has regularly incurred disciplinary reports;

(c)   s/he has caused serious damage to property in prison;

(d)   s/he has shown dangerous behaviour (such as roof top protests, hostage taking or self mutilation);

(e)   s/he has a history of mental illness; and/or

(f)   s/he has failed to respond to earlier measures to improve control;

2   there is past and recent evidence that the prisoner exhibits unacceptable levels of dangerous behaviour towards himself, staff and/or other prisoners;

3   on the basis of past and recent evidence, current management and control strategies are insufficient to protect the individual and others from harm.

A Transfer Case Conference, at which the Care and Management Plan will be discussed, will be held and the prisoner and his legal representative are invited to this.

Prisoners may be held on Rule 46 indefinitely. Their Care and Management Plans should be reviewed at three-monthly intervals at the CSC unit, and should be submitted to the

CSC SC regularly .Regular case conferences are held at the prison, and legal advisers are often invited to attend these with their clients. In addition, CSC prisoner's cases are reviewed on a monthly basis by the CSC SC at Headquarters and they are provided with a 'gist' of reports to be submitted to the meeting. Prisoners or their legal advisers may make written representations to the meeting.

9.14. Prisoner informants

Governors will often run into problems in providing prisoners with the reasons for their segregation under r 45 or their transfer under IG 28/93 because of the need to protect the identity of other prisoners. It is relatively common for one prisoner to provide information about the activities of another by having a private conversation with staff or by placing a 'note in the box'. Each prison wing has a box on it where prisoners post the correspondence that they wish to send out of the prison. Sometimes, a prisoner will also post an anonymous note informing the authorities of the activities of another prisoner, eg that an escape attempt is being planned, drugs are being sold, or someone is planning to take a hostage. The notes will be referred to the Security Department within the prison, and if information is thought to be reliable, the suspected prisoner will be segregated or transferred.

There is also a more formal Inmate Informant System, the mechanics of which are laid out in the Prison Service's Security Manual. The Inmate Informant System recognises that prisoners are one of the best sources of security intelligence, and that the best informants are 'prisoners who have the respect of other prisoners and who are regarded as above suspicion' Prison governors do not have to adopt the Inmate Informant System, although they are advised that to do so will maximise security intelligence and ensure that staff dealing with informants behave properly.

Each prison which adopts the Inmate Informant System should appoint a manager who is responsible for staff dealing with informants, available to advise and brief staff, and who ensures that all information received is processed and assessed for reliability. The manager also identifies likely informers, records rewards given to them and maintains secure records of the names of informants.

Prisoners who pass information to the prison authorities can expect to be rewarded for their trouble. Rewards given are supposed to relate to the usefulness of the information that they have provided. The following rewards are suggested:

(a) a commitment to report directly on the informant's work to third parties (including the Parole Board);

(b) acknowledgment that a prisoner's approach to criminal behaviour has changed, justifying progress to better regimes or lower security categorisation;

(c) the sympathetic consideration of transfer requests where security factors permit;

(d) additional facilities, eg longer visits, favourable job allocations, and access to other discretionary facilities available within the establishment;

(e) payments of incentive bonuses within the provisions of the prisoners' pay scheme;

(f) in particularly worthy cases, a recommendation may be made that the use of the Royal Prerogative of Mercy be considered to remit part of a sentence as a reward for meritorious acts .

Staff dealing with informants are warned that they should only offer the above rewards; that they must only reward a prisoner when information has been delivered and after they have received any necessary authority; that rewards may be visible to other prisoners and this may place the informant at risk. The risk of informers using the system for their own means and providing fabricated information in order to receive a reward is recognised.

Staff who 'handle' informants may be selected for their skills in developing relationships, their post within the prison, or their experience of working within prisons. In particular, staff who frequently deal with prisoners in privacy whilst they are conducting cell searches, acting in a personal officer role, or dealing with prisoners' applications are the best placed to extract good quality information without arousing the suspicion of other prisoners and thus putting the informant at risk.

CHAPTER 10 - CRIMINAL OFFENCES COMMITTED IN PRISON

10.1. INTRODUCTION

The Prison Rules were amended in 2005 after the case of *Ezeh and Connors v UK* (2004) 39 EHRR 1. The amended Prison Rules now allow an independent adjudicator to hear allegations of serious breaches of prison discipline where prisoners are at risk of being punished by the imposition of additional days of imprisonment.

10.2. REFERRING SERIOUS OFFENCES TO THE POLICE

Where it is believed that a serious criminal offence has been committed, this should be reported to the governor immediately, regardless of whether or not the offender has been identified. The governor should decide whether the police need be informed and should give details of the incident to the Intelligence and Incident Support Unit at Prison Service Headquarters (Prison Discipline Manual, para 11.1).

Any suspects should be charged with an offence against prison discipline within 48 hours of discovery of the alleged offence, but if the matter is being investigated by the police an adjudication should be opened and then adjourned pending the outcome of their enquiries. If the police or Crown Prosecution Service decide not to prosecute, the governor should decide whether to pursue the internal charge at that stage.

Circular Instruction 3/92 gives guidance to governors on when offences should be referred to the police for investigation. Broadly, offences falling within the following categories should be referred:

(a) Assault – alleged murder, manslaughter, non-consensual buggery and rape, attempts at the above, threats to kill if there appears to be intent, assaults with a weapon likely to cause serious injury, where serious violence has been used or serious injury caused, sexual assaults involving violence or where the victim was especially vulnerable, and hostage-taking.

(b) Escape – from closed establishments or secure escorts and alleged escape attempts, provided that the attempt is more than preparation.

(c) Possession of unauthorised articles – allegations that a prisoner was in possession of firearms or explosives, other offensive weapons if there is evidence that the weapon was to be used to commit a serious criminal offence, class A drugs, class B drugs if there appears to have been intention to supply.

(d) Criminal damage, arson – where the cost of the damage exceeds £2,000, or there was a risk of the fire taking hold.

(e) Robbery – with serious violence or the threat or use of a weapon.

(f) Major disturbances – involving a number of prisoners where the governor appears to be in danger of losing control or has lost control over any part of the establishment, and mass disobedience involving the use or threat of violence or the commission of serious criminal offences.

10.3.1. POWERS OF PRISON OFFICERS

Every prison officer while acting as such shall have the powers, authority, protection and privileges of a constable.

Section 8 is applied to prison officers (defined by section 92(1) as "an officer of a directly managed prison") on attachment to a contracted out prison by section 87(1) and (3) of the Criminal Justice Act 1991 (as amended by the CJPOA 1994, s.97 (3)). The powers and duties of prisoner custody officers are provided for by section 86 of the 1991 Act.

10.3.2. CPD Guidance to Prison Governors

Prison governors have been informed that the following offences must be referred to the police: murder and attempted murder; manslaughter; rape and attempted rape; threats to kill, where there appears a genuine intent; where there is the use of a weapon likely to cause serious injury; the occasioning of serious injury by any means; the use of serious violence even if minor injury only is caused; personal sexual violation, especially where the victim is vulnerable or there has been violence or a threat of violence; unlawful imprisonment (hostage taking); escape from a secure establishment or secure escort, and attempted escape from a secure establishment or secure escort; attempt to escape especially if it involved the possession of items intended to facilitate the escape (eg. weapons); escape from a non-secure environment will not normally be serious enough to refer to the police unless further offences were committed in the course of the escape; criminal damage by an individual (i.e. over £2000) or group action, even where the value is less; arson, unless there was little risk of the fire taking hold (a cell fire may be an attempt to commit harm - these cases should not normally be referred); robbery, especially where serious violence is used or threatened. (CPS Guidance).

It is to be noted that in cases of manslaughter of one prisoner by another, there may well be an offence by the prison itself under the Corporate Manslaughter Act 2007. The Corporate Manslaughter Act 2007 is in force and prisons can be charged with corporate manslaughter. An organisation to which this Act applies is guilty of the offence of corporate manslaughter if the way in which any of the organisation's activities are managed or organised by its senior managers –causes a person's death, and amounts to a gross breach of a relevant duty of care owed by the organisation to the deceased. The new offence also incorporates a requirement of grossness, taken from the existing law of involuntary manslaughter, which effectively raises the required level of culpability to a significantly higher level; the company's conduct in breaching health and safety law/guidance must fall *far* below the standards expected or required. This ensures that the new criminal offence involves a greater degree of culpability than the health and safety offence it is based on, and will also ensure that most breaches of '*guidance*' alone will not give rise to liability for the new offence. As regards grossness, *Adomako* established that negligence can be deemed 'gross' when it is '*so bad in all the circumstances as to amount ... to a criminal act or omission*' (*per* Lord Mackay at p187).

10.3.3. RACIALLY MOTIVATED CRIMINAL OFFENCES IN PRISON

If there is clear evidence of racial motivation in any of the offences described above, the case for referral to the police will be strengthened (Prison Discipline Manual, para 7). Otherwise, the governor should make a referral if any victim asks for a police investigation Prison governors are advised that the chances of successful prosecution of an offender will be enhanced if the police are called immediately when an offence is discovered. Any notes taken by staff in relation to an incident should be 'carefully preserved' and placed in prisoners' records . Once the police are called in to investigate a serious offence in prison, the prisoner must be allowed legal advice. (1999 Prison Rules 38 and 39).

10.4.1. EVIDENCE GATHERING PROCEDURE
Following the discovery of a serious offence in a prison establishment, prison staff is expected to follow a series of practical procedures in order to preserve physical evidence at the crime scene. However, staff are told that they must not take on the role of an investigating officer. Rather, they should take action, which will assist the police's task in the gathering of evidence. (Prison Discipline Manual, paras 1–10)

10.4.2. EVIDENCE GATHERING FROM OVERSEAS PRISONER
Evidence gathering can also include the transport of overseas prisoner to give evidence or assist in investigation in the United Kingdom (Criminal Justice (International Co-operation) Act 1990, s.5(4)-(8)) where - a witness order has been made or a witness summons or citation issued in criminal proceedings in the United Kingdom in respect of a person ("a prisoner") who is detained in custody in a country or territory outside the United Kingdom by virtue of a sentence or order of a court or tribunal exercising criminal jurisdiction in that country or territory; or it appears to the Secretary of State that it is desirable for a prisoner to be identified in, or otherwise by his presence to assist, such proceedings or the investigation in the United Kingdom of an offence. The effect of a warrant shall be to authorise - the bringing of the prisoner to the United Kingdom; the taking of the prisoner to, and his detention in custody at, such place or places in the United Kingdom as are specified in the warrant; and the returning of the prisoner to the country or territory from which he has come.

10.4.3. POLICE INTERVIEWS IN PRISON
Different police forces take different approaches with regard to interview arrangements. In practice, the majority of police interviews will take place in legal visiting rooms in prison, although in some cases prisoners may be taken to a police station. The 'spirit of' the Police and Criminal Evidence Act

1984 and Codes of Practice apply to all police interviews, which take place in prison. However, police officers can be particularly unaccommodating when it comes to the time constraints imposed by the prison regime, as the usual period for legal visits tends to be two or two-and-a-half hours long. Thus, if a solicitor meets police officers to obtain disclosure at the beginning of the visiting period, the police will often interrupt private consultation if they are of a view that the solicitor has been with the client so long that there will not be enough time left for the interview afterwards. In view of this, it is worth considering whether to meet the police to obtain disclosure before being taken to the legal visiting room in the prison, or booking two legal visits in succession.

10.4.4. DEROGATING THE PRIVILEGE AGAINST SELF-INCRIMINATION

Prisoners can be subjected to a 'compulsory' interview by the police (CI 10/88). Any prisoner who is to be interviewed by the police should be given an information notice (F2042) advising them that if the police consider that there are reasonable grounds for suspecting that they have committed an arrestable offence they must remain in an interview room whilst questions are put to them. The notice also advises prisoners that they have a right to have a solicitor of their choice present at interview and that legal aid should be available for this purpose. In view of this, prisoners cannot avoid the possibility of adverse inferences being drawn against them (under the Criminal Justice and Public Order Act 1994, s 34) by refusing to see the police at interview.

10.4.5. EVIDENCE MAY BE GATHERED AT A POLICE STATION

By the Police and Criminal Evidence Act 1984, s.118, a serving prisoner may be brought to a police station pursuant to a production order (issued under the Crime (Sentences) Act 1997, s.41 and Sched. 1, in order that the police may ask questions relating to evidence that the prisoner might give for the prosecution in another's trial, is not in police detention within the meaning of section 118.

10.5.1. CHARGING A PRISONER

Different police forces have different practices. In some geographical areas, prisoners are usually informed that they will be reported for summons, and they will then experience a period of uncertainty before a decision as to whether to summons them is made. Summonses are often used for serious offences such as prison mutiny, GBH under s 18 of the Offences against the Person Act 1861, and attempted murder.

In other geographical areas, the police will attend the prison and charge a prisoner in the normal way. Prisoners are entitled to have a solicitor with them when they are charged, and procedures are the same as outlined above for interviews.

10.5.2. THE PUBLIC INTEREST THAT THERE MUST BE A REALISTIC PROSPECT OF CONVICTION

In 1951, Lord Shawcross, Attorney General, said:"It has never been the rule in this country - I hope it never will be - that suspected criminal offences must automatically be the subject of prosecution". (House of Commons Debates, volume 483, column 681, 29 January 1951) .The public interest must be considered in each case where there is enough evidence to provide a realistic prospect of conviction. Although there may be public interest factors against prosecution in a particular case, often the prosecution should go ahead and those factors should be put to the court for consideration when sentence is being passed. A prosecution will usually take place unless there are public interest factors tending against prosecution which clearly outweigh those tending in favour, or it appears more appropriate in all the circumstances of the case to divert the person from prosecution. Crown Prosecutors must balance factors for and against prosecution carefully and fairly. Public interest factors that can affect the decision to prosecute usually depend on the seriousness of the offence or the circumstances of the suspect. Some factors may increase the need to prosecute but others may suggest that another course of action would be better. The following lists of some common public interest factors, both for and against prosecution, are not exhaustive. In cases of offences in prison, prosecution is likely to be needed if a weapon was used or violence was threatened during the commission of the offence; the offence was committed against a person serving the public, e.g. police or prison officer ;if the evidence shows that the defendant was a ringleader or an organiser of the offence; if there is evidence that the offence was premeditated; if there is evidence that the offence was carried out by a group; if the victim of the offence was vulnerable, has been put in considerable fear, or suffered personal attack, damage or disturbance; if the offence was motivated by any form of discrimination against the victim's ethnic or national origin, disability, sex, religious beliefs, political views or sexual orientation, or the suspect demonstrated hostility towards the victim based on any of those characteristic; if the defendant's previous convictions or cautions are relevant to the present offence; and if a prosecution would have a significant positive impact on maintaining community confidence.

It may be necessary for counsel to draw the background to the decision to prosecute in Crown Court cases to the attention of the trial or sentencing court. The points made are of equal application to agents and CPS advocates in the magistrates' courts.

10.6. Handcuffing of Prisoners

The Prison Service Security Manual (chapter 38) deals with all issues relating to security at court. Court escorts are often contracted out, and so the policy applies equally to private contractors and prison staff on escort duty. In practice, prison staff are generally used to escort category A prisoners to court; the lower security categories are normally escorted by private security companies. The decision as to whether any prisoner should be handcuffed in the dock is for the judge or the magistrate to make . Their decision must comply with the requirements of the European Convention on Human Rights, in particular Article 3, which prohibits degrading treatment

10.7. DEFENCE TEAM VISIT TO THE PRISON

The Prison Service is usually amenable to allowing defence lawyers to attend a prison to view the scene of the incident and to take photographs of it. Whilst it is generally appropriate to liaise with the police in relation to this, security governors at establishments can also be approached in order to arrange access. Views of prisons tend to take place over the lunchtime 'bang up' period. If it is important to see any area of the prison other than the one in which the incident took place (eg the segregation block, any sterile areas, sight lines from cells or from the grounds of the prison into the prison) it is advisable to make a written request to the governor beforehand in order that any security arrangements can be made.

10.8. THE DEFENCE CASE: DISCLOSURE OF PRISON DOCUMENTS TO DEFENCE SOLICITOR

Section 114 of the CJA 2003 is, available to both parties and it can provide the defence with opportunities to admit evidence that would previously have been inadmissible.(See *R v McLean)*. The evidence was admissible if the judge concluded that it was in the interests of justice that it should be admitted. In the decision in *Prosecution Appeal* (*No 2 of 2008*) *R v Y* [2008] EWCA Crim 10, [2008] 2 All ER 484,as to out-of-court statements under s 114(1)(*d*), it was genuinely in the interests of justice to admit the evidence.

In addition to the usual documents created in the course of a criminal enquiry, the Prison Service will also have a large amount of documentation in its possession. Whether or not the police have seized this will depend upon their diligence and/or their familiarity with prosecuting offences that have occurred within the confines of a prison. In the course of preparing the defence case, it may be helpful to request the following items from the prosecution:

(a) Forms relating to the charging of a prisoner for an internal disciplinary offence arising from the same incident and the transcript of any adjudication proceedings (F256 and F1127). These can be requested for the defendant(s) and suspects who have been eliminated.

(b) Records of segregation of the defendant(s), or prisoner witnesses/victims (F1299B/C/D).

(c) Medical records of the victim or the defendant if he was injured in the incident (it is common for prison staff to be attended by a prison doctor in the first instance, and so it is worth asking for the records of prison officer victims as well as prisoners).

(d) Prison history sheets (F2052A).

(e) Report of Injury to Inmate/Prison Staff.

(f) Serious Incident Reports completed by prison officers who are prosecution witnesses.

(g) Security Intelligence Reports completed by prison officers who are prosecution witnesses.

(h) Disciplinary findings against prison officer witnesses.

(i) Records of sick leave taken by prison officer victims.

(j) CICA (Criminal Injuries Compensation Authority) claims completed by victims.

(k) Reports of any internal enquiries conducted by the Prison Service in the aftermath of the incident (the presence of these will depend upon the seriousness of the incident).

(l) Requests/complaints forms relating to the incident (eg where a defendant has complained to the governor that s/he was assaulted by staff).

(m) Control and Restraint (use of force) records.

(n) Use of Special Cell forms (if it is not clear whether a prisoner was held in a special cell, the Cell Certificate, indicating type of cell, can be requested).

(o) Fifteen minute watch forms.

(p) Audio tapes of relevant telephone calls made by prisoners.

(q) Video tapes from any CCTV cameras in the vicinity of the incident.

(r) A list of all prisoners who were in the prison/on the wing at the time of the incident, and an up-to-date list of their locations. This information is held on computer at each prison and can be invaluable in tracking down witnesses.

(s) Prison disciplinary findings against prisoner victims/prisoner prosecution witnesses.

(t) Criminal convictions of prisoner and prison officer witnesses.

(u) Emergency Control Room logs. These are created in the course of more serious incidents or where incidents last for a protracted period of time, and should provide a contemporaneous record of the actions of prison staff involved in managing the incident, and information coming into the control room from other sources.

(v) Photographs/plans of the area of the prison in which the incident took place.

10.9. NON-DISCLOSURE RULES AS APPLIED TO THE PRISONER DEFENDANT

Where the police have not already seized those items, in some circumstances the CPS will instruct them to approach the prison in order to ask for disclosure. At other times, the CPS will refer requests for disclosure to the Treasury Solicitor. In such cases, the Treasury Solicitor will consider the rules on third party disclosure and may ask lawyers to address them on materiality and relevance before making any decision. If the Treasury Solicitor refuses to disclose the documentation, then an application for a third party witness summons should be considered.

10.10. EVIDENCE OF A PRISONER

In *R v Musone,* the victim, a serving prisoner, had been stabbed to death in his cell. The two defendants were running a 'cut throat' defence and at a late stage in the proceedings, the defendant sought to introduce evidence of his co-accused's confession of committing murder 12 years before under s 101(1)(*e*) (substantive probative value in relation to an important issue between the defendant and a co-defendant). The evidence was admitted on the basis that it suggested it was the co-accused who had committed the present offence. There was no express power for a court to exclude evidence of a defendant's bad character. The trial judge was concerned about the fairness of admitting the evidence and relied on the provisions of art 6 of the Human Rights Convention (the right to a fair trial and declined to extend the time limit for giving notice. In the Court of Appeal, Moses LJ concluded that there was no express power to exclude evidence, which by implication was of 'substantial probative value'.

10.11. JURY VISIT TO THE PRISON

Juries are sometimes taken to view the prison during the course of the trial. In such cases, it can be invaluable to have advance knowledge of the layout of the jail, as this will enable informed discussion with the prosecution as to which areas of the prison it would be useful for the jury to see.

10.12. PROSECUTION WITNESS WHO IS A PRISON OFFICER

The Prison Service is often anxious to secure convictions against prisoners for offences committed in custody, particularly if such offences have been widely reported in the media. Criminal practitioners should be aware that the desire for a successful prosecution has led to training sessions where prison officers who are due to be witnesses in criminal proceedings have been given briefings as to how to give their evidence.

10.13. DEFENCE WITNESS WHO IS A PRISONER

Applications to witness summons-serving prisoners should be made in the usual way. However, the summons should be directed to the governor of the relevant prison, and should ask him to produce a named prisoner at court. Prison governors will usually accept service of a summons by fax. In large trials involving several prisoners, it is likely that the prison will appoint a court/prison liaison officer. S/he will be responsible for ensuring that all prisoner witnesses are brought to court in good time to give their evidence.

10.14. PRISON DISCIPLINE IF THERE IS NO CRIMINAL CHARGE

Where an offence is reported to the police, but this does not result in a prosecution, the governor must decide whether or not to proceed with the adjudication. Governors are advised that, where the CPS has decided not to pursue a prosecution on the basis that there is insufficient evidence against the prisoner, they must dismiss the disciplinary charge. However, in other cases the governor may decide to proceed with the charge (Prison Discipline Manual, para 11.6). Likewise, governors may re-open adjudications where criminal proceedings are discontinued, or it is directed that the charge should lie on file (para 11.7). In cases where prisoners are cautioned by the police, governors are advised that they may still go ahead and hear an adjudication, on the basis that 'no formal proceedings will have taken place and no evidence will formally have been presented' (Prison Discipline Manual, para 11.8). It is to be noted that in July 2002, the European Court of Human Rights held that Article 6 was applicable to internal disciplinary hearings conducted by a prison governor. *((1) Okechukwiw Ezeh (2) Lawrence Connors v. United Kingdom* (application nos. 39665/98 and 40086/98)*)*. As a result of this judgment, such hearings are now held before District Judges who act as independent adjudicators.

10.15.1. CRIMINAL OFFENCES COMMITTED IN PRISON-PRISON MUTINY

The crime of prison mutiny was introduced following the disturbances at HMP Strangeways. The law is framed in such a way as to make it easier to achieve a successful prosecution for prison mutiny, which requires the involvement of a minimum of two prisoners, than riot, which requires 12 participants (Public Order Act 1986, s 1). The maximum period of imprisonment for the two offences is the same. The offence of prison mutiny, contrary Section 1 Prison Security Act 1992) is committed when two or more prisoners, on the premises of any prison, engage in conduct which is intended to further a common purpose of overthrowing lawful authority in that prison. The offence is aimed at behaviour intended to make a prison, or part of prison, ungovernable. Offences under section 1 require DPP consent . Guidance has been provided to prison governors by the Home Office concerning the type of conduct that should be referred to the police for investigation as a possible prison mutiny. The guidance provides guidance on types of behaviour in response to which internal measures are generally appropriate and those that may justify prosecution.

A charge of Prison Mutiny will be appropriate only when the disturbance is serious. It will be particularly appropriate where the evidence fails to show clearly an identifiable person who can be prosecuted for a substantive offence. In many circumstances the charging of public order offences, offences against the person or against property will be preferable, notwithstanding that they took place in prison.

Under Public Order Act s4(1), where a prisoner fails to submit to lawful authority without reasonable excuse, he will be regarded as taking part in the mutiny. The purpose of this subsection is to catch prisoners who, by their presence and refusal to disperse, make the role of the authorities who are attempting to restore lawful control more difficult. The s4(1) offence is confined to failure to submit etc., in the context of a prison mutiny and is not appropriate in cases of mere defiance of, or a challenge to, lawful authority in a prison in other contexts.

10.15.2. CONSPIRACY TO ESCAPE PRISON; AIDING & ABETTING A PRISON ESCAPE

There are many offences relating to escape – prisoners may be tried for escapes, conspiracies to escape and attempts; prison officers for permitting an escape; police officers for negligently permitting an escape; and others for aiding or assisting escapes (Prison Act 1953, s 39) or, at common law, for rescuing a prisoner in custody. Further offences relating to escape include harbouring escaped prisoners (Criminal Justice Act 1961, s 22(2)).

10.15.3. CRIMINAL OFFENCE OF 'ASSISTING PRISONERS TO ESCAPE'

Any person who aids any prisoner in escaping or attempting to escape from a prison or who, with intent to facilitate the escape of any prisoner, conveys anything into a prison or to a prisoner sends anything (by post or otherwise) into a prison or to a prisoner or places anything anywhere outside a prison with a view to its coming into the possession of a prisoner, shall be guilty of an offence and liable to imprisonment for a term not exceeding ten years. The offence under section 39 of the Prison Act 1952 is one of assisting prisoners to escape from naval detention quarters and the Army Act 1955,ss.54,56, concerns the escape from military prisons, whilst the Air Force Act 1955,ss.54,56, concerns the escape from air force prisons.

10.15.5. THE CRIMINAL OFFENCE OF PRISON MUTINY

Prison Security Act 1992, s.1 deals with the offence of prison mutiny. It states:

"(1) Any prisoner who takes part in a prison mutiny shall be guilty of an offence and liable, on conviction on indictment, to imprisonment for a term not exceeding ten years or to a fine or to both".

Criminal Damage Act 1971,ss.1(1),(3) deal with the criminal offence of damaging a prison and arson, making threats to destroy or damage the prison, or possessing anything with intent to destroy or damage property.

Criminal Justice Act 1961,s.22 deals with the criminal offence of harbouring escaped prisoners.

10.15.6. CRIMINAL OFFENCE OF HARBOURING ESCAPED PRISONERS

If any person knowingly harbours a person who has escaped from a prison or other institution to which said section 39 applies, or who, having been sentenced in any part of the United Kingdom or in any of the Channel Islands or the Isle of Man to imprisonment or detention, is otherwise unlawfully at large, or who gives to any such person any assistance with intent to prevent, hinder or interfere with his being taken into custody, he shall be liable on summary conviction, to imprisonment for a term not exceeding six months, or to a fine not exceeding the prescribed sum, or to both on conviction on indictment, to imprisonment for a term not exceeding ten years, or to a fine, or to both. In this context, "harbour" means to shelter a person, in the sense of giving or providing a refuge to that person. It is possible for a person to give shelter to a person within the category specified in section 22(2) even though the alleged harbourer has no interest in the relevant place and even if in fact he is a trespasser in that place

The word "prisoner" according to Prison Security Act 1992,

means any person for the time being in a prison as a result of any requirement imposed by a court or otherwise that he be detained in legal custody.

10.15.7. THE CRIMINAL OFFENCE OF ASSISTING A PRISONER TO ESCAPE, CONTRARY TO SECTION 39 OF THE PRISON ACT 1952.

The defendant must have conveyed or caused to be conveyed unto the said prisoner some article, eg. two steel files. It must be proved that the prisoner was in custody (see Prison Act 1952,s.13(2), and that that is the prisoner in the gaol mentioned in the indictment. The words of the statute are "any prisoner". It must then be proved that whilst this named prisoner was so in custody, the defendant conveyed to him one or more articles; and proved that such articles were intended to facilitate his escape. The mere delivery of such article to the person in custody is a fact from which the jury may well infer the intent, and it is immaterial, upon this statute, whether an escape is actually made or not.

10.15.8. COMMON LAW OFFENCE OF BREACH OF PRISON

It is an indictable offence at common law, punishable by fine and imprisonment, to breach prison. Breach of prison consists in the escape from lawful custody by the use of any force. It is immaterial whether the custody is criminal or civil and whether the prisoner is actually within a gaol, or is only in the constable's house or a lock-up, provided that he is lawfully imprisoned or restrained of his liberty. Other offences peculiar to prisons and prisoners include the common law offence of breaking prison, which requires the use of force in escaping, eg by cutting through fences or bars. Breaking prison is a more serious offence than escape.

10.15.9. CRIMINAL OFFENCE OF BREAKING PRISON.

A prisoner in Her Majesty's prison, serving a sentence of imprisonment passed on him, broke the said prison by cutting two iron bars of the prison, or similar act, by means whereof he escaped. It must be proved that the prisoner was in prison as alleged; and that, while in custody there, he broke the prison and escaped. The breaking proved must be an actual breaking; merely getting over the walls, or passing out through a door, or the like, is an escape only and not a breach of prison. For this reason, it would seem that the manner of the breaking should be stated in the indictment, as in the above precedent, in order that the court may see that it was such as is necessary in law to constitute a breach of prison. But the breaking need not be intentional; and therefore where a prisoner, in effecting his escape, by accident threw down some loose bricks at the top of the prison wall, placed there to impede escape and give alarm, it was held to be a prison breach(*R. v. Haswell* (1821)).

10.15.10. CRIMINAL OFFENCE OF PRISON MUTINY, CONTRARY TO PRISON SECURITY ACT 1992, S.1

The offence of prison mutiny is contained in the Prison Security Act 1992, s 1 which states that any prisoner who takes part in a prison mutiny shall be guilty of an offence and liable, on conviction on indictment, to imprisonment for a term not exceeding ten years or to a fine or both. Prison mutiny is a more serious offence than violent disorder (Public Order Act, s 2), which is also often used against prisoners following smaller disturbances within prisons.

10.15.11. CRIMINAL OFFENCE OF ASSAULT ON PRISONERS

The vast majority of offences committed in prison and referred to the police for prosecution are assaults on prisoners by prisoners. These will range from a very few cases of murder and false imprisonment (hostage-taking), and many reported offences of grievous bodily harm (Offences Against the Person Act 1861, ss 18 and 20) and actual bodily harm (Offences Against the Person Act 1861, s 47).

10.15.12. MISUSE OF DRUGS ACT OFFENCES BY PRISONERS

Mandatory drug testing (MDT) of a random sample of 5% or 10% (depending on prison capacity) of prisoners each month, to monitor and deter drug-misuse. Failing a mandatory drug test is a disciplinary offence that may lead to days being added to the sentence. MDT can also act as a useful trigger for referring into treatment individuals who fail tests. Taking these into account, around 80% report some drug-misuse prior to prison, and 55% report a severe. Added to this, some prisons that receive prisoners from Court report up to 80% of offenders testing positive for Class A drugs on arrival into custody – based on information obtained from healthcare screening on reception.

10.16. DEFENCE OF SELF-DEFENCE

In the trial of a criminal offence of violence in prison, a prisoner may bring a defence of self-defence. Where a defence of self-defence is raised, the burden of negating it rests on the prosecution, but the prosecution are not obliged to give evidence-in-chief to rebut a suggestion of self-defence before that issue is raised, or indeed to give any evidence on that issue at all. If, on consideration of the whole of the evidence, the jury are either convinced of the innocence of the prisoner or are left in doubt whether he was acting in necessary self-defence, they should acquit: *R. v. Lobell*[1957] 1 Q.B. 547,41 Cr.App.R. 100, CCA. Before the issue of self-defence is left to the jury, there must be evidence, whether from the prosecution or the defence, which, if accepted, could raise a prima facie case of self-defence; if there is such evidence, the issue must be left to the jury, whether it is relied on by the defence or not: see *DPP (Jamaica) v. Bailey*[1995] 1 Cr.App.R. 257, PC.

10.17. CONCLUSION

Criminal offences by prisoners in prison is handled under a regime fit to deal with such further offences . Nevertheless, it may be seen as a result of organisational failures in the management and supervision of offenders aggravated by environmental conditions in prisons.

BIBLIOGRAPHY

Argus Leader.com, *Prison Informant Charged with Perjury,* March 13, 2008

C. Moraff, *The Rat Trap-Death Row Exonerations Expose Failings of the 'Snitch System',* In These Times, July 30, 2008.

A. Rojas, *A hard look at jail snitches; Bill would require that their testimony be corroborated,* Sacramento Bee, May 18, 2007, at A3.

H. Weinstein, *A Fight 24 Years in the Making; A Man Wrongfully Imprisoned for Murder Because of a Jailhouse Informant is Seeking the Right to Sue the D.A.'s Office for Compensation,* Los AngelesTimes, April 4, 2006.

H. Weinstein, *D.A.s can be sued over jailhouse informants, court finds,* Los Angeles Times, March 29, 2007.

H. Weinstein, *Limited Use of Jail Informants Urged, State Blue Ribbon Panel Says the Legislature Should Enact Laws Requiring Corroborating Evidence if Such Testimony is Offered,* Los AngelesTimes, November 22, 2006.

V. Alter, *Jailhouse Informants: A Lesson in E-Snitching*, Issue 10, Journal of Technology Law and Politics, 223 (2005

R. M. Bloom, *Jailhouse Informants*, 18 Crim. Justice 20 (2003).

D. L. Martin, *Lessons About Justice from the "Laboratory" of Wrongful Convictions: Tunnel Vision, the Construction of Guilt and Informer Evidence*, 70 U.M.K.C. L. Rev. 847 (2002)

A. Natapoff, *Comment, Beyond Unreliable: How Snitches Contribute to Wrongful Convictions*, 37 Golden Gate U. L. Rev. 107 (2006).

A. Natapoff, *Snitching: The Institutional and Communal Consequences*, 73 U. Cin. L. Rev. 645 (2004).

E. Yaroshefsky, *Cooperation with Federal Prosecutors: Experiences of Truth Telling and Embellishment*, 68 Fordham L. Rev. 917 (1999)

R. Bloom, *Ratting: The Use and Abuse of Informants in the American Justice System*, Praeger Publishers, 2002

E. Brown, *Snitch: Informants, Cooperators and the Corruption of Justice*, PublicAffairs, 2007

T. P. Sullivan, *Police Experiences with Recording Custodial Interrogations*, Northwestern University School of Law, Center on Wrongful Convictions, Summer 2004.

APPENDIX 1 - THE PRISON (AMENDMENT) RULES 2008

Made 4th March 2008
Laid before Parliament
5th March 2008
In force since 1st April 2008

The Secretary of State, in exercise of the powers conferred by section 47 of the Prison Act 1952(1), makes the following Rules:

Citation and commencement

1. These Rules may be cited as the Prison (Amendment) Rules 2008 and shall come into force on 1st April 2008.

Amendment of the Prison Rules 1999

2. The Prison Rules 1999(2) are amended as follows.

3. In rule 2(1) (interpretation), the following definition shall be added in the appropriate place—

"information technology equipment" includes any laptop or notebook computer, desktop computer, gaming console, handheld computing device, personal organiser or any electronic device containing a computer processor and capable

of connecting to the internet, and any reference to information technology equipment includes a reference to–
(a) a component part of a device of that description; or
(b) any article designed or adapted for use with any information technology equipment (including any disk, film or other separate article on which images, sounds, computer code or other information may be stored or recorded)".
4. For "board of visitors" substitute "*independent monitoring board*" in—
(a) each place where it occurs in rules 11(1), 22(2), 35(6), 43(1), 49(2) and (4)(3), 73(2), 74(4), 75(2) and (4), 76(1), 77(1), 78(1) and 80(1);
(b) the title to Part 5 and the heading to rule 75.
5. In rule 61(2)(5) for "*governor or the board of visitors*" substitute "*or governor*".
6. In rule 70 omit "*money, clothing, food, drink, tobacco, letter, paper, book, tool, controlled drug, firearm, explosive, weapon or othe*r".
7. After rule 70 insert—
"*70A. List C Articles*
A List C article is any article or substance in the following list—
(a) tobacco;
(b) money;
(c) clothing;
(d) food;
(e) drink;
(f) letters;
(g) paper;
(h) books;
(i) tools;
(j) information technology equipment."

NOTES

These Rules amend the Prison Rules 1999 ("*the 1999 Rules*"). Rule 4 alters all references to "*boards of visitors*" in the 1999 Rules to "*independent monitoring boards*", following the renaming of the board by section 26(1) of the Offender Management Act 2007. Rule 5 removes the reference to 'boards of visitors' in rule 61(2) of the 1999 Rules. Boards of visitors, now independent monitoring boards, no longer have any role in imposing punishments for disciplinary offences.

Rule 6 provides for amendments to rule 70 (prohibited articles) to remove the illustrative list of unauthorised articles which may be confiscated by the governor.

Section 22 of the Offender Management Act 2007(c.21) inserted sections 40A to 40C of the Prison Act 1952. In consequence, Rule 7 inserts a new Rule 70A into the 1999 Rules. Rule 70A lists for the purposes of the new section 40C, the List C articles which it is an offence to bring, or attempt to bring into a prison intending to give to a prisoner, or intending it to come into a prisoner's possession, or to take out of a prison on a prisoner's behalf.

(1) 1952 c.52. Section 40A(6), which provides for List C articles to be prescribed by prison rules, was inserted by the Offender Management Act 2007 (2007 c.21).

(2) S.I. 1999/728 as amended by S.I. 2005/869 and S.I. 2005/3437. Rule 79(1) was amended by S.I. 2007/2954 to include reference to the independent monitoring board. There are other amending instruments but none is relevant.

(3) Rule 49(2) and (4) were amended by S.I. 2005/3437.

(4) Rule 74 was amended by S.I. 2000/1794.

(5) Rule 61(2) was amended by S.I. 2005/3437.

APPENDIX 2 - CONSOLIDATED PRISON RULES 1999

STATUTORY INSTRUMENTS 1999 No. 728

PRISONS
The Prison Rules 1999
as amended by the Prison (Amendment) Rules 2000, the Prison (Amendment) (No. 2) Rules 2000, the Prison (Amendment) Rules 2002, the Prison (Amendment) Rules 2003 and the Prison (Amendment) Rules 2005.
Revocations
PART I
1. Citation
These Rules came into force on 1st April 1999
Interpretation
2. (1) In these Rules, where the context so admits, the expression
"*adjudicator*" means a District Judge (Magistrates' Courts) or Deputy District Judge (Magistrates' Courts) approved by the Lord Chancellor for the purpose of inquiring into a charge which has been referred to him;
"*communication*" includes any written or drawn communication from a prisoner to any other person, whether intended to

be transmitted by means of a postal service or not, and any communication from a prisoner to any other person transmitted by means of a telecommunications system;" *controlled drug*" means any drug which is a controlled drug for the purposes of the Misuse of Drugs Act 1971.

"*convicted prisoner*" means, subject to the provisions of rule 7(3), a prisoner who has been convicted or found guilty of an offence or committed or attached for contempt of court or for failing to do or abstain from doing anything required to be done or left undone, and the expression "*unconvicted prisoner*" shall be construed accordingly;

"*governor*" includes an officer for the time being in charge of a prison;

"*intercepted material*" means the contents of any communication intercepted pursuant to these Rules;

"*intermittent custody order*" has the meaning assigned to it by section 183 of the Criminal Justice Act 2003.

"*legal adviser*" means, in relation to a prisoner, his counsel or solicitor, and includes a clerk acting on behalf of his solicitor;

"*officer*" means an officer of a prison and, for the purposes of rule 40(2), includes a prisoner custody officer who is authorised to perform escort functions in accordance with section 89 of the Criminal Justice Act 1991;

"*prison minister*" means, in relation to a prison, a minister appointed to that prison under section 10 of the Prison Act 1952;

"*short-term prisoner*" and "*long-term prisoner*" have the meanings assigned to them by section 33(5) of the Criminal Justice Act 1991, as extended by sections 43(1) and 45(1) of that Act.

"*telecommunications system*" means any system (including the apparatus comprised in it) which exists for the purpose of facilitating the transmission of communications by any means involving the use of electrical or electro-magnetic energy.

(2) In these Rules

(a) a reference to an award of additional days means additional days awarded under these Rules by virtue of section 42 of the Criminal Justice Act 1991;

(b) a reference to the Church of England includes a reference to the Church in Wales; and

(c) a reference to a numbered rule is, unless otherwise stated, a reference to the rule of that number in these Rules and a reference in a rule to a numbered paragraph is, unless otherwise stated, a reference to the paragraph of that number in that rule.

PART II
PRISONERS
Purpose of prison training and treatment
3. The purpose of the training and treatment of convicted prisoners shall be to encourage and assist them to lead a good and useful life.

Outside contacts
4.(1) Special attention shall be paid to the maintenance of such relationships between a prisoner and his family as are desirable in the best interests of both.
(2) A prisoner shall be encouraged and assisted to establish and maintain such relations with persons and agencies outside prison as may, in the opinion of the governor, best promote the interests of his family and his own social rehabilitation.

After care
5. From the beginning of a prisoner's sentence, consideration shall be given, in consultation with the appropriate after-care organisation, to the prisoner's future and the assistance to be given him on and after his release.

Maintenance of order and discipline

6. (1) Order and discipline shall be maintained with firmness, but with no more restriction than is required for safe custody and well ordered community life.

(2) In the control of prisoners, officers shall seek to influence them through their own example and leadership, and to enlist their willing co-operation.

(3) At all times the treatment of prisoners shall be such as to encourage their self-respect and a sense of personal responsibility, but a prisoner shall not be employed in any disciplinary capacity.

Classification of prisoners

7.(1) Prisoners shall be classified, in accordance with any directions of the Secretary of State, having regard to their age, temperament and record and with a view to maintaining good order and facilitating training and, in the case of convicted prisoners, of furthering the purpose of their training and treatment as provided by rule 3.

(2) Unconvicted prisoners:

(a) shall be kept out of contact with convicted prisoners as far as the governor considers it can reasonably be done, unless and to the extent that they have consented to share residential accommodation or participate in any activity with convicted prisoners; and

(b) shall under no circumstances be required to share a cell with a convicted prisoner.

(3) Prisoners committed or attached for contempt of court, or for failing to do or abstain from doing anything required to be done or left undone:

(a) shall be treated as a separate class for the purposes of this rule;

(b) notwithstanding anything in this rule, may be permitted to associate with any other class of prisoners if they are willing to do so; and

(c) shall have the same privileges as an unconvicted prisoner under rules 20(5), 23(1) and 35(1).

(4) Nothing in this rule shall require a prisoner to be deprived unduly of the society of other persons.

Privileges
8. (1) There shall be established at every prison systems of privileges approved by the Secretary of State and appropriate to the classes of prisoners there, which shall include arrangements under which money earned by prisoners in prison may be spent by them within the prison.
(2) Systems of privileges approved under paragraph (1) may include arrangements under which prisoners may be allowed time outside their cells and in association with one another, in excess of the minimum time which, subject to the other provisions of these Rules apart from this rule, is otherwise allowed to prisoners at the prison for this purpose.
(3) Systems of privileges approved under paragraph (1) may include arrangements under which privileges may be granted to prisoners only in so far as they have met, and for so long as they continue to meet, specified standards in their behaviour and their performance in work or other activities.
(4) Systems of privileges which include arrangements of the kind referred to in paragraph (3) shall include procedures to be followed in determining whether or not any of the privileges concerned shall be granted, or shall continue to be granted, to a prisoner; such procedures shall include a requirement that the prisoner be given reasons for any decision adverse to him together with a statement of the means by which he may appeal against it.
(5) Nothing in this rule shall be taken to confer on a prisoner any entitlement to any privilege or to affect any provision in these Rules other than this rule as a result of which any privilege may be forfeited or otherwise lost or a prisoner deprived of association with other prisoners.

Temporary release

9.(1) The Secretary of State may, in accordance with the other provisions of this rule, release temporarily a prisoner to whom this rule applies.

(2) A prisoner may be released under this rule for any period or periods and subject to any conditions.

(3) A prisoner may only be released under this rule:

 (a) on compassionate grounds or for the purpose of receiving medical treatment;

 (b) to engage in employment or voluntary work;

 (c) to receive instruction or training which cannot reasonably be provided in the prison;

 (d) to enable him to participate in any proceedings before any court, tribunal or inquiry;

 (e) to enable him to consult with his legal adviser in circumstances where it is not reasonably practicable for the consultation to take place in the prison;

 (f) to assist any police officer in any enquiries;

 (g) to facilitate the prisoner's transfer between prisons;

 (h) to assist him in maintaining family ties or in his transition from prison life to freedom; or

 (i) to enable him to make a visit in the locality of the prison, as a privilege under rule 8.

(4) A prisoner shall not be released under this rule unless the Secretary of State is satisfied that there would not be an unacceptable risk of his committing offences whilst released or otherwise failing to comply with any condition upon which he is released.

(5) The Secretary of State shall not release under this rule a prisoner serving a sentence of imprisonment if, having regard to:

 (a) the period or proportion of his sentence which the prisoner has served or, in a case where paragraph (10) does not apply to require all the sentences he is serving to be treated as a single term, the period or proportion of any such sentence he has served; and

(b) the frequency with which the prisoner has been granted temporary release under this rule,
the Secretary of State is of the opinion that the release of the prisoner would be likely to undermine public confidence in the administration of justice.
(6) If a prisoner has been temporarily released under this rule during the relevant period and has been sentenced to imprisonment for a criminal offence committed whilst at large following that release, he shall not be released under this rule unless his release, having regard to the circumstances of this conviction, would not, in the opinion of the Secretary of State, be likely to undermine public confidence in the administration of justice.
(7) For the purposes of paragraph (6), "*the relevant period*":
(a) in the case of a prisoner serving a determinate sentence of imprisonment, is the period he has served in respect of that sentence, unless, notwithstanding paragraph (10), the sentences he is serving do not fall to be treated as a single term, in which case it is the period since he was last released in relation to one of those sentences under Part II of the Criminal Justice Act 1991 ("*the 1991 Act);*
(b) in the case of a prisoner serving an indeterminate sentence of imprisonment, is, if the prisoner has previously been released on licence under Part II of the Crime (Sentences) Act 1997[5] or Part II of the 1991 Act, the period since the date of his last recall to prison in respect of that sentence or, where the prisoner has not been so released, the period he has served in respect of that sentence; or
(c) in the case of a prisoner detained in prison for any other reason, is the period for which the prisoner has been detained for that reason;
save that where a prisoner falls within two or more of sub-paragraphs (a) to (c), the "*relevant period*", in the case of that prisoner, shall be determined by whichever of the applicable sub-paragraphs produces the longer period.

(8) A prisoner released under this rule may be recalled to prison at any time whether the conditions of his release have been broken or not.

(9) This rule applies to prisoners other than persons committed in custody for trial or to be sentenced or otherwise dealt with before or by any Crown Court or remanded in custody by any court.

(10) For the purposes of any reference in this rule to a prisoner's sentence, consecutive terms and terms which are wholly or partly concurrent shall be treated as a single term if they would fall to be treated as a single term for the purposes of any reference to the term of imprisonment to which a person has been sentenced in Part II of the 1991 Act.

(11) In this rule:

 (a) any reference to a sentence of imprisonment shall be construed as including any sentence to detention or custody; and

 (b) any reference to release on licence or otherwise under Part II of the 1991 Act includes any release on licence under any legislation providing for early release on licence.

Information to prisoners

10.(1) Every prisoner shall be provided, as soon as possible after his reception into prison, and in any case within 24 hours, with information in writing about those provisions of these Rules and other matters which it is necessary that he should know, including earnings and privileges, and the proper means of making requests and complaints.

(2) In the case of a prisoner aged less than 18, or a prisoner aged 18 or over who cannot read or appears to have difficulty in understanding the information so provided, the governor, or an officer deputed by him, shall so explain it to him that he can understand his rights and obligations.

(3) A copy of these Rules shall be made available to any prisoner who requests it.

Requests and complaints

11. (1) A request or complaint to the governor or board of visitors relating to a prisoner's imprisonment shall be made orally or in writing by the prisoner.

(2) On every day the governor shall hear any requests and complaints that are made to him under paragraph (1).

(3) A written request or complaint under paragraph (1) may be made in confidence.

Women prisoners

12. (1) Women prisoners shall normally be kept separate from male prisoners.

(2) The Secretary of State may, subject to any conditions he thinks fit, permit a woman prisoner to have her baby with her in prison, and everything necessary for the baby's maintenance and care may be provided there.

Religious denomination

13. A prisoner shall be treated as being of the religious denomination stated in the record made in pursuance of section 10(5) of the Prison Act 1952 but the governor may, in a proper case and after due enquiry, direct that record to be amended.

Special duties of chaplains and prison ministers

14.(1) The chaplain or a prison minister of a prison shall -

 (a) interview every prisoner of his denomination individually soon after the prisoner's reception into that prison and shortly before his release; and

 (b) if no other arrangements are made, read the burial service at the funeral of any prisoner of his denomination who dies in that prison.

(2) The chaplain shall visit daily all prisoners belonging to the Church of England who are sick, under restraint or undergoing cellular confinement; and a prison minister shall do the same, as far as he reasonably can, for prisoners of his denomination.

(3) The chaplain shall visit any prisoner not of the Church of England who is sick, under restraint or undergoing cellular

confinement, and is not regularly visited by a minister of his denomination, if the prisoner is willing.

Regular visits by ministers of religion

15.(1) The chaplain shall visit the prisoners belonging to the Church of England.

(2) A prison minister shall visit the prisoners of his denomination as regularly as he reasonably can.

(3) Where a prisoner belongs to a denomination for which no prison minister has been appointed, the governor shall do what he reasonably can, if so requested by the prisoner, to arrange for him to be visited regularly by a minister of that denomination.

Religious services

16. (1) The chaplain shall conduct Divine Service for prisoners belonging to the Church of England at least once every Sunday, Christmas Day and Good Friday, and such celebrations of Holy Communion and weekday services as may be arranged.

(2) Prison ministers shall conduct Divine Service for prisoners of their denominations at such times as may be arranged.

Substitute for chaplain or prison minister

17.(1) A person approved by the Secretary of State may act for the chaplain in his absence.

(2) A prison minister may, with the leave of the Secretary of State, appoint a substitute to act for him in his absence.

Sunday work

18. Arrangements shall be made so as not to require prisoners of the Christian religion to do any unnecessary work on Sunday, Christmas Day or Good Friday, or prisoners of other religions to do any such work on their recognised days of religious observance.

Religious books

19. There shall, so far as reasonably practicable, be available for the personal use of every prisoner such religious books recognised by his denomination as are approved by the Secretary of State for use in prisons.

MEDICAL ATTENTION

Medical attendance

20. - (1) The medical officer of a prison shall have the care of the health, mental and physical, of the prisoners in that prison.

(2) Every request by a prisoner to see the medical officer shall be recorded by the officer to whom it is made and promptly passed on to the medical officer.

(3) The medical officer may consult a medical practitioner who is a fully registered person within the meaning of the Medical Act 1983[7]. Such a practitioner may work within the prison under the general supervision of the medical officer.

(4) The medical officer shall consult another medical practitioner, if time permits, before performing any serious operation.

(5) If an unconvicted prisoner desires the attendance of a registered medical practitioner or dentist, and will pay any expense incurred, the governor shall, if he is satisfied that there are reasonable grounds for the request and unless the Secretary of State otherwise directs, allow him to be visited and treated by that practitioner or dentist in consultation with the medical officer.

(6) Subject to any directions given in the particular case by the Secretary of State, a registered medical practitioner selected by or on behalf of a prisoner who is a party to any legal proceedings shall be afforded reasonable facilities for examining him in connection with the proceedings, and may do so out of hearing but in the sight of an officer.

Special illnesses and conditions

21. - (1) The medical officer or a medical practitioner such as is mentioned in rule 20(3) shall report to the governor on the case of any prisoner whose health is likely to be injuriously affected by continued imprisonment or any conditions of imprisonment. The governor shall send the report to the Secretary of State without delay, together with his own recommendations.

(2) The medical officer or a medical practitioner such as is mentioned in rule 20(3) shall pay special attention to any prisoner whose mental condition appears to require it, and make any special arrangements which appear necessary for his supervision or care.

Notification of illness or death

22. - (1) If a prisoner dies, becomes seriously ill, sustains any severe injury or is removed to hospital on account of mental disorder, the governor shall, if he knows his or her address, at once inform the prisoner's spouse or next of kin, and also any person who the prisoner may reasonably have asked should be informed.

(2) If a prisoner dies, the governor shall give notice immediately to the coroner having jurisdiction, to the board of visitors and to the Secretary of State.

PHYSICAL WELFARE AND WORK

Clothing

23. - (1) An unconvicted prisoner may wear clothing of his own if and in so far as it is suitable, tidy and clean, and shall be permitted to arrange for the supply to him from outside prison of sufficient clean clothing:

Provided that, subject to rule 40(3):

(a) he may be required, if and for so long as there are reasonable grounds to believe that there is a serious risk of his attempting to escape, to wear items of clothing which are distinctive by virtue of being specially marked or coloured or both; and

(b) he may be required, if and for so long as the Secretary of State is of the opinion that he would, if he escaped, be highly dangerous to the public or the police or the security of the State, to wear clothing provided under this rule.

(2) Subject to paragraph (1) above, the provisions of this rule shall apply to an unconvicted prisoner as to a convicted prisoner.

(3) A convicted prisoner shall be provided with clothing adequate for warmth and health in accordance with a scale approved by the Secretary of State.

(4) The clothing provided under this rule shall include suitable protective clothing for use at work, where this is needed.

(5) Subject to rule 40(3), a convicted prisoner shall wear clothing provided under this rule and no other, except on the directions of the Secretary of State or as a privilege under rule 8.

(6) A prisoner may be provided, where necessary, with suitable and adequate clothing on his release.

Food

24. - (1) Subject to any directions of the Secretary of State, no prisoner shall be allowed, except as authorised by the medical officer or a medical practitioner such as is mentioned in rule 20(3), to have any food other than that ordinarily provided.

(2) The food provided shall be wholesome, nutritious, well prepared and served, reasonably varied and sufficient in quantity.

(3) The medical officer, a medical practitioner such as is mentioned in rule 20(3) or any person deemed by the governor to be competent, shall from time to time inspect the food both before and after it is cooked and shall report any deficiency or defect to the governor.

(4) In this rule "food" includes drink.

Alcohol and tobacco

25. - (1) No prisoner shall be allowed to have any intoxicating liquor except under a written order of the medical officer or a medical practitioner such as is mentioned in rule 20(3) specifying the quantity and the name of the prisoner.

(2) No prisoner shall be allowed to smoke or to have any tobacco except as a privilege under rule 8 and in accordance with any orders of the governor.

Sleeping accommodation

26. - (1) No room or cell shall be used as sleeping accommodation for a prisoner unless it has been certified in the manner required by section 14 of the Prison Act 1952 in the case of a cell used for the confinement of a prisoner.

(2) A certificate given under that section or this rule shall specify the maximum number of prisoners who may sleep or be confined at one time in the room or cell to which it relates, and the number so specified shall not be exceeded without the leave of the Secretary of State.

Beds and bedding

27. Each prisoner shall be provided with a separate bed and with separate bedding adequate for warmth and health.
Hygiene

28. - (1) Every prisoner shall be provided with toilet articles necessary for his health and cleanliness, which shall be replaced as necessary.

(2) Every prisoner shall be required to wash at proper times, have a hot bath or shower on reception and thereafter at least once a week.

(3) A prisoner's hair shall not be cut without his consent.

Physical education

29. - (1) If circumstances reasonably permit, a prisoner aged 21 years or over shall be given the opportunity to participate in physical education for at least one hour a week.

(2) The following provisions shall apply to the extent circumstances reasonably permit to a prisoner who is under 21 years of age -

(a) provision shall be made for the physical education of such a prisoner within the normal working week, as well as evening and weekend physical recreation; the physical education activities will be such as foster personal responsibility and the prisoner's interests and skills and encourage him to make good use of his leisure on release; and

(b) arrangements shall be made for each such prisoner who is a convicted prisoner to participate in physical education for two hours a week on average.

(3) In the case of a prisoner with a need for remedial physical activity, appropriate facilities will be provided.

(4) The medical officer or a medical practitioner such as is mentioned in rule 20(3) shall decide upon the fitness of every prisoner for physical education and remedial physical activity and may excuse a prisoner from, or modify, any such education or activity on medical grounds.

Time in the open air

30. If the weather permits and subject to the need to maintain good order and discipline, a prisoner shall be given the opportunity to spend time in the open air at least once every day, for such period as may be reasonable in the circumstances.

Work

31. - (1) A convicted prisoner shall be required to do useful work for not more than 10 hours a day, and arrangements shall

be made to allow prisoners to work, where possible, outside the cells and in association with one another.

(2) The medical officer or a medical practitioner such as is mentioned in rule 20(3) may excuse a prisoner from work on medical grounds, and no prisoner shall be set to do work which is not of a class for which he has been passed by the medical officer or by a medical practitioner such as is mentioned in rule 20(3) as being fit.

(3) No prisoner shall be set to do work of a kind not authorised by the Secretary of State.

(4) No prisoner shall work in the service of another prisoner or an officer, or for the private benefit of any person, without the authority of the Secretary of State.

(5) An unconvicted prisoner shall be permitted, if he wishes, to work as if he were a convicted prisoner.

(6) Prisoners may be paid for their work at rates approved by the Secretary of State, either generally or in relation to particular cases.

EDUCATION AND LIBRARY

Education

32. - (1) Every prisoner able to profit from the education facilities provided at a prison shall be encouraged to do so.

(2) Educational classes shall be arranged at every prison and, subject to any directions of the Secretary of State, reasonable facilities shall be afforded to prisoners who wish to do so to improve their education by training by distance learning, private study and recreational classes, in their spare time.

(3) Special attention shall be paid to the education and training of prisoners with special educational needs, and if necessary they shall be taught within the hours normally allotted to work.

(4) In the case of a prisoner of compulsory school age as defined in section 8 of the Education Act 1996, arrangements shall be made for his participation in education or training

courses for at least 15 hours a week within the normal working week.

Library
33. A library shall be provided in every prison and, subject to any directions of the Secretary of State, every prisoner shall be allowed to have library books and to exchange them.

COMMUNICATIONS

Communications generally
34. - (1) Without prejudice to sections 6 and 19 of the Prison Act 1952 and except as provided by these Rules, a prisoner shall not be permitted to communicate with any person outside the prison, or such person with him, except with the leave of the Secretary of State or as a privilege under rule 8.
(2) Notwithstanding paragraph (1) above, and except as otherwise provided in these Rules, the Secretary of State may impose any restriction or condition, either generally or in a particular case, upon the communications to be permitted between a prisoner and other persons if he considers that the restriction or condition to be imposed -
(a) does not interfere with the convention rights of any person; or
(b)
(i) is necessary on grounds specified in paragraph (3) below;
(ii) reliance on the grounds is compatible with the convention right to be interfered with; and
(iii) the restriction or condition is proportionate to what is sought to be achieved.
(3) The grounds referred to in paragraph (2) above are -
(a) the interests of national security;
(b) the prevention, detection, investigation or prosecution of crime;
(c) the interests of public safety;

(d) securing or maintaining prison security or good order and discipline in prison;
(e) the protection of health or morals;
(f) the protection of the reputation of others;
(g) maintaining the authority and impartiality of the judiciary; or
(h) the protection of the rights and freedoms of any person.
(4) Subject to paragraph (2) above, the Secretary of State may require that any visit, or class of visits, shall be held in facilities which include special features restricting or preventing physical contact between a prisoner and a visitor.
(5) Every visit to a prisoner shall take place within the sight of an officer or employee of the prison authorised for the purposes of this rule by the governor (in this rule referred to as an "authorised employee"), unless the Secretary of State otherwise directs, and for the purposes of this paragraph a visit to a prisoner shall be taken to take place within the sight of an officer or authorised employee if it can be seen by an officer or authorised employee by means of an overt closed circuit television system.
(6) Subject to rule 38, every visit to a prisoner shall take place within the hearing of an officer or authorised employee, unless the Secretary of State otherwise directs.

(7) The Secretary of State may give directions, either generally or in relation to any visit or class of visits, concerning the day and times when prisoners may be visited.
(8) In this rule -
(a) references to communications include references to communications during visits;
(b) references to restrictions and conditions upon communications include references to restrictions and conditions in relation to the length, duration and frequency of communications; and

(c) references to convention rights are to the convention rights within the meaning of the Human Rights Act 1998..

Personal letters and visits

35. - (1) Subject to paragraph (8), an unconvicted prisoner may send and receive as many letters and may receive as many visits as he wishes within such limits and subject to such conditions as the Secretary of State may direct, either generally or in a particular case.

(2) Subject to paragraphs (2A) and (8), a convicted prisoner shall be entitled -

(a) to send and to receive a letter on his reception into a prison and thereafter once a week; and

(b) to receive a visit twice in every period of four weeks, but only once in every such period if the Secretary of State so directs.

(2A) A prisoner serving a sentence of imprisonment to which an intermittent custody order relates shall be entitled to receive a visit only where the governor considers that desirable having regard to the extent to which he has been unable to meet with his friends and family in the periods during which he has been temporarily released on licence.

(3) The governor may allow a prisoner an additional letter or visit as a privilege under rule 8 or where necessary for his welfare or that of his family.

(4) The governor may allow a prisoner entitled to a visit to send and to receive a letter instead.

(5) The governor may defer the right of a prisoner to a visit until the expiration of any period of cellular confinement.

(6) The board of visitors may allow a prisoner an additional letter or visit in special circumstances, and may direct that a visit may extend beyond the normal duration.

(7) The Secretary of State may allow additional letters and visits in relation to any prisoner or class of prisoners.

(8) A prisoner shall not be entitled under this rule to receive a visit from:

(a) any person, whether or not a relative or friend, during any period of time that person is the subject of a prohibition imposed under rule 73; or

(b) any other person, other than a relative or friend, except with the leave of the Secretary of State.

(9) Any letter or visit under the succeeding provisions of these Rules shall not be counted as a letter or visit for the purposes of this rule.

Interception of communications

35A. - (1) The Secretary of State may give directions to any governor concerning the interception in a prison of any communication by any prisoner or class of prisoners if the Secretary of State considers that the directions are -

(a) necessary on grounds specified in paragraph (4) below; and

(b) proportionate to what is sought to be achieved.

(2) Subject to any directions given by the Secretary of State, the governor may make arrangements for any communication by a prisoner or class of prisoners to be intercepted in a prison by an officer or an employee of the prison authorised by the governor for the purposes of this rule (referred to in this rule as an "authorised employee") if he considers that the arrangements are -

(a) necessary on grounds specified in paragraph (4) below; and

(b) proportionate to what is sought to be achieved.

(3) Any communication by a prisoner may, during the course of its transmission in a prison, be terminated by an officer or an authorised employee if he considers that to terminate the communication is -

(a) necessary on grounds specified in paragraph (4) below; and
(b) proportionate to what is sought to be achieved by the termination.
(4) The grounds referred to in paragraphs (1)(a), (2)(a) and (3)(a) above are -
(a) the interests of national security;
(b) the prevention, detection, investigation or prosecution of crime;
(c) the interests of public safety;
(d) securing or maintaining prison security or good order and discipline in prison;
(e) the protection of health or morals; or
(f) the protection of the rights and freedoms of any person.
(5) Any reference to the grounds specified in paragraph (4) above in relation to the interception of a communication by means of a telecommunications system in a prison, or the disclosure or retention of intercepted material from such a communication, shall be taken to be a reference to those grounds with the omission of sub-paragraph (f).
(6) For the purposes of this rule "interception" -
(a) in relation to a communication by means of a telecommunications system, means any action taken in relation to the system or its operation so as to make some or all of the contents of the communications available, while being transmitted, to a person other than the sender or intended recipient of the communication; and the contents of a communication are to be taken to be made available to a person while being transmitted where the contents of the communication, while being transmitted, are diverted or recorded so as to be available to a person subsequently; and

(b) in relation to any written or drawn communication, includes opening, reading, examining and copying the communication.

Permanent log of communications

35B. - (1) The governor may arrange for a permanent log to be kept of all communications by or to a prisoner.

(2) The log referred to in paragraph (1) above may include, in relation to a communication by means of a telecommunications system in a prison, a record of the destination, duration and cost of the communication and, in relation to any written or drawn communication, a record of the sender and addressee of the communication.

Disclosure of material

35C. The governor may not disclose to any person who is not an officer of a prison or of the Secretary of State or an employee of the prison authorised by the governor for the purposes of this rule any intercepted material, information retained pursuant to rule 35B or material obtained by means of an overt closed circuit television system used during a visit unless -

(a) he considers that such disclosure is -

(i) necessary on grounds specified in rule 35A(4); and

(ii) proportionate to what is sought to be achieved by the disclosure; or

(b) (i) in the case of intercepted material or material obtained by means of an overt closed circuit television system used during a visit, all parties to the communication or visit consent to the disclosure; or

(ii) in the case of information retained pursuant to rule 35B, the prisoner to whose communication the information relates, consents to the disclosure.

Retention of material

35D. - (1) The governor shall not retain any intercepted material or material obtained by means of an overt closed circuit television system used during a visit for a period longer

than 3 months beginning with the day on which the material was intercepted or obtained unless he is satisfied that continued retention of it is -
(a) necessary on grounds specified in rule 35A(4); and
(b) proportionate to what is sought to be achieved by the continued retention.
(2) Where such material is retained for longer than 3 months pursuant to paragraph (1) above the governor shall review its continued retention at periodic intervals until such time as it is no longer held by the governor.
(3) The first review referred to in paragraph (2) above shall take place not more than 3 months after the decision to retain the material taken pursuant to paragraph (1) above, and subsequent reviews shall take place not more than 3 months apart thereafter.
(4) If the governor, on a review conducted pursuant to paragraph (2) above or at any other time, is not satisfied that the continued retention of the material satisfies the requirements set out in paragraph (1) above, he shall arrange for the material to be destroyed.

Police interviews

36. A police officer may, on production of an order issued by or on behalf of a chief officer of police, interview any prisoner willing to see him.

Securing release

37. A person detained in prison in default of finding a surety, or of payment of a sum of money, may communicate with and be visited at any reasonable time on a weekday by any relative or friend to arrange for a surety or payment in order to secure his release from prison.

Legal advisers

38. - (1) The legal adviser of a prisoner in any legal proceedings, civil or criminal, to which the prisoner is a party shall be afforded reasonable facilities for interviewing him in connection with those proceedings, and may do so out of hearing but in the sight of an officer.

(2) A prisoner's legal adviser may, subject to any directions given by the Secretary of State, interview the prisoner in connection with any other legal business out of hearing but in the sight of an officer.

Correspondence with legal advisers and courts

39. - (1) A prisoner may correspond with his legal adviser and any court and such correspondence may only be opened, read or stopped by the governor in accordance with the provisions of this rule.

(2) Correspondence to which this rule applies may be opened if the governor has reasonable cause to believe that it contains an illicit enclosure and any such enclosures shall be dealt with in accordance with the other provision of these Rules.

(3) Correspondence to which this rule applies may be opened, read and stopped if the governor has reasonable cause to believe its contents endanger prison security or the safety of others or are otherwise of a criminal nature.

(4) A prisoner shall be given the opportunity to be present when any correspondence to which this rule applies is opened and shall be informed if it or any enclosure is to be read or stopped.

(5) A prisoner shall on request be provided with any writing materials necessary for the purposes of paragraph (1).

(6) In this rule, "court" includes the European Commission of Human Rights, the European Court of Human Rights and the European Court of Justice; and "illicit enclosure" includes any article possession of which has not been authorised in accordance with the other provisions of these Rules and any

correspondence to or from a person other than the prisoner concerned, his legal adviser or a court.

REMOVAL, SEARCH, RECORD AND PROPERTY

Custody outside prison

40. - (1) A person being taken to or from a prison in custody shall be exposed as little as possible to public observation, and proper care shall be taken to protect him from curiosity and insult.

(2) A prisoner required to be taken in custody anywhere outside a prison shall be kept in the custody of an officer appointed or a police officer.

(3) A prisoner required to be taken in custody to any court shall, when he appears before the court, wear his own clothing or ordinary civilian clothing provided by the governor.

Search

41. - (1) Every prisoner shall be searched when taken into custody by an officer, on his reception into a prison and subsequently as the governor thinks necessary or as the Secretary of State may direct.

(2) A prisoner shall be searched in as seemly a manner as is consistent with discovering anything concealed.

(3) No prisoner shall be stripped and searched in the sight of another prisoner, or in the sight of a person of the opposite sex.

Record and photograph

42. - (1) A personal record of each prisoner shall be prepared and maintained in such manner as the Secretary of State may direct.

(2) Every prisoner may be photographed on reception and subsequently, but no copy of the photograph or any other

personal record shall be given to any person not authorised to receive it.

(2A) In this rule "personal record" may include personal information and biometric records (such as fingerprints or other physical measurements).

Prisoners' property

43. - (1) Subject to any directions of the Secretary of State, an unconvicted prisoner may have supplied to him at his expense and retain for his own use books, newspapers, writing materials and other means of occupation, except any that appears objectionable to the board of visitors or, pending consideration by them, to the governor.

(2) Anything, other than cash, which a prisoner has at a prison and which he is not allowed to retain for his own use shall be taken into the governor's custody. An inventory of a prisoner's property shall be kept, and he shall be required to sign it, after having a proper opportunity to see that it is correct.

(2A) Where a prisoner is serving a sentence of imprisonment to which an intermittent custody order relates, an inventory as referred to in paragraph (2) shall only be kept where the value of that property is estimated by the governor to be in excess of £100.

(3) Any cash which a prisoner has at a prison shall be paid into an account under the control of the governor and the prisoner shall be credited with the amount in the books of the prison.

(4) Any article belonging to a prisoner which remains unclaimed for a period of more than 3 years after he leaves prison, or dies, may be sold or otherwise disposed of; and the net proceeds of any sale shall be paid to the National Association for the Care and Resettlement of Offenders, for its general purposes.

(5) The governor may confiscate any unauthorised article found in the possession of a prisoner after his reception into prison, or concealed or deposited anywhere within a prison.

Money and articles received by post
44. - (1) Any money or other article (other than a letter or other communication) sent to a convicted prisoner through the post office shall be dealt with in accordance with the provisions of this rule, and the prisoner shall be informed of the manner in which it is dealt with.

(2) Any cash shall, at the discretion of the governor, be -
(a) dealt with in accordance with rule 43(3);
(b) returned to the sender; or
(c) in a case where the sender's name and address are not known, paid to the National Association for the Care and Resettlement of Offenders, for its general purposes:
Provided that in relation to a prisoner committed to prison in default of payment of any sum of money, the prisoner shall be informed of the receipt of the cash and, unless he objects to its being so applied, it shall be applied in or towards the satisfaction of the amount due from him.

(3) Any security for money shall, at the discretion of the governor, be -
(a) delivered to the prisoner or placed with his property at the prison;
(b) returned to the sender; or
(c) encashed and the cash dealt with in accordance with paragraph (2).

(4) Any other article to which this rule applies shall, at the discretion of the governor, be -
(a) delivered to the prisoner or placed with his property at the prison;
(b) returned to the sender; or
(c) in a case where the sender's name and address are not known or the article is of such a nature that it would be unreasonable

to return it, sold or otherwise disposed of, and the net proceeds of any sale applied in accordance with paragraph (2).

SPECIAL CONTROL, SUPERVISION AND RESTRAINT AND DRUG TESTING

Removal from association

45. - (1) Where it appears desirable, for the maintenance of good order or discipline or in his own interests, that a prisoner should not associate with other prisoners, either generally or for particular purposes, the governor may arrange for the prisoner's removal from association accordingly.

(2) A prisoner shall not be removed under this rule for a period of more than 3 days without the authority of a member of the board of visitors or of the Secretary of State. An authority given under this paragraph shall be for a period not exceeding one month, but may be renewed from month to month except that, in the case of a person aged less than 21 years who is detained in prison such an authority shall be for a period not exceeding 14 days, but may be renewed from time to time for a like period.

(3) The governor may arrange at his discretion for such a prisoner as aforesaid to resume association with other prisoners, and shall do so if in any case the medical officer or a medical practitioner such as is mentioned in rule 20(3) so advises on medical grounds.

(4) This rule shall not apply to a prisoner the subject of a direction given under rule 46(1).

Close supervision centres

46. - (1) Where it appears desirable, for the maintenance of good order or discipline or to ensure the safety of officers, prisoners or any other person, that a prisoner should not associate with other prisoners, either generally or for particular purposes, the Secretary of State may direct the prisoner's

removal from association accordingly and his placement in a close supervision centre of a prison.

(2) A direction given under paragraph (1) shall be for a period not exceeding one month, but may be renewed from time to time for a like period., and shall continue to apply notwithstanding any transfer of a prisoner from one prison to another.

(3) The Secretary of State may direct that such a prisoner as aforesaid shall resume association with other prisoners, either within a close supervision centre or elsewhere.

(4) In exercising any discretion under this rule, the Secretary of State shall take account of any relevant medical considerations which are known to him.

(5) A close supervision centre is any cell or other part of a prison designated by the Secretary of State for holding prisoners who are subject to a direction given under paragraph (1).

Use of force

47. - (1) An officer in dealing with a prisoner shall not use force unnecessarily and, when the application of force to a prisoner is necessary, no more force than is necessary shall be used.

(2) No officer shall act deliberately in a manner calculated to provoke a prisoner.

Temporary confinement

48. - (1) The governor may order a refractory or violent prisoner to be confined temporarily in a special cell, but a prisoner shall not be so confined as a punishment, or after he has ceased to be refractory or violent.

(2) A prisoner shall not be confined in a special cell for longer than 24 hours without a direction in writing given by a member of a board of visitors or by an officer of the Secretary of State (not being an officer of a prison). Such a direction shall

state the grounds for the confinement and the time during which it may continue.

Restraints

49. - (1) The governor may order a prisoner to be put under restraint where this is necessary to prevent the prisoner from injuring himself or others, damaging property or creating a disturbance.

(2) Notice of such an order shall be given without delay to a member of the board of visitors, and to the medical officer or to a medical practitioner such as is mentioned in rule 20(3).

(3) On receipt of the notice, the medical officer, or the medical practitioner referred to in paragraph (2), shall inform the governor whether there are any medical reasons why the prisoner should not be put under restraint. The governor shall give effect to any recommendation which may be made under this paragraph.

(4) A prisoner shall not be kept under restraint longer than necessary, nor shall he be so kept for longer than 24 hours without a direction in writing given by a member of the board of visitors or by an officer of the Secretary of State (not being an officer of a prison). Such a direction shall state the grounds for the restraint and the time during which it may continue.

(5) Particulars of every case of restraint under the foregoing provisions of this rule shall be forthwith recorded.

(6) Except as provided by this rule no prisoner shall be put under restraint otherwise than for safe custody during removal, or on medical grounds by direction of the medical officer or of a medical practitioner such as is mentioned in rule 20(3).

No prisoner shall be put under restraint as a punishment.

(7) Any means of restraint shall be of a pattern authorised by the Secretary of State, and shall be used in such manner and under such conditions as the Secretary of State may direct.

Compulsory testing for controlled drugs

50. - (1) This rule applies where an officer, acting under the powers conferred by section 16A of the Prison Act 1952 (power to test prisoners for drugs), requires a prisoner to provide a sample for the purpose of ascertaining whether he has any controlled drug in his body.

(2) In this rule "sample" means a sample of urine or any other description of sample specified in the authorisation by the governor for the purposes of section 16A of the Prison Act 1952.

(3) When requiring a prisoner to provide a sample, an officer shall, so far as is reasonably practicable, inform the prisoner:
(a) that he is being required to provide a sample in accordance with section 16A of the Prison Act 1952; and
(b) that a refusal to provide a sample may lead to disciplinary proceedings being brought against him.

(4) An officer shall require a prisoner to provide a fresh sample, free from any adulteration.

(5) An officer requiring a sample shall make such arrangements and give the prisoner such instructions for its provision as may be reasonably necessary in order to prevent or detect its adulteration or falsification.

(6) A prisoner who is required to provide a sample may be kept apart from other prisoners for a period not exceeding one hour to enable arrangements to be made for the provision of the sample.

(7) A prisoner who is unable to provide a sample of urine when required to do so may be kept apart from other prisoners until he has provided the required sample, save that a prisoner may not be kept apart under this paragraph for a period of more than 5 hours.

(8) A prisoner required to provide a sample of urine shall be afforded such degree of privacy for the purposes of providing the sample as may be compatible with the need to prevent

or detect any adulteration or falsification of the sample; in particular a prisoner shall not be required to provide such a sample in the sight of a person of the opposite sex.

Observation of prisoners by means of an overt closed circuit television system

50A. - (1) Without prejudice to his other powers to supervise the prison, prisoners and other persons in the prison, whether by use of an overt closed circuit television system or otherwise, the governor may make arrangements for any prisoner to be placed under constant observation by means of an overt closed circuit television system while the prisoner is in a cell or other place in the prison if he considers that -
(a) such supervision is necessary for -
(i) the health and safety of the prisoner or any other person;
(ii) the prevention, detection, investigation or prosecution of crime; or
(iii) securing or maintaining prison security or good order and discipline in the prison; and
(b) it is proportionate to what is sought to be achieved.
(2) If an overt closed circuit television system is used for the purposes of this rule, the provisions of rules 35C and 35D shall apply to any material obtained.

Compulsory testing for alcohol

50B. - (1) This rule applies where an officer, acting under an authorisation in
 force under section 16B of the Prison Act 1952 (power to test prisoners
 for alcohol), requires a prisoner to provide a sample for the purpose of
 ascertaining whether he has alcohol in his body.
(2) When requiring a prisoner to provide a sample an officer shall, so
 far as is reasonably practicable, inform the prisoner—

(a) that he is being required to provide a sample in accordance with
section 16B of the Prison Act 1952; and
(b) that a refusal to provide a sample may lead to disciplinary
proceedings being brought against him.
(3) An officer requiring a sample shall make such arrangements and give
the prisoner such instructions for its provision as may be reasonably
necessary in order to prevent or detect its adulteration or falsification.
(4) Subject to paragraph (5) a prisoner who is required to provide a
sample may be kept apart from other prisoners for a period not exceeding
one hour to enable arrangements to be made for the provision of the
sample.
(5) A prisoner who is unable to provide a sample of urine when required
to do so may be kept apart from other prisoners until he has provided the
required sample, except that a prisoner may not be kept apart under this
paragraph for a period of more than 5 hours.
(6) A prisoner required to provide a sample of urine shall be afforded
such degree of privacy for the purposes of providing the sample as may be
compatible with the need to prevent or detect any adulteration or
falsification of the sample; in particular a prisoner shall not be

required to provide such a sample in the sight of a person of the opposite
sex.".

OFFENCES AGAINST DISCIPLINE

Offences against discipline

51. A prisoner is guilty of an offence against discipline if he -

(1) commits any assault;

(1A) commits any racially aggravated assault;

(2) detains any person against his will;

(3) denies access to any part of the prison to any officer or any person (other than a prisoner) who is at the prison for the purpose of working there;

(4) fights with any person;

(5) intentionally endangers the health or personal safety of others or, by his conduct, is reckless whether such health or personal safety is endangered;

(6) intentionally obstructs an officer in the execution of his duty, or any person (other than a prisoner) who is at the prison for the purpose of working there, in the performance of his work;

(7) escapes or absconds from prison or from legal custody;

(8) fails to comply with any condition upon which he is temporarily released under rule 9;

(9) is found with any substance in his urine which demonstrates that a controlled drug has, whether in prison or while on temporary release under rule 9, been administered to him by himself or by another person (but subject to rule 52);

(10) is intoxicated as a consequence of consuming any alcoholic beverage (but subject to rule 52A);

(11) consumes any alcoholic beverage whether or not provided to him by another person (but subject to rule 52A);

(12) has in his possession -

(a) any unauthorised article, or

(b) a greater quantity of any article than he is authorised to have;

(13) sells or delivers to any person any unauthorised article;

(14) sells or, without permission, delivers to any person any article which he is allowed to have only for his own use;

(15) takes improperly any article belonging to another person or to a prison;

(16) intentionally or recklessly sets fire to any part of a prison or any other property, whether or not his own;

(17) destroys or damages any part of a prison or any other property, other than his own;

(17A) causes racially aggravated damage to, or destruction of, any part of a prison or any other property, other than his own;

(18) absents himself from any place he is required to be or is present at any place where he is not authorised to be;

(19) is disrespectful to any officer, or any person (other than a prisoner) who is at the prison for the purpose of working there, or any person visiting a prison;

(20) uses threatening, abusive or insulting words or behaviour;

(20A) uses threatening, abusive or insulting racist words or behaviour;

(21) intentionally fails to work properly or, being required to work, refuses to do so;

(22) disobeys any lawful order;

(23) disobeys or fails to comply with any rule or regulation applying to him;

(24) receives any controlled drug, or, without the consent of an officer, any other article, during the course of a visit (not being an interview such as is mentioned in rule 38);

(24A) displays, attaches or draws on any part of a prison, or on any other property, threatening, abusive or insulting racist words, drawings, symbols or other material;

(25)

(a) attempts to commit,

(b) incites another prisoner to commit, or

(c) assists another prisoner to commit or to attempt to commit, any of the foregoing offences.

51A. Interpretation of rule 51

(2) For the purposes of rule 51 words, behaviour or material are racist if they demonstrate, or are motivated (wholly or partly) by, hostility to members of a racial group (whether identifiable or not) based on their membership (or presumed membership) of a racial group, and "membership", "presumed", "racial group" and "racially aggravated" shall have the meanings assigned to them by section 28 of the Crime and Disorder Act 1998(a).

Defences to rule 51(9)

52. It shall be a defence for a prisoner charged with an offence under rule 51(9) to show that:

(a) the controlled drug had been, prior to its administration, lawfully in his possession for his use or was administered to him in the course of a lawful supply of the drug to him by another person;

(b) the controlled drug was administered by or to him in circumstances in which he did not know and had no reason to suspect that such a drug was being administered; or

(c) the controlled drug was administered by or to him under duress or to him without his consent in circumstances where it was not reasonable for him to have resisted.

Defences to rule 51(10) and rule 51(11)

52A. It shall be a defence for a prisoner charged with an offence under rule

51(10) or (11) to show that—

(a) the alcohol was consumed by him in circumstances in which he did not know and had no reason to suspect that he was consuming alcohol;

(b) the alcohol was consumed by him without his consent in circumstances where it was not reasonable for him to have resisted; or

(c) the alcohol was provided to him pursuant to a written order under rule 25(1).

Disciplinary charges

53. - (1) Where a prisoner is to be charged with an offence against discipline, the charge shall be laid as soon as possible and, save in exceptional circumstances, within 48 hours of the discovery of the offence.

(2) Every charge shall be inquired into by the governor or, as the case may be, the adjudicator.

(3) Every charge shall be first inquired into not later, save in exceptional circumstances or in accordance with rule 55A(5), than:

(a) where it is inquired into by the governor, the next day, not being a Sunday or public holiday, after it is laid;

(b) where it is referred to the adjudicator under rule 53A(2), 28 days after it is so referred.

(4) A prisoner who is to be charged with an offence against discipline may be kept apart from other prisoners pending the governor's first inquiry or determination under rule 53A.

Determination of mode of inquiry

53A - (1) Before inquiring into a charge the governor shall determine whether it is so serious that additional days should be awarded for the offence, if the prisoner is found guilty.

(2) Where the governor determines:

(a) that it is so serious, he shall:

(i) refer the charge to the adjudicator forthwith for him to inquire
    into it;
  (ii) refer any other charge arising out of the same incident to the
    adjudicator forthwith for him to inquire into it; and
  (iii) inform the prisoner who has been charged that he has done so;
 (b) that it is not so serious, he shall proceed to inquire into the
   charge.
  (3) If:
 (a) at any time during an inquiry into a charge by the governor; or
 (b) following such an inquiry, after the governor has found the prisoner
   guilty of an offence but before he has imposed a punishment for that
     offence,
   it appears to the governor that the charge is so serious that additional
     days should be awarded for the offence if (where sub-paragraph (a)
     applies) the prisoner is found guilty, the governor shall act in
       accordance with paragraph (2)(a)(i) to (iii) and the adjudicator shall
     first inquire into any charge referred to him under this paragraph not
     later than, save in exceptional circumstances, 28 days after the charge
       was referred.".

Rights of prisoners charged

ENGLISH PRISON LAW

54. - (1) Where a prisoner is charged with an offence against discipline, he shall be informed of the charge as soon as possible and, in any case, before the time when it is inquired into by the governor or, as the case may be, the adjudicator.

(2) At an inquiry into a charge against a prisoner he shall be given a full opportunity of hearing what is alleged against him and of presenting his own case.

(3) At an inquiry into a charge which has been referred to the adjudicator, the prisoner who has been charged shall be given the opportunity to be legally represented.

Governor's punishments

55. - (1) If he finds a prisoner guilty of an offence against discipline the governor may, subject to paragraph (2) and to rule 57, impose one or more of the following punishments:
(a) caution;
(b) forfeiture for a period not exceeding 42 days of any of the privileges under rule 8;
(c) exclusion from associated work for a period not exceeding 21 days;
(d) stoppage of or deduction from earnings for a period not exceeding 84 days;
(e) cellular confinement for a period not exceeding 21 days;
(f) [revoked by 2002 amd]
(g) in the case of a prisoner otherwise entitled to them, forfeiture for any period of the right, under rule 43(1), to have the articles there mentioned.
(h) removal from his wing or living unit for a period of 28 days.

(2) A caution shall not be combined with any other punishment for the same charge.

(3) If a prisoner is found guilty of more than one charge arising out of an incident, punishments under this rule may be ordered to run consecutively but, in the case of a punishment

of cellular confinement, the total period shall not exceed 21 days.

(4) In imposing a punishment under this rule, the governor shall take into account any guidelines that the Secretary of State may from time to time issue as to the level of punishment that should normally be imposed for a particular offence against discipline.

Adjudicator's punishments

55A. - (1) If he finds a prisoner guilty of an offence against discipline the adjudicator may, subject to paragraph (2) and to rule 57, impose one or more of the following punishments:
(a) any of the punishments mentioned in rule 55(1);
(b) in the case of a short-term prisoner or long-term prisoner, an award of additional days not exceeding 42 days.

(2) A caution shall not be combined with any other punishment for the same charge.

(3) If a prisoner is found guilty of more than one charge arising out of an incident, punishments under this rule may be ordered to run consecutively but, in the case of an award of additional days, the total period added shall not exceed 42 days and, in the case of a punishment of cellular confinement, the total period shall not exceed 21 days.

(4) This rule applies to a prisoner who has been charged with having committed an offence against discipline before the date on which the rule came into force, in the same way as it applies to a prisoner who has been charged with having committed an offence against discipline on or after that date, provided the charge is referred to the adjudicator no later than 60 days after that date.

(5) Rule 53(3) shall not apply to a charge where, by virtue of paragraph (4), this rule applies to the prisoner who has been charged..

Review of adjudicator's punishment

55B. - (1) A reviewer means a Senior District Judge (Chief Magistrate) approved
by the Lord Chancellor for the purposes of conducting a review under this rule or any deputy of such a judge as nominated by that judge.

(2) Where a punishment is imposed by an adjudicator under rule 55A(1), a
prisoner may, within 14 days of receipt of the punishment, request in writing that a reviewer conducts a review.

(3) The review must be commenced within 14 days of receipt of the request and must be conducted on the papers alone.

(4) The review must only be of the punishment imposed and must not be a review of the finding of guilt under rule 55A.

(5) On completion of the review, if it appears to the reviewer that the punishment imposed was manifestly unreasonable he may—

(a) reduce the number of any additional days awarded;

(b) for whatever punishment has been imposed by the adjudicator,
substitute another punishment which is, in his opinion, less severe; or

(c) quash the punishment entirely.

(6) A prisoner requesting a review shall serve any additional days
awarded under rule 55A(1)(b) unless and until they are reduced.".

Forfeiture of remission to be treated as an award of additional days

56. - (1) In this rule, "existing prisoner" and "existing licensee" have the meanings assigned to them by paragraph 8(1) of Schedule 12 to the Criminal Justice Act 1991.

(2) In relation to any existing prisoner or existing licensee who has forfeited any remission of his sentence, the provisions of Part II of the Criminal Justice Act 1991 shall apply as if he had been awarded such number of additional days as equals the numbers of days of remission which he has forfeited.

Offences committed by young persons

57. - (1) In the case of an offence against discipline committed by an inmate who was under the age of 21 when the offence was committed (other than an offender in relation to whom the Secretary of State has given a direction under section 13(1) of the Criminal Justice Act 1982[13] that he shall be treated as if he had been sentenced to imprisonment) rule 55 or, as the case may be, rule 55A shall have effect, but -

(a) the maximum period of forfeiture of privileges under rule 8 shall be 21 days;

(b) the maximum period of stoppage of or deduction from earnings shall be 42 days;

(c) the maximum period of cellular confinement shall be ten days.

(d) the maximum period of removal from his cell or living unit shall be 21 days.

(2) In the case of an inmate who has been sentenced to a term of youth custody or detention in a young offender institution, and by virtue of a direction of the Secretary of State under section 99 of the Powers of Criminal Courts (Sentencing) Act 2000, is treated as if he had been sentenced to imprisonment for that term, any punishment imposed on him for an offence against discipline before the said direction was given shall, if it has not been exhausted or remitted, continue to have effect:

(a) if imposed by a governor, as if made pursuant to rule 55;

(b) if imposed by an adjudicator, as if made pursuant to rule 55A".

Cellular confinement

58. When it is proposed to impose a punishment of cellular confinement, the medical officer, or a medical practitioner such as is mentioned in rule 20(3), shall inform the governor whether there are any medical reasons why the prisoner should not be so dealt with. The governor shall give effect to any recommendation which may be made under this rule.

Prospective award of additional days

59. - (1) Subject to paragraph (2), where an offence against discipline is committed by a prisoner who is detained only on remand, additional days may be awarded by the adjudicator notwithstanding that the prisoner has not (or had not at the time of the offence) been sentenced.

(2) An award of additional days under paragraph (1) shall have effect only if the prisoner in question subsequently becomes a short-term or long-term prisoner whose sentence is reduced, under section 67 of the Criminal Justice Act 1967[14], by a period which includes the time when the offence against discipline was committed.

Removal from a cell or living unit

59A. Following the imposition of a punishment of removal from his cell or living unit, a prisoner shall be accommodated in a separate part of the prison under such restrictions of earnings and activities as the Secretary of State may direct..

Suspended punishments

60. - (1) Subject to any directions given by the Secretary of
State, the power to impose a disciplinary punishment (other than a
caution) shall include power to direct that the punishment is not to
take effect unless, during a period specified in the direction (not

being more than six months from the date of the direction), the prisoner
 commits another offence against discipline and a direction is given

(2) Where a prisoner commits an offence against discipline during
the period specified the person
dealing with that offence may -
(a) direct that the suspended punishment shall take effect;
(b) reduce the period or amount of the suspended punishment and direct
that it shall take effect as so reduced;
(c) vary the original direction by substituting for the period specified
a period expiring not later than six months from the date of variation;
or
(d) give no direction with respect to the suspended punishment.

(3) Where an award of additional days has been suspended under paragraph (1) and a prisoner is charged with committing an offence against discipline during the period specified in a direction given under that paragraph, the governor shall either:
 (a) inquire into the charge and give no direction with respect to the
    suspended award; or
 (b) refer the charge to the adjudicator for him to inquire into it

Remission and mitigation of punishments and quashing of findings of
guilt

61. - (1) Except in the case of a finding of guilt made, or a punishment imposed,

by an adjudicator under rule 55A(1), the Secretary of State may quash any finding of guilt and may remit any punishment or mitigate it either by reducing it or by
substituting another award which is, in his opinion, less severe.

(2) Subject to any directions given by the Secretary of State, the governor may, on the grounds of good behaviour, remit or mitigate any punishment already imposed by an adjudicator, governor or the board of visitors.

PART III
OFFICERS OF PRISONS

General duty of officers
62. - (1) It shall be the duty of every officer to conform to
these Rules and the rules and regulations of the prison, to assist and
support the governor in their maintenance and to obey his lawful
instructions.

(2) An officer shall inform the governor promptly of any abuse or
impropriety which comes to his knowledge.

Gratuities forbidden
63. No officer shall receive any unauthorised fee, gratuity or
other consideration in connection with his office.

Search of officers

64. An officer shall submit himself to be searched in the prison if
the governor so directs. Any such search shall be conducted in as seemly

a manner as is consistent with discovering anything concealed.

Transactions with prisoners

65. - (1) No officer shall take part in any business or pecuniary
transaction with or on behalf of a prisoner without the leave of the
Secretary of State.

(2) No officer shall without authority bring in or take out, or
attempt to bring in or take out, or knowingly allow to be brought in or
taken out, to or for a prisoner, or deposit in any place with intent
that it shall come into the possession of a prisoner, any article whatsoever.

Contact with former prisoners

66. No officer shall, without the knowledge of the governor,
communicate with any person whom he knows to be a former prisoner or a
relative or friend of a prisoner or former prisoner.

Communications to the press

67. - (1) No officer shall make, directly or indirectly, any unauthorised communication to a representative of the press or any other
person concerning matters which have become known to him in the course
of his duty.

(2) No officer shall, without authority, publish any matter or make

any public pronouncement relating to the administration of any
institution to which the Prison Act 1952 applies or to any of its
inmates.

Code of discipline

68. The Secretary of State may approve a code of discipline to have
effect in relation to officers, or such classes of officers as it may
specify, setting out the offences against discipline, the awards which
may be made in respect of them and the procedure for dealing with
charges.

Emergencies

69. Where any constable or member of the armed forces of the Crown
is employed by reason of any emergency to assist the governor of a
prison by performing duties ordinarily performed by an officer of a
prison, any reference in Part II of these Rules to such an officer
(other than a governor) shall be construed as including a reference to a
constable or a member of the armed forces of the Crown so employed.

PART IV
PERSONS HAVING ACCESS TO A PRISON

Prohibited articles

70. No person shall, without authority, convey into or throw into
or deposit in a prison, or convey or throw out of a prison, or convey to
a prisoner, or deposit in any place with intent that it shall come into
the possession of a prisoner, any money, clothing, food, drink, tobacco,
letter, paper, book, tool, controlled drug, firearm, explosive, weapon
or other article whatever. Anything so conveyed, thrown or deposited may
be confiscated by the governor.

Control of persons and vehicles

71. - (1) Any person or vehicle entering or leaving a prison may be stopped,
examined and searched and in addition any such person may be photographed,
fingerprinted or required to submit to other physical measurement.

(1A) Any such search of a person shall be carried out in as seemly a manner as is consistent with discovering anything concealed about the person or their belongings.

(2) The governor may direct the removal from a prison of any person
who does not leave on being required to do so.

Viewing of prisons

72. - (1) No outside person shall be permitted to view a prison
unless authorised by statute or the Secretary of State.

(2) No person viewing the prison shall be permitted to take a

photograph, make a sketch or communicate with a prisoner unless
authorised by statute or the Secretary of State.

Visitors

73. - (1) Without prejudice to any other powers to prohibit or restrict entry to prisons, or his powers under rules 34 and 35, the Secretary of State may prohibit visits by a person to a prison or to a prisoner in a prison for such periods of time as he considers necessary if the Secretary of State considers that such a prohibition is -
(a) necessary on grounds specified in rule 35A(4); and
(b) is proportionate to what is sought to be achieved by the prohibition.

(2) Paragraph (1) shall not apply in relation to any visit to a
prison or prisoner by a member of the board of visitors of the prison,
or justice of the peace, or to prevent any visit by a legal adviser for
the purposes of an interview under rule 38 or visit allowed by the board
of visitors under rule 35(6).

PART V
BOARDS OF VISITORS

Disqualification for membership

74. Any person, directly or indirectly interested in any contract
for the supply of goods or services to a prison, shall not be a member
of the board of visitors for that prison and any member who becomes so
interested in such a contract shall vacate office as a member.

Board of visitors

75. - (1) A member of the board of visitors for a prison appointed
by the Secretary of State under section 6(2) of the Prison Act 1952
shall subject to paragraphs (3) and (4) hold office for three years, or
such lesser period as the Secretary of State may appoint.

(2) A member -
(a) appointed for the first time to the board of visitors for a particular prison; or
(b) reappointed to the board following a gap of a year or more in his
membership of it,
shall, during the period of 12 months following the date on which he is
so appointed or (as the case may be) reappointed, undertake such
training as may reasonably be required by the Secretary of State.

(3) The Secretary of State may terminate the appointment of a member
if he is satisfied that -
(a) he has failed satisfactorily to perform his duties;
(b) he has failed to undertake training he has been required to
undertake under paragraph (2), by the end of the period specified in
that paragraph;
(c) he is by reason of physical or mental illness, or for any other
reason, incapable of carrying out his duties;
(d) he has been convicted of such a criminal offence, or his conduct has

been such, that it is not in the Secretary of State's opinion fitting
that he should remain a member; or
(e) there is, or appears to be or could appear to be, any conflict of
interest between the member performing his duties as a member and any
interest of that member, whether personal, financial or otherwise.

(4) Where the Secretary of State:
(a) has reason to suspect that a member of the board of visitors for a
prison may have so conducted himself that his appointment may be liable
to be terminated under paragraph (3)(a) or (d); and
(b) is of the opinion that the suspected conduct is of such a serious
nature that the member cannot be permitted to continue to perform his
functions as a member of the board pending the completion of the
Secretary of State's investigations into the matter and any decision as
to whether the member's appointment should be terminated, he may suspend the member from office for such period or periods as he
may reasonably require in order to complete his investigations and
determine whether or not the appointment of the member should be so
terminated; and a member so suspended shall not, during the period of
his suspension, be regarded as being a member of the board, other than

for the purposes of this paragraph and paragraphs (1) and (3).

(5) A board shall have a chairman and a vice chairman who shall be
members of the board.

(6) The Secretary of State shall -
(a) upon the constitution of a board for the first time, appoint a
chairman and a vice chairman to hold office for a period not exceeding
twelve months;
(b) thereafter appoint, before the date of the first meeting of the
board in any year of office of the board, a chairman and vice chairman
for that year, having first consulted the board; and
(c) promptly fill, after first having consulted the board, any casual
vacancy in the office of chairman or vice chairman.

(7) The Secretary of State may terminate the appointment of a member
as chairman or vice chairman of the board if he is satisfied that the
member has -
(a) failed satisfactorily to perform his functions as chairman (or as
the case may be) vice chairman;
(b) has grossly misconducted himself while performing those functions.

Proceedings of boards

76. - (1) The board of visitors for a prison shall meet at the
prison once a month or, if they resolve for reasons specified in the

resolution that less frequent meetings are sufficient, not fewer than
eight times in twelve months.

(2) The board may fix a quorum of not fewer than three members for
proceedings.

(3) The board shall keep minutes of their proceedings.

(4) The proceedings of the board shall not be invalidated by any
vacancy in the membership or any defect in the appointment of a member.

General duties of boards

77. - (1) The board of visitors for a prison shall satisfy themselves as to the state of the prison premises, the administration of
the prison and the treatment of the prisoners.

(2) The board shall inquire into and report upon any matter into
which the Secretary of State asks them to inquire.

(3) The board shall direct the attention of the governor to any
matter which calls for his attention, and shall report to the Secretary
of State any matter which they consider it expedient to report.

(4) The board shall inform the Secretary of State immediately of any
abuse which comes to their knowledge.

(5) Before exercising any power under these Rules the board and any
member of the board shall consult the governor in relation to any matter
which may affect discipline.

Particular duties

78. - (1) The board of visitors for a prison and any member of the
board shall hear any complaint or request which a prisoner wishes to
make to them or him.

(2) The board shall arrange for the food of the prisoners to be
inspected by a member of the board at frequent intervals.

(3) The board shall inquire into any report made to them, whether or
not by a member of the board, that a prisoner's health, mental or
physical, is likely to be injuriously affected by any conditions of his
imprisonment.

Members visiting prisons

79. - (1) The members of the board of visitors for a prison shall
visit the prison frequently, and the board shall arrange a rota whereby
at least one of its members visits the prison between meetings of the
board.

(2) A member of the board shall have access at any time to every
part of the prison and to every prisoner, and he may interview any
prisoner out of the sight and hearing of officers.

(3) A member of the board shall have access to the records of the
prison.

Annual report

80. - (1) The board of visitors for a prison shall, in accordance with paragraphs (2) and (3) below, from time to time make a report to the Secretary of State concerning the state of the prison and its administration, including in it any advice and suggestions they consider appropriate.

(2) The board shall comply with any directions given to them from time to time by the Secretary of State as to the following matters:

(a) the period to be covered by a report under paragraph (1);

(b) the frequency with which such a report is to be made; and

(c) the length of time from the end of the period covered by such a report within which it is to be made;

either in respect of a particular report or generally; providing that no directions may be issued under this paragraph if they would have the effect of requiring a board to make or deliver a report less frequently than once in every 12 months.

(3) Subject to any directions given to them under paragraph (2), the board shall, under paragraph (1), make an annual report to the Secretary of State as soon as reasonably possible after 31st December each year, which shall cover the period of 12 months ending on that date or, in the

case of a board constituted for the first time during that period, such
part of that period during which the board has been in existence.

PART VI
SUPPLEMENTAL

Delegation by governor
81. The governor of a prison may, with the leave of the Secretary
of State, delegate any of his powers and duties under these Rules to
another officer of that prison.
Contracted out prisons
82. - (1) Where the Secretary of State has entered into a contract
for the running of a prison under section 84 of the Criminal Justice Act
1991 ("the 1991 Act") these Rules shall have effect in relation to
that prison with the following modifications -
(a) references to an officer in the Rules shall include references to a
prisoner custody officer certified as such under section 89(1) of the
1991 Act and performing custodial duties;
(b) references to a governor in the Rules shall include references to a
director approved by the Secretary of State for the purposes of section
85(1)(a) of the 1991 Act except -
(i) in rules 45, 48, 49, 53, 53A, 54, 55, 57, 60, 61 and 81 where references to a

governor shall include references to a controller appointed by the
Secretary of State under section 85(1)(b) of the 1991 Act, and
(ii) in rules 62(1), 66 and 77 where references to a governor shall
include references to the director and the controller;
 (c) rule 68 shall not apply in relation to a prisoner custody officer
certified as such under section 89(1) of the 1991 Act and performing
custodial duties.
   (2) Where a director exercises the powers set out in section 85(3)
(b) of the 1991 Act (removal from association, temporary confinement and
restraints) in cases of urgency, he shall notify the controller of that
fact forthwith.

Contracted out parts of prisons

   83. Where the Secretary of State has entered into a contract for
the running of part of a prison under section 84(1) of the Criminal
Justice Act 1991, that part and the remaining part shall each be treated
for the purposes of Parts II to IV and Part VI of these Rules as if they
were separate prisons.

Contracted out functions at directly managed prisons

   84. - (1) Where the Secretary of State has entered into a contract

under section 88A(1) of the Criminal Justice Act 1991 ("the 1991 Act")
for any functions at a directly managed prison to be performed by
prisoner custody officers who are authorised to perform custodial duties
under section 89(1) of the 1991 Act, references to an officer in these
Rules shall, subject to paragraph (2), include references to a prisoner
 custody officer who is so authorised and who is performing contracted
out functions for the purposes of, or for purposes connected with, the
prison.

(2) Paragraph (1) shall not apply to references to an officer in
rule 68.

(3) In this rule, "directly managed prison" has the meaning assigned
to it by section 88A(5) of the 1991 Act.

Revocations and savings

85. - (1) Subject to paragraphs (2) and (3) below, the Rules
specified in the Schedule to these Rules are hereby revoked.

(2) Without prejudice to the Interpretation Act 1978 where a
prisoner committed an offence against discipline contrary to rule 47 of
the Prison Rules 1964 prior to the coming into force of these Rules,
those rules shall continue to have effect to permit the prisoner to be

charged with such an offence, disciplinary proceedings in relation to
such an offence to be continued, and the governor to impose punishment
for such an offence.

(3) Without prejudice to the Interpretation Act 1978, any award of
additional days or other punishment or suspended punishment for an
offence against discipline awarded or imposed under any provision of the
rules revoked by this rule, or those rules as saved by paragraph (2), or
treated by any such provision as having been awarded or imposed under
the rules revoked by this rule, shall have effect as if awarded or
imposed under the corresponding provision of these Rules.

SCHEDULE
Rule 85
Rules Revoked
S.I. number The Prison Rules 1964/388
The Prison(Amendment) Rules 1968/440
The Prison (Amendment) Rules 1971/2019
The Prison (Amendment) Rules 1972/1860
The Prison (Amendment) Rules 1974/713
The Prison (Amendment) Rules 1976/503
The Prison (Amendment) Rules 1981/70
The Prison (Amendment) Rules 1982/260
The Prison (Amendment) Rules 1983/568
The Prison (Amendment) Rules 1987/1256
The Prison (Amendment) Rules 1988/89
The Prison (Amendment) (No. 2) Rules 1988/747
The Prison (Amendment) (No. 3) Rules 1988/1421

The Prison (Amendment) Rules 1989/330
The Prison (Amendment) (No. 2) Rules 1989/2141
The Prison (Amendment) Rules 1990/1762
The Prison (Amendment) Rules 1992/514
The Prison (Amendment) (No. 2) Rules 1992/2080
The Prison (Amendment) Rules 1993/516
The Prison (Amendment) (No. 2) Rules 1993/3075
The Prison (Amendment) Rules 1994/3195
The Prison (Amendment) Rules 1995/983
The Prison (Amendment) (No. 2) Rules 1995/1598
The Prison (Amendment) Rules 1996/1663
The Prison (Amendment) Rules 1998/23
The Prison (Amendment) (No. 2) Rules 1998/1544

EXPLANATORY NOTE
(This note is not part of the Rules)
These Rules make provision for the management of prisons, including the
treatment of prisoners, the conduct of prison officers and the powers
and duties of boards of visitors.
They revoke and replace the Prison Rules 1964 (S.I. 1964/388), as amended.
The provisions of the new Rules generally re-enact those of the previous
Rules, but certain modifications have been made to the latter.
The principal changes of substance are listed below.
Provision is made to provide for the possibility of distance learning in
rule 32 (Education).
In rule 34 (Communications) references to restrictions on telecommunications and visits have been added.
A search under rule 41(3) shall not take place in the sight of a person

of the opposite sex. Any confinement in a special cell which lasts
beyond 24 hours has to be authorised by a member of the board of
visitors (rule 48).
In rule 51 (Offences against discipline) a new offence of receiving an
article or controlled drugs during a visit has been added, and the
general offence of "in any way offends against good order and discipline" has been removed.
Rule 55 (Governor's punishments) has been changed so that a caution
shall not be combined with any other punishment and the total award of
cellular confinement shall not exceed 14 days, and the Secretary of
State has been given a power to issue guidelines for punishments.
Rule 73 (Visitors) adds powers to prohibit certain visitors.
Rules 74 and 75 (Boards of visitors) have been changed so as to amplify
the circumstances in which a person is prohibited from being a member of
a board of visitors and to give to the Secretary of State a discretion
to terminate the appointment of a board member with a conflict of
interest. In addition to these and other minor changes, certain
provisions from the Prison Rules 1964 are omitted as obsolete, for
example, the rules dealing with prisoners under sentence of death.

Appendix 3 - Prison Act 1952

1 General control over prisons
All powers and jurisdiction in relation to prisons and prisoners which before the commencement of the Prison Act 1877 were exercisable by any other authority shall, subject to the provisions of this Act, be exercisable by the Secretary of State. This section does not extend to Scotland.

2 Repealed by SI 1963/597.

3 Officers and servants of the Secretary of State
(1) The Secretary of State [may, for the purposes of this Act, appoint such officers and [employ such other persons] as he] may, with the sanction of the Treasury as to number, determine.
(2) There shall be paid out of moneys provided by Parliament to [the officers and servants appointed under this section] such salaries as the Secretary of State may with the consent of the Treasury determine. This section does not extend to Scotland.

4 General duties of the Secretary of State.
(1) The Secretary of State shall have the general superintendence of prisons and shall make the contracts and do the other acts

necessary for the maintenance of prisons and the maintenance of prisoners.

(2) Officers of the Secretary of State duly authorised in that behalf shall visit all prisons and examine the state of buildings, the conduct of officers, the treatment and conduct of prisoners and all other matters concerning the management of prisons and shall ensure that the provisions of this Act and of any rules made under this Act are duly complied with.

(3) The Secretary of State and his officers] may exercise all powers and jurisdiction exercisable at common law, by Act of Parliament, or by charter by visiting justices of a prison.

5 Annual report of the Secretary of State

(1)   The Secretary of State shall issue an annual report on every prison and shall lay every such report before Parliament.

(2)   The report shall contain--

(a)   a statement of the accommodation of each prison and the daily average and highest number of prisoners confined therein;

(b)   such particulars of the work done by prisoners in each prison, including the kind and quantities of articles produced and the number of prisoners employed, as may in the opinion of the Secretary of State give the best information to Parliament;

(c)   a statement of the punishments inflicted in each prison and of the offences for which they were inflicted . . .

This section does not extend to Scotland.

Amendment

Section heading: words in square brackets substituted by virtue of SI 1963/597, art 3(2), Sch 1.

Sub-s (1): substituted by SI 1963/597, art 3(2), Sch 1.

Sub-s (2): words omitted repealed by the Criminal Justice Act 1967, s 103(2), Sch 7, Part I.

5A Appointment and functions of Her Majesty's Chief Inspector of Prisons.

(1) Her Majesty may appoint a person to be Chief Inspector of Prisons.

(2) It shall be the duty of the Chief Inspector to inspect or arrange for the inspection of prisons in England and Wales and to report to the Secretary of State on them.

(3) The Chief Inspector shall in particular report to the Secretary of State on the treatment of prisoners and conditions in prisons.

(4) The Secretary of State may refer specific matters connected with prisons in England and Wales and prisoners in them to the Chief Inspector and direct him to report on them.

(5) The Chief Inspector shall in each year submit to the Secretary of State a report in such form as the Secretary of State may direct, and the Secretary of State shall lay a copy of that report before Parliament.

(5A) Subsections (2) to (5) shall apply--

(a) in relation to removal centres within the meaning of section 147 of the Immigration and Asylum Act 1999 (c 33),

(b) in relation to short-term holding facilities within the meaning of that section, and

(c) in relation to escort arrangements within the meaning of that section.

(5B) In their application by virtue of subsection (5A) subsections (2) to (5)--

(a) shall apply to centres, facilities and arrangements anywhere in the United Kingdom, and

(b) shall have effect--

(i) as if a reference to prisons were a reference to removal centres, short-term holding facilities and escort arrangements,

(ii) as if a reference to prisoners were a reference to detained persons and persons to whom escort arrangements apply, and

(iii) with any other necessary modifications.

(6) The Chief Inspector shall be paid such salary and allowances as the Secretary of State may with the consent of the Treasury determine.

(7) Schedule A1 to this Act (which makes further provision about the Chief Inspector) has effect.

This section does not extend to Scotland.

Amendment inserted by the Criminal Justice Act 1982, s 57.

Sub-ss (5A), (5B): substituted, for sub-s (5A) (as inserted by the Immigration and Asylum Act 1999, s 152(5)), by the Immigration, Asylum and Nationality Act 2006, s 46(1). Sub-s (7): inserted by the Police and Justice Act 2006, s 28(1).

Amendment

Cross-heading: substituted by virtue of the Offender Management Act 2007, s 26(1), (2)(a).

6 Independent monitoring boards

(1) ...

(2) The Secretary of State shall appoint for every prison ... a group of independent monitors

[(2A) The groups so appointed are to be known as independent monitoring boards.

(3) Rules made as aforesaid shall prescribe the functions of ... [independent monitoring boards] and shall among other things require members to pay frequent visits to the prison and hear any complaints which may be made by the prisoners and report to the Secretary of State any matter which they consider it expedient to report; and any member of ... an independent monitoring board may at any time enter the prison and shall have free access to every part of it and to every prisoner.

(4) ...

This section does not extend to Scotland.

Amendment

Section heading: substituted by the Offender Management Act 2007, s 26(1), (2)(a).

Sub-s (1): repealed by the Courts Act 1971, ss 53(3), 56(4), Sch 7, Pt II, para 4(1), Sch 11, Pt IV.

Sub-s (2): first words omitted repealed by the Courts Act 1971, ss 53(3), 56(4), Sch 7, Pt II, para 4(2), Sch 11, Pt IV.
Sub-s (2): words "group of independent monitors" in square brackets substituted by the Offender Management Act 2007, s 26(1), (2)(b).
Sub-s (2): final words omitted repealed by the Offender Management Act 2007, ss 26(3), 39, Sch 5, Pt 2.
Sub-s (2A): inserted by the Offender Management Act 2007, s 26(1), (2)(c).
Sub-s (3): words omitted repealed by the Courts Act 1971, ss 53(3), 56(4), Sch 7, Pt II, para 4(3), Sch 11, Pt IV.
Sub-s (3): words "independent monitoring boards" and "an independent monitoring board" in square brackets substituted by the Offender Management Act 2007, s 26(1), (2)(d).
Sub-s (4): repealed by the Courts Act 1971, ss 53(3), 56(4), Sch 7, Pt II, para 4(4), Sch 11, Pt IV.

Prison officers

7 Prison officers

(1) Every prison shall have a governor, a chaplain . . . and such other officers as may be necessary.

(2) Every prison in which women are received shall have a sufficient number of women officers; . . .

(3) A prison which in the opinion of the Secretary of State is large enough to require it may have a deputy governor or an assistant chaplain or both.

(4) The chaplain and any assistant chaplain shall be a clergyman of the Church of England . . ..

(5) . . .

This section does not apply to Scotland.

Amendment

Sub-s (1): words omitted repealed by Offender Management Act 2007, ss 25(1), 39, Sch 5, Pt 2.

Sub-s (2): words omitted repealed by the Sex Discrimination Act 1975, s 18(2).
Sub-s (4): words omitted repealed by the Offender Management Act 2007, s 39, Sch 5, Pt 2.
Sub-s (5): repealed by SI 1963/597, art 3(2), Sch 1.
Modification
Modified, in relation to contracted out prisons, by the Criminal Justice Act 1991, s 87.

8 Powers of prison officers
Every prison officer while acting as such shall have all the powers, authority, protection and privileges of a constable.
This section does not extend to Scotland.
Modification
Modified, in relation to contracted out prisons, by the Criminal Justice Act 1991, s 87.

8A Powers of search by authorised persons.
(1) An authorised [person] at a prison shall have the power to search any prisoner for the purpose of ascertaining whether he has any unauthorised property on his person.
(2) An authorised [person] searching a prisoner by virtue of this section--
(a) shall not be entitled to require a prisoner to remove any of his clothing other than an outer coat, jacket, headgear, gloves and footwear;
(b) may use reasonable force where necessary; and
(c) may seize and detain any unauthorised property found on the prisoner in the course of the search.
(3) In this section "[authorised person]" means [a person working at the prison,] of a description for the time being authorised by the governor to exercise the powers conferred by this section.
(4) The governor of a prison shall take such steps as he considers appropriate to notify to prisoners the descriptions of

persons who are for the time being authorised to exercise the powers conferred by this section.

(5) In this section "unauthorised property", in relation to a prisoner, means property which the prisoner is not authorised by prison rules or by the governor to have in his possession or, as the case may be, in his possession in a particular part of the prison.

This section does not extend to Scotland.

Amendment Inserted by the Criminal Justice and Public Order Act 1994, s 152(1).

Section heading: word "persons" in square brackets substituted by the Offender Management Act 2007, s 27(1), (2).

Sub-s (1): word "person" in square brackets substituted by the Offender Management Act 2007, s 27(1), (3).

Sub-s (2): word "person" in [] substituted by the Offender Management Act 2007, s 27(1), (3).

Sub-s (3): words "authorised person" in square brackets substituted by the Offender Management Act 2007, s 27(1), (4)(a).

Sub-s (3): words "a person working at the prison," in square brackets substituted by the Offender Management Act 2007, s 27(1), (4)(b).

Modification

Modified, in relation to contracted out prisons, by the Criminal Justice Act 1991, s 87.

9 Exercise of office of chaplain

(1) A person shall not officiate as chaplain of two prisons unless the prisons are within convenient distance of each other and are together designed to receive not more than one hundred prisoners.

(2) Notice of the nomination of a chaplain or assistant chaplain to a prison shall, within one month after it is made, be given to the bishop of the diocese in which the prison is situate; and the chaplain or assistant chaplain shall not officiate

in the prison except under the authority of a licence from the bishop.
Extent
This section does not extend to Scotland.

10 Appointment of prison ministers

(1) Where in any prison the number of prisoners who belong to a religious denomination other than the Church of England is such as in the opinion of the Secretary of State to require the appointment of a minister of that denomination, the Secretary of State may appoint such a minister to that prison.

(2) The Secretary of State may pay a minister appointed under the preceding subsection such remuneration as he thinks reasonable.

(3) The Secretary of State may allow a minister of any denomination other than the Church of England to visit prisoners of his denomination in a prison to which no minister of that denomination has been appointed under this section.

(4) No prisoner shall be visited against his will by such a minister as is mentioned in the last preceding subsection; but every prisoner not belonging to the Church of England shall be allowed, in accordance with the arrangements in force in the prison in which he is confined, to attend chapel or to be visited by the chaplain.

(5) The governor of a prison shall on the reception of each prisoner record the religious denomination to which the prisoner declares himself to belong, and shall give to any minister who under this section is appointed to the prison or permitted to visit prisoners therein a list of the prisoners who have declared themselves to belong to his denomination; and the minister shall not be permitted to visit any other prisoners.

This section does not extend to Scotland.
Amendment

Sub-s (3): words in square brackets substituted by SI 1963/597, art 3(2), Sch 1.

Modification
Modified, in relation to contracted out prisons, by the Criminal Justice Act 1991, s 87.

11 Ejectment of prison officers and their families refusing to quit

(1) Where any living accommodation is provided for a prison officer or his family by virtue of his office, then, if he ceases to be a prison officer or is suspended from office or dies, he, or, as the case may be, his family, shall quit the accommodation when required to do so by notice of the Secretary of State.

(2) Where a prison officer or the family of a prison officer refuses or neglects to quit the accommodation forty-eight hours after the giving of such a notice as aforesaid, any two justices of the peace, on proof made to them of the facts authorising the giving of the notice and of the service of the notice and of the neglect or refusal to comply therewith, may, by warrant under their hands and seals, direct any constable, within a period specified in the warrant, to enter by force, if necessary, into the accommodation and deliver possession of it to a person acting on behalf of the Secretary of State.

This section does not extend to Scotland.

Amendment
Sub-ss (1), (2): words in square brackets substituted by SI 1963/597, art 3(2), Sch 1.

Modification
Modified, in relation to contracted out prisons, by the Criminal Justice Act 1991, s 87.

Confinement and treatment of prisoners

12 Place of confinement of prisoners

(1) A prisoner, whether sentenced to imprisonment or committed to prison on remand or pending trial or otherwise, may be lawfully confined in any prison.
(2) Prisoners shall be committed to such prisons as the Secretary of State may from time to time direct; and may by direction of the Secretary of State be removed during the term of their imprisonment from the prison in which they are confined to any other prison.
(3) A writ, warrant or other legal instrument addressed to the governor of a prison and identifying that prison by its situation or by any other sufficient description shall not be invalidated by reason only that the prison is usually known by a different description.
This section does not extend to Scotland.
Modification
Modified, in relation to contracted out prisons, by the Criminal Justice Act 1991, s 87.

13 Legal custody of prisoner

(1) Every prisoner shall be deemed to be in the legal custody of the governor of the prison.
(2) A prisoner shall be deemed to be in legal custody while he is confined in, or is being taken to or from, any prison and while he is working, or is for any other reason, outside the prison in the custody or under the control of an officer of the prison [and while he is being taken to any place to which he is required or authorised by or under this Act [or *section 95, 98, 99 or 108(5) of the Powers of Criminal Courts (Sentencing) Act 2000* section 99 of the Powers of Criminal Courts (Sentencing) Act 2000 or section 61 of the Criminal Justice and Court Services Act 2000 to be taken, or is kept in custody in pursuance of any such requirement or authorisation.
This section does not extend to Scotland.
Amendment

Sub-s (2): words from "and while he is being taken" to "such requirement or authorisation" in square brackets inserted by the Criminal Justice Act 1961, s 41(1), Sch 4.

Sub-s (2): words "or section 95, 98, 99 or 108(5) of the Powers of Criminal Courts (Sentencing) Act 2000" in square brackets substituted by the Powers of Criminal Courts (Sentencing) Act 2000, s 165(1), Sch 9, para 4.

Sub-s (2): words "section 95, 98, 99 or 108(5) of the Powers of Criminal Courts (Sentencing) Act 2000" in italics repealed and subsequent words in square brackets substituted by the Criminal Justice and Court Services Act 2000, s 74, Sch 7, Pt II, paras 7, 8.

Modification

Modified, in relation to contracted out prisons, by the Criminal Justice Act 1991, s 87.

Modified, in relation to contracted out functions at directly managed prisons, by the Criminal Justice Act 1991, s 88A.

Modified, in relation to contracted out functions at directly managed secure training centres, by the Criminal Justice and Public Order Act 1994, s 11(3).

14 Cells

(1) The Secretary of State shall satisfy himself from time to time that in every prison sufficient accommodation is provided for all prisoners.

(2) No cell shall be used for the confinement of a prisoner unless it is certified by an inspector that its size, lighting, heating, ventilation and fittings are adequate for health and that it allows the prisoner to communicate at any time with a prison officer.

(3) A certificate given under this section in respect of any cell may limit the period for which a prisoner may be separately confined in the cell and the number of hours a day during which a prisoner may be employed therein.

(4) The certificate shall identify the cell to which it relates by a number or mark and the cell shall be marked by that number or mark placed in a conspicuous position; and if the number or mark is changed without the consent of an inspector the certificate shall cease to have effect.
(5) An inspector may withdraw a certificate given under this section in respect of any cell if in his opinion the conditions of the cell are no longer as stated in the certificate.
(6) In every prison special cells shall be provided for the temporary confinement of refractory or violent prisoners.
This section does not extend to Scotland.
Modification
Modified, in relation to contracted out prisons, by the Criminal Justice Act 1991, s 87.
Modified, in relation to contracted out functions at directly managed prisons, by the Criminal Justice Act 1991, s 88A.
Modification: references to an inspector to be construed as references to an officer (not being an officer of the prison) acting on behalf of the Secretary of State, by virtue of the Prison Commissioners Dissolution Order 1963, SI 1963/597, art 3(2), Sch 1.
Amendment Repealed by the Criminal Justice Act 1967, ss 66(2), 103(2), Sch 7, Pt I.

15. repealed.

16 Photographing and measuring of prisoners

The Secretary of State may make regulations as to the measuring and photographing of prisoners and such regulations may prescribe the time or times at which and the manner and dress in which prisoners shall be measured and photographed and the number of copies of the measurements and photographs of each prisoner which shall be made and the persons to whom they shall be sent.
This section does not extend to Scotland.

Subordinate Legislation

Regulations for the Measuring and Photographing of Criminal Prisoners 1896, SI 1896/762.

Regulation for the Measuring and Photographing of Prisoners 1906, SI 1906/160.

Regulation regarding the Measuring and Photographing of Prisoners (1913), SI 1913/987.

16A Testing prisoners for drugs

(1) If an authorisation is in force for the prison, any prison officer may, at the prison, in accordance with prison rules, require any prisoner who is confined in the prison to provide a sample of urine for the purpose of ascertaining whether he has any drug in his body.

(2) If the authorisation so provides, the power conferred by subsection (1) above shall include power to require a prisoner to provide a sample of any other description specified in the authorisation, not being an intimate sample, whether instead of or in addition to a sample of urine.

(3) In this section--

"authorisation" means an authorisation by the governor;

"drug" means any drug which is a controlled drug for the purposes of the Misuse of Drugs Act 1971;

"intimate sample" has the same meaning as in Part V of the Police and Criminal Evidence Act 1984;

"prison officer" includes a prisoner custody officer within the meaning of Part IV of the Criminal Justice Act 1991; and

"prison rules" means rules under section 47 of this Act.

This section does not extend to Scotland.

Amendment

Inserted by the Criminal Justice and Public Order Act 1994, s 151(1).

Modification

Modified, in relation to contracted out prisons, by the Criminal Justice Act 1991, s 87.

16B Power to test prisoners for alcohol.
(1) If an authorisation is in force for the prison, any prison officer may, at the prison, in accordance with prison rules, require any prisoner who is confined in the prison to provide a sample of breath for the purpose of ascertaining whether he has alcohol in his body.
(2) If the authorisation so provides, the power conferred by subsection (1) above shall include power--
(a) to require a prisoner to provide a sample of urine, whether instead of or in addition to a sample of breath, and
(b) to require a prisoner to provide a sample of any other description specified in the authorisation, not being an intimate sample, whether instead of or in addition to a sample of breath, a sample of urine or both.
(3) In this section--
"authorisation" means an authorisation by the governor;
"intimate sample" has the same meaning as in Part V of PACE 1984;
"prison officer" includes a prisoner custody officer within the meaning of Part IV of the Criminal Justice Act 1991;
"prison rules" means rules under section 47 of this Act.
This section does not extend to Scotland.
Amendment Inserted by the Prisons (Alcohol Testing) Act 1997, s 1.
Amendment Repealed by the Offender Management Act 2007, ss 25(3), 39, Sch 5, Pt 2.
Amendment Repealed by the Criminal Justice Act 1967, ss 66(2), 103(2), Sch 7, Pt I.

17. repealed.

18. repealed.

19 Right of justice to visit prison

(1) A justice of the peace [assigned to any local justice area] . . . may at any time visit any prison in that [area] . . . and any prison in which a prisoner is confined in respect of an offence committed in that area . . . , and may examine the condition of the prison and of the prisoners and enter in the visitors' book, to be kept by the governor of the prison, any observations on the condition of the prison or any abuses.

(2) Nothing in the preceding subsection shall authorise a justice of the peace to communicate with any prisoner except on the subject of his treatment in the prison. . ..

(3) The governor of every prison shall bring any entry in the visitors' book to the attention of the [independent monitoring board] at their next visit.

This section does not extend to Scotland.

Amendment

Sub-s (1): words "assigned to any local justice area" in square brackets substituted by the Courts Act 2003, s 109(1), Sch 8, para 94(1), (2).

Sub-s (1): words omitted repealed by the Local Government Act 1972, s 272(1), Sch 30.

Sub-s (1): word "area" in square brackets in both places it occurs substituted by the Access to Justice Act 1999, s 76(2), Sch 10, para 21(b).

Sub-s (2): words omitted repealed by the Courts Act 2003, s 109(1), (3), Sch 8, para 94(1), (3), Sch 10.

Sub-s (3): words "independent monitoring board" in square brackets substituted by the Offender Management Act 2007, s 39, Sch 3, Pt 2, para 6.

Modification

Modified, in relation to contracted out prisons, by the Criminal Justice Act 1991, s 87.

20 ...

Amendment Repealed by the Courts Act 1971, s 56, Sch 11, Pt IV.

21 Expenses of conveyance to prison

A prisoner shall not in any case be liable to pay the cost of his conveyance to prison.

This section does not extend to Scotland.

See Further

This section does not apply in relation to the conveyance to prison at the end of any licence period of an offender to whom an intermittent custody order relates: see the Criminal Justice Act 2003, s 186(1).

22 Removal of prisoners for judicial and other purposes

(1) Rules made under section forty-seven of this Act may provide in what manner an appellant within the meaning of [Part I of the Criminal Appeal Act 1968], when in custody, is to be taken to, kept in custody at, and brought back from, any place at which he is entitled to be present for the purposes of that Act, or any place to which the Court of Criminal Appeal or any judge thereof may order him to be taken for the purpose of any proceedings of that court.

(2) The Secretary of State may--

(a) ...repealed.

(b) if he is satisfied that a person so detained requires [medical investigation or observation or medical or surgical treatment of any description, direct him to be taken to a hospital or other suitable place for the purpose of the [investigation, observation or treatment;

and where any person is directed under this subsection to be taken to any place he shall, unless the Secretary of State otherwise directs, be kept in custody while being so taken, while at that place, and while being taken back to the prison in which he is required in accordance with law to be detained.

This section does not extend to Scotland.

Amendment

Sub-s (1): words in square brackets substituted by the Criminal Appeal Act 1968, s 52, Sch 5, Part I.
Sub-s (2): para (a) repealed by the Criminal Justice Act 1961, s 41(2), Sch 5; in para (b) words in square brackets inserted by the Criminal Justice Act 1982, s 77, Sch 14, para 5.
Modification
Modification: references to the Court of Criminal Appeal to be construed as a reference to the criminal division of the Court of Appeal, by virtue of the Supreme Court Act 1981, s 151(4), Sch 4, para 3.

23 Power of constable etc to act outside his jurisdiction

For the purpose of taking a person to or from any prison under the order of any authority competent to give the order a constable or other officer may act outside the area of his jurisdiction and shall notwithstanding that he is so acting have all the powers, authority, protection and privileges of his office.
This section does not extend to Scotland.

Length of sentence, release on licence and temporary discharge

24 Calculation of term of sentence

(1)   In any sentence of imprisonment the word "month" shall, unless the contrary is expressed, be construed as meaning calendar month.
(2)   . . .
This section does not extend to Scotland.
Amendment
Sub-s (2): repealed by the Criminal Justice Act 1961, s 41(2), Sch 5.
See further: in relation to the disapplication of this section in relation to a person detained in England and Wales in pursuance of a sentence of the International Criminal Court:

see the International Criminal Court Act 2001, s 42(6), Sch 7, paras 1, 2(1)(a).
Amendment
Repealed in part by the Criminal Justice Act 1967, s 103(2), Sch 7, Pt I; remainder repealed by the Criminal Justice Act 1991, s 101(2), Sch 13.

25. repealed.

26 ...
Amendment
Repealed by the Criminal Justice Act 1967, s 103(2), Sch 7, Pt I.

27 ...
Repealed by the Criminal Justice Act 1967, s 103(2), Sch 7, Pt I.

28 Power of Secretary of State to discharge prisoners temporarily on account of ill health

(1) If the Secretary of State is satisfied that by reason of the condition of a prisoner's health it is undesirable to detain him in prison, but that, such condition of health being due in whole or in part to the prisoner's own conduct in prison, it is desirable that his release should be temporary and conditional only, the Secretary of State may, if he thinks fit, having regard to all the circumstances of the case, by order authorise the temporary discharge of the prisoner for such period and subject to such conditions as may be stated in the order.

(2) Where an order of temporary discharge is made in the case of a prisoner not under sentence, the order shall contain conditions requiring the attendance of the prisoner at any further proceedings on his case at which his presence may be required.

(3) Any prisoner discharged under this section shall comply with any conditions stated in the order of temporary discharge, and shall return to prison at the expiration of the period stated in the order, or of such extended period as may be fixed by any subsequent order of the Secretary of State, and if the prisoner fails so to comply or return, he may be arrested without warrant and taken back to prison.

(4) Where a prisoner under sentence is discharged in pursuance of an order of temporary discharge, the currency of the sentence shall be suspended from the day on which he is discharged from prison under the order to the day on which he is received back into prison, so that the former day shall be reckoned and the latter shall not be reckoned as part of the sentence.

(5) ...

This section does not extend to Scotland.

Amendment

Sub-s (5): repealed by the Offender Management Act 2007, ss 25(3), 39, Sch 5, Pt 2.

See Further

See further: in relation to the disapplication of this section in relation to a person detained in England and Wales in pursuance of a sentence of the International Criminal Court: see the International Criminal Court Act 2001, s 42(6), Sch 7, paras 1, 3(1).

Discharged prisoners
29 ...

Amendment

Repealed by the Criminal Justice Act 1961, ss 21, 41(2), Sch 5.

30 Payments for discharged prisoners

The Secretary of State may make such payments to or in respect of persons released or about to be released from prison as he may with the consent of the Treasury determine.

This section does not extend to Scotland.

Amendment

Substituted for existing ss 30-32 by the Criminal Justice Act 1967, s 66(3).

31 ...

Amendment

Substituted, together with original ss 30, 32, by new s 30, by the Criminal Justice Act 1967, s 66(3).

32 ...

Amendment

Substituted, together with original ss 30, 31, by new s 30, by the Criminal Justice Act 1967, s 66(3).

Provision, maintenance and closing of prisons

33 Power to provide prisons, etc

(1)   The Secretary of State may with the approval of the Treasury alter, enlarge or rebuild any prison and build new prisons.

(2)   The Secretary of State may provide new prisons by declaring to be a prison--

(a)   any building or part of a building built for the purpose or vested in him or under his control; or

(b)   any floating structure or part of such a structure constructed for the purpose or vested in him or under his control.

(3)   A declaration under this section may with respect to the building or part of a building declared to be a prison make the same provisions as an order under the next following section may make with respect to an existing prison.

(4) A declaration under this section may at any time be revoked by the Secretary of State.

(5) A declaration under this section shall not be sufficient to vest the legal estate of any building in the [Secretary of State]. This section does not extend to Scotland.

Amendment

Sub-s (5): words in square brackets substituted by SI 1963/597, art 3(2), Sch 1.

Sub-s (2): substituted by the Criminal Justice and Public Order Act 1994, s 100(1).

Modification

Modification: sub-s (2) modified, in relation to contracted out prisons, by the Criminal Justice and Public Order Act 1994, s 100(2), (3).

Subordinate Legislation

Declaration of the Home Secretary, dated 30 July 1887, constituting

the New Prison Buildings at Norwich a Prison under the Prison Act 1865 and the Prison Act 1877.

Declaration of the Secretary of State, dated 1 October 1890, constituting

Wormwood Scrubs Prison a Prison under the Prison Act 1865 and the Prison Act 1887.

UK Parliament Acts/P/PO-PT/Prison Act 1952 (1952 c 52)/34 Jurisdiction of sheriff, etc

34 Jurisdiction of sheriff, etc

(1) The transfer under the Prison Act 1877 of prisons and of the powers and jurisdiction of prison authorities and of justices in sessions assembled and visiting justices shall not be deemed to have affected the jurisdiction of any sheriff or coroner or, except to the extent of that transfer, of any justice of the peace or other officer.

(2) The Secretary of State may by order direct that, for the purpose of any enactment, rule of law or custom dependent

on a prison being the prison of any county or place, any prison situated in that county or in the county in which that place is situated, or any prison provided by him in pursuance of this Act, shall be deemed to be the prison of that county or place. This section does not extend to Scotland.

35 Prison property

(1) Every prison and all real and personal property belonging to a prison shall be vested in the Secretary of State for Justice and may be disposed of in such manner as the Secretary of State [for Justice, with the consent of the Treasury, may determine.
(2) . . .repealed.
(3) . . .repealed.
(4) . . .repealed.
This section does not extend to Scotland.
Amendment
Substituted by SI 1963/597, art 3(2), Sch 1.
Sub-s (1): words "for Justice" in square brackets in both places they occur inserted by SI 2007/2128, art 8, Schedule, Pt 1, para 2(1), (2).
Sub-ss (2)-(4): repealed by SI 2007/2128, art 8, Schedule, Pt 1, para 2(1), (3).
See further, in relation to contracted out prisons: the Criminal Justice Act 1991, s 87 and the Criminal Justice and Public Order Act 1994, s 100(2), (4).

36 Acquisition of land for prisons

(1) The Secretary of State may purchase by agreement or] compulsorily, any land required for the alteration, enlargement or rebuilding of a prison or for establishing a new prison or for any other purpose connected with the management of a prison (including the provision of accommodation for officers or servants employed in a prison).

(2) The Acquisition of Land Act 1981 shall apply to the compulsory purchase of land by the Secretary of State under this section . . .

(3) In relation to the purchase of land by agreement under this section, [the provisions of Part I of the Compulsory Purchase Act 1965 (so far as applicable) other than sections 4 to 8, section 10, and section 31, shall apply.

This section does not extend to Scotland.

Amendment

Sub-s (1): words in square brackets substituted by SI 1963/597, art 3(2), Sch 1.

Sub-s (2): substituted by SI 1963/597, art 3(2), Sch 1; words in square brackets substituted, and words omitted repealed, by the Acquisition of Land Act 1981, s 34, Sch 4, para 1, Sch 6, Part I.

Sub-s (3): words in[] substituted by the Compulsory Purchase Act 1965, s 38, Sch 6.

See further: the Criminal Justice Act 1988, s 167.

37 Closing of prisons

(1) Subject to the next following subsection, the Secretary of State may by order close any prison.

(2) Where a prison is the only prison in the county, the Secretary of State shall not make an order under this section in respect of it except for special reasons, which shall be stated in the order.

(3) In this section the expression "county" means a county at large.

(4) For the purposes of this and the next following section a prison shall not be deemed to be closed by reason only of its appropriation for use as a *remand centre*, [or young offender institution or secure training centre..

This section does not extend to Scotland.

Amendment

Sub-s (4): words "remand centre" in italics repealed by the Criminal Justice and Court Services Act 2000, ss 74, 75, Sch 7, Pt II, paras 7, 9, Sch 8.

Sub-s (4): words "or young offender institution" in square brackets substituted by virtue of the Criminal Justice Act 1988, s 123, Sch 8, para 1.

Sub-s (4): words "or secure training centre" in square brackets inserted by the Criminal Justice and Public Order Act 1994, s 168(2), Sch 10, para 8.

Subordinate Legislation

Closure of Prisons (HM Prison Northeye) Order 1992, SI 1992/2250.

Closure of Prisons (HM Young Offender Institution Lowdham Grange) Order 1992, SI 1992/2867.

Closure of Prisons (H M Young Offender Institution Campsfield House) Order 1993, SI 1993/2104.

Closure of Prisons (HM Young Offender Institution Finnamore Wood) Order 1996, SI 1996/1551.

Closure of Prisons (HM Prison Oxford) Order 1996, SI 1996/2126.

Closure of Prisons (HM Prison Haslar) Order 2002, SI 2002/77.

Closure of Prisons (HM Young Offender Institution Dover) Order 2002, SI 2002/78.

Amendment Repealed with a saving by the Criminal Justice Act 1972, ss 59, 64(2), Sch 6, Pt II.

38 repealed.

Offences

39 Assisting a prisoner to escape
(1)   A person who--
(a)   assists a prisoner in escaping or attempting to escape from a prison, or

(b) intending to facilitate the escape of a prisoner--
(i) brings, throws or otherwise conveys anything into a prison,
(ii) causes another person to bring, throw or otherwise convey anything into a prison, or
(iii) gives anything to a prisoner or leaves anything in any place (whether inside or outside a prison), is guilty of an offence.
(2) A person guilty of an offence under this section is liable on conviction on indictment to imprisonment for a term not exceeding ten years.
This section does not extend to Scotland.
Amendment Substituted by the Offender Management Act 2007, s 21.

40A Sections 40B and 40C: classification of articles.

(1) This section defines the categories of articles which are referred to in sections 40B and 40C.
(2) A List A article is any article or substance in the following list ("List A")--
(a) a controlled drug (as defined for the purposes of the Misuse of Drugs Act 1971);
(b) an explosive;
(c) any firearm or ammunition (as defined in section 57 of the Firearms Act 1968);
(d) any other offensive weapon (as defined in section 1(9) of the Police and Criminal Evidence Act 1984).
(3) A List B article is any article or substance in the following list ("List B")--
(a) alcohol (as defined for the purposes of the Licensing Act 2003);
(b) a mobile telephone;
(c) a camera;
(d) a sound-recording device.
(4) In List B--

"camera" includes any device by means of which a photograph (as defined in section 40E) can be produced;

"sound-recording device" includes any device by means of which a sound-recording (as defined in section 40E) can be made.

(5) The reference in paragraph (b), (c) or (d) of List B to a device of any description includes a reference to--

(a) a component part of a device of that description; or

(b) an article designed or adapted for use with a device of that description (including any disk, film or other separate article on which images, sounds or information may be recorded).

(6) A List C article is any article or substance prescribed for the purposes of this subsection by prison rules.

(7) The Secretary of State may by order amend this section for the purpose of--

(a) adding an entry to List A or List B;

(b) repealing or modifying any entry for the time being included in List A or List B;

(c) adding, repealing or modifying any provision for the interpretation of any such entry.

This section does not extend to Scotland.

Amendment

Substituted, together with ss 40B, 40C, for s 40 as originally enacted, by the Offender Management Act 2007, s 22(1).

40B Conveyance etc of List A articles into or out of prison

(1) A person who, without authorisation--

(a) brings, throws or otherwise conveys a List A article into or out of a prison,

(b) causes another person to bring, throw or otherwise convey a List A article into or out of a prison,

(c) leaves a List A article in any place (whether inside or outside a prison) intending it to come into the possession of a prisoner, or

(d) knowing a person to be a prisoner, gives a List A article to him,
is guilty of an offence.

(2) In this section "authorisation" means authorisation given for the purposes of this section--

(a) in relation to all prisons or prisons of a specified description, by prison rules or by the Secretary of State; or

(b) in relation to a particular prison, by the Secretary of State or by the governor or director of the prison.

In paragraph (a) "specified" means specified in the authorisation.

(3) Authorisation may be given to specified persons or persons of a specified description--

(a) in relation to specified articles or articles of a specified description;

(b) in relation to specified acts or acts of a specified description; or

(c) on such other terms as may be specified.

In this subsection "specified" means specified in the authorisation.

(4) Authorisation given by the Secretary of State otherwise than in writing shall be recorded in writing as soon as is reasonably practicable after being given.

(5) Authorisation given by the governor or director of a prison shall--

(a) be given in writing; and

(b) specify the purpose for which it is given.

(6) A person guilty of an offence under this section is liable on conviction on indictment to imprisonment for a term not exceeding ten years or to a fine (or both).]

This section does not extend to Scotland: see s 55(4).

Amendment

Substituted, together with ss 40A, 40C, for s 40 as originally enacted, by the Offender Management Act 2007, s 22(1).

40C Conveyance etc of List B or C articles into or out of prison

(1) A person who, without authorisation--

(a) brings, throws or otherwise conveys a List B article into or out of a prison,

(b) causes another person to bring, throw or otherwise convey a List B article into or out of a prison,

(c) leaves a List B article in any place (whether inside or outside a prison) intending it to come into the possession of a prisoner, or

(d) knowing a person to be a prisoner, gives a List B article to him,

is guilty of an offence.

(2) A person who, without authorisation--

(a) brings, throws or otherwise conveys a List C article into a prison intending it to come into the possession of a prisoner,

(b) causes another person to bring, throw or otherwise convey a List C article into a prison intending it to come into the possession of a prisoner,

(c) brings, throws or otherwise conveys a List C article out of a prison on behalf of a prisoner,

(d) causes another person to bring, throw or otherwise convey a List C article out of a prison on behalf of a prisoner,

(e) leaves a List C article in any place (whether inside or outside a prison) intending it to come into the possession of a prisoner, or

(f) while inside a prison, gives a List C article to a prisoner,

is guilty of an offence.

(3) A person who attempts to commit an offence under subsection (2) is guilty of that offence.

(4) In proceedings for an offence under this section it is a defence for the accused to show that-

(a) he reasonably believed that he had authorisation to do the act in respect of which the proceedings are brought, or

(b) in all the circumstances there was an overriding public interest which justified the doing of that act.

(5) A person guilty of an offence under subsection (1) is liable--

(a) on conviction on indictment, to imprisonment for a term not exceeding two years or to a fine (or both);

(b) on summary conviction, to imprisonment for a term not exceeding 12 months or to a fine not exceeding the statutory maximum (or both).

(6) A person guilty of an offence under subsection (2) is liable on summary conviction to a fine not exceeding level 3 on the standard scale.

(7) In this section "authorisation" means authorisation given for the purposes of this section; and subsections (1) to (3) of section 40E apply in relation to authorisations so given as they apply to authorisations given for the purposes of section 40D.

This section does not extend to Scotland: see s 55(4).

Amendment

Substituted, together with ss 40A, 40B, for s 40 as originally enacted, by the Offender Management Act 2007, s 22(1).

40D Other offences relating to prison security

[(1) A person who, without authorisation--

(a) takes a photograph, or makes a sound-recording, inside a prison, or

(b) transmits, or causes to be transmitted, any image or any sound from inside a prison by electronic communications for simultaneous reception outside the prison,

is guilty of an offence.

(2) It is immaterial for the purposes of subsection (1)(a) where the recording medium is located.

(3) A person who, without authorisation--

(a) brings or otherwise conveys a restricted document out of a prison or causes such a document to be brought or conveyed out of a prison, or

(b) transmits, or causes to be transmitted, a restricted document (or any information derived from a restricted document) from inside a prison by means of electronic communications,

is guilty of an offence.

(4) In proceedings for an offence under this section it is a defence for the accused to show that-

(a) he reasonably believed that he had authorisation to do the act in respect of which the proceedings are brought, or

(b) in all the circumstances there was an overriding public interest which justified the doing of that act.

(5) A person guilty of an offence under this section is liable--

(a) on conviction on indictment, to imprisonment for a term not exceeding two years or to a fine (or both); or

(b) on summary conviction, to imprisonment for a term not exceeding 12 months or to a fine not exceeding the statutory maximum (or both).]

This section does not extend to Scotland: see s 55(4).

Amendment Inserted by the Offender Management Act 2007, s 23(1).

40E Section 40D: meaning of "authorisation" and other interpretation

(1) In section 40D (and the following provisions of this section) "authorisation" means authorisation given for the purposes of that section--

(a) in relation to all prisons or prisons of a specified description, by prison rules or by the Secretary of State;

(b) in relation to a particular prison--

(i) by the Secretary of State;

(ii) by the governor or director of the prison;

(iii) by a person working at the prison who is authorised by the governor or director to grant authorisation on his behalf.
In paragraph (a) "specified" means specified in the authorisation.
(2) Authorisation may be given--
(a) to persons generally or to specified persons or persons of a specified description; and
(b) on such terms as may be specified.
In this subsection "specified" means specified in the authorisation.
(3) Authorisation given by or on behalf of the governor or director of a prison must be in writing.
(4) In section 40D "restricted document" means the whole (or any part of)--
(a) a photograph taken inside the prison;
(b) a sound-recording made inside the prison;
(c) a personal record (or a document containing information derived from a personal record);
(d) any other document which contains--
(i) information relating to an identified or identifiable relevant individual, if the disclosure of that information would or might prejudicially affect the interests of that individual; or
(ii) information relating to any matter connected with the prison or its operation, if the disclosure of that information would or might prejudicially affect the security or operation of the prison.
(5) In subsection (4)--
"personal record" means any record which is required by prison rules to be prepared and maintained in relation to any prisoner (and it is immaterial whether or not the individual concerned is still a prisoner at the time of any alleged offence);
"relevant individual" means an individual who is or has at any time been--
(a) a prisoner or a person working at the prison; or

(b) a member of such a person's family or household.

(6) In section 40D and this section--

"document" means anything in which information is recorded (by whatever means);

"electronic communications" has the same meaning as in the Electronic Communications Act 2000 (c 7);

"photograph" means a recording on any medium on which an image is produced or from which an image (including a moving image) may by any means be produced; and

"sound-recording" means a recording of sounds on any medium from which the sounds may by any means be reproduced.

This section does not extend to Scotland: see s 55(4).

Amendment

Inserted by the Offender Management Act 2007, s 23(1).

40D extension of Crown immunity

40F Offences under sections 40B to 40D: extension of Crown immunity

[(1) An individual who--

(a) works at a prison;

(b) does not do that work as a servant or agent of the Crown; and

(c) has been designated by the Secretary of State for the purposes of this section,

shall be treated for the purposes of the application of sections 40B to 40D as if he were doing that work as a servant or agent of the Crown.

(2) A designation for the purposes of this section may be given--

(a) in relation to persons specified in the designation or persons of a description so specified; and

(b) in relation to all work falling within subsection (1)(a) or only in relation to such activities as the designation may provide.

This section does not extend to Scotland: see s 55(4).
Amendment
Inserted by the Offender Management Act 2007, s 24.
Amendment
Repealed by the Offender Management Act 2007, ss 23(2), 39, Sch 5, Pt 2.
UK Parliament Acts/P/PO-PT/Prison Act 1952 (1952 c 52)/42 Display of notice of penalties

41 repealed.

42 Display of notice of penalties
The Prison Commissioners shall cause to be affixed in a conspicuous place outside every prison a notice of the penalties to which persons committing offences under [sections 39 to 40D] are liable.
This section does not extend to Scotland.
Amendment
Words "sections 39 to 40D" in square brackets substituted by the Offender Management Act 2007, s 23(3).

Transfer of Functions
Functions of the Prison Commissioners transferred to the Secretary of State for the Home Department, by the Prison Commissioners Dissolution Order 1963, SI 1963/597.
UK Parliament Acts/P/PO-PT/Prison Act 1952 (1952 c 52)/ [43 Remand centres and young offender institutions
Remand centres [and young offender institutions

Amendment
Reference to "young offender institutions" substituted by virtue of the Criminal Justice Act 1988, s 123(6), Sch 8, para 1.

43 Remand centres [and young offender institutions

(1) The Secretary of State may provide--

(a) *remand centres, that is to say places for the detention of persons not less than fourteen but under 21 years of age who are remanded or committed in custody for trial or sentence;*

[(aa) young offender institutions, that is to say places for the detention of offenders sentenced to detention in a young offender institution [or to custody for life][or other persons who may be lawfully detained there;

(b), (c)   . . . ; and

(d) secure training centres, that is to say places in which offenders in respect of whom detention and training orders have been made under [section 100 of the Powers of Criminal Courts (Sentencing) Act 2000] may be detained and given training and education and prepared for their release.

(2) The Secretary of State may from time to time direct--

(a) that a woman aged *21* [18] years or over who is serving a sentence of imprisonment or who has been committed to prison for default shall be detained in *a remand centre or* a [young offender institution] instead of a prison;

(b) *that a woman aged 21 years or over who is remanded in custody or committed in custody for trial or sentence shall be detained in a remand centre instead of a prison;*

(c) *that a person under 21 but not less than 17 years of age who is remanded in custody or committed in custody for trial or sentence shall be detained in a prison instead of a remand centre or a remand centre instead of a prison, notwithstanding anything in section 27 of the Criminal Justice Act 1948 or section 23(3) of the Children and Young Persons Act 1969.*

(3) *Notwithstanding subsection (1) above, any person required to be detained in an institution to which this Act applies may be detained in a remand centre for any temporary purpose [and a person [aged 18 years] or over may be detained in such a centre] for the purpose of providing maintenance and domestic services for that centre.*

(4) Sections 5A, 6(2) and (3), 16, 22, 25 and 36 of this Act shall apply to *remand centres* [and young offender institutions and to persons detained in them as they apply to prisons and prisoners.

(4A) Sections 16, 22 and 36 of this Act shall apply to secure training centres and to persons detained in them as they apply to prisons and prisoners.

(5) The other provisions of this Act preceding this section, except sections 28 and 37(2) above, shall apply to [centres of the descriptions specified in subsection (4) above and to persons detained in them as they apply to prisons and prisoners, but subject to such adaptations and modifications as may be specified in rules made by the Secretary of State.

(5A) The other provisions of this Act preceding this section, except sections 5, 5A, 6(2) and (3), 12, 14, 19, 25, 28 and 37(2) and (3) above, shall apply to secure training centres and to persons detained in them as they apply to prisons and prisoners, but subject to such adaptations and modifications as may be specified in rules made by the Secretary of State.

(6) References in the preceding provisions of this Act to imprisonment shall, so far as those provisions apply to institutions provided under this section, be construed as including references to detention in those institutions.

(7) *Nothing in this section shall be taken to prejudice the operation of* [*section 108(5) of the Powers of Criminal Courts (Sentencing) Act 2000.*

(8) The application of this Act to a person on whom a custodial sentence (within the meaning of the Armed Forces Act 2006) has been passed in respect of a service offence (within the meaning of that Act) is not affected by the omission from subsection (1) of a reference to that sentence.

This section does not extend to Scotland.

Amendment

Substituted by the Criminal Justice Act 1982, s 11.

Section heading: reference to "young offender institutions" substituted by virtue of the Criminal Justice Act 1988, s 123(6), Sch 8, para 1.

Sub-s (1): para (a) repealed by the Criminal Justice & Court Services Act 2000, ss 59, 75, Sch 8.

Sub-s (1): para (aa) inserted by the Criminal Justice Act 1988, s 170, Sch 15, para 11.

Sub-s (1): in para (aa) words "or to custody for life" in square brackets inserted by the Criminal Justice and Public Order Act 1994, s 18(3).

Sub-s (1): in para (aa) words "or other persons who may be lawfully detained there" in square brackets inserted by Criminal Justice and Immigration Act 2008, s 148(1), Sch 26, Pt 2, para 3.

Sub-s (1): para (b) repealed by the Criminal Justice Act 1988, s 170, Sch 16.

Sub-s (1): word "and" after para (b) repealed by the Criminal Justice and Public Order Act 1994, s 168(3), Sch 11.

Sub-s (1): para (c) repealed by the Criminal Justice Act 1988, s 170, Sch 16.

Sub-s (1): para (d) and word "and" preceding it inserted by the Criminal Justice and Public Order Act 1994, s 5(2).

Sub-s (1): para (d) substituted by the Crime and Disorder Act 1998, s 119, Sch 8, para 6.

Sub-s (1): in para (d) words "section 100 of the Powers of Criminal Courts (Sentencing) Act 2000" in square brackets substituted by the Powers of Criminal Courts (Sentencing) Act 2000, s 165(1), Sch 9, para 5(1), (2).

Sub-s (2): in para (a) number "21" in italics repealed and subsequent number in[] substituted by the Criminal Justice and Court Services Act 2000, s 74, Sch 7, Pt II, paras 7, 10(a)(i).

Sub-s (2): in para (a) words "a remand centre or" in italics repealed by the Criminal Justice and Court Services Act 2000, ss 74, 75, Sch 7, Pt II, paras 7, 10(a)(i), Sch 8.

Sub-s (2): in para (a) words "young offender institution" in square brackets substituted by virtue of the Criminal Justice Act 1988, s 123(6), Sch 8, para 1.

Sub-s (2): paras (b), (c) repealed by the Criminal Justice and Court Services Act 2000, ss 74, 75, Sch 7, Pt II, paras 7, 10(a)(ii), Sch 8.

Sub-s (3): repealed by the Criminal Justice and Court Services Act 2000, ss 74, 75, Sch 7, Pt II, paras 7, 10(b), Sch 8.

Sub-s (3): words in square brackets beginning with the words "and a person" substituted by the Criminal Justice Act 1988, s 170(1), Sch 15, para 12.

Sub-s (3): words "aged 18 years" in square brackets substituted by the Criminal Justice Act 1991, s 68, Sch 8, para 2.

Sub-s (4): words "remand centres" in italics repealed by the Criminal Justice and Court Services Act 2000, ss 74, 75, Sch 7, Pt II, paras 7, 10(c), Sch 8.

Sub-s (4): words "and young offender institutions" in square brackets substituted by virtue of the Criminal Justice Act 1988, s 123(6), Sch 8, para 1.

Sub-ss (4A), (5A): inserted by the Criminal Justice and Public Order Act 1994, s 5(3), (5).

Sub-s (5): words in square brackets substituted by the Criminal Justice and Public Order Act 1994, s 5(4).

Sub-s (7): repealed by the Criminal Justice and Court Services Act 2000, ss 74, 75, Sch 7, Pt II, paras 7, 10(d), Sch 8.

Sub-s (7): words "section 108(5) of the Powers of Criminal Courts (Sentencing) Act 2000" in square brackets substituted by the Powers of Criminal Courts (Sentencing) Act 2000, s 165(1), Sch 9, para 5(1), (3).

Rules for the management of prisons and other institutions

47 Rules for the management of prisons, remand centres and young offender institutions

(1) The Secretary of State may make rules for the regulation and management of prisons, *remand centres*[, young offender institutions or secure training centres] respectively, and for the classification, treatment, employment, discipline and control of persons required to be detained therein.

(2) Rules made under this section shall make provision for ensuring that a person who is charged with any offence under the rules shall be given a proper opportunity of presenting his case.

(3) Rules made under this section may provide for the training of particular classes of persons and their allocation for that purpose to any prison or other institution in which they may lawfully be detained.

(4) Rules made under this section shall provide for the special treatment of the following persons whilst required to be detained in a prison, that is to say--

(a)-(c) . . .

(d) any . . . person detained in a prison, not being a person serving a sentence or a person imprisoned in default of payment of a sum adjudged to be paid by him on his conviction [or a person committed to custody on his conviction].

(4A) Rules made under this section shall[provide for the inspection of secure training centres and the appointment of independent persons to visit secure training centres and to whom representations may be made by offenders detained in secure training centres.

(5) Rules made under this section may provide for the temporary release of persons [detained in a prison, *[remand centre]*[, young offender institution or secure training centre not being persons committed in custody for trial (before the Crown Court] or committed to be sentenced or otherwise dealt with by [the Crown Court or remanded in custody by any court)

This section does not extend to Scotland.

Amendment

Provision heading: words "remand centres" in italics repealed by the Criminal Justice and Court Services Act 2000, s 74, Sch 7, Pt II, paras 7, 11(a).

Provision heading: reference to "young offender institutions" substituted by virtue of the Criminal Justice Act 1988, s 123(6), Sch 8, paras 1, 3(2).

Sub-s (1): words "remand centres" in italics repealed by the Criminal Justice and Court Services Act 2000, ss 74, 75, Sch 7, Pt II, paras 7, 11(a), Sch 8.

Sub-s (1): words ", young offender institutions or secure training centres" in square brackets substituted by the Criminal Justice and Public Order Act 1994, s 6(2).

Sub-s (4): words omitted repealed and words in square brackets inserted, by the Criminal Justice Act 1967, ss 66(5), 103(2), Sch 7, Part I.

Sub-s (4A): inserted by the Criminal Justice and Public Order Act 1994, s 6(3).

Sub-s (5): words in square brackets beginning with the words "detained in a prison," substituted by the Criminal Justice Act 1961, s 41(1), (3), Sch 4.

Sub-s (5): words "remand centre" in square brackets substituted by the Criminal Justice Act 1982, s 77, Sch 14, para 7.

Sub-s (5): words "remand centre" in italics repealed by the Criminal Justice and Court Services Act 2000, ss 74, 75, Sch 7, Pt II, paras 7, 11(b), Sch 8.

Sub-s (5): words ", young offender institution or secure training centre" in square brackets substituted by the Criminal Justice and Public Order Act 1994, s 6(4).

Sub-s (5): words "before the Crown Court" in square brackets substituted by the Courts Act 1971, s 56(1), Sch 8, Pt II, para 33.

Sub-s (5): words "the Crown Court" in square brackets substituted by the Courts Act 1971, s 56(1), Sch 8, Pt II, para 33.

See further: in relation to the disapplication of provisions of Rules made under this section permitting temporary release on licence, in relation to a person detained in England and Wales in persuance of a sentence of the Internation Criminal Court: see the International Criminal Court Act 2001, s 42(6), Sch 7, paras 1, 3(1).

Subordinate Legislation

Secure Training Centre Rules 1998, SI 1998/472.
Prison Rules 1999, SI 1999/728.
Prison (Amendment) Rules 2000, SI 2000/1794.
Prison (Amendment) (No 2) Rules 2000, SI 2000/2641.
Young Offender Institution Rules 2000, SI 2000/3371.
Prison (Amendment) Rules 2002, SI 2002/2116.
Young Offender Institution (Amendment) Rules 2002, SI 2002/2117.
Secure Training Centre (Amendment) Rules 2003, SI 2003/3005.
Prison (Amendment) Rules 2003, SI 2003/3301.
Prison (Amendment) Rules 2005, SI 2005/869.
Young Offender Institution (Amendment) Rules 2005, SI 2005/897.
Prison (Amendment) (No 2) Rules 2005, SI 2005/3437.
Young Offender Institution (Amendment) (No 2) Rules 2005, SI 2005/3438.
Secure Training Centre (Amendment) Rules 2007, SI 2007/1709.
Young Offender Institution (Amendment) Rules 2007, SI 2007/2953.
Prison (Amendment) Rules 2007, SI 2007/2954.
Prison (Amendment No 2) Rules 2007, SI 2007/3149.
Young Offender Institution (Amendment No 2) Rules 2007, SI 2007/3220.
Prison (Amendment) Rules 2008, SI 2008/597.
Young Offender Institution (Amendment) Rules 2008, SI 2008/599.

Miscellaneous

Amendment
Repealed by the Criminal Justice Act 1961, s 41(2), (3), Sch 5.
UK Parliament Acts/P/PO-PT/Prison Act 1952 (1952 c 52)/49 Persons unlawfully at large

49 Persons unlawfully at large

(1) Any person who, having been sentenced to [imprisonment or custody for life or ordered to be detained in [youth detention] accommodation or in a young offenders institution], or having been committed to a prison or remand centre, is unlawfully at large, may be arrested by a constable without warrant and taken to the place in which he is required in accordance with law to be detained.

(2) Where any person sentenced to [imprisonment, or ordered to be detained in [youth detention] accommodation or in a young offenders institution], is unlawfully at large at any time during the period for which he is liable to be detained in pursuance of the sentence or order, then, unless the Secretary of State otherwise directs, no account shall be taken, in calculating the period for which he is liable to be so detained, of any time during which he is absent from the place in which he is required in accordance with law to be detained:

Provided that--

(a) this subsection shall not apply to any period during which any such person as aforesaid is detained in pursuance of the sentence or order or in pursuance of any other sentence of any court [in the United Kingdom] [in a prison or remand centre, in youth detention accommodation or in a young offenders institution;

(b), (c) . . .

(3) The provisions of the last preceding subsection shall apply to a person who is detained in custody in default of payment of any sum of money as if he were sentenced to imprisonment.

(4) For the purposes of this section a person who, after being temporarily released in pursuance of rules made under subsection (5) of section forty-seven of this Act, is at large at any time during the period for which he is liable to be detained in pursuance of his sentence shall be deemed to be unlawfully at large if the period for which he was temporarily released has expired or if an order recalling him has been made by the [Secretary of State] in pursuance of the rules.

(4A) For the purposes of this section a person shall also be deemed to be unlawfully at large if, having been temporarily released in pursuance of an intermittent custody order made under section 183 of the Criminal Justice Act 2003, he remains at large at a time when, by reason of the expiry of the period for which he was temporarily released, he is liable to be detained in pursuance of his sentence.

(5) In this section ["youth detention accommodation"] means--

(a) a young offender institution;
(b) a secure training centre; or
(c) any other accommodation that is [youth detention] accommodation within the meaning given by section 107(1) of the Powers of Criminal Courts (Sentencing) Act 2000] (detention and training orders).

This section does not extend to Scotland.

Amendment

Sub-s (1): words from "imprisonment or custody for life" to "a young offenders institution" in square brackets substituted by the Crime and Disorder Act 1998, s 119, Sch 8, para 7(1).

Sub-s (1): words "youth detention" in square brackets substituted by the Offender Management Act 2007, s 39, Sch 3, Pt 3, para 11(1), (2).

Sub-s (2): words "imprisonment, or ordered to be detained in secure accommodation or in a young offenders institution" in square brackets substituted by the Crime and Disorder Act 1998, s 119, Sch 8, para 7(2)(a).

Sub-s (2): words "place in which he is required in accordance with law to be detained" in square brackets substituted by the Criminal Justice Act 1982, s 77, Sch 14, para 8(b)(ii).

Sub-s (2): in para (a) words "in the United Kingdom" in square brackets inserted by the Criminal Justice Act 1961, s 30(4), Sch 4.

Sub-s (2): in para (a) words "in a prison or remand centre, in secure accommodation or in a young offenders institution" in square brackets substituted by the Crime and Disorder Act 1998, s 119, Sch 8, para 7(2)(b).

Sub-s (2): in para (a) words "youth detention" in square brackets substituted by the Offender Management Act 2007, s 39, Sch 3, Pt 3, para 11(1), (3).

Sub-s (2): para (b) repealed by the Criminal Justice Act 1982, s 78, Sch 16.

Sub-s (2): para (c) repealed by the Criminal Justice Act 1961, s 41, Sch 5.

Sub-s (4): words "Secretary of State" in [] substituted by SI 1963/597, art 3(2), Sch 1. Sub-s (4A): inserted by the Criminal Justice Act 2003, s 186(3).

Sub-s (5): inserted by the Crime and Disorder Act 1998, s 119, Sch 8, para 7(3).

Sub-s (5): words ""youth detention accommodation"" in square brackets substituted by the Offender Management Act 2007, s 39, Sch 3, Pt 3, para 11(1), (4)(a).

Sub-s (5): in para (c) words "youth detention" in square brackets substituted by the Offender Management Act 2007, s 39, Sch 3, Pt 3, para 11(1), (4)(b).

Sub-s (5): in para (c) words "section 107(1) of the Powers of Criminal Courts (Sentencing) Act 2000" in square brackets substituted by the Powers of Criminal Courts (Sentencing) Act 2000, s 165(1), Sch 9, para 6.

See further: in relation to the disapplication of sub-s (2) above in relation to a person detained in England and Wales in pursuance of a sentence of the International Criminal Court: see the International Criminal Court Act 2001, s 42(6), Sch 7, paras 1, 2(1)(b).

50 Amendment
Repealed in part by the Children and Young Persons Act 1969, s 72(4), Sch 6; remainder is spent.

UK Parliament Acts/P/PO-PT/Prison Act 1952 (1952 c 52)/51 Payment of expenses out of moneys provided by Parliament.

Supplemental

51 Payment of expenses out of moneys provided by Parliament
All expenses incurred in the maintenance of prisons and in the maintenance of prisoners and all other expenses of the Secretary of State . . . incurred under this Act shall be defrayed out of moneys provided by Parliament.

This section does not extend to Scotland.

UK Parliament Acts/P/PO-PT/Prison Act 1952 (1952 c 52)/52 Exercise of power to make orders, rules and regulations.

52 Exercise of power to make orders, rules and regulations
(1) Any power of the Secretary of State to make rules or regulations under this Act and the power of the Secretary of State to make an order under section thirty-four [, 37 or 40A] of this Act [or under Schedule A1 to this Act] shall be exercisable by statutory instrument.

(2) Any statutory instrument containing regulations made under section sixteen or an order made under section thirty-seven of this Act, . . . shall be laid before Parliament.

(2A) A statutory instrument containing an order under Schedule A1 to this Act shall be subject to annulment in pursuance of a resolution of either House of Parliament.

(2A) A statutory instrument containing an order under section 40A(7) which relates to List A (whether or not it also relates to List B) shall not be made unless a draft of it has been laid before, and approved by a resolution of, each House of Parliament.

(2B) A statutory instrument containing an order under section 40A(7) which relates only to List B is subject to annulment in pursuance of a resolution of either House of Parliament.

(3) The power of the Secretary of State to make an order under section six or section thirty-four of this Act [or under Schedule A1 to this Act] shall include power to revoke or vary such an order.

This section does not extend to Scotland.

Amendment

Sub-s (1): words ", 37 or 40A" in square brackets substituted by the Offender Management Act 2007, s 22(2)(a).

Sub-s (1): words "or under Schedule A1 to this Act" in square brackets inserted by the Police and Justice Act 2006, s 52, Sch 14, para 1(1), (2).

Sub-s (2): words omitted repealed by the Criminal Justice Act 1967, ss 66(4), 103(2), Sch 7, Pt I.

First sub-s (2A): inserted by the Police and Justice Act 2006, s 52, Sch 14, para 1(1), (3).

Second sub-s (2A), sub-s (2B): inserted by the Offender Management Act 2007, s 22(2)(b).

Sub-s (3): words "or under Schedule A1 to this Act" in square brackets inserted by the Police and Justice Act 2006, s 52, Sch 14, para 1(1), (4).

Subordinate Legislation
Rules made by the Secretary of State in pursuance of the Prison Act 1877.

53 Interpretation

(1) In this Act the following expressions have the following meanings:--

"Attendance centre" means a centre provided by the Secretary of State under [section 221 of the Criminal Justice Act 2003];

"Prison" does not include a naval, military or air force prison;

(2) For the purposes of this Act the maintenance of a prisoner shall include all necessary expenses incurred in respect of the prisoner for food, clothing, custody and removal from one place to another, from the period of his committal to prison until his death or discharge from prison.

(3) References in this Act to the Church of England shall be construed as including references to the Church in Wales.

(4) References in this Act to any enactment shall be construed as references to that enactment as amended by any other enactment.

Amendment

Sub-s (1): in definition "Attendance centre" words "section 221 of the Criminal Justice Act 2003" in square brackets substituted by the Criminal Justice Act 2003, s 304, Sch 32, Pt 1, para 3.

Sub-s (1): definition "Remand home" (omitted) repealed by the Children and Young Persons Act 1969, s 72(4), Sch 6.

54 Consequential amendments, repeals and savings

(1), (2) . . .

(3) Nothing in this repeal shall affect any rule, order, regulation or declaration made, direction or certificate given or thing done under any enactment repealed by this Act and every such rule, order, regulation, direction, certificate or thing

shall, if in force at the commencement of this Act, continue in force and be deemed to have been made, given or done under the corresponding provision of this Act.

(4) Any document referring to any Act or enactment repealed by this Act shall be construed as referring to this Act or to the corresponding enactment in this Act.

(5) The mention of particular matters in this section shall not be taken to affect the general application to this Act of section thirty-eight of the Interpretation Act 1889 (which relates to the effect of repeals).

This section does not extend to Scotland or to Northern Ireland except for section 5a (5A) and (5B) and 5A(2) to (5) by virtue of vsection 5A(5A).

Sub-s (1): repealed by the Statute Law (Repeals) Act 1993.

Sub-s (2): repealed by the Statute Laws (Repeals) Act 1974.

Act commenced on 1 October 1952.

Amendment

Sub-s (3): repealed by the Statute Law (Repeals) Act 1993.

Sub-s (4): words omitted repealed by the Statute Law (Repeals) Act 1993; words in square brackets substituted by the Criminal Justice Act 1961, s 41, Sch 4.

Sub-s (4A): inserted by the Immigration and Asylum Act 1999, s 169(1), Sch 14, para 33.

Sub-s (4A): repealed by the Immigration, Asylum & Nationality Act 2006, ss 46(2)(a), 61,Sch 3..

Sub-s (6): inserted by the Immigration, Asylum and Nationality Act 2006, s 46(2)(b).

Amendment Inserted by the Police and Justice Act 2006, s 28(2).

Delegation of functions

(1) The Chief Inspector may delegate any of his functions (to such extent as he may determine) to another public authority.

(2) If the carrying out of an inspection is delegated under sub-paragraph (1) above it is nevertheless to be regarded for the purposes of section 5A of this Act and this Schedule as carried out by the Chief Inspector.

(3) In this Schedule "public authority" includes any person certain of whose functions are functions of a public nature.

Inspection programmes and inspection frameworks

(1) The Chief Inspector shall from time to time, or at such times as the Secretary of State may specify by order, prepare--

(a) a document setting out what inspections he proposes to carry out (an "inspection programme");

(b) a document setting out the manner in which he proposes to carry out his functions of inspecting and reporting (an "inspection framework").

(2) Before preparing an inspection programme or an inspection framework the Chief Inspector shall consult the Secretary of State and (subject to sub-paragraph (3) below)--

(a) Her Majesty's Chief Inspector of Constabulary,

(b) Her Majesty's Chief Inspector of the Crown Prosecution Service,

(c) [Her Majesty's Chief Inspector of Probation for England and Wales],

(d) Her Majesty's Chief Inspector of Court Administration,

(e) Her Majesty's Chief Inspector of Education, Children's Services and Skills,

(f) *the Commission for Healthcare Audit and Inspection,*

(g) the Commission for Social Care Inspection,

(h) the Audit Commission for Local Government and the National Health Service in England.

(i) the Auditor General for Wales, and

(j) any other person or body specified by an order made by the Secretary of State,

and he shall send to each of those persons or bodies a copy of each programme or framework once it is prepared.

ENGLISH PRISON LAW

(3) The requirement in sub-paragraph (2) above to consult, and to send copies to, a person or body listed in paragraphs (a) to (j) of that sub-paragraph is subject to any agreement made between the Chief Inspector and that person or body to waive the requirement in such cases or circumstances as may be specified in the agreement.

(4) The Secretary of State may by order specify the form that inspection programmes or inspection frameworks are to take.

(5) Nothing in any inspection programme or inspection framework is to be read as preventing the Chief Inspector from making visits without notice.

Inspections by other inspectors of organisations within Chief Inspector's remit

(1) If--

(a) a person or body within sub-paragraph (2) below is proposing to carry out an inspection that would involve inspecting a specified organisation, and

(b) the Chief Inspector considers that the proposed inspection would impose an unreasonable burden on that organisation, or would do so if carried out in a particular manner,

the Chief Inspector shall, subject to sub-paragraph (7) below, give a notice to that person or body not to carry out the proposed inspection, or not to carry it out in that manner.

(2) The persons or bodies within this sub-paragraph are--

(a) Her Majesty's Inspectorate of Probation for England and Wales;

(b) Her Majesty's Chief Inspector of Education, Children's Services and Skills;

(c) *the Commission for Healthcare Audit and Inspection;*

(d) *the Commission for Social Care Inspection;*

(e) the Audit Commission for Local Government and the National Health Service in England .

(3) The Secretary of State may by order amend sub-paragraph (2) above.

(4) In sub-paragraph (1)(a) above "specified organisation" means a person or body specified by an order made by the Secretary of State.

(5) A person or body may be specified under sub-paragraph (4) above only if it exercises functions in relation to any prison or other institution or matter falling with the scope of the Chief Inspector's duties under section 5A of this Act.

(6) A person or body may be specified under sub-paragraph (4) above in relation to particular functions that it has.

In the case of a person or body so specified, sub-paragraph (1)(a) above is to be read as referring to an inspection that would involve inspecting the discharge of any of its functions in relation to which it is specified.

(7) The Secretary of State may by order specify cases or circumstances in which a notice need not, or may not, be given under this paragraph.

(8) Where a notice is given under this paragraph, the proposed inspection is not to be carried out, or (as the case may be) is not to be carried out in the manner mentioned in the notice.

This is subject to sub-paragraph (9) below.

(9) The Secretary of State, if satisfied that the proposed inspection--

(a) would not impose an unreasonable burden on the organisation in question, or

(b) would not do so if carried out in a particular manner, may give consent to the inspection being carried out, or being carried out in that manner.

(10) The Secretary of State may by order make provision supplementing that made by this paragraph, including in particular--

(a) provision about the form of notices;

(b) provision prescribing the period within which notices are to be given;
(c) provision prescribing circumstances in which notices are, or are not, to be made public;
(d) provision for revising or withdrawing notices;
(e) provision for setting aside notices not validly given.

Co-operation

The Chief Inspector shall co-operate with--
(a) Her Majesty's Inspectors of Constabulary,
(b) Her Majesty's Chief Inspector of the Crown Prosecution Service,
(c) [Her Majesty's Inspectorate of Probation for England and Wales],
(d) Her Majesty's Inspectorate of Court Administration,
(e) Her Majesty's Chief Inspector of Education, Children's Services and Skills,
(f) the Commission for Healthcare Audit and Inspection,
(g) the Commission for Social Care Inspection,
(h) the Audit Commission for Local Government and the National Health Service in England .
(i) the Auditor General for Wales, and
(j) any other public authority specified by an order made by the Secretary of State,
where it is appropriate to do so for the efficient and effective discharge of his functions.

Joint action

(1) The Chief Inspector may act jointly with another public authority where it is appropriate to do so for the efficient and effective discharge of his functions.

(2) The Chief Inspector, acting jointly with the chief inspectors within sub-paragraph (3) below, shall prepare a document (a "joint inspection programme") setting out--
(a) what inspections he proposes to carry out in the exercise of the power conferred by sub-paragraph (1) above, and
(b) what inspections the chief inspectors within sub-paragraph (3) below (or their inspectorates) propose to carry out in the exercise of any corresponding powers conferred on them.
(3) The chief inspectors within this sub-paragraph are--
(a) Her Majesty's Chief Inspector of Constabulary;
(b) Her Majesty's Chief Inspector of the Crown Prosecution Service;
(c) [Her Majesty's Chief Inspector of Probation for England and Wales];
(d) Her Majesty's Chief Inspector of Court Administration.
(4) A joint inspection programme shall be prepared from time to time or at such times as the Secretary of State, the Lord Chancellor and the Attorney General may jointly direct.
(5) Sub-paragraphs (2), (3) and (5) of paragraph 2 above apply to a joint inspection programme as they apply to a document prepared under that paragraph.
(6) The Secretary of State, the Lord Chancellor and the Attorney General may by a joint direction specify the form that a joint inspection programme is to take.

Assistance for other public authorities
(1) The Chief Inspector may if he thinks it appropriate to do so provide assistance to any other public authority for the purpose of the exercise by that authority of its functions.
(2) Assistance under this paragraph may be provided on such terms (including terms as to payment) as the Chief Inspector thinks fit).

Amendment Inserted by the Police and Justice Act 2006, s 28(2).

Para 2: in sub-para (2)(c) words "Her Majesty's Chief Inspector of Probation for England and Wales" in square brackets substituted by SI 2008/912, art 3, Sch 1, Pt 2, para 27(1), (2)(a).

Para 2: sub-para (2)(f) repealed by the Health and Social Care Act 2008, ss 95, 166, Sch 5, Pt 3, para 53(1), (2)(a), Sch 15, Pt 1.

Para 2: sub-para (2)(g) substituted by the Health and Social Care Act 2008, s 95, Sch 5, Pt 3, para 53(1), (2)(b).

Para 2: in sub-para (2)(h) words omitted repealed by the Local Government and Public Involvement in Health Act 2007, ss 146(3), 241, Sch 9, para 1(1), (2)(a), Sch 18, Pt 9.

Para 3: in sub-para (2)(a) words "Her Majesty's Inspectorate of Probation for England and Wales" in square brackets substituted by SI 2008/912, art 3, Sch 1, Pt 2, para 26(1), (2)(a).

Para 3: sub-para (2)(c) repealed by the Health and Social Care Act 2008, ss 95, 166, Sch 5, Pt 3, para 53(1), (3)(a), Sch 15, Pt 1.

Para 3: sub-para (3)(d) substituted by the Health and Social Care Act 2008, s 95, Sch 5, Pt 3, para 53(1), (3)(b).

Para 3: in sub-para (2)(e) words omitted repealed by the Local Government and Public Involvement in Health Act 2007, ss 146(3), 241, Sch 9, para 1(1), (2)(a), Sch 18, Pt 9.

Para 4: in para (c) words "Her Majesty's Inspectorate of Probation for England and Wales" in square brackets substituted by SI 2008/912, art 3, Sch 1, Pt 2, para 26(1), (2)(b).

Para 4: in sub-para (h) words omitted repealed by the Local Government and Public Involvement in Health Act 2007, ss 146(3), 241, Sch 9, para 1(1), (2)(a), Sch 18

Para 5: in sub-para (3)(c) words "Her Majesty's Chief Inspector of Probation for England and Wales" in square brackets substituted by SI 2008/912, art 3, Sch 1, Pt 2, para 27(1), (2)(a).

Subordinate Legislation

Her Majesty's Chief Inspector of Prisons (Specified Organisations) Order 2007, SI 2007/1173 (made under para 3(4)).

Amendment Repealed by the Criminal Justice Act 1961, s 41(2), (3), Sch 5.

Amendment Repealed by the Statute Law (Repeals) Act 1993.

Amendment Repealed by the Statute Law (Repeals) Act 1974.

Amendment Repealed by the Statute Law (Repeals) Act 1974.

Prisons (Scotland) Act 1952

This Act was repealed by the Prisons (Scotland) Act 1989, s 45(2), Sch 3.

UK Parliament SIs 1950-1979/1952/1401-1450/[R] Prison Rules 1952 (SI 1952/1405)

Prison Rules 1952

These Rules were revoked by SI 1964/388.

APPENDIX 4 - THE PRISON (AMENDMENT) RULES 2005

2005 No. 869 (Statutory Instrument 2005 No. 869)

PRISONS

The Prison (Amendment) Rules 2005 in force from 18th April 2005.

The Secretary of State, in exercise of the powers conferred upon him by section 47 of the Prison Act 1952 hereby makes the following Rules:

1.

(1) These Rules may be cited as the Prison (Amendment) Rules 2005 and shall come into force on 18th April 2005.

(2) The requirement in rule 2 (as substituted by paragraph 1 of the Schedule) of the approval of the Lord Chancellor for the appointment of a District Judge (Magistrates' Courts) or Deputy District Judge (Magistrates' Courts) as an adjudicator does not apply to a person who is approved to act as an adjudicator on the date when these Rules come into force, and

such a person may continue to act as an adjudicator for so long as he holds office as a District Judge (Magistrates' Courts) or Deputy District Judge (Magistrates' Courts).

2. The Prison Rules 1999 shall have effect subject to the amendments set out in the Schedule to these Rules.

SCHEDULE 1-Rule 2

AMENDMENTS TO THE PRISON RULES 1999

1. In paragraph (1) of rule 2 (interpretation), for the definition of "adjudicator" substitute – ""adjudicator" means a District Judge (Magistrates' Courts) or Deputy District Judge (Magistrates' Courts) approved by the Lord Chancellor for the purpose of inquiring into a charge which has been referred to him;".

2. In rule 42 (record and photograph) - (a) in paragraph (2) after the word "photograph" insert "or any other personal record";

(b) after paragraph (2) insert - " (2A) In this rule "personal record" may include personal information and biometric records (such as fingerprints or other physical measurements).".

3. After rule 50A, insert - " **Compulsory testing for alcohol 50B.** –

(1) This rule applies where an officer, acting under an authorisation in force under section 16B of the Prison Act 1952[4] (power to test prisoners for alcohol), requires a prisoner to provide a sample for the purpose of ascertaining whether he has alcohol in his body.

(2) When requiring a prisoner to provide a sample an officer shall, so far as is reasonably practicable, inform the prisoner - (a) that he is being required to provide a sample in accordance with section 16B of the Prison Act 1952; and (b) that a refusal

to provide a sample may lead to disciplinary proceedings being brought against him.

(3) An officer requiring a sample shall make such arrangements and give the prisoner such instructions for its provision as may be reasonably necessary in order to prevent or detect its adulteration or falsification.

(4) Subject to paragraph (5) a prisoner who is required to provide a sample may be kept apart from other prisoners for a period not exceeding one hour to enable arrangements to be made for the provision of the sample.

(5) A prisoner who is unable to provide a sample of urine when required to do so may be kept apart from other prisoners until he has provided the required sample, except that a prisoner may not be kept apart under this paragraph for a period of more than 5 hours.

(6) A prisoner required to provide a sample of urine shall be afforded such degree of privacy for the purposes of providing the sample as may be compatible with the need to prevent or detect any adulteration or falsification of the sample; in particular a prisoner shall not be required to provide such a sample in the sight of a person of the opposite sex.".

4. In rule 51 (offences against discipline) - (a) for paragraph (9) substitute -   " (9) is found with any substance in his urine which demonstrates that a controlled drug has, whether in prison or while on temporary release under rule 9, been administered to him by himself or by another person (but subject to rule 52);";(b) for paragraph (10) substitute -   " (10) is intoxicated as a consequence of consuming any alcoholic beverage (but subject to rule 52A);";(c) for paragraph (11) substitute -   " (11) consumes any alcoholic beverage whether or not provided to him by another person (but subject to rule 52A);".

5. After rule 52 insert - " **Defences to rule 51(10) and rule 51(11) 52A.** It shall be a defence for a prisoner charged with an offence under rule 51(10) or (11) to show that - (a) the alcohol was consumed by him in circumstances in which he did not know and had no reason to suspect that he was consuming alcohol;(b) the alcohol was consumed by him without his consent in circumstances where it was not reasonable for him to have resisted; or (c) the alcohol was provided to him pursuant to a written order under rule 25(1).".

6. After rule 55A insert - " **Review of adjudicator's punishment 55B.** –
(1) A reviewer means a Senior District Judge (Chief Magistrate approved by the Lord Chancellor for the purposes of conducting a review under this rule or any deputy of such a judge as nominated by that judge.
(2) Where a punishment is imposed by an adjudicator under rule 55A(1), a prisoner may, within 14 days of receipt of the punishment, request in writing that a reviewer conducts a review.
(3) The review must be commenced within 14 days of receipt of the request and must be conducted on the papers alone.
(4) The review must only be of the punishment imposed and must not be a review of the finding of guilt under rule 55A.
(5) On completion of the review, if it appears to the reviewer that the punishment imposed was manifestly unreasonable he may - (a) reduce the number of any additional days awarded;
(b) for whatever punishment has been imposed by the adjudicator, substitute another punishment which is, in his opinion, less severe; or (c) quash the punishment entirely.
(6) A prisoner requesting a review shall serve any additional days awarded under rule 55A(1)(b) unless and until they are reduced.".

7. In rule 61 (remission and mitigation of punishments and quashing of findings of guilt) - (a) at the beginning of paragraph (1) insert - " Except in the case of a finding of guilt made, or a punishment imposed, by an adjudicator under rule 55A(1)";(b) for paragraph (2) substitute - " (2) Subject to any directions given by the Secretary of State, the governor may, on the grounds of good behaviour, remit or mitigate any punishment already imposed by an adjudicator, governor or the board of visitors.".

8. In rule 71 (control of persons and vehicles) - (a) for paragraph (1) substitute - " (1) Any person or vehicle entering or leaving a prison may be stopped, examined and searched and in addition any such person may be photographed, fingerprinted or required to submit to other physical measurement.";(b) after paragraph (1) insert - " (1A) Any such search of a person shall be carried out in as seemly a manner as is consistent with discovering anything concealed about the person or their belongings.".

APPENDIX 5 – PRISON DISCIPLINE MANUAL 1995

PRISON DISCIPLINE MANUAL 1995
'All institutions....require means of enforcing their rules and procedures and effective sanction for those who disobey'.
White Paper: ' Custody, care and justice' 1991
'Our suggestions (on disciplinary procedures) are directed to one of the themes which has run through this report, the theme of justice in prison secured through the exercise of responsibility and respect. The achievement of justice will itself enhance security and control'
Woolf Report (1991)
Much misconduct in Prison Service establishments can be dealt with informally through good management or good staff-prisoner relations. However, the formal discipline system is central to the maintenance of good order and discipline. Discipline procedures are provided for by the Prison Rules 1999 and the Young Offender Institution Rules 2000, both as amended. The Rules set out all disciplinary offences and punishments. They empower governors and controllers of contracted out prisons to investigate all charges and they require prisoners to have a full opportunity to hear what is alleged against them and to present their case. Where alleged

indiscipline amounts to a serious criminal offence the police will be asked to investigate and a prosecution may result.

References in this Manual to the Prison Rules should be taken to refer also to the YOI Rules except where a distinction is made. Similarly, references to prisoners and to prisons should be taken to refer also to young offenders and to YOIs except where a distinction is made.

This Manual contains both instructions and guidance on procedures related to the discipline system. Governors and controllers must comply with the instructions and must take account of the advice. The Manual should help all those involved - adjudicators, staff, prisoners and their representatives - in understanding the process. Its contents have been shaped by the decisions of the courts and by experience in the field. Adjudicators must manage hearings in accordance with the rules of natural justice and following the guidance in this Manual will offer the best prospect of that.

H.M. Prison Service Directorate of Programmes Policy Group 1995

1. THE PRISON DISCIPLINARY SYSTEM

PURPOSE OF THE ADJUDICATION

1.1 An adjudication has two purposes:

(a) to help maintain order, control, discipline and a safe environment

(b) to ensure that the use of authority in the establishment is lawful, reasonable and fair.

THE ROLE AND RESPONSIBILITIES OF THE ADJUDICATOR

1.2 The role of the adjudicator is to inquire into a report of alleged events and to decide whether a breach of Prison Rule 51 or YOI Rule 55 has been established beyond reasonable doubt. The adjudicator must ascertain the facts and must be prepared to question, in a spirit of impartial inquiry, the accused, the reporting officer and any witnesses. The role is thus different from that of a magistrate or judge.

1.3 The adjudicator is responsible for his or her own procedure and the parts of this Manual that deal with procedure during hearings are advisory. Adjudicators must act fairly and justly. If they depart from the guidance and, in doing so, compromise fairness and justice, their decisions will be at risk of being overturned if the adjudication is reviewed.

WHO MAY ADJUDICATE AND WHEN ?

1.4 The Prison Rules give authority to adjudicators and the governor of an establishment to conduct adjudications. Adjudicators are independent people appointed by the Secretary of State for the purpose of hearing charges referred to them by the governor. The governor may delegate adjudication powers and duties to any prison service manager grade F or above who has operational experience and who has received authorised training in adjudication procedures. This includes anyone on temporary promotion but not anyone substituting. Under Prison Rule 82(1)(b)(i) and YOI rule 86(1)(b)(i), adjudications in contracted out prisons and YOIs are conducted by the controller who may delegate that task to his/her deputy. Officers not below the rank of principal officer who have completed appropriate authorised training may hear minor reports.

1.5 – 1.7 Omitted.

1.8 Minor reports may be heard by officers not below the rank of principal officer who have been trained for that purpose. Minor report hearings are a form of adjudication and are subject to the same principles though their procedures are simpler.

1.9 Under Prison Rule 53(3) and YOI Rule 58(3) except where the charge is referred to the adjudicator, the governor must adjudicate on every charge and, save in exceptional circumstances, must do so not later than the next day after it has been laid, unless that day is a Sunday or a public holiday. When the charge is referred to the independent adjudicator the adjudicator must begin enquiries within 28 days of the charge being referred. The date of the referral counts as the first day of this 28 day period.

1.10   Omitted.

1.11   The training referred to in this section is that provided or approved by the Prison Service to meet the needs of adjudicators or those conducting minor reports.

2. CHARGING AND PRELIMINARIES

CHARGES

2.1   Normally a charge will be drawn up by the prison officer or prisoner custody officer against whom the alleged offence was committed or who witnessed or dealt with the incident during which the alleged offence took place. It can however be laid by another officer, for example where no member of staff was present or where a prisoner who was unlawfully at large is taken to another establishment.

2.2   Reporting officers should be advised to consult a principal officer, usually in their own management line, before a charge is laid. The principal officer should offer guidance to reporting officers on whether to lay charges and, if so, the correct charges to lay. Governors should ensure that at least one of their senior staff is nominated adjudication liaison officer and has received training in the proper interpretation of offences. The adjudication liaison officer should be a source of advice and, with the training principal officer, of training for staff. He or she may also act as a point of reference for principal officers so that they are fully equipped to carry out their role.

2.3 A charge is formally laid when form F1127 (Notice of Report) is handed to the accused. Prison Rule 53 and YOI Rule 58 require that a disciplinary charge against a prisoner shall be laid as soon as possible and save in exceptional circumstances within 48 hours of the alleged offence being discovered. This applies irrespective of whether any part of those 48 hours includes a weekend or public holiday. Failure to charge within 48 hours renders any subsequent hearing void unless there are exceptional circumstances. The interpretation of exceptional is strict and does not, for example, allow for the period to be extended whilst an escapee is brought back to the establishment from which he or she escaped to face charges. It is essential that, as soon as the alleged offence is discovered or an escapee is returned to prison custody, arrangements are made promptly to lay a charge, if necessary on the basis of information telephoned to the holding establishment. It may be that, on occasion, the substantive hearing of a `charge has to be delayed whilst the detailed evidence to support it is prepared.

2.4 The charge must be of an offence described in Prison Rule 51 or YOI Rule 55. If not, it must be dismissed. A charge may not be changed after the form F1127 has been served, though its details may be amended by the adjudicator at the hearing provided the amendment does not result in any injustice or unfairness to the accused. The accused must be told of any amendment made.

2.5 A charge may not be reduced at a hearing, for example from assault to attempted assault. If there is insufficient evidence to support the charge that has been laid it must be dismissed. If during the hearing it becomes clear that the accused's behaviour may have amounted to a lesser or to a different offence the prisoner may be charged with that offence provided that this is done as soon as possible and that it is still within 48 hours of the alleged offence being discovered. The subsequent hearing should be before a different adjudicator who comes to the hearing afresh.

2.6   If it is unclear at charging stage whether or not alleged behaviour amounts to one or more of possible alternative offences, more than one charge may be laid. The accused should be advised as to why this is being done. The hearings may commence simultaneously. As evidence is presented it will become clear to the adjudicator which, if any, of the charges is correct. The charges for which there is insufficient evidence must be dismissed and the course of events should be clearly recorded on the principal record of the hearing (form F256). This practice should be exceptional.

2.7   A prisoner must be charged under the correct Rules. Each establishment operates under Rules governing its designation. Thus a prison or remand centre will operate under Prison Rules, even though it may contain some young offenders (with the provisions of Prison Rule 57 operating). Some establishments have a dual designation as a prison and as a YOI and therefore operate under both sets of Rules. The accused must then be charged under the Rules applying to him or her. A sentenced YOI/Juvenile must be detained in YOI designated accommodation at all times.

Thus a sentenced young offender escapes from a YOI and is returned to a prison/YOI where he assaults a officer in reception. He must be located in YOI designated accommodation. He will be charged under YOI Rule 55. Where the accused is located in a common area, such as the health care unit or segregation unit, s/he must be charged under the Rules that would apply if s/he were on normal location.

2.8   Before a disciplinary charge is laid for an offence committed at court it must be established that the prisoner was in the custody of the prison at the material time, that is that the prisoner was required to be detained in the prison and was under the control of prison officers or prison custody officers. Charges should not be laid if the prisoner has been or is to be dealt with by the court for the conduct constituting the offence

2.9 Form F1127 should be served on the prisoner at least two hours before the adjudication is due to begin. A written record should be kept of when and by whom form F1127 was issued to the accused in case the form is lost or destroyed. Good practice would be for form F1127 and the form explaining the procedure to be followed (form F1145) to be served the day before the adjudication. In the case of resuming an adjourned hearing the prisoner should also be given at least two hours notice by way of a fresh or renewed form F1127. Exceptionally it may be possible to proceed without the two hours notice for example where a prisoner is well aware that he or she is to face the resumed hearing and is prepared to proceed. In this case it must be recorded in the record of the hearing (form F256) that the prisoner has been offered the chance to delay the resumption of the hearing for a further two hours but has declined.

2.10 Where a prisoner is taken to court before a charge is either laid or heard and will possibly, on recommittal, be taken direct to another establishment, arrangements should be made for the prisoner to return initially to the establishment from which he or she came, so that the outstanding charge can be dealt with if its importance merits that course. If the transfer takes place before the charge can be dealt with and if the receiving establishment operates under a different set of Rules from those allegedly broken, care should be taken to follow the guidance.

2.11 The charge as recorded on form F1127 should contain sufficient explanatory detail to leave the accused in no doubt as to what is alleged. A charge of failing to comply with a condition of temporary release should, for example, make it quite clear which condition is alleged to have been broken. Similarly, if the charge is one of attempt, incitement or assisting (under Prison Rule 25a, 25b or 25c or YOI Rule 29a, 29b or 29c) forms F1127 and F256 should make it clear which offence the accused is alleged to have attempted to commit (see Section 6).

2.12   More than one charge may be laid in respect of offences arising from a single incident, and if the evidence supports it, the prisoner may be found guilty in each case provided that the acts are separate ones and that the charges do not duplicate each other. If the prisoner appears to have been charged twice for the same act, he or she cannot be found guilty of both offences. So a prisoner who swears at an officer, for example, should not be charged both with being disrespectful and using threatening, abusive or insulting words. Similarly, continuing charges are to be avoided. Thus a prisoner who, at 0800 refused to obey an order to go to work and is placed on report, should not be charged with a separate offence if ordered to do the same thing at 0900.

2.13   If a prisoner who is charged with an offence has difficulty in understanding English, he or she should be given assistance by staff or, if necessary, an interpreter. If an interpreter is not readily available the governor may wish to use the Language Line translation service. The Prisoners Information Books published jointly by the Prison Service and the Prison Reform Trust is available in 16 languages. One section is about the disciplinary system. Further information about translation and interpreting facilities is to be found in the staff section of the Foreign Prisoners' Resource Pack, also published jointly as above.

SELF HARM

2.14   Disciplinary charges should not normally be brought either in respect of deliberate self harm or of preparations for this. This applies equally to repetitive acts of self harm. The Prison Service's response to self harm or attempted self harm must be to look to the care of the individual prisoner as its priority. If early signs of a tendency to self harm are overlooked or met with a punitive response, the risk of eventual tragedy may be increased. The threat of punishment should not form part of the strategy for dealing with such behaviour. Exceptionally a disciplinary charge may be brought if, in attempting self harm (for example by starting a fire) the health and safety of others is endangered. The person managing the incident must decide whether it is likely that the prisoner intended to cause injury to others or was reckless as to this. If he or she is satisfied about intention or recklessness, a charge may be brought. Otherwise the events should be interpreted as an indication of severe distress not calling for a punitive response.

MEDICAL EXAMINATION BEFORE THE HEARING

2.15 A punishment of cellular confinement must not be imposed unless the medical officer has certified on the form 256 that the prisoner is fit to undergo the punishment (as required by Prison Rule 58 and YOI Rule 61(1). The Segregation Safety Algorithm must be completed as part of this assessment and the final result recorded on the form F256, regardless of whether the cellular confinement takes place in the segregation unit or elsewhere. The medical officer and adjudicator must take particular care over the decision where the prisoner has a condition which may preclude cellular confinement, for example being on an open F2052SH or pregnant. 2.16 Omitted.
2.17 The final decision as to whether or not the accused is fit for the hearing rests with the adjudicator. This applies also to the punishment, except where the medical officer has assessed that the prisoner is unfit for cellular confinement. (See paragraphs 2.15 and 7.20).
2.18 Omitted.
2.19 Omitted.

PRELIMINARIES TO THE HEARING

2.20 If the accused, or his or her legal representative, asks before the hearing for a copy of all statements to be submitted in evidence so as to prepare a defence or mitigation these should be supplied at public expense. Arrangements should be made by a member of staff not conducting the hearing who should also provide the names of any witnesses to the incident of which the accused may not know. Copies should also be provided of any statements made or other material discovered in the course of investigation unless there are compelling grounds for nondisclosure. This might be the case where disclosure could present a real risk to its author or where a medical report constitutes one of the exclusions from disclosure under sections 4 or 5 of the Access to Health Records Act 1990. The latter exclusions are records or parts of records which in the opinion of the medical officer or other health professional concerned would disclose information likely to cause serious harm to the physical or mental health of the patient or of any other individual, or information provided by an individual other than the patient who could be identified from that information. A health care officer is not regarded as a health professional within the meaning of the Act unless he or she is nurse-qualified.

2.21 Where a prisoner asks before a hearing to interview prisoners or other witnesses who may have relevant evidence, in or out of hearing of prison staff, the governor should allow such interviews if he or she judges it reasonable and the witnesses are willing. Where it is decided that such interviews must take place within the hearing of staff, the officer supervising the interview must not be the reporting officer or any other officer who may be called to give evidence at the adjudication. The supervising officer must not disclose the nature of the discussion unless it presents a threat to security or unless there is a clear intention to defeat the ends of justice; in these circumstances the interview should be terminated.

2.22 A prisoner should be granted reasonable access to reference books to help prepare a defence and a request for an adjournment of a hearing for that purpose should be allowed.
2.23 Where a prisoner asks, before a hearing, for the names of witnesses or others involved in the incident which gave rise to the charge, whether of staff or prisoners, the names, if known, must be supplied. The governor should take steps, which do not disrupt the orderly running of the establishment, to identify the people the accused can describe. Members of staff will not be required to take part in an identification parade against their will

An adjudicator can decide not to proceed with a charge or to dismiss it, for example if the alleged offence is trivial or if medical evidence makes it clear that the accused is unfit for adjudication. The reason should be noted in the record of the hearing.

3.APPLICATIONS FOR ASSISTANCE OR LEGAL REPRESENTATION

ACCESS TO A SOLICITOR
3.1 Any prisoner whose charge is referred to the independent adjudicator must be offered the opportunity to seek legal representation. A copy of the F1127, as issued to the prisoner, must be put with the adjudication papers.
3.1A The adjudicator must adjourn a hearing if:
• after a charge has been read out, a prisoner who has requested legal assistance has not had
reasonable time to contact a solicitor; or
• the first time a prisoner asks to consult his/her solicitor is during the hearing.
Any further requests by an accused to consult a solicitor should be considered as they arise. In setting time limits for such consultation, the adjudicator will be guided by the nature of the charge and any impending date of release. The prisoner

must be advised when the hearing will resume. If by then s/he has not asked for or received advice the adjudicator may proceed providing s/he is satisfied that the prisoner has had reasonable opportunity to obtain advice.

3.1B A prisoner who does not know of a solicitor who will act for him/her should be advised to approach the Legal Services Officer for help in selecting one.

REQUEST FOR LEGAL HELP OR FOR A MCKENZIE FRIEND

3.2 At the start of every hearing the adjudicator must ask the prisoner whether he or she wishes to have additional assistance and, if the prisoner expresses interest, must explain about the possibilities of legal assistance or representation or of assistance from a friend or adviser (also known as a McKenzie friend .

3.3 Requests for assistance or legal representation may also be made at any later point in the adjudication. Circumstances during the hearing may also persuade an adjudicator to reverse a decision to refuse representation. Granting representation at a later stage will require an adjournment and possibly a new hearing with a different adjudicator who comes to the case afresh.

3.4 The prisoner may ask for assistance from an adviser or friend even if legal representation is refused. It is the prisoner's responsibility to nominate such a person who must be willing to act in the role. Adjudicators must consider such requests afresh, independently of any decision to refuse legal representation.

3.5 A McKenzie friend's role is limited to attending the hearing, taking notes, quietly making suggestions and giving advice to the prisoner and in this way assisting the latter in presenting the case and giving support. An adjudicator may allow greater participation, but if the McKenzie friend interferes or participates in the proceedings without the permission of the adjudicator, the latter may require him or her to leave.

CONSIDERING REQUESTS

3.6 The adjudicator may reach a decision on granting a McKenzie friend or legal representation on the basis of the charge, the reporting officer's statement and any statement the prisoner wishes to make or read out. The adjudicator should ask for other information where this appears to be necessary.

3.7 In considering requests for assistance or representation it is enough for the adjudicator to be satisfied, on balance, that they should or should not be granted. Adjudicators do not need to be sure beyond reasonable doubt that assistance or representation is not needed before rejecting a request.

3.8 Adjudicators must take account of the following six considerations, listed in the Divisional Court ruling in the Tarrant case (see Appendix 4), in deciding whether to grant legal representation or a McKenzie friend. The list is not exhaustive. The circumstances of individual cases might produce other considerations which should be taken into account when coming to a decision.

(a) The seriousness of the charge and of the potential penalty

There is no hard and fast rule as to how to determine seriousness. It is a matter of degree whether the seriousness of the charge or the potential penalty (including cases where several charges in combination will produce a combined maximum penalty that is serious), or a combination of both, points to legal representation, a McKenzie friend or neither. In the most serious cases, legal representation will no doubt be appropriate. In the least serious cases probably neither is necessary. In practice the adjudicator will consider this point in combination with the others.

(b) Where any points of law are likely to arise

This might indicate the need for legal representation rather than a McKenzie friend. Points of law could include cases where the prisoner's intentions or the definition of the offence are in question.

(c) The capacity of a particular prisoner to present his or her own case

This may indicate the need for either a legal representative or a friend or adviser. The decision will depend on the circumstances of the case and the judgement of the adjudicator. Prisoners who are incapable of preparing a written reply to the charge, those who are unlikely to be able to follow the proceedings or those who have difficulty expressing themselves verbally might need such help.

(d) Procedural difficulties

The adjudicator should take into account any special difficulties prisoners might have. For example, the prisoner may have been segregated under Rule 45 or Rule 46 and thus have had no opportunity to interview potential witnesses. An accused may have difficulty in cross-examining witnesses (particularly those giving evidence of an expert nature). How far a friend or legal adviser will be necessary, or able to help, will depend on the circumstances of the case and on who that person is. An adjudicator should tend to favour a legal representative rather than a McKenzie friend in cases where the prisoner will have difficulty in calling and questioning witnesses, since a McKenzie friend does not represent the prisoner and may not be allowed to question them.

(e) The need for reasonable speed

Delay is an inevitable consequence of granting legal representation since solicitors will wish to consult their clients, interview potential witnesses and generally prepare their case. McKenzie friends should be readily available but even so some deGlays may result from granting such assistance. This has to be balanced with other considerations and the overriding necessity is to ensure that the requirements of natural justice are respected.

(f) The need for fairness

Where, for example, a number of prisoners are alleged to have taken part in the same incident, the granting of assistance or legal representation to one may imply the need to grant it to others. Where help is granted to a prisoner for one charge it should also be allowed for other charges against the prisoner arising from the same incident.

3.9 For all McKenzie friend requests there is a further requirement that anyone agreed is both readily available and a suitable person. Both must be matters for the adjudicator's judgement. Should an accused ask for the assistance of a fellow prisoner who is willing and available to assist, a member of his or her family or of a friend from among the general public the request should be given proper consideration. If the prisoner nominates a solicitor, the latter must accept the role of friend and not of legal representative and may not be able to charge costs to public funds.

MATTERS ARISING FROM THE DECISION

3.10 Where legal representation or a McKenzie friend is agreed, it will be necessary to adjourn the hearing. It is the prisoner's responsibility to select a solicitor and to approach the latter or McKenzie friend. Where requests are refused it should normally be possible for the adjudicator to proceed with the adjudication forthwith. This is stated in the explanation of procedure at adjudications (form F1145) which must be made available to prisoners before adjudications.

3.11 Where a request for legal representation or for an adviser is refused the adjudication record (form F256) must be sufficiently detailed to show that the adjudicator has properly considered the request. The adjudicator must record that he or she has explained to the prisoner that the request has been considered in the light of the Tarrant criteria although the judgement need not be mentioned by name.

THE DE NOVO PRINCIPLE

3. 12 Adjudicators must not proceed to conduct adjudications if, in hearing and considering applications for legal

representation, legal advice or a McKenzie friend, they receive information or evidence (for example, details of the prisoner's defence or some relevant incriminating admissions of criminal, disciplinary or behavioural history) which make it impossible to hear the charge afresh (de novo). The test is whether the adjudicator can come to the adjudication proper without having been prejudiced by anything heard in considering a request for representation or advice.

3.13 An adjudicator who feels it is impossible to hear the charge de novo must adjourn the hearing so that it can be conducted by another adjudicator .

PRISON SERVICE LEGAL REPRESENTATION

3. 14 Consideration must be given to whether the Prison Service requires legal representation. This is most likely to be appropriate in cases where points of law or procedural difficulty are likely to arise. If it is decided that the Prison Service should be legally represented then a member of staff who will not adjudicate at the hearing must make arrangements through the Treasury Solicitor's agents as necessary. The adjudicator must have no direct involvement in these arrangements. It should be remembered that at a legally represented hearing the adjudicator remains the master of his/her own procedure and that procedure remains inquisitorial and not adversarial in nature.

ARRANGEMENTS FOR LEGAL REPRESENTATIVES

3.15 Legal representatives may ask for certain facilities in advance of the hearing which may have a bearing on security or good order and discipline. Examples are a visit to the scene of an alleged incident or interviews with prisoners or staff. Such requests must be considered by a member of staff not involved in the adjudication; it would be wrong for the adjudicator to decide on the security aspect of facilities requested.

3.16   When such an interview is requested with other prisoners or with staff, and they are willing to be interviewed, the member of staff making the arrangements should normally allow the interview. Where such requests are made during the hearing, the adjudicator, provided he or she considers the request reasonable, should ask a member of staff not involved in the adjudication to make suitable arrangements and, where necessary, should adjourn the proceedings for that purpose.

3.17   Where the governor considering the request for facilities cannot provide them and the adjudicator believes that this prejudices a fair hearing, there may be no alternative but to dismiss the charge.

3.18   Interviews between the prisoner's legal representative and potential witnesses should normally take place in sight but out of hearing of prison officers.

3.19   Where the member of staff considering the request for facilities decides that interviews must take place within the hearing of staff for reasons of security or because of the possibility of coercion or collusion between witnesses, the officer supervising the interview must not disclose the nature of the discussion unless it presents a threat to security (in which case, the interview should be terminated) or unless there is a clear intention to defeat the ends of justice. In these circumstances the adjudicator must be informed at the adjudication.

ARRANGEMENTS FOR McKENZIE FRIENDS

3.20   McKenzie friends may ask for arrangements to be made before the hearing for access to various facilities in order to help the accused prepare the case. Requests must be considered by a member of staff not involved in the adjudication and such facilities as appear reasonable for the purpose should be offered. Should the McKenzie friend come from outside the establishment it will not be necessary, for example, to provide unlimited visiting orders so that a case may be prepared. The

McKenzie friend, by definition, is not a legal representative and should not be permitted to use facilities offered as if they were simply opportunities for, say, extra personal visits.

4.GENERAL MANAGEMENT OF ADJUDICATIONS AND MINOR REPORTS

ADJUDICATIONS IN PRISONER'S ABSENCE

4.1   If a prisoner refuses to attend an adjudication it should be explained by the adjudicator or by a member of staff appointed by the adjudicator, that the hearing will proceed in the prisoner's absence. It should be noted on the record of the hearing that he or she has been seen and informed. If the accused still refuses to attend a not guilty plea should be entered. The adjudicator should consider keeping the prisoner informed at key points in the proceedings, for example, to allow him or her to attend to explain mitigation if a finding of guilt is reached. Such approaches to the prisoner should be noted on the record of the hearing. The prisoner must be informed of the result of the hearing and of any punishment imposed as soon as possible after its conclusion.

4.2   A prisoner who is prepared to attend an adjudication who is indecently dressed, or is in a condition which is offensive to the adjudicator or others (for example on dirty protest), should be told that the adjudication will proceed in his or her absence. The record of the adjudication should be noted to show that the warning had been issued, by whom, and when.

4.3   When a prisoner has been granted legal representation the legal representative should be present at an adjudication where the client is to be adjudicated upon in his or her absence.

MULTIPLE CHARGES

4.4 Where more than one charge is laid against a prisoner in respect of a single incident it will be safest to hear all the evidence on all the charges before reaching a finding on any of them. There is otherwise a risk that the adjudicator will appear prejudiced on subsequent charges by the decision reached on the first. When a prisoner is charged with two or more offences arising out of separate incidents these may be heard consecutively by the same adjudicator. He or she must consider the need for all cases to start afresh (the de novo principle) and decide whether it would appear biased to continue. The test for bias is neither whether the adjudicator feels biased or unbiased nor how the accused feels but whether a reasonable person observing the hearing with full knowledge of the relevant facts would consider it fair. If one of a series of multiple charges is to be referred to the independent adjudicator, then all charges arising from a single incident must also be referred.

CHARGES WITH MORE THAN ONE ACCUSED

4.5 Where more than one prisoner has been charged, cases may be dealt with either at a single hearing at which all accused are present or separately and in stages, using adjournments, to allow two or more cases to proceed concurrently to virtually simultaneous conclusions. Should one of the prisoners charged with an incident have the case referred to an independent adjudicator, then all other prisoners charged in connection with the same incident should also normally have their charges referred.

4.6 Where more than one prisoner is charged with an offence relating to one incident and the adjudicator decides to hear the cases separately care must be taken to ensure that the accused is not found guilty on evidence that the adjudicator has heard elsewhere. Evidence heard at one adjudication must not be taken into account in reaching a decision at another adjudication unless the evidence is presented at that other hearing too.

PHYSICAL ARRANGEMENTS

4.7 Adjudicators should ensure that the general atmosphere is as relaxed as possible whilst maintaining sufficient formality to emphasise the importance of the proceedings.

4.8 In determining the number and deployment of staff during a hearing account will be taken of the general demeanour of the prisoner and the nature of the alleged offence.

4.9 Upon commencing or resuming a hearing, the prisoner and escort (if any) should enter the adjudication room before the reporting officer and witnesses. At any adjournment the reporting officer and witnesses should leave the adjudication room before the prisoner and escort. This is to preclude suggestions that evidence may have been given to the adjudicator in the absence of the accused.

4.10 The prisoner must be allowed to sit and should be offered writing materials to take notes. Arrangements should be made for all other participants in the proceedings to be seated if possible.

4.11 There must be two escorting officers in every hearing before the independent adjudicator. In hearings before Prison Service personnel, the governor will decide if escorting officers are necessary. Any escorting officers must sit to the side(s) of the accused. They must not be in front of or facing the prisoner. They must not maintain eye contact with the prisoner during the proceedings or indulge in any other behaviour that may seem intimidatory or an obstruction to the stating of a defence or mitigation. This could constitute grounds for an application for judicial review or grounds for quashing under Prison Rule 61 or YOI Rule 64 on appeal.

4.12 The prisoner's record (F2050) should not be in the adjudication room. Its presence might raise the suspicion in the mind of the accused or his or her representative that the adjudicator had access to it beforehand and thus could not come to the hearing *de novo*.

ADJOURNMENTS

4.13 Adjournments may be necessary for a number of reasons. Examples might be when a material witness is sick, when it is necessary to arrange for the attendance of an interpreter (see 2.13), when legal representation has been granted and the accused needs time to make arrangements, when it is necessary to obtain the results of forensic analysis or simply because an accused is not in a position to proceed. An adjudicator should always offer an adjournment to the accused if it has been necessary to amend the detail of a charge or if the accused has misunderstood its nature. Where a material witness is sick the adjudicator may proceed with written evidence if the accused does not wish to question it. A reporting officer or other officer witness who is on sick leave may nevertheless be invited to participate in the adjudication. There will be occasions upon which officers may be fit enough to attend for this purpose whilst remaining unfit for the full range of duties. Adjudicators should consider whether or not prolonged adjournment endangers the requirement of being fair to the accused. If there is likely to be undue delay it may be that natural justice will require the adjudicator not to proceed with the hearing. Circumstances will vary and it will be up to the adjudicator to decide in a particular case whether or not it is fair to proceed.

4.14 When legal representation has been granted there is likely to be some delay whilst legal representatives are appointed and they make their preparations. It is important therefore that the adjudicator should set a date for the represented hearing at the time that legal representation is granted. As a standard, it is recommended that the hearing should be resumed at a date no later than six weeks after representation has been granted. If legal representatives are not then ready to proceed, the adjudicator should consider whether an adjournment is justified. If it is, a further and final date no more than three weeks later should be set. Adjudicators should always consider requests for adjournments carefully in order to ensure that prisoners are given a fair chance to prepare their case before a hearing. If adjudicators do not feel that the request is justified they may reject it and conclude the hearing. Adjudicators must bear in mind that delay can become a serious impediment to achieving a fair hearing and that on occasions it may therefore be necessary to press on in the face of objections from legal representatives.

4.15 If the charge is criminal in character and the governor believes it is sufficiently serious to be reported to the police, the hearing should be opened and adjourned until the outcome of the police investigation or subsequent prosecution is known. The accused must be informed of the reason for the adjournment. (For guidance on referral to the police see Section 11 and Appendix 3).

4.16 Omitted.

SEGREGATION

4.17 Prison Rule 53(4) or YOI Rule 58(4) allows for a prisoner to be segregated pending adjudication on the authority of the governor or controller. This term includes the officer for the time being in charge of the establishment. The authority to segregate can be delegated to any senior operational manager (Grade F and above). Rule 53(4) or YOI Rule 58(4) can only be used for the period between the alleged offence and the initial hearing. It should not be an automatic measure but be used where there is a real need, such as the risk of collusion or intimidation relating to the alleged offence which segregation of the accused might prevent.

When deciding upon segregation under this Rule, the governor/ controller or senior operational manager must take into account information from the Segregation Safety Algorithm (see PSO 1700). Segregation under Prison Rule 53(4) or YOI Rule 58(4) and the reasons for it must be recorded on the prisoner's main record (F2050).

4.18 If the adjudicator's initial hearing is inconclusive, but the need for segregation is still felt to exist, it may only then be authorized under Prison Rule 46, YOI Rule 49. Prisoners thus segregated :

(a) will be given the reasons for their segregation both orally and in writing by a senior operational manager;

(b) will not be deprived of any facilities to which s/he is normally entitled;

(c) will be visited daily by a healthcare professional if the medical officer has not visited or is not visiting. The medical officer must visit each prisoner in cellular confinement as often as his/her individual health needs dictate.

4.19 It is recommended that governors should review the need for continued segregation at least every seven days and decisions should be noted in the prisoner's main record.

4.20 If continued segregation is necessary and the adjudication cannot take place for some time, the governor should consider the need to transfer the prisoner temporarily elsewhere where he or she may be held on ordinary location pending the adjudication.

4.21 If legal representation has been granted and the governor believes that temporary transfer would be appropriate, he or she should seek the views of the prisoner's solicitor. If and when a transfer is arranged, the solicitor must be informed of the prisoner's new location.

4.22 A prisoner segregated as above should only be located in a segregation unit or any part of the establishment normally used for prisoners undergoing punishment when there is no suitable cell available elsewhere. However, where the adjudication room is in the punishment block a prisoner may be held in the punishment block on the morning of the adjudication.

RECORDS

4.23 The adjudicator must ensure that a record of proceedings is taken down on form F256. Form F256 is a document that may be required for a formal review of the hearing. It need not be a verbatim transcript but it must record the essence of the case and indicate the way in which the adjudicator pursued the inquiry. If the prisoner is found guilty it should be clear from the record why the adjudicator rejected any defence put forward. The salient points of procedure will vary from hearing to hearing but form F256 must record:

- action taken in response to the accused's answers to the preliminaries
- action taken in response to any written statement by the prisoner - is it read out ?
- requests for witnesses and how they are dealt with
- the adjudicator's own consideration of the need to call any witnesses on his or her own account
- requests for legal or other representation or assistance, the reasons for those requests, and the ground for the adjudicator's decision
- the adjudicator's response to any other requests, for example for an adjournment or for access to this Manual, and the grounds for decisions made
- the reason for any other adjournment
- any mitigating evidence the adjudicator has taken into consideration in deciding a punishment. Mitigation should be recorded as it is decided, whether in part 3 or part 4 of the record of the hearing.

4.24 Where two cases proceed together, the bulk of the hearing can be recorded on one form F256, and the form F256 relating to the other prisoner charged can simply refer to that record in part 3.

4.25 Verdicts and punishments must be recorded separately.

4.26 Although the record must eventually be on form F256, it does not necessarily have to be taken down on form F256 at the time but may be entered subsequently, for example from contemporaneous notes. An example might be if the record of the hearing is later typed by a member of staff. The adjudicator must be satisfied that the subsequent note is an accurate record of the hearing. It should then be signed by the adjudicator who is responsible for the adequacy and accuracy of the record. Should it prove necessary to amend the record of the hearing this may only be done for the purposes of accuracy. This should be done by striking through the original text and entering amendments above or adjacent to the deletions. Snopake, Liquid Paper or similar products should not be used for this purpose.

4.27 Immediately after an adjudication:

(a) details of the offence, the finding and any punishment should be entered on the prisoner's adjudication record (F2050E) in the same terms as those entered on the record of the adjudication

(b) the F2050E entry will be checked and initialled by the senior officer attending the adjudication and present when the punishment was imposed who will also initial the relevant space provided on form F256

(c) where an earlier suspended punishment has been dealt with the decision on that punishment should be recorded on the relevant previous form F256 and on the relevant F2050E.

4.28 The prisoner's record and form F256 should be made available to the appropriate member of staff who will:

(a) make any necessary amendments to the prisoner's key release dates

(b) inform the prisoner of any changes and record this on the back of the F2052A Inmate History

(c) take any other consequential action, for example notify the parole authorities.

4.29 The record of the hearing must be retained at the establishment for three years after the adjudication in case of a subsequent complaint being made.

MINOR REPORTS

4.30 The Home Secretary has authorised governors to operate minor reports systems to deal with certain charges against young prisoners and young offenders. It is for governors to decide whether to operate minor reporting systems in their establishments.

4.31 The charges which may be heard are those under paragraphs 6, 7 and 18, 20 –22, 24 – 26 and 29 of YOI Rule 55 for those in YOIs or part of a prison designated as a YOI, and under paragraphs 5, 6, 17-23, and 25 of Prison Rule 51 (excluding 17a, 20a, and 24a) for remand prisoners aged under 21 (whether unconvicted or unsentenced) held in local prisons and remand centres. To qualify for inclusion in the minor systems, charges brought under YOI Rule 55 paragraph 29, or Prison Rule 51 paragraph 25 may only refer to other offences specified in this paragraph.

4.32 The punishments available for those found guilty at minor report hearings are:

a caution

forfeiture of specified facilities for a period not exceeding three days

stoppage of earnings for a period not exceeding three days

extra work outside the normal working week for a period not exceeding three days and for not more than two hours on any day.

4.33 Those conducting minor reports hearings must have specific delegated authority from the governing governor, must be not below the rank of principal officer and must have received training provided or approved by the Prison Service for the purpose.

4.34 Minor reports hearings are subject to all Prison or YOI Rules relating to adjudications, modified by the above restrictions on offences and punishments. Because the system should not be used for serious offences it should not be necessary to use the power to segregate the accused before the hearing.

4.35 Procedures must be conducted fairly in accordance with the rules of natural justice. Adjudicators must be satisfied beyond reasonable doubt of guilt before finding a charge proved.

4.36 Those responsible for minor reports procedures should base them on simplified versions of adjudication procedures contained in this Manual. The accused must be told in advance that he or she is on report, and be informed of the nature and detail of the charge. The adjudicator must be satisfied that the accused has had sufficient time to consider a reply to the charge.

4.37 Medical examination is not necessary for every hearing but if, during the hearing, the adjudicator considers that medical advice about the accused is needed, the hearing should be adjourned and resumed after a medical examination has been carried out.

4.38 A record of the hearing should be kept in the minor report book and noted in the prisoner's record (F2050). Minor report books should be examined and initialled by the governing governor or next most senior governor each week. There should be regular standardisation meetings chaired by one of the latter which officers authorised to conduct hearings should attend.

4.39 Where minor reports systems operate, the option remains to hear any specific charge under the relevant paragraphs either at a minor report hearing or at a governor's adjudication. However it is not possible for a governor to rehear a case already the subject of a minor report hearing or to set aside the findings: any quashing or mitigation would need to be under the arrangements for adjudications set out in Section 8. Nor has the adjudicating officer any authority to refer to the governor the adjudication of any charge that has been laid as a minor report.

INDEPENDENT ADJUDICATIONS

4.40 Responsibility for the daily operation of the independent adjudications scheme rests with Bow Street Magistrate's Court. Any queries, including those about referrals or bookings, or requests to Independent Adjudicators, including those from legal representatives, must be made via telephone number, 020 7853 9254 or fax 020 7853 9298. Establishments must use the dedicated intranet email address for referrals and notification of transfers and outcomes.

5. EVIDENCE

GENERAL

5.1 It is for the adjudicator to assess the truth of each statement given in evidence and, where there is doubt, to try to obtain further information that will help an assessment. An example is where a prisoner's defence is a simple contradiction of the evidence of a member of staff.

5.2 An adjudicator may need to assist an unrepresented prisoner who has difficulty framing questions and will then be responsible for discovering from witnesses the information the accused seeks.

5.3 The accused or his or her legal representative must hear, and have the opportunity to challenge, all the evidence. The adjudicator must not consider anything relevant to the alleged offence which was not brought out in the course of the hearing, although he or she may of course have regard to general knowledge of the background of the prison in which the incident is alleged to have taken.

5.4 The accused may ask questions directly of witnesses. Only if he or she in any way abuses that opportunity should the adjudicator insist on questions being put through him or her.

WRITTEN EVIDENCE
5.5 The adjudicator may accept written evidence but if the accused denies or contests it, its reliability may be put in doubt. Thus a previously written statement may be accepted only if it is read out, and either the writer is present at the hearing so that the accused may have an opportunity of questioning, or the accused consents to it being accepted without having such an opportunity. The reporting officer may read his or her evidence from form F254 which will be incorporated in the record of the hearing. The accused may present a written defence on the reverse of form F1127. In this case he or she may read it out at the hearing or ask that it be read out by the adjudicator.

PHYSICAL EVIDENCE
5.6 It is important that physical evidence is retained and produced at the hearing. The accused must be allowed to ask questions about it in the same way as any other evidence. If there is a dispute relating to the location of an alleged offence it may be necessary to visit the location in order to ascertain the facts. In this case the hearing should be adjourned and all relevant parties should attend the location. A note of the visit and what was discovered should be entered on the record of the hearing

HEARSAY EVIDENCE
5.7 The adjudicator may decide to hear hearsay evidence subject to the overriding requirement to be fair to the accused. First hand evidence is obviously preferable to hearsay evidence but there will be occasions, for instance where no members of staff witnessed the alleged offence or where an absconder from

another establishment is being dealt with, when a reporting officer has to rely on what he or she has been told. If the accused pleads not guilty, a finding of guilt based solely on hearsay evidence would clearly be unsafe. Where an accused disputes the hearsay evidence and for this purpose wishes to question the witness, and where there are insuperable or very serious difficulties in arranging attendance, the adjudicator should refuse to admit that evidence or, if it has already come to notice, should expressly dismiss it from consideration. If there are prisoner witnesses who are called but who refuse to give evidence the adjudicator must assess whether, in the light of their refusal to give evidence at first hand, the hearsay evidence is credible. The adjudicator should disregard the hearsay evidence where there is any doubt.

CIRCUMSTANTIAL EVIDENCE

5.8   There may be occasions when, in the absence of sufficient first hand evidence, it will be proper for an adjudicator to take circumstantial evidence into account. Circumstantial evidence is that which tends to suggest that the accused committed the offence as opposed to direct evidence that he or she did. It is unlikely that this alone will ever be sufficient upon which to reach a finding but it will add to the sum of available information, and thus help to explain more fully the context of the alleged offence.

WITNESS ISSUES

5.9   The accused should be asked to indicate in advance of the hearing the witnesses he or she would like to call so that arrangements can be made to make them available. The accused may still, during the course of the hearing, ask to call additional witnesses.

5.10   Any person employed by the Prison Service may be required to appear as a witness and give evidence as part of his or her duties (but see 5.21]). The same is true of directors and prisoner custody officers in the case of contracted out prisons and services. Prisoner witnesses may be required to attend the adjudication but cannot be compelled to give evidence. If they decline, this must be recorded in the record of the hearing. Other people may be invited to attend as witnesses but there is no power to compel their attendance. Copies of the letter of invitation and of the reply, if any, should be made available to the accused and form part of the record of the hearing. If their presence is required by the accused and their evidence is deemed relevant to the hearing, and yet there are compelling security reasons why they should not be admitted to the prison or they decline to attend, charges against the prisoner may have to be dismissed.

5.11 An adjudicator has the discretion to refuse to call witnesses named by the prisoner or by the reporting officer but this must be done reasonably and on proper grounds and not, for example, for reasons of administrative convenience or because the adjudicator considers the case against the prisoner is already made out. The accused should first be asked what assistance or evidence the accused believes the witness might give. If the request is refused the adjudicator should give reasons and these should be noted on the record of the hearing. A witness may be refused, for example, if it is clear that he or she was not present at a material time and had no relevant information to offer, if the adjudicator believes that the request is simply part of an attempt to render the hearing unmanageable, or if the adjudicator already accepts the evidence that the accused hopes the witness will confirm.

5.12 If, unknown to the accused, someone has witnessed the incident, and a member of staff knows this, he or she must bring this to the attention of the adjudicator. If the accused knows of a witness but refuses to help to identify that person, the adjudicator is under no duty to adjourn to allow for an investigation as to who the alleged witness may be.

5.13 It is important to consider whether material evidence could be given by a witness who has not been called by the accused or the reporting officer. The adjudicator is able to request a witness of his or her own volition and should do so if he or she believes the witness has material evidence to give.

5.14 If during an adjudication the adjudicator is in doubt about the prisoner's capacity or state of mind at the time of an alleged offence, the medical officer should be asked if he or she can assist. The medical officer can properly relate relevant confidential information as evidence at the hearing. Such information can be challenged in the same way as any other evidence. The adjudicator should dismiss a charge against a prisoner if it is considered, having heard all the evidence, that at the time of the alleged offence the accused could not, on medical grounds, be held responsible for his or her actions.

5.15 If the adjudicator is not satisfied that the accused is fit enough to take part in the hearing the medical officer should be called to give evidence on the point. If the adjudicator is still not satisfied, a second medical opinion can be sought, usually after such a request has been made by the accused's representative, although this will not always be the case. Ultimately, the adjudicator must decide, having listened to expert evidence, whether or not a prisoner is fit for adjudication. An adjournment may be appropriate if any incapacity is thought to be temporary.

5.16 It is important that, on leaving the adjudication room, no witness should have the opportunity to talk to those waiting to give evidence.

EXAMINATION OF WITNESSES

5.17 An accused must be allowed to ask questions of the reporting officer and witnesses. These questions should be asked directly and only if the accused abuses this should the adjudicator require questions to be put through him or her. The accused must not be prevented from asking questions of witnesses unless the adjudicator is convinced that they are irrelevant to the point at issue. The adjudicator, the reporting officer and the accused may all question witnesses.

ALLEGATIONS AGAINST STAFF MADE BEFORE OR AT AN ADJUDICATION

5.18 If an allegation is made before or during an adjudication, whether by the accused or by a witness, the adjudicator should consider whether it is relevant to the charge being heard (either as part of a defence or mitigation). If the allegation is clearly not relevant the prisoner should be advised of the need to make it in writing if he or she has not already done so; the adjudication may continue, and the allegation should be investigated separately in the normal way.

5.19 If it is not clear whether the allegation is relevant, or if it is clearly relevant to the charge being heard, the adjudicator should consider what steps need to be taken to allow a full investigation to take place. It will often be the case that the adjudicator can thoroughly investigate the allegation at the hearing by calling witnesses and questioning the prisoner making the allegation. In these cases the adjudication may be concluded without a separate investigation being carried out.

5.20 In the remaining cases, where the allegation appears too weighty or complicated to be investigated adequately during the hearing, the adjudicator should open but then adjourn the proceedings to allow for a full investigation to take place separately. The adjudicator must ensure that any evidence that he or she subsequently takes into account when the hearing is resumed is made available to the prisoner and that witnesses are called if necessary. The adjudicator must ensure that he or she is not influenced by any matters arising out of the investigation of which he or she may become aware and which are not presented as evidence. If there is a danger of such influence the resumed hearing should be conducted by a different adjudicator who comes to the proceedings afresh thus preserving the de novo principle.

5.21 A member of staff cannot be compelled to incriminate himself or herself at a hearing. If allegations are made by an accused and a member of staff thereby becomes suspected of misconduct which could lead to a disciplinary charge any further statement made by the member of staff would be inadmissible in disciplinary proceedings unless he or she had first been cautioned under paragraph 1.3v of the document Conduct and Discipline in the Prison Service. The options would be either to stop questioning the member of staff pending a formal disciplinary investigation into the allegation or to continue the adjudication in the knowledge that whatever the member of staff says must not be used in subsequent disciplinary action against him or her.

6. OFFENCES

6.1 The guidance in this section is not comprehensive but presents an outline of the essential elements of disciplinary offences under the paragraphs in Prison Rule 51 and YOI Rule 55.

6.2 Intent and recklessness are defined in Appendix 4. Of the Prison Discipline Rules.

(In the following paragraph headings where there are two reference numbers the first reference number refers to the Prison Rule paragraph and the second reference number to the YOI Rule paragraph.).

PARAGRAPH 1 - COMMITS ANY ASSAULT

6.3 Specimen charge. Under Prison Rule 51/YOI Rule 50, paragraph 1, commits any assault. At [time] on [date] in [place] you assaulted [name] by punching him.

6.4 A prisoner will be guilty of assault if he or she intentionally or recklessly applies unlawful force to another person. Under the criminal law an accused may also be guilty of assault if, without applying unlawful force, he or she causes another person to fear the application of immediate unlawful force to that person. However, since Prison Rule 51, paragraph 20 or YOI Rule 55, paragraph 22 provides a ready alternative for this type of behaviour, it is recommended that a charge under one of these paragraphs would be preferable.

6.5   Evidence. Before an adjudicator can be satisfied of guilt beyond reasonable doubt the following must be established.

a)   The accused applied force to another (or, subject to the guidance above, committed an act which caused another person to fear the immediate application of force to that person).
b)   The accused intended this, or was reckless as to whether it would happen.
c)   The force was unlawful, in other words the accused did not use only that force which was reasonable in self-defence or to prevent the commission of a serious crime. What is reasonable will vary according to the circumstances of each offence as the accused honestly believed them to be, and bearing in mind that in a moment of attack an accused cannot always weigh exactly the amount of force required to resist.

PARAGRAPH 2/3 - DETAINS ANY PERSON AGAINST HIS WILL

6.6   Specimen charge. Under Prison Rule 51 paragraph 2/ YOI Rule 55, paragraph 3, detains any person against his will. At [time] (OR between [time] and [time]) on [date] in [place] you detained [name] against his will.

6.7   This charge is designed to deal with the hostage taker. It is important when laying and dealing with these charges to decide whether or not the victim colluded in events. Where collusion is suspected it may be appropriate to lay a charge under paragraph 3/4 either instead of or in addition to one under paragraph 2/3 if the incident has also involved a refusal to allow officers or anyone else working at the prison to enter a cell or any other part of the establishment.

6.8   Evidence. Before an adjudicator can be satisfied of guilt beyond reasonable doubt the following must be established.

a)   The victim was detained. Freedom of movement must have been curtailed in some way by force or threat of force. Any item used as apparatus for restricting movement should be produced in evidence. The detention may be in the open.

b)   The detention was against the victim's will. Collusion amounts to a complete defence. Collusion means that the incident was planned and executed as a joint venture freely entered into by all parties and remained in that state throughout. Details of injuries sustained by the victim would tend to negate collusion as would matters such as evidence of previous enmity between victim and accused. The adjudicator will wish to investigate whether or not there has been any attempt by the accused to pressurise the victim into saying he or she was colluding. A hostage-taking may begin with collusion and yet develop into an unlawful detention where one party changes his or her mind and wishes to surrender but is prevented from doing so by the other. The evidence of negotiators will be of importance in proving the lack of consent.

c)   The accused intended the victim to be detained against his or her will, or was reckless as to whether this would happen.

PARAGRAPH 3/4 - DENIES ACCESS TO ANY PART OF THE PRISON TO ANY OFFICER OR ANY PERSON (OTHER THAN A PRISONER) WHO IS AT THE PRISON FOR THE PURPOSE OF WORKING THERE

6.9   Specimen charge. Under Prison Rule 51 paragraph 3/ YOI Rule 55, paragraph 4, denies access to any part of the prison to any officer or any person (other than a prisoner) who is at the prison for the purpose of working there. At [time] (OR between [time] and [time]) on [date] in [place] you denied access to [part of prison] to [name], an officer of the prison (OR a person who was at the prison for the purpose of working there), by barricading your door.

6.10 This charge is designed to deal with barricades but is also appropriate, for instance, where the prisoner denies access without constructing a physical barrier.

6.11 Evidence. Before an adjudicator can be satisfied of guilt beyond reasonable doubt the following must be established.

a) Access was denied.
b) The site was part of a prison or YOI.
c) The person denied access was an officer (which in this context means a prison governor, prison officer, chaplain, medical officer, controller, prison director or prisoner custody officer) or anyone else (other than a prisoner) who was at the prison for the purpose of working there.
d) The accused intended such a person to be denied access, or was reckless as to whether this would happen.

PARAGRAPH 4/5 - FIGHTS WITH ANY PERSON

6.12 Specimen charge. Under Prison Rule 51 paragraph 4/ YOI Rule 55, paragraph 5, fights with any person. At [time] on [date] in [place] you were fighting with [name].

6.13 Evidence. Before an adjudicator can be satisfied of guilt beyond reasonable doubt the following must be established.

a) The accused intentionally committed an assault by inflicting unlawful force on another person. Fighting is similar to assault or any other charge in that self-defence is a complete defence. If the accused acted only in self-defence the force will not have been unlawful. It is not however a defence to a charge of fighting or assault that a prisoner consented to be injured.

b) The assault must have been committed in the context of a fight with the other person. It is for the adjudicator and not the witness to decide whether the conduct did or did not amount to a fight. Unlike an assault, a fight must involve more than a single blow or a single act of forcible resistance: it must continue for a sufficient rime to amount to a fight in the ordinary sense of that word. It is also implicit in the idea of a fight that another person must also have been involved in events. This does not mean that the accused can be found guilty only if the other person is also found guilty. The latter may have a defence, for example acting in self-defence. But it does mean that the other person must have applied force, whether by blows or forceful resistance, to the accused.

PARAGRAPH 5/6 - INTENTIONALLY ENDANGERS THE HEALTH OR PERSONAL SAFETY OF OTHERS OR, BY HIS CONDUCT, IS RECKLESS WHETHER SUCH HEALTH OR PERSONAL SAFETY IS ENDANGERED.

6.14 Specimen charge. Under Prison Rule 51 paragraph 5/ YOI Rule 55, paragraph 6, intentionally endangers the health or personal safety of others or, by his conduct, is reckless whether such health or personal safety is endangered. At [time] on [date] in [place] you intentionally endangered (OR by your conduct you recklessly endangered) the health or personal safety of [name or names] by throwing a can of corrosive fluid to the ground.

6.15 A charge under this paragraph may, on occasion, be correct when a prisoner is alleged unlawfully to have abstracted electricity by tampering with the mains supply to wire up a radio or other electrical item. This should be done only when the criteria in 6.16 are established. In most cases the recommended action however is to have in operation a local rule and then to lay a charge under paragraph 23 or YOI Rule, paragraph 26 (see below).

6.16 Evidence. Before an adjudicator can be satisfied of guilt beyond reasonable doubt the following must be established.

a) The health or personal safety of at least one person other than the accused was endangered, in other words there was a definite and serious risk of harm to the health and safety of such a person.

b) The danger was caused by the accused's conduct.

c) The accused intended this to occur, or was reckless as to whether it would.

PARAGRAPH 6/7 - INTENTIONALLY OBSTRUCTS AN OFFICER IN THE EXECUTION OF HIS DUTY, OR ANY PERSON (OTHER THAN A PRISONER) WHO IS AT THE PRISON FOR THE PURPOSE OF WORKING THERE, IN THE PERFORMANCE OF HIS WORK

6.17 Specimen charge. Under Prison Rule 51 paragraph 6/ YOI Rule 55, paragraph 7, intentionally obstructs an officer in the execution of his duty, or any person (other than a prisoner) who is at the prison for the purpose of working there, in the performance of his work. At [time] on [date] in [place] you intentionally obstructed [name], an officer of the prison, in the execution of his duty (OR a person who was at the prison for the purpose of working there, in the performance of his work), by placing your foot in the door.

6.18 This charge covers physical obstruction but not exclusively so. A prisoner who deliberately provides false information to an officer might be charged with this offence.

6.19 Evidence. Before an adjudicator can be satisfied of guilt beyond reasonable doubt the following must be established.

a) There was an obstruction of some sort, physical or otherwise.

b) The person obstructed was an officer (as defined in 6.11 above) or anyone else (other than a prisoner) who was at the prison for the purpose of working there.

c) The officer was attempting to carry out his or her duty, or the person was attempting to perform his or her work.
d) The accused intended such a person to be obstructed in such a way.

PARAGRAPH 7/8 - ESCAPES OR ABSCONDS FROM PRISON OR FROM LEGAL CUSTODY.

6.20 Specimen charge. Under Prison Rule 51 paragraph 7/ YOI Rule 55, paragraph 8, escapes or absconds from prison or from legal custody. At [time] (OR between [time] and [time]) on [date] in [place] you escaped from HMP [name] (OR you absconded from the farm party OR you escaped from an escort).

6.21 Escaping or absconding refers to the act of getting clean away from the prison or legal custody. If the prisoner did not get beyond the boundary of the establishment in trying to escape, a charge under paragraph 25 or YOI Rule, paragraph 29, would be correct. If a prisoner at an open establishment absents himself or herself for a specific purpose, such as buying something in a nearby shop, with every intention of returning to the prison, then a charge under paragraph 18 or YOI Rule, paragraph 20 would apply.

6.22 Evidence. Before an adjudicator can be satisfied of guilt beyond reasonable doubt the following must be established.

a) The prisoner was held in prison or in legal custody. The latter includes being escorted to or from a prison by a prison officer or a prisoner custody officer, or working on an outside party. A copy of the committal warrant should be produced in evidence together with the details of the provisional automatic release date or conditional release date at the time of the escape.

b) The prisoner escaped or absconded. These terms are interchangeable since they are the same in law. It is for the adjudicator to decide whether the conduct alleged amounted to an escape, therefore the details of the charge should contain details of the events alleged and not merely "he escaped from HMP [name]".

c) The prisoner had no lawful authority to do what he or she did. It would be a defence that he or she had been authorised by the governor to leave the prison or the control of the officer.

d) The prisoner intended to escape. It must be shown that the prisoner knew he or she was leaving lawful custody without lawful authority. This may be proved by all the circumstances, for example the tools used, the actions of the accused after the escape, and explanations given on return to custody. It is a defence if the prisoner genuinely believed that he or she had authority to go where he or she did. Where an accused states that this is the case, the reasonableness or otherwise of the belief is a matter which may affect the credibility of the accused's evidence.

PARAGRAPH 8/9 -FAILS TO COMPLY WITH ANY CONDITION UPON WHICH HE IS TEMPORARILY RELEASED UNDER RULE 9 OF THESE RULES, OR RULE 5 OF YOI RULES

6.23 Specimen charge. Under Prison Rule 51 paragraph 8/ YOI Rule 55, paragraph 9, fails to comply with any condition upon which he is temporarily released, under Rule 9, or YOI Rule 5. At [time] (OR between [time] and [time]) on [date] in [place], having been temporarily released, you failed to comply with the condition that you should [condition].

6.24 Where a prisoner is charged with failing to return, a frequently used defence is that he or she was not well enough to do so. Every licence issued under Rule 9/5 should include a statement to be signed by a doctor if he or she considers that the prisoner is not fit to travel or to be conveyed to a prison health care centre. If the statement is signed by a doctor before the licence expires the accused has a complete defence to the charge. However, if the statement has not been signed by a doctor but some other form of medical certificate has been produced, the adjudicator must consider the terms of that certificate to establish whether or not it shows that the prisoner was unfit to travel or be conveyed to a prison health care centre. A prisoner who was physically prevented from returning due to circumstances that were genuinely beyond his or her control would also have a defence to a charge of failure to return.

6.25 If it has been made a condition of the licence that it must be presented to a doctor if the prisoner feels too ill to return from temporary release failure to do so amounts to a breach of the conditions of the licence and therefore justifies a charge in those specific terms.

6.26 Prisoners who are alleged to have misbehaved whilst on any form of release on temporary licence may only be charged under Rule 51(8) or YOI Rule 55(9). It is important to establish that the licence made clear what was expected of the prisoner whilst on release on temporary licence and that the alleged behaviour contravened those conditions. For example, it will not be sufficient to say that the prisoner "was arrested whilst released on temporary licence" - a charge can only be brought if there is evidence that an accused contravened the conditions laid down. Prosecution for an alleged criminal offence whilst released on temporary licence does not debar disciplinary proceedings for other breaches of conditions of the licence.

6.27 Evidence. Before an adjudicator can be satisfied of guilt beyond reasonable doubt the following must be established.

a) A temporary release licence signed by a governor with authority to do so had been issued, its terms were clear and unambiguous and the prisoner was made aware of them. A copy of the licence, preferably the original, should be produced in evidence.

b) The accused failed to comply with any of the conditions. This includes the condition as to time of return.

c) The accused intended not to comply with any condition or was reckless as to whether this would happen (for example the accused took a late bus or train knowing that he or she might not therefore be back at the prison on time).

d) There was no justification for the failure to comply with any condition.

6.28 In punishing a prisoner found guilty of an offence relating to absence outside the establishment or a failure to return after being released on temporary licence the length of time the prisoner has been unlawfully at large should not automatically influence the level of the punishment. However it may be taken into account as an indicator of attitude in conjunction with others, such as whether the prisoner resisted arrest or surrendered himself or herself, the pressures on the accused to surrender or not to return, the extent to which plans were made to stay at large indefinitely and so on. No account should be taken of any criminal offences committed by the prisoner while at large as such offences can be dealt with by the police. Failure to return from release on temporary licence can be referred to the police.

PARAGRAPH 9/10- ADMINISTERS A CONTROLLED DRUG TO HIMSELF OR FAILS TO PREVENT THE ADMINISTRATION OF A CONTROLLED DRUG TO HIM BY ANOTHER PERSON (BUT SUBJECT TO PRISON RULE 52/YOI RULE 56

6.29 See 6.88 onwards for details of this offence. Rule 52/56 states It shall be a defence for a prisoner charged with an offence under Rule 51(9)/55(10) to show that:

(a) the controlled drug has been, prior to its administration, lawfully in his possession for his use or was administered to him in the course of a lawful supply of the drug to him by another person;

(b) the controlled drug was administered by or to him in circumstances in which he did not know and had no reason to suspect that such a drug was being administered; or

(c) the controlled drug was administered by or to him under duress or to him without his consent in circumstances where it was not reasonable for him to have resisted.

6.30 Specimen charge. Under Rule 51 paragraph 10/ YOI Rule 55, paragraph 11 is intoxicated as a consequence of knowingly consuming any alcoholic beverage. At [time observed by reporting officer] you were seen to be intoxicated following the cessation of visits.

6.31 This is the more serious of the two alcohol related disciplinary offences which will remain in place until primary legislation authorises mandatory alcohol testing. It concerns the prisoner who is clearly intoxicated in contrast to the one who may merely have consumed a small amount of alcohol.

6.32 Evidence. Before an adjudicator can be satisfied of guilt the following elements must be established beyond reasonable doubt.

PARAGRAPH 10/11 - IS INTOXICATED AS A CONSEQUENCE OF KNOWINGLY CONSUMING ANY ALCOHOLIC BEVERAGE

a) The accused was intoxicated. If the adjudicator is satisfied after hearing the evidence that the accused's behaviour was elated beyond the point of self- control this will satisfy the test of intoxication. It will not be sufficient evidence for a finding of guilt for example, if it is demonstrated that the behaviour was caused by skylarking or by an excess of high spirits.

b) The intoxication was wholly or partly as a consequence of consuming any alcoholic beverage. The evidence must be based upon the observations of the reporting officer or other relevant member of staff. Indicators such as the slurring of speech, unstable gait or the smell of alcohol on the breath will be of significance. It will be important for the adjudicator to enquire into any other possible cause for the reported behaviour, for example the prisoner's medical condition or whether or not prescribed medicine could account for the behaviour.

c) The accused knowingly consumed the alcoholic beverage. If the adjudicator believes after hearing all the evidence that the accused had no knowledge that a beverage contained alcohol, for example because a drink was "spiked" and because he or she reasonably believed the drink to be other than alcoholic, the charge must be dismissed.

6.33 A defence to a charge under Rule 51, paragraph 11, or YOI Rule 55, paragraph 12 may be that the alcohol was taken under the order of a medical officer. Rule 51, paragraph 10, YOI Rule 55, paragraph 11 charges can be distinguished from those under Rule 51, paragraph 11 or YOI Rule, paragraph 12, since it can be assumed that no medical officer, properly informing himself, would ever prescribe alcohol in such quantities as to cause intoxication.

PARAGRAPH 11/12 - KNOWINGLY CONSUMES ANY ALCOHOLIC BEVERAGE OTHER THAN ANY PRESCRIBED TO HIM PURSUANT TO A WRITTEN ORDER OF THE MEDICAL OFFICER UNDER PRISON RULE 25(1)/YOI RULE 21(1)

6.34 Specimen charge. Under Prison Rule 51 paragraph 11/YOI Rule 55 paragraph 12, knowingly consumes any alcoholic beverage other than any prescribed to him pursuant to a written order of the medical officer under Prison Rule 25(1)/YOI Rule 21(1). At [time observed by reporting officer] you were seen to have consumed an alcoholic beverage. This was at the cessation of visits.

6.35 This is the less serious of the two alcohol related disciplinary offences which will remain in place until primary legislation authorises mandatory alcohol testing. It concerns the prisoner, who whilst not intoxicated, has knowingly consumed alcohol which had not been prescribed to him or her.

6.36 Before an adjudicator can be satisfied of guilt the following must be established beyond reasonable doubt.

a) The observed behaviour was the consequence of consuming alcoholic beverage. Similar indicators to those noted at paragraph 6.32 will be of significance though, under this paragraph it will not be necessary to prove intoxication. The evidence should be such as would lead a reasonable person to conclude that the accused had consumed alcohol.
b) If the alcohol had been prescribed by the medical officer this will be a complete defence to the charge. If the accused wishes to raise this defence he or she should be invited to sign a consent to medical disclosure form which will allow the medical officer to disclose the nature of any relevant treatment. If the accused will not do this it should be remembered that it is not up to him or her to prove innocence but for the adjudicator to decide, after hearing all the evidence, whether or not the prisoner is innocent or guilty. The adjudicator may make such inferences as appear reasonable should the accused raise this defence but decline to substantiate it.
c) The accused knowingly consumed the alcoholic beverage. The same arguments apply as at paragraph 6.32.

PARAGRAPH 12/13 - HAS IN HIS POSSESSION (A) ANY UNAUTHORISED ARTICLE, OR (B) A GREATER QUANTITY OF ANY ARTICLE THAN HE IS AUTHORISED TO HAVE.

6.37 Specimen charge. Under Prison Rule 51 paragraph 12/YOI Rule 55, paragraph 13, has in his possession any unauthorised article [a greater quantity of any article than he is authorised to have]. At [time] (OR between [time] and [time]) on [date] in [place] you had in your possession an unauthorised article, namely a razor blade (OR a greater quantity of pillow cases than you were authorised to have, namely 12 pillow cases).

6.38 This paragraph is intended to cover in the case of (a) the possession of an article (for example drugs) which is unauthorised in itself, an article which may be authorised (such as a radio) but which is, in the particular case, unauthorised (perhaps, because it has been smuggled in), or an article which may have been authorised to a certain prisoner but not to the one in whose possession it is found. In the case of (b) the offence is intended to cover possession of more of certain articles than a prisoner is entitled to have. See 6.79 onwards for guidance on drug possession.

6.39 Evidence. Before an adjudicator can be satisfied of guilt the following three elements must each be established beyond reasonable doubt.

a) Presence: the article exists; it is what it is alleged to be and is found where it is so alleged.

b) Knowledge: the accused knew of the presence of the article and its nature, for example that a substance was a controlled drug. Knowledge of its nature can be properly inferred from all the circumstances for instance whether it was hidden or whether the prisoner attempted to dispose of it before it was found. It is good practice for a reporting officer to question the prisoner as soon as an article is found so that his or her immediate reaction to its presence can be adduced in evidence.

c) Control: the accused exercised sole or joint control over the article. A prisoner who drops or throws away an article simply because he or she believes that it is about to be discovered may still be guilty of possession at an earlier stage if there is sufficient evidence that it was in his or her control before it was abandoned. Care will be needed in specifying the time the offence is alleged to have occurred on such a case.

6.40 In the case of charges under either section of paragraph 12/13 it will be necessary to show that the accused was aware of the restrictions on authorisation or quantity or was reckless as to whether there were such restrictions. A genuine belief that the article was authorised or that there were no restrictions on quantity allowed in possession would be a defence. Where an accused states that he or she held such a belief, the reasonableness or otherwise of the belief is a matter which may affect the credibility of the accused's evidence.

6.41 If a prisoner is found in possession of a number of unauthorised articles the reporting officer should consider a charge in respect of each. The reason is that, should all the articles be incorporated into the one charge and the prisoner later has a complaint upheld in respect of one of the articles, the whole adjudication would be quashed. If separate charges are laid, only the adjudication in respect of that one article would be quashed.

6.42 Specimen charge. Under Prison Rule 51 paragraph 13/ YOI Rule 55, paragraph 14, sells or delivers to any person any unauthorised article. At [time] on [date] in [place] you delivered an unauthorised article, namely a razor blade to [name].

6.43 This charge is to be used for articles which in themselves are unauthorised, for example drugs, or articles which are not authorised for the giver. The charge represents a single offence which may be committed in two separate ways: selling or delivering. It is not necessary to show which of the two is involved.

6.44 Evidence. Before an adjudicator can be satisfied of guilt beyond reasonable doubt the following must be established.

PARAGRAPH 13/14 - SELLS OR DELIVERS TO ANY PERSON ANY UNAUTHORISED ARTICLE.

a) The article was sold or delivered by the accused to another person. The person to whom the article was sold or delivered does not have to be a prisoner.

b) The item was unauthorised (see 6.31).

c) The accused intended to sell or deliver an unauthorised article, or was reckless as to whether he or she was doing so. A genuine belief that he or she was authorised to dispose of the item in that way would be a defence. Where an accused states that he or she held such a belief, the reasonableness or otherwise of the belief is a matter which may affect the credibility of the accused's evidence.

PARAGRAPH 14/15 - SELLS OR, WITHOUT PERMISSION, DELIVERS TO ANY PERSON ANY ARTICLE WHICH HE IS ALLOWED TO HAVE ONLY FOR HIS OWN USE.

6.45 Specimen charge. Under Prison Rule 51 paragraph 14/YOI Rule 55, paragraph 15, sells or, without permission, delivers to any person any article which he is allowed to have only for his own use. At [time] on [date] in [place] you sold (OR delivered without permission) a radio which you were allowed to have only for your own use to [name].

6.46 The charge is to be used for articles which the prisoner is allowed to have but not pass on. As in the case of charges under Rule 51, paragraph 13, YOI Rule 55, paragraph 14, it is not necessary to prove whether the article was sold or whether it was delivered. The charge represents a single offence which may be committed in two separate ways.

6.47 Evidence. Before an adjudicator can be satisfied of guilt beyond reasonable doubt the following must be established.

a) The item was sold or delivered to another (see 6.37).

b) The item was allowed only for the accused's own use.

c) In the case of delivering, that the accused did not have permission.

d) The accused intended to sell or deliver such an item in such a way, or was reckless as to whether he or she was doing so. A genuine belief that the item was not only for his or her own use, or that he or she had permission to deliver it, would be a defence. Where an accused states that he or she held such a belief, the reasonableness or otherwise of the belief is a matter which may affect the credibility of the accused's evidence.

PARAGRAPH 15/16 - TAKES IMPROPERLY ANY ARTICLE BELONGING TO ANOTHER PERSON OR TO A PRISON (OR YOUNG OFFENDER INSTITUTION)

6.48 Specimen charge. Under Prison Rule 51 paragraph 15/YOI Rule 55, paragraph 16, takes improperly any article belonging to another person or to a prison (or young offender institution). At [time] (OR between [time] and [time]) on [date] in [place] you took improperly a radio belonging to [name] (OR a cigarette belonging to Officer [name] OR a ruler belonging to the Education Department OR a sign belonging to HMP [name]).

6.49 This charge covers exclusively articles belonging to people other than the accused and can be considered as similar to the criminal charge of theft.

6.50 Evidence. Before an adjudicator can be satisfied of guilt beyond reasonable doubt the following must be established.

a) There was an article.

b) The article belonged to another person or to a prison. This charge covers exclusively articles belonging to people other than the accused and in many cases the only way of proving the charge beyond reasonable doubt will be to show to whom the article does belong.

c) The accused assumed physical control of the article. Consequently, if an accused has signed for another prisoner's pay but has not yet collected that pay or equivalent goods he or she cannot be guilty of an offence under this paragraph. In these circumstances a charge of attempt under Rule 51, paragraph 25, YOI Rule 55, paragraph 29 might be appropriate.

d) The article was taken improperly. This means that the accused did not have permission to take it.
e) The accused intended to take such an article improperly, or was reckless as to whether he was doing so. It will be a defence to a charge under this paragraph that the accused genuinely believed he or she owned the article or had permission to take it. Of course, where an accused gives evidence that he held such a belief, the reasonableness or otherwise of the belief is a matter which may affect the credibility of the accused's evidence.

PARAGRAPH 16/17 - INTENTIONALLY OR RECKLESSLY SETS FIRE TO ANY PART OF A PRISON [OR YOUNG OFFENDER INSTITUTION] OR ANY OTHER PROPERTY, WHETHER OR NOT HIS OWN.

6.51 Specimen charge. Under Prison Rule 51 paragraph 16/ YOI Rule 55, paragraph 17, intentionally or recklessly sets fire to any part of a prison [or young offender institution] or any other property, whether or not his own. At [time] on [date] in [place] you intentionally (OR recklessly) set fire to the gymnasium at HMP [name] (OR a blanket OR a book).

6.52 Evidence. Before an adjudicator can be satisfied of guilt beyond reasonable doubt the following must be established.

a) The accused set fire to a part of an establishment or other property: property is to be taken as meaning property of a tangible nature, whether real (for example land or buildings) or personal, including money, and also including creatures which are held in ownership.
b) The accused intended to set fire to the property, or was reckless as to whether this would happen.

PARAGRAPH 17/18 - DESTROYS OR DAMAGES ANY PART OF A PRISON [OR YOUNG OFFENDER INSTITUTION] OR ANY OTHER PROPERTY, OTHER THAN HIS OWN.

6.53   Specimen charge. Under Prison Rule 51 paragraph 17/ YOI Rule 55, paragraph 18, destroys or damages any part of a prison [or young offender institution] or any other property, other than his own. At [time] on [date] in [place] you destroyed (OR damaged) a television set belonging to HMP [name] (OR a radio belonging to [name]).

6.54   The adjudicator must be satisfied that the article was damaged by the accused and that guilt is not determined merely on the basis of being in possession of a damaged article.

6.55   Evidence. Before an adjudicator can be satisfied of guilt beyond reasonable doubt the following must be established.

a)   Part of an establishment or other property was destroyed or damaged (for a definition of property see 6.45a).
b)   The property did not belong to the accused.
c)   There was no lawful excuse to damage the property.
d)   The accused intended such property to be destroyed or damaged in such a way, or was reckless as to whether this would happen. A genuine belief that he or she owned the property or was entitled to damage it would be a defence. Where an accused states that he held such a belief, the reasonableness or otherwise of the belief is a matter which may affect the credibility of the accused's evidence.

PARAGRAPH 18/20 - ABSENTS HIMSELF FROM ANY PLACE WHERE HE IS REQUIRED TO BE OR IS PRESENT AT ANY PLACE WHERE HE IS NOT AUTHORISED TO BE.

6.56   Specimen charge. Under Prison Rule 51 paragraph 18/ YOI Rule 55, paragraph 20 , absents himself from any place where he is required to be or is present at any place where he is not authorised to be. At time on date you were absent from the dining hall where you were required to be (OR you were in the cell of name where you were not authorised to be).

6.57   This charge can apply to incidents either within or outside the prison. If a prisoner absents himself or herself without permission for a specific purpose, such as buying something in a local shop, with every intention of returning to the prison, then a charge under this paragraph would apply. Such incidents outside the prison are only usually applicable to open establishments. A prisoner would have a difficult task to show that he or she intended to return directly if found outside a closed prison unless, of course, he or she had absented himself or herself from an outside working party.

6.58 Evidence. Before an adjudicator can be satisfied of guilt beyond reasonable doubt the following must be established.

a) The accused was required to be in a particular place or was not authorised to be in the place he or she was found. It will be important to be able to show that any local instructions to prisoners are passed to them and to the accused in particular or that reasonable steps have been taken to pass instructions to the accused.

b) The accused was in fact absent from the place he or she was required to be or was in fact present at the place he or she was not authorised to be.

c) The accused had no justification for his or her actions.

d) The accused intended this to happen, or was reckless as to whether it would. A genuine belief that the accused was not required to be somewhere or was authorised to be in the place he or she was found would be a defence. Where an accused states that he or she held such a belief, the reasonableness or otherwise of the belief is a matter which may affect the credibility of the accused's evidence.

PARAGRAPH 19/21 - IS DISRESPECTFUL TO ANY OFFICER, OR ANY PERSON (OTHER THAN A PRISONER) WHO IS AT THE PRISON FOR THE PURPOSE OF WORKING THERE, OR ANY PERSON VISITING A PRISON.

6.59 Specimen charge. Under Prison Rule 51 paragraph 19/ YOI Rule 55, paragraph 21, is disrespectful to any officer, or any person (other than a prisoner) who is at the prison for the purpose of working there, or any person visiting a prison. At time on date in place you were disrespectful to name an officer of the prison (OR a person who was at the prison for the purpose of working there OR a member of the board of visitors OR a visitor to another prisoner) by making a two-fingered gesture towards him.

6.60 This charge can include verbal, written and physical behaviour.

6.61 Evidence. Before an adjudicator can be satisfied of guilt beyond reasonable doubt the following must be established.

a) There was an act.

b) The disrespect was directed towards a specific individual or group. This will be proved by all the circumstances, or perhaps by the content of verbal abuse.

c) The act was disrespectful in the ordinary meaning of the term. This is for the adjudicator to decide in all the circumstances. What is disrespectful in some circumstances may not be in others.

d) The person to whom the act was disrespectful was an officer (as defined in 6.11 above) or anyone else (other than a prisoner) who was at the prison for the purpose of working there, or a visitor to the prison.

e) The accused intended to be disrespectful to such a person, or was reckless as to whether he or she was being so. A genuine belief that, for example, the conduct was not disrespectful would be a defence. Where an accused states that he or she held such a belief, the reasonableness or otherwise of the belief is a matter which may affect the credibility of the accused's evidence.

PARAGRAPH 20/22 - USES THREATENING, ABUSIVE OR INSULTING WORDS OR BEHAVIOUR.

6.62 Specimen charge. Under Prison Rule 51 paragraph 20/YOI Rule 55, paragraph 22, uses threatening, abusive or insulting words or behaviour. At [time] on date in place you used threatening (OR abusive OR insulting) words or behaviour towards name namely by saying "you wait till I get out I'll come round and kill you."

6.63 It is important that it is shown how the action was threatening, abusive or insulting, but it may not always be necessary to establish at whom the action was aimed and it is not necessary to name an individual in every charge.

6.64 Evidence. Before an adjudicator can be satisfied of guilt beyond reasonable doubt the following must be established.

a) The accused performed a specific act or adopted a general pattern of behaviour or said specific words. This need not be a single incident as in the above specimen but may have continued over a period of time.

b) The act, pattern of behaviour or words were either threatening, abusive or insulting. These terms should be given their ordinary meanings, taking account of the circumstances of the case. It should be borne in mind that words or behaviour may be annoying or rude without necessarily being abusive or insulting. To find guilt it is only necessary to be satisfied that a reasonable person at the scene would consider the words or behaviour threatening, abusive or insulting.

c) The accused intended to be threatening, abusive or insulting or was reckless as to whether his or her words or behaviour might be so.

PARAGRAPH 21/24 - INTENTIONALLY FAILS TO WORK PROPERLY OR, BEING REQUIRED TO WORK, REFUSES TO DO SO

6.65 Specimen charge. Under Prison Rule 51 paragraph 21/ YOI Rule 55, paragraph 24, intentionally fails to work properly or, being required to work, refuses to do so. At time on date in place you intentionally failed to work properly, by talking with other prisoners when you should have been cleaning (OR At time on date]in place, being required to work in the metal shop you refused to do so).

6.66 This paragraph covers two distinct offences and it is important that the correct one is chosen.

6.67 Evidence of intentional failure to work properly. Before an adjudicator can be satisfied of guilt beyond reasonable doubt the following must be established.

a) The accused was lawfully required to work at the time and in the circumstances specified (for example he or she was not an unconvicted prisoner who could not be required to work in the first place).

b) The accused failed to work properly, in other words the alleged failure should be measured against a standard.

c) The prisoner intended not to work properly, or was reckless as to whether he was not doing so. This means that the prisoner must have known his or her work was not up to the standard, or might not be. A genuine belief that the work was adequate would be a defence to this charge. Where an accused states that he or she held such a belief, the reasonableness or otherwise of the belief is a matter which may affect the credibility of the accused's evidence.

6.68 Evidence of refusing to work. Before an adjudicator can be satisfied of guilt beyond reasonable doubt the following must be established.

a) The accused was lawfully required to work at the time and in the circumstances specified (for example that he or she was not an unconvicted prisoner who could not be required to work in the first place).

b) The accused refused to work. This may be either by an act or an omission. The accused does not have to say "I refuse" but his or her actions may amount to such refusal.

c) The accused intended to refuse to do such work, or was reckless as to whether he or she was doing so. This means that the accused must have known that he or she was required to work at the time and in the circumstances alleged, or been aware that this might be the case. A genuine belief that he or she was not required to work there and then would be a defence to this charge. Where an accused states that he or she held such a belief, the reasonableness or otherwise of the belief is a matter which may affect the credibility of the accused's evidence.

6.69 If the prisoner claims to have been medically certified unfit to carry out the work he or she is required to do, care must be taken to investigate fully such a defence. If the prisoner claims to have been unfit to carry out such work but has not been medically certified as unfit the adjudicator may wish to seek evidence on the point.

6.70 This is the correct charge to bring in respect of alleged offences at the place of work. A refusal to attend a place of work would constitute an offence under paragraphs 18 or 22/20 or 25.

PARAGRAPH 22/25 - DISOBEYS ANY LAWFUL ORDER.

6.71 Specimen charge. Under Prison Rule 51 paragraph 22/ YOI Rule 55, paragraph 19, disobeys any lawful order. At time on date in place you disobeyed a lawful order to return to your cell.

6.72 A lawful order is one which is reasonable and which a member of staff has authority to give in the execution of his or her duties.

6.73 Evidence. Before an adjudicator can be satisfied of guilt beyond reasonable doubt the following must be established.

a) The action of a member of staff amounted to an order. An order is a clear indication by word and/or action given in the course of his or her duties by a member of prison staff requiring a specific prisoner to do or refrain from doing something. Whilst it is desirable that such an instruction should be given verbally it need not be so to amount to an order. What is necessary is that there is a clear indication of what is required of the prisoner concerned. It is not necessary to preface any such instruction by words "this is an order", "I am giving you a direct order", or the like.

b)   The order was lawful.

c)   The accused did not comply with the order. The prisoner need not have said "I refuse" but it is important to be satisfied that he or she did not comply with the order within a reasonable period of time. Even if a prisoner eventually complies with an order, there may nevertheless be sufficient evidence to find him or her guilty under this paragraph where the adjudicator can be satisfied that the accused deliberately delayed compliance. This will depend on the particular circumstances of any case.

d)   The accused intended not to comply with a lawful order, or was reckless as to whether he or she was not doing so. This means the accused must have understood what was being required of him of her.

PARAGRAPH 23/26 - DISOBEYS OR FAILS TO COMPLY WITH ANY RULE OR REGULATION APPLYING TO HIM.

6.74   Specimen charge. Under Prison Rule 51 paragraph 23/ YOI Rule 55, paragraph 26, disobeys or fails to comply with any rule or regulation applying to him. At time on date in place you disobeyed (OR failed to comply with) the regulation requiring you to attend roll check.

6.75   Rules or regulations of the prison can range from the requirements of Prison Rules to a local regulation of that particular establishment or wing. This is the recommended charge to bring when a prisoner is alleged unlawfully to have abstracted electricity by tampering with the mains supply to wire up a radio or other electrical item, although one under paragraph 5/6 may also be possible on occasion. For such a charge a local rule must be in force stating that prisoners must not

tamper with cell electrical fittings, mains supply or circuitry

wire up any equipment or article to cell electrical fittings, main supply or circuitry
allow their property to be or continue to be so connected
use any equipment or article so connected.
In this way, prisoners using their radio when it is connected to the mains, but not having made the connection themselves, would nevertheless be in breach of the local rule.

6.76 **Evidence.** Before an adjudicator can be satisfied of guilt beyond reasonable doubt the following must be established.

a) The rule or regulation applied to the accused. The accused must have been aware of the rule or regulation or reasonable steps must have been taken to make him or her aware. The latter may be shown, for example, by evidence from an induction unit or a member of wing staff that the rule in question has been explained or pointed out to the prisoner at some time in the past, or that the rule or regulation was displayed in such a fashion that it should have been clear to a prisoner passing it. In the latter case, the burden of proof will obviously be greater in the case of an illiterate or non-English speaking prisoner. It may be proved (perhaps in the case of kitchen workers or the like) that the prisoner had been given training and that the rules or regulations had been explained to him. Evidence that the prisoner had complied with the rule on previous occasions might be sufficient in any given case. However, a genuine belief, reasonably held, that the rule or regulation did not apply to the prisoner in question would be a defence to this charge.

b) The rule or regulation was lawful. As is the case with paragraphs 21 and 22/ paragraphs 24 and 25, it is important to show that the rule or regulation was lawful in respect of the particular prisoner concerned. Lawful has the same meaning as it does in relation to orders. A lawful rule or regulation is one which prison staff have the authority to impose in keeping prisoners in custody or one contained in Prison or YOI Rules or in Standing Orders.

c) The accused did not comply with the rule or regulation.

d) The accused intended not to comply with such a rule or regulation, or was reckless as to whether he or she was not doing so.

PARAGRAPH 24/27- RECEIVES ANY CONTROLLED DRUG, OR, WITHOUT THE CONSENT OF AN OFFICER, ANY OTHER ARTICLE, DURING THE COURSE OF A VISIT (NOT BEING AN INTERVIEW AS IS MENTIONED IN RULE 38/YOI RULE 13)

6.77 Specimen charge. Under Prison Rule 51 paragraph 24/ YOI Rule 55 paragraph 27, receives any controlled drug, or without the consent of an officer, any other article, during the course of a visit (not being an interview such as mentioned in Prison Rule 38/YOI Rule 16). At time on date] during the course of your visit you did receive an article believed to be a controlled drug or an article without the consent of an officer, namely a £5 note.

6.771 This charge is specifically for prisoners who receive controlled drugs and articles during the course of a visit, that is, from when the visitor and prisoner first meet until the visitor leaves the visits area, and immediately after a visit, including the searching area. Where the drug or article is discovered after the visit but not in the visits or searching areas, or there is some doubt the article was received during the visit then a charge under paragraph 12 should be used. However if CCTV evidence shows that the drug or article was received during the visit then this charge should be used.

6.772 Evidence. Before an adjudicator can be satisfied of guilt beyond reasonable doubt the following must be established.

a) that the prisoner received a controlled drug or other article during the course of the visit;

b) that the prisoner knew the controlled drug or article existed;

c) that the prisoner knew they did not have permission to have that article.

6.773 In the case of an article received during the visit, it must be established that the prisoner knew they did not have permission to accept such an article from their visitor. A genuine belief by the prisoner that permission had been granted to have that article (not being a controlled drug) would be a defence to the charge.

6.774 If a prisoner used the defence that they were passed the controlled drug or article from another prisoner during the visit, the charge may still be proved providing the adjudicator can establish beyond reasonable doubt that the controlled drug or article was received during the course of the visit.

6.78 When awarding a punishment against a prisoner under this charge, adjudicators must take into account the guidelines issued by the Secretary of State in

Appendix o the Prison Discipline Rules

PARAGRAPH 25/29-
(A) ATTEMPTS TO COMMIT,
(B) INCITES ANOTHER PRISONER TO COMMIT, OR
(C) ASSISTS ANOTHER PRISONER TO COMMIT OR TO ATTEMPT TO COMMIT.

ANY OF THE FOREGOING OFFENCES

6.79 Whether (a),(b) or (c) is used the charge must specify by number one of the other paragraphs of Prison Rule 51 or YOI Rule 55.

6.80 Specimen charge (a). Under Prison Rule 51, paragraphs 25(a) and 7/YOI Rule 55, paragraphs 29(a) and 8, attempts to escape or abscond from prison or from legal custody. At

[time] on [date] in [place] you attempted to escape by running for the fence.

6.81   Evidence of attempting. Before an adjudicator can be satisfied of guilt beyond reasonable doubt the following must be established.

a)   The accused did an act which was more than merely preparatory to the commission of the intended offence. An example might be that the manufacture of a rope out of knotted sheets would not constitute an attempted escape but using the same rope to descend into the grounds might well.

b)   The accused intended to commit the full offence. It is not necessary to show that it was one that he or she would be able to carry out (because, for example, the level of security was such that an attempted escape could not possibly have succeeded).

6.82   Specimen charge (b). Under Prison Rule 51, paragraphs 25(b) and 17/YOI Rule 55, paragraphs 29(b) and 18, incites another prisoner to destroy or damage any part of a prison or any other property, other than his own. At [time] on [date] in [place] you incited a group of prisoners to commit damage to a holding room in Reception.

6.83   Evidence of inciting. Before an adjudicator can be satisfied of guilt beyond reasonable doubt the following must be established.

a)   The accused's action was communicated to other prisoners. It is necessary to show that other prisoners were sufficiently near to be able to react to the incitement.

b)   The act was capable of inciting other prisoners to commit the full offence. Incitement in this context means seeking to persuade another prisoner to commit a disciplinary offence, whether this is done by suggestion, persuasion, threats, pressure, words or implication. It does not matter that nobody in fact attempted to commit the full offence. It is for the adjudicator to decide whether the act was capable of inciting other prisoners and he or she should take into account the nature of the prisoners involved in deciding this.

c) The full offence was either the subject of the incitement or the consequence of it.

d) The accused intended to incite or was reckless whether he or she did so.

6.84 Specimen charge (c). Under Prison Rule 51, paragraphs 25(c) and 7/YOI Rule 55, paragraphs 29(c) and 8, assists another prisoner to escape or abscond from prison or from legal custody. At [time] on [date] in [place] you assisted [name] to escape by supplying him with sheets.

6.85 Evidence of assisting. Before an adjudicator can be satisfied of guilt beyond reasonable doubt the following must be established.

a) An offence was committed by another prisoner. This may include an attempt. However, since paragraph 25(c)/29(c) is dependent upon the commission of another offence, it would be a defence that the other prisoner was found not guilty of the substantive offence.

b) The accused actively assisted in the commission of the offence. It is not sufficient that the accused was aware of and did not prevent the offence occurring. It is important that he or she did an act which made the commission of the offence easier.

c) The accused intended to assist the other prisoner.

DRUG POSSESSION OFFENCES IN PARTICULAR

6.86 There is no specific disciplinary offence under the Rules which refers to the possession or supply of controlled drugs; charges may be laid under paragraphs 12, 13, or 15/13, 14, or 16 depending on the circumstances of the alleged offence. Such cases can also be referred to the police. Guidance is in Appendix 3.

6.87 As for other disciplinary offences a finding of guilt must not be reached unless the adjudicator is satisfied beyond reasonable doubt that the accused committed the offence with which s/he is charged. The offence of possessing an unauthorised article under paragraph 12/13 can apply not only to drugs themselves but also to articles used in connection with them, for

example, a pen which has been in contact with cannabis resin. A charge under paragraph 12/13 is the normal one to be used in respect of articles such as the above notwithstanding that only traces of the drug, not amounting to a measurable quantity, are found.

6.88 Charges should be laid immediately on discovery of the alleged offence and the charge must be formulated as 'had in his possession a controlled drug...' or 'had in his possession an article containing traces of a controlled drug namely...' and not ' had in his possession a substance believed to be a controlled drug' or ' had in his possession a substance which when tested with a British Drug Houses (BDH) or similar kit proved positive as a controlled drug'. A BDH test can screen out the possibility that the substance analysed is a controlled drug but it cannot prove it that it is one. Any charge or evidence that implies that it can prove this is misleading and may undermine the adjudicator's subsequent finding. In addition to the laying of a charge a governor or director may refer the matter to the police for investigation and an adjudication will be opened and adjourned pending the outcome

6.89 If discovery of a controlled drug is not referred to the police for investigation, an adjudication may proceed. If a prisoner makes a clear and unambiguous admission of guilt, it is unnecessary to send the suspected substance for forensic analysis. If, however, during the course of the hearing evidence is put forward which casts doubts upon the nature of the substance the adjudicator may decide to send it for forensic analysis.

6.90 Where a prisoner makes a not guilty or equivocal plea or changes a guilty plea to one which is equivocal or not guilty, the substance must immediately be sent for forensic analysis. A forensic test will not be required if it is quite clear that the prisoner is not contesting the nature of the substance but pleads not guilty to the charge.

6.91 A statement by the prisoner in defence of a charge that s/he 'did not know the article was there' or 'did not know the article had been used for smoking a controlled drug' is a defence. Equally, a statement to the effect that s/he was exercising no degree of control over an article in the cell is a defence, even if the prisoner admitted knowing the article was there or had been used for smoking drugs. Whether these defences are believed is a matter for judgement by the adjudicator.

6.92 Wherever possible, a sample should not be destroyed until after the proceedings have been completed and a finding has been reached, as additional analysis may be required in the course of the hearing. The only instance where this would not be possible is where the amount was so small that it was consumed in the original analysis.

6.93 Any sample retained after a hearing must be secured in the governor's/director's safe until it is handed over to the police to be destroyed. A receipt must be obtained when it is handed over.

6.94 In the case of any subsequent request or complaint by the prisoner where the nature of the sample is called into question production of the forensic analysis report will be put forward as evidence that the article was that which it was alleged to be.

DRUG USE OFFENCES IN PARTICULAR

6.95 Specimen charge Under Prison Rule 51 paragraph 9/ YOI Rule 55, paragraph 10, administers a controlled drug to himself or fails to prevent the administration of a controlled drug to him by another person. Between [date] and [date] you administered cannabis to yourself or failed to prevent another person administering it to you.

6.96   Prisoners are to be charged under paragraph 9 /10 only as a result of samples taken under mandatory drug testing provisions. The test must have been of the accused's urine or other authorised sample, which is not an intimate sample. Prisoners should not be charged on the basis of positive test results obtained by way of any voluntary testing arrangement for example under a compact.

6.97   Discovery of an alleged offence occurs when two elements have been established. First that an initial screening test has given a positive result for a controlled drug and second that at all material times the prisoner was in prison custody when the drug was administered.

6.98   If the controlled drug was alleged to have been taken whilst the prisoner was released temporarily under Prison Rule 9 or YOI Rule 5, paragraph 9/10 cannot be used. The charge should then be laid under paragraph 8/9, since the prisoner would thus be alleged to have broken a licence condition expressly prohibiting the misuse of controlled drugs provided, of course, that the licence contained such a condition. Where it is uncertain at what point the drug was taken (whether in prison custody or on licence) the prisoner may be charged with alternative offences, one under paragraph 8/9 and one under paragraph 9/10, and the procedure at 2.6 should be followed. If the adjudicator is satisfied beyond reasonable doubt that a controlled drug was taken but cannot be certain as to when it was taken, both charges must be dismissed.

6.99   At the start of a hearing, if the accused enters an unequivocal plea of guilt, the adjudicator may proceed on that basis. If he or she pleads not guilty or equivocates over a plea the hearing should be adjourned and the sample sent for a secondary, confirmation, test. At a resumed hearing the result of the latter test must be admitted as evidence. If the accused contests the results of the confirmation test he or she may ask for the relevant laboratory scientist to attend as a witness and ask questions on the evidence. Further, the prisoner may arrange for an independent analysis of his or her sample (part of which will have been retained under mandatory drug testing procedures) and submit the results in evidence.

6.991 Evidence. Before an adjudicator can be satisfied of guilt beyond reasonable doubt the following must be established.

a) A controlled drug was administered. There must have been a test of an approved sample from the accused prisoner made under mandatory testing arrangements, and a positive result. There must have been no significant irregularities in the chain of custody procedures so that it can be confirmed that the sample provided by the accused was the one tested and is the one referred to in the test report presented to the adjudicator. The correctness of these points should have been checked before charging by the adjudication liaison officer but if anything becomes apparent at the hearing which throws doubt on the correctness of procedures, it should be investigated and, if significant, the charge should be dismissed. It is for the adjudicator to decide what would amount to a significant irregularity. Clerical errors, such as a wrong spelling of a name or an incorrect digit in a number, might not be significant. A failure to record a name or number at all, however, would almost certainly be so.

b) The controlled drug must have been taken at a time when the accused was subject to Prison or YOI Rules. Correct dates entered in the particulars of the charge are thus essential. The later date should be the date of collecting the sample; the former date should be 31 days before that (see 6.98 regarding minimum waiting periods).

c) The prisoner had not been charged previously for misusing the same drug within a period of time which might mean that the current charge could have arisen from the same act of administration as the earlier charge (see 6.98 regarding minimum waiting periods).

6.992 The express defences. These are set out at Prison Rule 52 and YOI Rule 56 (see Appendix 5). It shall be a defence for a prisoner charged with an offence under paragraph 9 /10, to show that:

a) the controlled drug had been, prior to its administration, lawfully in the accused's possession for his or her use or was administered to the accused in the course of a lawful supply of the drug to him or her by another person;

b) the controlled drug was administered by or to him or her in circumstances in which he or she did not know and had no reason to suspect that such a drug was being administered; or

c) the controlled drug was administered by or to the accused under duress or to him or her without consent in circumstances where it was not reasonable for the accused to have resisted.

6.993 The wording of the offence together with the existence of the express defences assist in clarifying what has to be established before there can be a finding of guilt. The existence of the express defences permit the adjudicator, in the absence of any credible explanation from the accused, or from any witness, to find guilt on the basis of the positive test without the need to find additional evidence as to knowledge or intent. The express defences do not remove the duty of the adjudicator to enquire into the offence but he or she is not obliged to enquire into a defence unless there is sufficient credible evidence produced in the course of the hearing to cast reasonable doubt on those elements.

6.994 There can be additional defences to the three express ones. It will, for example, be a defence to a current charge if the accused has already been charged with using the same drug within the minimum waiting period which could account for the current positive test.

6.995 If a potential defence, including one of the express defences, is raised in some way other than by the accused, it must be investigated.

6.996 The table of minimum waiting periods required before a prisoner may be charged or charged again should be available to the adjudicator and to the accused and be referred to in evidence .

RACIALLY AGGRAVATED & RACIST OFFENCES

6.997 There are four new offences that deal with racially aggravated and racist offences against prison discipline. The offences cover: racially aggravated assault; racially aggravated damage or destruction of property; threatening, abusive or insulting racist words or behaviour; and displaying any threatening, abusive or insulting racist material. Specimen charges are set out below at paragraphs 6.999c - 6.999r.

6.998 That an offence is racist or racially aggravated clearly indicates that it is more serious e.g. all other things being equal, a racially aggravated assault is more serious than a non-racially aggravated assault. The more serious nature of such offences should be reflected in the punishments given.

6.999 An offence under paragraph 1(A) or 17 (A) is racially aggravated if

a) at the time of committing the offence, or immediately before or after doing so, the offender demonstrates towards the victim of the offence hostility based on the victim's membership (or presumed membership) of a racial group; or
b) the offence is motivated (wholly or partly) by hostility towards members of a racial group based on their membership of that group.

6.999a A "racial group" means a group of persons defined by reference to race, colour, nationality (including citizenship) or ethnic or national origins. Membership of a racial group includes association with members of that group and "presumed" membership of that group means presumed by the accused. It is immaterial in defining "racially aggravated" whether or not the accused's hostility is also based on the fact or presumption that any person or group of persons belongs to any religious group; or any other factor not mentioned in paragraph b) above.

6.999b An offence under paragraph 20 (A) or 24 (A) is racist under the Prison and YOI Rules if:

the words, behaviour or material demonstrate or are motivated (either partly or wholly) by hostility to members of a racial group (whether identifiable or not) based on their membership or presumed membership) of a racial group.

PARAGRAPH 1(A) /2- COMMITS ANY RACIALLY AGGRAVATED ASSAULT

6.999c Specimen charge. Under Prison Rule 51 paragraph 1A (or YOI Rule 55, paragraph 2), commits any racially aggravated assault. At [time] on [date] in [place] you assaulted [name] by punching him whilst shouting "you black bastard".

6.999d The criteria for the act of assault remain as detailed in paragraph 1, commits any assault: an offence will be racially aggravated if, in addition, the criteria at paragraph 6.999 above are met.

6.999e Evidence. Before an adjudicator can be satisfied of guilt beyond reasonable doubt the following must be established.:

a) The accused applied force to another (or, subject to the guidance above, committed an act which caused another person to fear the immediate application of force to that person) and was demonstrating racially aggravated hostility before, during, or after the offence was committed; (see paragraph 6.999 above)

b) The accused intended this, or was reckless as to whether it would happen.

c) The force was unlawful, in other words the accused did not use only that force which was reasonable in self-defence or to prevent the commission of a serious crime. What is reasonable will vary according to the circumstances of each offence as the accused honestly believed them to be, and bearing in mind that, in a moment of attack, an accused cannot always weigh exactly the amount of force required to resist.

6.999f Where a prisoner is charged with committing a racially aggravated assault, s/he should also, at the same time, be charged with committing an assault under paragraph 1 (see paragraph 2.6 for advice on simultaneous charging). If the adjudicator is satisfied beyond reasonable doubt that the accused committed an assault, but is not satisfied beyond reasonable doubt that the offence was racially aggravated, then the adjudicator must dismiss the charge under paragraph 1A/2. The adjudicator then can find the prisoner guilty of the charge under paragraph 1 (commits any assault). Similarly, if the adjudicator is satisfied beyond reasonable doubt that the accused committed a racially aggravated assault then the adjudicator must dismiss the charge under paragraph 1 and find the accused guilty of the charge under paragraph 1A/2.

PARAGRAPH 17(A) / 19 - CAUSES RACIALLY AGGRAVATED DAMAGE TO ANY PART OF A PRISON /OR YOUNG OFFENDER INSTITUTION OR ANY OTHER PROPERTY, OTHER THAN HIS OWN

6.999g Specimen charge. Under Prison Rule 51 paragraph 17(A) /YOI Rule 55, paragraph 19, causes racially aggravated damage to any part of a prison /or young offender institution or any other property, other than his own. At time on date] in [place] you damaged a radio belonging to [name] which was playing Indian music whilst shouting "bloody Paki music".

6.999h The adjudicator must be satisfied that the article was damaged by the accused and that guilt is not determined merely on the basis of being in possession of a damaged article. In addition, the offence will be racially aggravated if the criteria at paragraph above are met.

Evidence. Before an adjudicator can be satisfied of guilt beyond reasonable doubt the following must be established:

a) Part of an establishment or other property was destroyed or damaged (for a definition of property see 6.45a);
b) The destruction or damage was racially aggravated;
c) The property did not belong to the accused;
d) There was no lawful excuse to damage or destroy the property;
e) The accused intended such property to be destroyed or damaged or was reckless as to whether this would happen. A genuine belief that he or she owned the property or was entitled to damage it would be a defence. Where an accused states that he held such a belief, the reasonableness or otherwise of the belief is a matter which may affect the credibility of the accused's evidence. Where a prisoner is charged with causing racially aggravated damage to any part of a prison or young offender institution or any other property, other than his own, s/he should also at the same time be charged under paragraph 17/18 with damaging any part of a prison [or young offender institution] or any other property, other than his own (see paragraph 2.6 for advice on simultaneous charging). If the adjudicator is satisfied beyond reasonable doubt that the accused committed an offence under paragraph 17/18, but is not satisfied beyond reasonable doubt that the offence was racially aggravated, then the adjudicator must dismiss the charge under paragraph 17A/19. The adjudicator can find then the prisoner guilty of the charge under paragraph 17/18. Similarly, if the adjudicator is satisfied beyond reasonable doubt that the accused caused racially aggravated damage then the adjudicator must dismiss the charge

under paragraph 17/18 and find the accused guilty of the charge under paragraph 17A/19.
PARAGRAPH 20(A) / 23 - USES THREATENING, ABUSIVE OR INSULTING RACIST WORDS OR BEHAVIOUR.

6.999k Specimen charge. Under Prison Rule 51 paragraph 20(A)/YOI Rule 55, paragraph 23, uses threatening, abusive, or insulting racist words or behaviour towards [name] namely by saying: "You wait till I get out I'll come round and kill you, you black bastard."

6.999l The criteria for whether words or actions are threatening or abusive or insulting remain the same as for an offence under paragraph 20/22. However, in order to prove a charge under paragraph 20A/23 it must also be proved that the threatening, abusive or insulting behaviour was racist, in accordance with the definition given at paragraph 6.999b above.

6.999m Evidence. Before an adjudicator can be satisfied of guilt beyond reasonable doubt the following must be established:

a) The accused performed a specific act or adopted a general pattern of behaviour or said specific words. This need not be a single incident as in the above specimen but may have continued over a period of time;

b) The act, pattern of behaviour or words were threatening, abusive or insulting. These terms should be given their ordinary meanings, taking account of the circumstances of the case. It should be borne in mind that words or behaviour may be annoying or rude without necessarily being abusive or insulting. To find guilt it is necessary to be satisfied that a reasonable person at the scene would consider the words threatening, abusive or insulting;

c) In addition, the pattern of behaviour or words were racist as set out at paragraph 6.999b above;

d) The accused intended to be racist and either threatening, or abusive or insulting or was reckless as to whether his or her words or behaviour might be so.

6.999n Where a prisoner is charged with the racist version of the offence s/he should at the same time also be charged under paragraph 20 / 22 with using threatening, abusive or insulting words or behaviour (see paragraph 2.6 for advice on simultaneous charging). If the adjudicator is satisfied beyond reasonable doubt that the accused committed an offence under paragraph 20/22, but is not satisfied beyond reasonable doubt that the offence was racist, then the adjudicator must dismiss the charge under paragraph 20A /23. The adjudicator can find then the prisoner guilty of the charge under paragraph 20 / 22. Similarly, if the adjudicator is satisfied beyond reasonable doubt that the accused used threatening, abusive or insulting racist words or behaviour then the adjudicator must dismiss the charge under paragraph 20 /22 and find the accused guilty of the charge under paragraph 20A / 23.

PARAGRAPH 24(A)/28 - DISPLAYS, ATTACHES TO OR DRAWS ON ANY PART OF A PRISON THREATENING, ABUSIVE OR INSULTING RACIST WORDS, DRAWINGS, SYMBOLS OR OTHER MATERIAL.

6.999o Specimen charge. Under Prison Rule 51 paragraph 24(A)/YOI Rule 55, paragraph 28), displays, attaches or draws threatening, abusive or insulting racist words, drawings, symbols or other material. At [time] on [date] in [place] you displayed, attached or drew threatening, abusive or racist words, drawings, symbols or other material aimed towards [name or [group] namely by writing "graffiti" saying " Kill all blacks."

6.999p The criteria for defining threatening or abusive or insulting remains the same as for an offence under paragraph 20/22). However, in order to prove a charge under paragraph 24A/28) it must also be proved that the words, drawings, symbols or other material were racist, in accordance with the definition given at paragraph 6.999b above.

6.999q Evidence. Before an adjudicator can be satisfied of guilt beyond reasonable doubt the following must be established:

a)   The accused either drew, displayed, circulated or attached the material (or words) set out in the charge;

b)   The displayed, or circulated material was threatening, abusive or insulting and racist. It should be borne in mind that words, behaviour or slogans can be annoying or rude without necessarily being abusive or insulting. To find guilt it is necessary to be satisfied that a reasonable person at the scene would consider the circulated or displayed material either threatening, or abusive or insulting. In addition, the material (or words) must come within the definition of racist set out at paragraph 6.999b above;

c) The accused intended to be racist and either threatening, or abusive or insulting and intended to act in such a way, or was reckless as to whether his or her words or behaviour might be so

6.999r There is no directly comparable charge not involving a racist element. Consideration should be given to laying one of two other charges at the same time; either paragraph 20/22) uses threatening, abusive or insulting words or behaviour; or destroys or damages any part of a prison, depending on the circumstances of the alleged offence (see paragraph 2.6 on simultaneous charging). If the adjudicator is not satisfied beyond reasonable doubt that the offence was racist s/he must dismiss the charge. If the prisoner has also been charged with any offence under either paragraph 20 or 17 /22 and 18), the adjudicator may find the prisoner guilty of the charge provided s/he is satisfied beyond reasonable doubt of the accused's guilt. Similarly, if the accused is found guilty of the racist charge under paragraph 24A /28 then any alternative charge must be dismissed.

7. **VERDICTS and PUNISHMENTS**
THE STANDARD OF PROOF .

7.1 An adjudicator must be satisfied beyond reasonable doubt that the accused has committed the offence which is the subject of the charge before finding guilt. Otherwise the finding must be one of not guilty regardless of how the accused has pleaded.

MITIGATION AND CONDUCT REPORT

7.2 If the finding is one of guilt the prisoner should be asked whether he or she wishes to say anything in mitigation. There is no need to use the word 'mitigation' so long as the prisoner understands that this is an opportunity to explain his or her actions. If the prisoner asks to call any person to support a plea in mitigation this should be allowed unless the adjudicator is satisfied that the witness will not be able to give relevant evidence. If no plea in mitigation is put forward this fact must be recorded on form F256.

7.3   After the mitigation. if any, has been taken into account, the adjudicator should ask the prisoner's personal officer or a member of staff who knows the prisoner for a report about him or her. If a written report is submitted its authorship should be made clear since the prisoner should be given every opportunity to ask any question in connection with it. The report will form a part of the record of the hearing and should be about the prisoner's behaviour during the current period of imprisonment. Reports should be based on facts about the prisoner's behaviour. They should not include subjective assessments which cannot be given to the adjudicator in the absence of the prisoner except, of course, where the hearing has been in the prisoner's absence. A verbal report is acceptable, but it must not be taken directly from the prisoner's prison record (F2050) which should not be present in the adjudication room.

GIVING REASONS FOR DECISIONS

7.4   Since a prisoner has the right, both internally and through the courts to challenge an adjudication it is reasonable that he or she should be given sufficient reasons for the decision in order to exercise that right effectively.

CONSISTENCY OF PUNISHMENTS

7.5   Punishments available are those contained in Prison Rules 55, 57 and 59 and in YOI Rules 60 and 63 (see Appendix 5). No other punishment may be imposed. It would, for example, be outside the Rules to disallow a privilege visit as privilege visits are granted at the governor's discretion under Prison Rule 35(3) and not Prison Rule 8. The disallowing of such facilities constitutes an administrative decision which stands aside from the disciplinary system.

7.6 There is no central tariff of punishments. A punishment should take account of the circumstances and seriousness of the offence and of the prisoner's behaviour during the present sentence. It should also take account of the type of establishment, the circumstances of the prisoner, the effect of the offence on the regime, the general order and discipline of a closed community, and the need to discourage the prisoner and others from repeating the offence.

7.7 Levels of punishments should be consistent within an establishment and governors may wish to establish a local tariff system. It is also desirable for adjudicators to ensure that when two or more prisoners are charged with offences arising out of the same incident, but the adjudications are carried out at different establishments, the punishments are consistent. The adjudicator should have available a list of recent offences and punishments. Governors should discuss with adjudicators on a regular basis what they consider to be aggravating or mitigating factors for certain offences.

7.8 Particular difficulties can arise where prisoners who have absconded or failed to return from temporary release are dealt with by the governor of the establishment other than that from which they absconded or to which they failed to return. Here adjudicators should inform themselves about the normal range of punishments at the original establishment with the aim of keeping discrepancies between the punishments received by prisoners in similar cases to a minimum.

7.9 Adjudicators must satisfy themselves that any punishment imposed is proportionate, taking into account the nature of the offence, its effect on the victim, the impact on the running of the prison, the likely impact of the punishment on the prisoner, the age of the prisoner, the conduct during the current period of imprisonment, and the length of time remaining to the prisoner's release. The key question to address is whether the punishment is justified, and also proportionate in the sense that a sledgehammer is not being used to crack a nut.

7.9A Independent adjudicators may use the full range of punishments contained within Prison Rules or YOI Rules, as applicable. Prison Service adjudicators may use the full range with the exception of additional days.

THE APPLICATION OF PUNISHMENTS

7.10 No prisoner will be punished about whose fitness for the punishment the adjudicator has any doubt.

7.11 Punishments must be within the range of and expressed in terms of the Prison or YOI Rules. Any punishment other than additional days will start immediately unless:

a) it was ordered to be suspended or
b) it was ordered to start at the end of a period of punishment already being served or just imposed.

7.12 If two or more punishments of the same kind are imposed at the same time for separate offences they may be ordered to run concurrently or consecutively to one another. Generally it will be good practice to impose concurrent punishments if the offences are part of the same incident. If consecutive punishments are imposed the adjudicator should ensure that the result is not excessive for all the offences taken together. Records should clearly show whether punishments are concurrent or consecutive.

7.13 If a pregnant woman is serving a punishment which involves segregation there is no reason why she should not be located in the segregation unit during the day, provided that there is a bell and she is observed at regular intervals. Governors must ensure that only a minimum loss of facilities results. The adjudicator would, however, normally be expected to impose a punishment which does not include segregation.

7.14 The adjudicator should ensure that the prisoner fully understands the effect of any punishment imposed.

Caution

7.15 Caution is available for any case where a warning seems sufficient to mark an offence and to discourage its repetition.

Forfeiture of facilities

7.16 Only the privileges that fall within Prison Rule 8 or YOI Rule 6 may be withdrawn as a punishment, for a maximum period of 42 days for adult prisoners and 21 days for young offenders. Radios, newspapers and magazines, general and educational notebooks, drawing books, attendance at educational classes, and correspondence courses should not normally be forfeited. If, exceptionally, any of these are to be forfeited, they must be specified. The purchase of postage stamps and phone cards should not normally be forfeited unless the circumstances of the offence are directly related to their abuse. Statutory gym is not a privilege and must not be withdrawn as a punishment. Where classes are a paid activity they may not be forfeited as a privilege. (See paragraph 7.21) Religious activities, whether attendance at worship or other activities organised by chaplains and visiting ministers, are not a privilege

Exclusion from associated work or activities

7.17 Exclusion from associated work may be given as a punishment for adult prisoners for a period not exceeding 21 days and should, where possible be served on normal location. The punishment should not in itself involve forfeiture of any other facilities except those which are incompatible with exclusion from associated work. For young offenders the corresponding punishment is up to 21 days removal from any particular activity of the YOI, other than training courses, work, education or physical education provided under YOI Rules 38 - 41.

Stoppage of earnings

7.18   The adjudicator may stop all or part of a prisoner's daily pay earned while in prison custody up to a maximum amount equivalent to 84 days full pay for adult offenders and 42 days full pay for young offenders. Prisoners should normally be able to purchase postage stamps and telephone cards or their equivalent. The amount must be calculated as a percentage of the pay the prisoner is due to receive during the period indicated in the punishment. It must not be stated as a fixed amount as there is no guarantee that a prisoner will earn that amount in future. 'Pay' is gross prison earnings exclusive of bonuses but inclusive of performance related or piece rate earnings. A bonus is an ad hoc payment for exceptional work, doing extra hours or work which is in addition to the prisoner's paid work. There is no power under the Prison/YOI Rules to impose a fine and any stoppage of earnings must not be expressed as a fine or as a fixed amount. It may, however, be expressed as 'Stoppage of earnings of 100 per cent less £1.25 (or whatever amount the adjudicator decides upon)'.

7.19   One day's pay should be treated for punishment purposes as one seventh of a week's pay (being gross earnings exclusive of bonuses) regardless of the number of days actually worked each week.

Cellular confinement

7.20   An adjudicator may impose cellular confinement for a maximum period of 21 days for adult prisoners and 10 days for young offenders. Consecutive punishments of cellular confinement, including punishments given for new offences whilst the prisoner is undergoing a period of cellular confinement, must not exceed 21 days in total for adults and 10 days for young offenders. Suspended punishments, when activated, count towards the maximum 21 or 10 days period. No cellular confinement will be imposed unless the medical officer has indicated that there are no reasons why the prisoner should not undergo the punishment. **A medical officer must**

undertake this duty. Staff should be alert to any potential deterioration of a prisoner's mental health while undergoing a period of cellular confinement. Cellular confinement must not be given as a method of enforcing other punishments, for example, forfeiture of privileges.

7.21   Prisoners serving a punishment of cellular confinement will be located in an ordinary cell set aside for the purpose. A bed and bedding, a table and a stool or chair must be provided in the cell and there must be access to sanitary facilities at all times. Other furnishing and fittings may be provided at the governor's discretion.

7.22   Prisoners serving a punishment of cellular confinement will be allowed all normal facilities except those which are incompatible with cellular confinement unless a punishment of forfeiture of facilities has also been imposed. Facilities which should normally be compatible are a reasonable number of personal possessions, cell hobbies and activities, entering public competitions, and own clothes and footwear where these have already been allowed. Facilities which will normally be incompatible are use of the canteen, use of private cash (although exceptions might be needed, for example to send money home or to purchase replacement radio batteries, phone cards or postage stamps) and association.

7.23   Prisoners' entitlements to correspond, to exercise, and to make applications to the governor, seconded probation officer, chaplain and board of visitors, are unaffected by cellular confinement. Prisoners will be allowed to attend the main service of their religion unless prevented under Standing Order 7A. Prisoners will be allowed to have books within the limits set out in Standing Orders. Visits and access to a telephone should be allowed unless the prisoner's behaviour and attitude make removal from cellular confinement impracticable or undesirable. Visits should take place at a time or place away from other prisoners.

7.24 A prisoner serving a punishment of cellular confinement, wherever the punishment is taking place, must be observed by an officer at least once an hour and must be visited by the chaplain daily. The governor or a senior operational manager (grade F or above) must visit all prisoners in cellular confinement daily. Where there are concerns about the potential deterioration of a prisoner's mental health, they should be drawn to the attention of the healthcare staff. The medical officer must visit each prisoner in cellular confinement as often as his/her individual health needs dictate. A daily visit must be made by a healthcare professional if the medical officer has not visited or is not visiting. At each visit the prisoner's physical, mental and emotional well-being must be assessed to ascertain continuing fitness for punishment. A note of each visit must be made on the prisoner's medical record. Any concerns about the health of a particular prisoner must be brought to the attention of the rest of the healthcare team. Where a medical officer considers that there are clinical reasons why the punishment should not continue, s/he must inform the governor, who must terminate the punishment.

7.25 The governor must ensure that the medical officer and chaplain are informed daily of prisoners in cellular confinement.

Additional Days

7.25A Additional days may only be imposed an independent adjudicator. Where a governor or Prison Service adjudicator considers that a charge warrants a punishment of additional days, the charge must be referred to an independent adjudicator. The prisoner must be informed as soon as the decision is made and given the opportunity to seek legal representation. Where s/he does not know a legal adviser they must be referred to the Legal Services Officer for help.

7.26 An independent adjudicator may impose a punishment of up to 42 additional days upon a sentenced prisoner .Two or more punishments imposed at the same time for separate offences will be treated as consecutive unless ordered to run concurrently. Punishments for related offences arising from a single incident may not exceed 42 days in total. The full term of a determinate sentence cannot, of course, be extended by punishments of additional days.

7.27 A prisoner serving an indeterminate sentence cannot receive additional days. However if at the time of the adjudication, he or she has been given a provisional date of release, the adjudicator may inform the prisoner that a recommendation will be made to the Parole Board or Home Secretary that the date of release should be postponed.

7.28 Additional days will not change the parole eligibility dates of prisoners sentenced before 1 October 1992, but such punishments must be notified to Prison Service Headquarters immediately so that any approved parole date may reflect the additional days. Parole eligibility dates of long term prisoners sentenced after 1 October 1992 will be automatically extended by any punishment of additional days.

Prospective punishment of additional days

7.29 Unconvicted and unsentenced prisoners may receive a prospective punishment of additional days which will be taken into account in calculating the date of release if a custodial sentence is imposed. Such a punishment must not exceed 42 days in respect of each offence. Prospective punishments of additional days may only be imposed by the independent adjudicator.

Extra work

7.30 This is available only under the YOI Rules. The extra work will be outside normal working hours for a maximum period of 21 days from the date punishment is imposed, and with not more than two hours extra work on any day. The work is to be carried out at a normal pace.

Removal from wing or living unit

7.31   The maximum period for removal from wing or living unit is 28 days for adults and 14 days for young offenders. The prisoner or young offender will take part in normal compulsory regime activities, including work, education, physical education and training, but will be held in a cell or room away from his or her wing or living unit for the rest of the time. Governors and controllers must ensure that only the minimum loss of facilities results.

Possessions of unconvicted and unsentenced prisoners

7.32   Unconvicted or unsentenced prisoners may be punished by forfeiture for any period of their right to have books, writing materials and other means of occupation and, if found guilty of escaping or attempting to escape, of the right to wear their own clothing.

Suspended punishments

7.33   An adjudicator may order any punishment other than a caution to be suspended up to six months so that it cannot take effect unless the prisoner commits another disciplinary offence in the suspension period. An individual punishment may not be suspended in part. A Prison Service adjudicator cannot activate a suspended punishment of additional days. If s/he considers that the charge warrants such an activation, s/he must refer the charge to the independent adjudicator.

7.34   If a prisoner commits a further offence against discipline during the period of suspension of an earlier punishment the activation of a suspended punishment should not be automatic and each case must be decided on its merits. An adjudicator may, irrespective of the punishment given for the later offence:

(a)   activate the suspended punishment in full

(b)   activate the suspended punishment in part, in which case the remainder will lapse

c)   change the suspension period by directing the punishment to remain suspended for up to six months from the date of the current adjudication

ENGLISH PRISON LAW

(d) take no action on the suspended punishment.

7.35   A punishment partly or fully activated can be directed to take effect immediately or to be consecutive to a punishment imposed for the subsequent offence .

7.35A A Prison Service adjudicator cannot activate a suspended pnishment of additional days. If s/he considers that the charge warrants such an activation, s/he must refer the charge to the independent adjudicator.

Interruptions to punishments

7.36   Time spent either in hospital or as an admitted patient in a prison health care centre will count as part of a punishment period.

7.37   Days on which a prisoner attends court will count as part of a punishment period.

7.38 When a punishment is interrupted by the prisoner being on bail or unlawfully at large, the balance of the punishment will be served if the prisoner returns to custody in connection with the same legal proceedings or is recaptured.

7.39   When the start of punishment is delayed more than 24 hours or is interrupted for any reason the prisoner will be examined by the medical officer before the punishment is started or resumed.

ADMINISTRATIVE ACTION

7.40   Neither the punishment nor any entry on form F256 should include reference to administrative action or recommendation for such action (for example placing on Rule 43, return to a closed prison, or disposal of exhibits). If such an action is to be taken it would be appropriate to tell the prisoner after the hearing has been concluded.

8. TERMINATION, MITIGATION AND REMISSION OF PUNISHMENTS

POWERS OF THE HOME SECRETARY

8.1   Prison Rule 61(1) and YOI Rule 64(1) give the Home Secretary the power to quash any finding of guilt and to terminate or mitigate any punishment. Authority to do so is delegated to area managers. Prisoners who wish to complain about adjudications on grounds of unfairness or error should complete a written requests and complaints form. The governor must forward this to the area manager together with copies of all relevant documents (form F256, statements of evidence etc.) and a report from the adjudicator commenting on the prisoner's claims. This action will be urgent when the prisoner is currently serving the punishment. Adjudicators must also ask the area manager to take action if they later discover a reason to doubt a finding or punishment. Area managers may also carry out a review on the recommendation of other interested parties for example the prisoner's solicitor or Member of Parliament.

POWERS OF GOVERNORS AND CONTROLLERS

8.2   A governor or controller may terminate or mitigate any partly served punishment other than additional days either on medical advice or where it appears that the effect of the punishment already served has been such that the prisoner is unlikely to repeat the offence. A governor or controller may remit additional days subject to directions under Prison Rule 61(2) and YOI Rule 64(2) set out below.

8.3   A governor or controller may not remit a caution, nor remit or mitigate any punishment on grounds of error or unfairness. This can only be done by area managers on behalf of the Home Secretary (see 8.1).

REMISSION OF ADDITIONAL DAYS

8.4   The prisoner concerned is responsible for applying for remission of additional days. A governor or controller is responsible for deciding on remission.

8.5   Eligibility. An adult prisoner is eligible for consideration or reconsideration for remission of actual or prospective additional days provided that, in the last six months
(a)   the prisoner has not committed any offence for which additional days were given, or for which suspended additional days were activated and
(b)   the prisoner has not submitted any other application for remission for which he or she was eligible.

The period is four months for young offenders and for prisoners who were young offenders at the time of the last offence for which additional days were given or activated

8.6   The only time that counts towards these periods is that spent in prison establishments, special hospitals, community homes and youth centres, on temporary release under Prison Rule 9 or YOI Rule 5 or in police custody if this occurs because no prison accommodation is available or because the prisoner is voluntarily helping the police with their enquiries. Time spent, for example, unlawfully at large or on parole does not count towards the period.

8.7   Punishments other than additional days do not remove eligibility. A punishment of suspended additional days does not remove eligibility, but its activation does.

8.8   Detainees held in community homes or youth centres under section 53(2) of the Children and Young Persons Act 1933 or section 92 of the Powers of Criminal Courts (Sentencing) Act 2000, are eligible to apply for remission of additional days received whilst on remand at prison establishments and should apply to Prison Service Headquarters, Section 53/92 Unit, Juvenile Group.

8.9   Governors must ensure that all prisoners know about the remission procedure, and that application form F2129A is available to them on request.

8.10 Preparation of prisoner's report. On receiving a completed application form the prisoner's personal officer or staff on the prisoner's wing must produce a report on form F2129B about the offences which led to the punishment of additional days and the prisoner's subsequent conduct. This report must draw on the experience of other members of staff who regularly see the prisoner and should be countersigned by the wing manager. Normally it should include the views of at least one member of staff not on the wing with whom the prisoner regularly comes into contact.

8.11 Reports must be obtained from any other establishments at which the prisoner has spent at least half of the period of six or four months before the application, and should be attached to form F2129B. It is not necessary to seek the views of the governor or panel giving the original punishment.

8.12 The information on form F2129B must be accurate and unbiased, even though the assessment has to be subjective in some respects, and must exclude opinions or suspicions that cannot be substantiated. The governor or controller will normally disclose the report to the prisoner so information that is confidential for reasons of security, for example where disclosure could place a third party at risk, should be clearly marked as such. Reports should include any evidence of a constructive attitude towards imprisonment. The extent to which the prisoner genuinely seeks or takes up opportunities for work, education and other regime activities will be relevant, as will a good response to a decision to grant temporary release. If the prisoner is judged to be a disruptive influence within the establishment specific examples must be given to back up this judgement. Information about the prisoner's criminal history is not relevant and must not appear in the form.

8.13 Considering the application. A governor or controller should consider applications for remission of additional days within one month of their submission by prisoners, taking account of factors up to the time of consideration. Prisoners wishing to support their applications orally should be allowed to do so. In this event, any reports considered by the governor or controller should be read to them unless security reasons prevent this and prisoners should be given an opportunity to comment on the reports. The officer completing the report on the prisoner should be present where practicable, and this will be necessary where, for example, a prisoner challenges the officer's report or where further amplification is required.

8.14 Applications from prisoners transferred to special hospitals should normally be made when they return to prison custody. Occasionally it may be necessary for the governor or controller to consider the application while the prisoner is in hospital, for example when the discharge is to be into the community by the hospital. It may be possible to deal with such applications by correspondence, in which case the prisoner should see in advance any information that would otherwise be available. In exceptional cases the governor may have to visit the hospital.

8.15 In reaching a decision, the governor or controller must take account of the following.

(a) Where it is considered appropriate to do so in accordance with (c) below, the power to remit additional days should be used to reward prisoners who take a constructive approach towards their imprisonment. Prisoners who genuinely seek or make the most of opportunities for work, education, PE, and other regime activities, and those who respect trust placed in them (for example in the granting of temporary release) could benefit from these arrangements.

(b) Where it is considered appropriate to do so in accordance with (c) below, remission of additional days should also be used to acknowledge a genuine change of attitude on the prisoner's part, whether or not this is made apparent in the prisoner's participation in regime or other activities. Simply keeping out of trouble may not always be an indication of such a change of heart, but for some prisoners it will be a significant achievement that could deserve recognition.

(c) Governors and controllers must take full account of the original offence for which additional days were given. In view of the nature of the offence they should consider whether, and to what extent, remission is appropriate to reward a constructive approach and significant change of attitude. For additional days imposed by a governor or controller, the normal expectation will be that any remission whether approved on one or over several occasions will be limited to a maximum of 50% of the additional days imposed for each offence, unless the remitting governor or controller takes the view that the offence was not a serious one or that there are exceptional circumstances. This expectation does not apply to additional days resulting from punishments given by boards of visitors under their former disciplinary powers.

8.16 There must be a consistent approach within each establishment and a record should be kept containing brief details of all applications and the outcomes.

8.17 Action after the decision is taken. Governors and controllers may inform prisoners immediately of their decisions. They must in any case give a written decision, with reasons, to the prisoner, using form F2129C, within seven days of considering the application. The form shows the prisoner's earliest release date following the decision and, if applicable, when the prisoner will next be eligible to apply for remission.

RECORDS

8.18 A record of any variation of a punishment must be made in the Actions/Events box relating to the charge on the prisoner's adjudication record (F2050E). Applications for remission of additional days, and the outcome, must also be recorded in the custodial documents file (F2051) and in the release dates box on page 3 of the core record (F2050).

9. REVIEW OF ADJUDICATIONS: THE APPLICATION OF THE RULES OF NATURAL JUSTICE

9.1 An adjudication may be reviewed at the request of a prisoner or his or her representative in a number of ways. First, the prisoner may use the internal requests and complaints procedure in which case the record of the hearing will be reviewed by the area manager. The area manager does not have the authority to rehear the case but if it is evident from the record that there was some error amounting to more than a mere technicality he or she may quash the adjudication exercising the authority of the Home Secretary under Prison Rule 61 or YOI Rule 64. Likewise, should the punishment imposed appear too severe, given all the circumstances, it may be mitigated under the same Rule.

9.2 Secondly a prisoner may express his or her concern about a hearing to those outside the Prison Service for example to a solicitor, Member of Parliament, or to a special interest group. If the matter is so raised by such an outsider on the prisoner's behalf the hearing will be reviewed by the area manager in the same manner. A prisoner may also ask a Member of Parliament to submit a grievance to the Parliamentary Commissioner for Administration at any stage in a complaint.

9.3 Thirdly, if the prisoner is dissatisfied with the area manager's decision, he or she may then take the complaint to the independent Prisons Ombudsman who has the authority to make recommendations to the Director General and to the Home Secretary including that a finding of guilt should be quashed or that a punishment should be remitted or mitigated.

9.4 Finally, the prisoner may seek leave of the Divisional Court to apply for judicial review of the adjudication or the area manager's decision following a complaint (see Appendix 4). Governors who receive notification or advance warning of an application for judicial review should immediately send all papers together with the record of the relevant hearing to the area manager for attention.

9.5 If at any time a prisoner found guilty at adjudication asks for copies of the record of the hearing, including statements of witnesses, the governor should allow this. No charge for photocopies should be made since a prisoner ought not to be impeded in any way should he or she wish to consider seeking a review of the hearing. The same goes for copies of documents supplied to a prisoner's legal representative. Charges may be made in respect of multiple copies, the first being supplied free.

GROUNDS FOR REVIEW

9.6 In every case, whether the review takes place by the area manager, the Prisons Ombudsman, or by the court, the crucial consideration will be whether the proceedings were conducted in accordance with legal requirements of fairness. However the Prisons Ombudsman and area managers have a wider brief and will also look at the merits of any particular decision. On a judicial review, the grounds for challenge are illegality, irrationality (unreasonableness) and procedural impropriety.

ILLEGALITY

9.7 At judicial review the Divisional Court will consider whether or not the adjudicator got the law wrong. Examples might be: did he or she find guilt in the case of unauthorised possession under the mistaken belief that it is an absolute offence? Was a McKenzie friend disallowed under the mistaken belief that such a person must not be a fellow prisoner? Is there a misinterpretation of the concepts of intent or recklessness? (See Appendix 4).

IRRATIONALITY (UNREASONABLENESS)

9.8 This is based on the Wednesbury principle (see Appendix 4). A decision is likely to be quashed at judicial review if it is such that no authority properly directing itself on the relevant law and acting reasonably could have reached it.

This may be so where the adjudicator has taken into account irrelevant considerations or failed to take into account relevant considerations, has applied the wrong test in reaching a finding or if the punishment imposed was indefensibly severe.

PROCEDURAL IMPROPRIETY

9.9 Primarily this relates to the question of whether or not the accused has been given a fair hearing; has it been in accordance with the rules of natural justice? A number of factors may constitute procedural impropriety, as follows.

9.10 The de novo principle: the adjudicator must come to the adjudication afresh with an uncluttered mind. The adjudicator should start the proceedings without reference to any previous hearing of the charge, for example one at which the question of legal representation was decided. There is one exception to this and that is if, during the course of the second hearing, the accused disputes evidence saying that it is at variance with that offered at the preliminary hearing. The record of the preliminary hearing may then be admitted as evidence at the represented hearing so that the evidence may be challenged. (See 3.12 and 3.13).

9.11 The rule against bias. The basis of this is the legal maxim that no one is to be a judge in his or her own cause. Bias may be suggested if, for example, the accused prisoner were to be a friend of the adjudicator or where an adjudicator had been the victim of a previous offence by the accused. It points to a personal involvement in an incident going beyond an interest in maintaining good order and discipline. A general good knowledge of the prisoner's history would not be sufficient to amount to bias.

9.12 The fettering of discretion. An adjudicator has discretion in a number of areas, particularly as to whether or not to admit evidence, to hear witnesses, or to allow legal representation or other assistance. He or she must act fairly in exercising that discretion. This is not to imply that it would be wrong to develop a local tariff of punishments for certain types of offence to ensure consistency. It is legitimate for decision makers to have a policy as to how like cases are to be treated but they must not allow the policy to close their minds to the circumstances of a particular case which might lead to the policy not being applied in that case. To do so would amount to an improper fettering of discretion.

9.13 The audi alteram partem rule. An adjudicator must hear both sides of the case. Each party to a hearing must have the opportunity to present their version of the facts and to ask questions of each other to substantiate their side of the events. Likewise, each party must be allowed to comment on all the material considered by adjudicator and be given an opportunity to explain, contradict or correct it. Each party must be allowed to call witnesses to corroborate their evidence. It would be improper for an adjudicator to refuse to call a witness on the grounds, say, that the accused had already called a number who had been unable to corroborate the defence or mitigation.

9.14 Legitimate expectation. In recent years the courts have developed a doctrine of legitimate expectation to indicate entitlements to which they will give effect over and above rights enshrined in law. When considering the duty to act in any particular case it is necessary to look at the conduct of the adjudicator as a whole in order to decide whether the circumstances are such that the accused has acquired a legitimate expectation that the adjudicator should act towards him or her in a particular way.

9.15 Excess of jurisdiction: ultra vires: An adjudication will be quashed if the adjudicator acts outside the Rules and this may occur in a variety of ways. Examples might be where the offence of which the prisoner has been found guilty is not an offence specified at Prison Rule 51/YOI Rule 55; where an adjudicator hears charges without the proper delegated authority so to do; where punishment is in excess of that allowed by the statutory instruments; or where the charges were laid outside the specified time limits, in the absence of exceptional circumstances.

10. MODEL PROCEDURE FOR THE CONDUCT OF AN ADJUDICATION
GENERAL

10.1 Proceedings must start afresh without reference to any previous hearing of the charge (for example one at which the question of legal or other representation or assistance was decided). This is to enable the adjudicator to determine the case solely on the evidence presented at the hearing.

10.2 The proceedings should be started without access to the accused's prison record or record of any previous prison offences committed by him or her.

10.3 An adjudicator may adjourn a hearing either to a later time or date if he or she considers it desirable, for example for further information or enquiries or for the presence of a witness who is not available. Any adjudicator who grants legal representation or the assistance of an adviser will almost certainly need to adjourn the hearing. If a prisoner has been segregated from others prior to an adjudication, segregation during any adjournment should not be automatic.

10.4 The adjudicator should check the following.

a. The charge has been properly laid, in other words that it has been laid under the correct Rules, as soon as possible after the discovery of the alleged offence and, save in exceptional circumstances, within 48 hours of its discovery.

b. Form F256 has been prepared for the hearing and each charge, as recorded on that form, is one that is provided for in, and follows, the wording of the correct paragraph of Prison Rule 51 or YOI Rule 55.

c. In addition to the formal wording under the Rules, each charge contains sufficient additional explanatory detail to leave the accused in no doubt as to the precise nature of the charge.

d. In the case of a renewed hearing, for example after the granting of representation, the adjudicator must be satisfied that a fresh or renewed form F1127 (Notice of Report) has been issued to the accused in sufficient time to prepare a defence. Brief particulars of the charge should be noted on this form. Form F1127, the charge recorded on form F256 and the charge as heard at any previous hearing (as recorded on form F256) should all be identical.

e. Form F1145 (Explanation of the Procedure at a hearing of a Disciplinary Charge by a Governor) has been issued in sufficient time for the accused to study it and normally at least two hours in advance of the hearing.

f. The medical officer has certified on form F256 that the accused is fit for adjudication and cellular confinement and that any report prepared by him or her for the attention of the adjudicator is available. If it is offered in evidence the content of any such report must be made known to the accused who should be permitted to challenge it as in the case of any other evidence.

OPENING PROCEDURE

10.6 The officer in charge of managing the hearing should ensure that the prisoner and escort enter the adjudication room before the reporting officer and witnesses and that at any adjournment they should leave before the prisoner and escort (see 4.9) He or she should also ensure that eyeballing of the accused is avoided at all times. (see 4.11)

10.7 The adjudicator must take the following steps and record them and the responses of the accused on form F256.

i) Identify the accused.
ii) Ascertain that the accused has received forms F1127 and F1145 and that he or she understands the procedure.
iii) Read out the charge.
iv) Ascertain that the accused understands the charge.

v) Ask the accused whether he or she has had sufficient time to prepare an answer to the charge.

vi) Ask whether or not the accused has made a written answer to the charge.

vii) Ask whether or not the accused would like the question of legal representation, or the assistance of a McKenzie friend to be considered.

viii) Ask whether the accused pleads guilty or not guilty to the charge. When a prisoner pleads guilty the governor should hear sufficient evidence to be satisfied that he or she fully understands the charge. If it becomes clear that the prisoner's plea of guilt is based on a misunderstanding he or she should be advised to plead not guilty. If the prisoner declines the advice the adjudicator may nevertheless inform the accused that the hearing will proceed on the basis of a not guilty plea. (A charge may be dismissed notwithstanding a guilty plea.)

ix) Ask whether or not the accused wishes to call witnesses.

1. 10.8 The adjudicator has no power to change a charge during the course of the hearing. If the evidence does not support the charge that has been brought it must be dismissed. Simple particulars of a charge may be amended.

2. 10.9 If the adjudicator is satisfied that the accused needs more information on the procedure or the charge, more time to prepare an answer, or to make out a case for representation or assistance the hearing should be adjourned so that this can be remedied.

3.

4. 10.10 Only stages i – iv of the procedure in 10.7 should be followed if one or more of the offences with which the accused has been charged has been referred to the police, or in the case of drug offences a substance or article has been sent for forensic analysis. In these circumstances the hearing should then be adjourned pending the outcome

of those enquiries and, when it is subsequently resumed, it will be necessary to follow the opening procedure.

5.   10.11   The record of the hearing must show that, where any application for legal assistance or representation was refused, the Tarrant principles were properly considered (see 3.8).

6.   10.12   The adjudicator should hear the evidence of the reporting officer and invite the accused to question the officer on that evidence or on relevant matters which the officer has not covered. The adjudicator may also wish to ask questions for clarification.

7.   10.13   If any exhibit is produced during the hearing this should be described and recorded on form F256 at the time it is produced.

8.   10.14   The adjudicator should invite the accused to offer a defence to the charge, or explain his or her actions, and to give oral evidence if he or she wishes. This is the appropriate time for the accused to comment on the evidence.

9.   10.15   If the accused asks to call witnesses, whether named in advance or during the hearing, the adjudicator should ask what the accused thinks their evidence will show or prove. Unless the adjudicator is satisfied that the witnesses will not be able to give relevant evidence, they should be called. If the adjudicator decides not to call a witness requested by the accused he or she should be told why and given the opportunity to comment. The reason for the decision should be noted in the record of the hearing.

10.   10.16   The adjudicator should invite the accused's witnessess to say what they know of the affair and invite the accused, if he or she so wishes, to question them on their evidence or on anything else that appears relevant to the case.

11.   10.17   The reporting officer should also be given the opportunity to question the accused and witnesses.

12. 10.18 The witnesses should not remain in the room after they have given their evidence and been questioned on it, except where the witness is a co-accused and the charges are being heard in tandem.

13. 10.19 If the adjudicator agrees to hear a witness who is not readily available to give evidence in person the hearing should be adjourned so that the witness can be present.

14. 10.20 The adjudicator may also wish to ask questions of witnesses or to call witnesses even though they have not been named by the accused or the reporting officer if by doing so it may be possible to discover the truth of the situation.

15. 10.21 After all the witnesses have been heard the adjudicator should ask the accused whether he or she wishes to say anything further about the case, to comment on the evidence, or to draw attention to any relevant considerations. If the accused tries to bring up points in mitigation at this stage, they should be noted and considered carefully at the appropriate time.

16. 10.22 The adjudicator must consider the question of guilt and may wish to adjourn the hearing for this purpose. The adjudicator should find the accused guilty only if he or she is satisfied beyond reasonable doubt that the prisoner is guilty of all the essential elements of the charge (see Appendix 4 regarding reasonable doubt).

17. 10.23 The adjudicator has no power to reduce a charge or to substitute a lesser charge during a hearing. If an adjudicator is satisfied that a prisoner is guilty only in respect of a part of the charge (for example that some items in possession were unauthorised but that some were authorised) it is possible to announce a finding of guilt in respect of part of the charge only. The prisoner should be left in no doubt in respect of which parts of the charge have been proved and this should be recorded on form F256. If the evidence does

not support a finding of guilt, the charge must be dismissed. It may be possible to lay new charges arising out of the same events provided that it is done within 48 hours of the alleged offence being discovered. In such a case the new hearing should be before a different adjudicator.

18.   10.24   The adjudicator must announce the decision and this must be recorded on form F256. When more than one charge is being heard at the same time the finding on each charge should be clearly stated and recorded, by cross-referencing, if necessary, on form F256.

19.   10.25   If the finding is one of guilt the prisoner should be asked if he or she has anything to say in mitigation and may ask to call witnesses in support of the mitigation.

20.   10.26   Before deciding upon punishment the adjudicator should ask for a conduct report. The prisoner should be allowed to ask questions of the officer giving the report.

21.   10.27   The adjudicator must now consider the punishment and may wish to adjourn for that purpose. No punishment of cellular confinement may be imposed unless the medical officer has certified that day that the prisoner is fit for it.

22.   10.28   The adjudicator must announce the punishments and if they are being imposed in respect of more than one charge, whether the punishments are to be consecutive or concurrent with other punishments.

23.   10.29   If the prisoner is currently subject to a suspended punishment, the adjudicator's decision on the suspended punishment must be announced and explained to the prisoner and recorded on form F256.

24.   10.30   The adjudicator must ensure that the punishments are correctly entered on form F256 and must sign and date the forms to complete the record.

25.   11.   REFERRING SERIOUS CRIMINAL OFFENCES TO THE POLICE

26.   11.1   Any serious criminal offence, whether or not there is an identifiable suspect, should be reported immediately to the governor to decide whether the police should be informed. Details should also be reported to the Intelligence and Incident Support Unit in Prison Service Headquarters under the normal incident reporting procedures. Where the police are asked to investigate, a disciplinary charge should nevertheless be laid within 48 hours of discovery of the alleged offence. In such cases the governor should open the adjudication and adjourn the hearing pending the outcome of the police investigation.

27.   11.2   Appendix 3 sets out guidelines for referrals which have been agreed with the Association of Chief Police Officers, Crown Prosecution Service and Lord Chancellor's Department. Governors must nevertheless judge each case on its merits and in the light of experience.

28.   11.3   Governors should ensure that they have effective arrangements locally for liaison with the police, Crown Prosecution Service and the courts, that communication is good and that there is a common understanding of how the arrangements should operate based on the referral guidelines. The Crown Prosecution Service cannot and should not be expected to account in detail for every decision that they take.

29.   11.4   The key to the success of the arrangements is likely to be the quality of the relationship with the police, and governors should work through existing police/prison liaison channels. Governors should maintain contact at a suitable level, probably with the head of the local CID.

30.   11.5   Good practice in prisons can increase the likelihood of successful prosecution of a serious offence. Staff must be aware of the need to:

INVESTIGATING THE CHARGE
-   notify the police immediately in appropriate cases

- make a precise note as soon as possible after an incident has occurred, using form F2147 for this purpose
- avoid contaminating physical evidence if at all possible
- leave the taking of statements to the police.

Advice to staff is contained in the pocket card Serious Criminal Offences in Prison Establishments reproduced in Appendix 3.

1. 11.6 If no prosecution results from the referral, or if the Crown Prosecution Service decide that a prosecution cannot continue, the governor should consider whether to proceed with the disciplinary charge. If it is clear that the police or Crown Prosecution Service have decided that a prosecution cannot be brought because the available evidence is insufficient, and the disciplinary charge is similar to and relies on the same evidence as the potential prosecution, the governor must dismiss the disciplinary charge. In other cases, for example where it is likely that witnesses may cooperate with the internal hearing but not with the police, it is open to the governor to proceed with the charge.

2. 11.7 If proceedings at court are discontinued or if charges are directed to lie on file at some point before the presenting of evidence the governor may similarly consider whether to proceed with the adjourned internal hearing.

3. 11.8 If the police decide to caution a prisoner a governor or controller must not proceed with a disciplinary hearing. The charge must be dismissed. It is not necessary to reconvene the hearing although the prisoner must be informed and this must be noted on the F256. (To

continue with a charge would be double jeopardy. A police caution forms part of a person's criminal record.)

11.9 If a prosecution does not go ahead it is essential that governors or controllers ensure that any adjudication is conducted as soon as possible. Unjustifiable delay may prevent a fair hearing of the charge. It will therefore be necessary for governors to press the Crown Prosecution Service for a rapid response as to the outcome of any trial or decision on their part.

1. 11.10 If the Crown Prosecution Service prosecute and present evidence in court, the governor must inform the prisoner that the disciplinary charge will not go ahead.
2. 11.11 Where a prisoner is prosecuted for causing criminal damage to prison property consideration should be given to applying to the court for a compensation order.

APPENDIX 1- omitted.

APPENDIX 2 HEARINGS WITH LEGAL REPRESENTATION
ROLE AND FUNCTIONS OF THE SOLICITOR REPRESENTING THE PRISON SERVICE

A2.1 The principal function of the solicitor representing the Prison Service is to present the evidence in support of the charge. He or she has an important part to play in protecting the witnesses from unfair cross-examination and in presenting the other side of the case if the prisoner's solicitor attacks the conduct of prison officers or the way the prisoner has been treated in prison. The solicitor does, of course, have an important role to play, along with the prisoner's solicitor, in assisting the adjudicator to get at the truth

A2.2 The solicitor representing the Prison Service will also be available to assist the adjudicator when points of law are raised. It will be sensible, when a legal point is made, to seek comments from both lawyers present so that when it has been elucidated the adjudicator will be able to form a judgement.

A2.3 A solicitor representing the Prison Service will receive instructions locally from, and will put requests for information or facilities to, a member of staff at the prison who is not adjudicating on the case.

A2.4 Before the solicitor receives instructions, the prisoner will have been charged and have appeared before the adjudicator.

The alleged offence will have been investigated by prison officers and some statements may have been taken from witnesses. The solicitor should consider the charge in the light of the evidence to see whether it is appropriate and whether further evidence is required to support it. If further evidence is needed, the solicitor should ask the instructing member of staff to arrange for him or her to see the witnesses and he or she should ask the adjudicator for an adjournment if this is necessary.

A2.5 If the charge is not appropriate, the solicitor should suggest to the instructing member of staff that he or she will not be calling evidence in support of that charge, and invite the adjudicator to dismiss it.

A2.6 If the offences charged are appropriate but the particulars are wrong or inadequate, the solicitor should raise the matter at the beginning of the hearing and suggest that the adjudicator should proceed on the basis of the solicitor's formulation of the particulars.

A2.7 A solicitor not satisfied with the evidence set out in the statements supplied should inform the instructing member of staff who will arrange for him or her to take further statements from the relevant witnesses.

ROLE AND FUNCTIONS OF THE SOLICITOR REPRESENTING THE PRISONER

A2 8 Solicitors acting for prisoners may make a number of requests. Examples are discussed below. In relation to each, it must be remembered that it is not proper for the adjudicator to require the attendance of witnesses from within the prison or the production of documents, nor to impose duties upon prison officers or the instructing member of staff simply because the solicitor for the prisoner has requested it. The adjudicator remains master of his or her procedure and must decide on the merits of each request what action should be taken.

A2.9 The solicitor acting for the prisoner may ask to see copies of all statements which it is intended to use at the hearing. Where there are such statements, the solicitor representing the Prison Service will no doubt wish to anticipate this request by providing copies as soon as possible. Copies should also be provided of any other statements made in the course of the investigation unless there are compelling reasons for nondisclosure, for example a real risk to the maker of the statement.

A2.10 The solicitor for the prisoner may request facilities to interview prison officers or other prisoners. This request should be made first to the instructing member of staff but if it is repeated, to the adjudicator, the solicitor representing the Prison Service should seek to establish which prisoners it is sought to interview and why it is thought that they may be able to give evidence for the defence.

A2.11 The solicitor representing the prisoner may ask for a list of names of prisoners in the wing or in particular cells or for a list of officers on duty at the time. This is a matter for the instructing member of staff and the solicitor representing the Prison Service who should seek to narrow the request as far as possible and to find its justification.

A2.12 The solicitor for the prisoner may ask for an opportunity for his or her client to identify prisoners or prison officers. How this is arranged is a matter for the instructing member of staff. An officer of the prison will not be compelled to take part in an identification parade against his or her will.

A2.13 After an adjudication with legal representation has been concluded the prisoner's solicitor should be allowed to meet with his or her client if this is requested.

MODEL LETTER TO THE SOLICITOR REPRESENTING THE ACCUSED

A2.14 To be sent from the instructing member of staff.

I understand that you will be representing (name) at an adjudication at this establishment on (date). If you have any queries about preparing your client's case including the possibility of interviewing witnesses or for seeing your client beforehand, please contact me.

If you are not familiar with the disciplinary system in prisons and YOIs, you will almost certainly find it helpful to consult the Prison Discipline Manual, which is published by the Prison Service and can be seen on the web-site at www.hmprisonservice.gov.uk. The document is also available to your client to consult in the prison library.

Adjudications are inquisitorial disciplinary hearings and whilst governed by the principles of natural justice, are not subject to the same procedural rules as a hearing in the courts. The adjudicator will conduct the inquiry and may well expect to pursue his or her own line of questioning, as well as listening to the questions you ask on your client's behalf.

The adjudicator will also be concerned to ensure that your client's case is heard promptly. We will make every effort to ensure that you have the opportunity to prepare your case in advance of the hearing, because the adjudicator will wish to avoid further adjournments if at all possible.

The documentation relating to the charge brought against your client is enclosed. The adjudication will take place at [time] on [date]. You should arrive at [place] at least [time] before the hearing, from where you will be shown either to your client or to the adjudications rooms, according to your preference.

APPENDIX 3 CRIMINAL OFFENCES IN PRISON SERVICE ESTABLISHMENTS

A) GUIDELINES FOR REFERRAL TO THE POLICE (AGREED WITH THE POLICE, THE CROWN PROSECUTION SERVICE AND THE LORD CHANCELLOR'S DEPARTMENT)

INTRODUCTION

1. These guidelines are to help governors decide when to ask the police to investigate alleged criminal offences committed in Prison Service establishments. They have been distributed

to all governors, police forces and offices of the Crown Prosecution Service.
2. The guidelines cannot be comprehensive and are not mandatory. There will be circumstances that they do not cover and particular factors in individual cases that may justify taking a different approach.
The governor will be the best judge of the balance to be struck in any individual case. But the guidelines are intended to cover the great majority of behaviour by prisoners which may warrant involving the police.
3. When they have completed their investigation the police will decide whether or not papers should be forwarded to the Crown Prosecution Service. There can be no guarantee that the Crown Prosecution Service will decide that an alleged offence warrants court proceedings. To prosecute the Crown Prosecution Service will need to be satisfied both that there is admissible, substantial and reliable evidence that a criminal offence has been committed by an identifiable person and that the public interest requires a prosecution. The Crown Prosecution Service must comply with the Code for Crown Prosecutors issued under section 10 of the Prosecution of Offences Act 1985 - governors may find it helpful to familiarise themselves with the Code. The aim of these referral guidelines, however, is to promote a shared understanding amongst all the agencies involved of the relative seriousness of offences committed in prison. Where a governor feels that the prison context is particularly relevant to the way an individual case is considered, it is his or her responsibility to explain that significance to the police and the Crown Prosecution Service.
DISCIPLINARY PROCEEDINGS
4. The great majority of offences against the prison disciplinary code will continue to be dealt with solely within the governor's powers. When the police are asked to investigate, however, a disciplinary charge should still be laid within 48 hours of discovery of the alleged offence. The adjudication should be

opened and the governor should satisfy himself or herself that there is a case to answer. If so, the hearing should be adjourned pending the outcome of the police investigation (provided the governor is satisfied that there is a case to answer). During this period, the prisoner charged should not be segregated unless the governor considers it essential for the maintenance of good order and discipline. If segregation is essential, it must be under Prison Rule 45 or YOI Rule 49 and therefore be subject to regular and critical review. The grounds for segregation must be clearly recorded; "pending the outcome of police investigation" will not be sufficient (see 4.17-4.22 in the body of the Manual).

5. If no prosecution results from the police investigation or if the Crown Prosecution Service decide that a prosecution cannot continue the governor should consider whether to proceed with the disciplinary charge. Where the resumption of internal proceedings is likely to create an appearance of unfairness out of proportion to the seriousness of the alleged disciplinary offence, however, governors should consider whether the charge should be dismissed. As a general principle governors should avoid lengthy adjournments wherever possible and should look to the police and the Crown Prosecution Service for an early prognosis of the likelihood of a criminal prosecution.

THE VICTIM'S WISHES

6. If the victim of any alleged criminal act requires that the matter to be referred to the police the governor should accede to that request. The governor will clearly wish to relay quickly any advice from the police that disciplinary proceedings are likely to be more appropriate. As with all other referrals, the

governor should only proceed with a disciplinary charge after a decision has been made not to prosecute under the criminal law.

RACIAL MOTIVATION

7. Clear evidence of a racial motivation in any of the offences described here will strengthen the case for referral.

ACTION TO BE TAKEN WHEN AN OFFENCE FALLING WITHIN THESE GUIDELINES IS COMMITTED

8. The prospects of securing a conviction where a serious offence has been committed will be greatly increased if the police are called immediately when an offence comes to light. It is important that there is efficient local liaison between the establishment and the police. Separate advice is being issued to staff about the preservation of evidence, but governors should be particularly aware that some statements given to prison officers by prisoners may not be admissible under Police and Criminal Evidence Act 1984 or comply with the formal requirements of the criminal justice legislation for evidence used in criminal proceedings. The sooner the police are involved, therefore, the better.

9. The notes which staff take immediately after an incident and any other papers, such as interview notes, which are relevant must be carefully preserved and a copy placed with the record of the prisoner(s) involved. If they are required to give evidence in court, staff may be permitted to refresh their memories by reference to any written notes made or verified by themselves, and made contemporaneously with the facts to which they can testify. Moreover, if a prosecution results, the Crown Prosecution Service is under a duty to disclose relevant all unused material. Whilst there is a discretion to withhold certain types of material, it is vital that the Crown Prosecution Service has easy access to everything.

ADVICE

10. The most important liaison point for governors will be the local police. If difficulties arise in interpreting the guidelines, governors can contact Prison Service Headquarters (Directorate of Resettlement, Prisoner Administration Group 020-7217-2908).

THE GUIDELINES

11. The guidelines that follow are arranged by broad category of alleged offence and deal primarily with circumstances in which referral to the police is likely to be appropriate. Where it seems helpful also to describe circumstances in which referral is not likely to be appropriate, this advice appears as a note.

1. ASSAULT
REFER
i) alleged offences and attempted offences of murder, manslaughter, non-consensual buggery or rape, and threats to kill where there appears to be genuine intent
ii) other alleged assaults if any of the following elements are present:
- the use of a weapon likely to cause, or causing, serious injury
- the occasioning of serious injury by any means
- the use of serious violence against any person (providing that more than minor injury was the intended or likely outcome of such an assault, the actual extent of the injuries received may not be significant; minor injury means minor bruising, sprains and minor cuts; serious injury will be more than this)

- personal sexual violation other than rape but where the victim is especially vulnerable or there has been the use or threat of violence
iii) any alleged assault that amounts to unlawful imprisonment (hostage-taking).

2. ESCAPE
REFER
i) any alleged escape from a closed establishment or secure escort
ii) any alleged attempted escape from a closed establishment or secure escort, provided that the attempt amounts to more

than an intention to escape and the act done can be regarded as more than mere preparation for the offence

iii) any other serious case where the means of escape have been found and where referral is needed to discover how they were obtained and to prosecute those responsible: the nature of the means and the category of the prisoner will be relevant in deciding whether referral is justified

iv) any alleged escape or abscond from open conditions where the prisoner has been absent for a substantial period of time (normally any period over eight weeks)

v) any alleged escape or abscond from open conditions where the prisoner has made determined efforts to avoid recapture (such as by changing his or her name).

Note Additional aggravating factors which may justify a decision to refer an incident to the police include

* a carefully planned and premeditated decision to abscond by the prisoner, involving the deception of staff

* a previous escape or abscond by the prisoner during the current sentence

Further alleged offences committed either in the course of the alleged escape or whilst unlawfully at large may make it preferable to refer the whole incident to the police for investigation.

3. POSSESSION OF UNAUTHORISED ARTICLES
REFER Weapons
i) alleged possession of firearms or explosives capable of inflicting serious injury or damage, whether manufactured or locally produced

    ii) alleged possession of other offensive weapons (knives, kitchen or workshop implements,

    home-made weapons etc) if there is evidence to suggest that the weapon was intended for

    use in the commission of a further serious criminal offence (such as a serious assault or an

    escape)

Drugs

iii) Class A Drugs: alleged supply and possession with or without intent to supply

iv) Class B Drugs: alleged supply and possession with intent to supply unless there is only

| small scale supply for no payment; | possession alone should be referred only when the |

quantity is substantial

Note

Alleged possession or supply of Class C Drugs, and alleged possession of a small quantity of Class B Drugs, without intent to supply, should not normally be referred.
A current list of drugs under the Misuse of Drugs Act 1971 appears at Annex C of the Security Manual.

4. CRIMINAL DAMAGE/ARSON
REFER
Criminal Damage
i) if damage to the property of the prison or other prisoners is very serious, normally to a value in excess of £2,000; evidence of concerted action by a group of prisoners will strengthen the case for referral; it is essential that any estimate of the value of damage done represents the full cost of repair; it may therefore be appropriate to obtain an estimate, including materials and labour, from a contractor
Arson
ii) unless it is clear that there was little or no risk of the fire taking hold Note However, governors will wish to be particularly aware of the possibility that cell-fires may in fact be
evidence of a prisoner's highly disturbed or suicidal state of mind. Acts that amount in reality to attempts at self injury

should not normally be referred, nor dealt with under the internal disciplinary system.

5. ROBBERY

REFER where the alleged theft is accompanied by the use or threat of serious violence or of a weapon.

6. MAJOR DISTURBANCES REFER

i) incidents involving a number of prisoners where the governor has lost, or seems likely to lose, control of all or part of the establishment; this may arise because the staff have had to withdraw for their own protection, or the prisoners have barricaded themselves into part of the prison, or for some other reason

ii) mass disobedience involving the use or threat of violence, resulting in assaults or criminal damage serious enough to be referred under section 1 and 4(i) above, or in the commission of other serious criminal offences.

Major disturbances that satisfy these criteria may constitute a basis for a charge of prison mutiny under the Prison Security Act 1992, or a charge of one of the public order offences under the Public Order Act 1986, or another criminal offence. A charge of prison mutiny is likely to be particularly appropriate for incidents involving a large number of prisoners where it is difficult to establish which prisoner did any specific act.

Note

The following should not be referred:

i) small, localised incidents where no criminal offence is committed and which the governor is able to contain without difficulty

ii) passive disobedience, even on a large scale, where it is clear that the prisoners are protesting about a particular grievance and where there seems to be no intention to overthrow lawful authority

iii) other disturbances for which the governor believes his or her powers under the disciplinary system to be adequate.

7. FAILURE TO RETURN FROM RELEASE ON TEMPORARY LICENCE OR FOLLOWING NOTICE OF RECALL

REFER

i) any alleged failure to return where the prisoner was unlawfully at large for a substantial period of time (normally any period over eight weeks)

ii) any alleged failure to return where the prisoner made significant efforts to avoid recapture, for example by changing addresses, assuming a different name, or previously misleading staff.

Note

Additional aggravating factors may justify a decision to refer an alleged incident to the police.

Further alleged offences committed whilst the prisoner was unlawfully at large may make it preferable to refer the whole incident to the police for investigation even if the failure to return in itself is not particularly serious.

Prisoners who have a reasonable excuse for failure to return on time after a period of release on temporary licence, or following notice of recall, should not normally be referred. (A reasonable excuse might include any case where the prisoner's failure to return was not intentional but was due to unforeseen circumstances or factors beyond his or her control).

B) SERIOUS CRIMINAL OFFENCES IN PRISON ESTABLISHMENTS

INFORMATION FOR STAFF

Disciplinary charges that involve criminal offences will be dealt with by the governor or the controller or by the courts, depending on their seriousness.

Guidelines on referral to the police are given above.

The police are responsible for gathering evidence for prosecution and it is vital that any action staff take after an incident assists the police in that duty. Staff must not seek to take on the role of the investigating police officer.

The Crown Prosecution Service decide whether to prosecute following the police investigation. They judge both whether the evidence is sufficient and whether prosecution is in the public interest. If prosecution results, the reporting officer becomes a witness to the alleged offence in the same way as any other person present. If there is no prosecution, the governor or controller may consider dealing with the matter under the disciplinary system provided a charge was laid properly at the outset.

GOOD PRACTICE FOR STAFF

1. The prison officer first on the scene must take charge of the incident until assistance arrives.

2. If identified the alleged offender must be detained and removed from the scene as early as practicable.

3. The identity of any witnesses, whether staff or prisoners, must be noted.

4. Questioning of victims, alleged offenders and witnesses must be limited to establishing what has happened. Prison officers must not conduct lengthy interviews or take written statements from prisoners.

This should be left to the police where criminal proceedings are a possibility. A court may exclude evidence if correct procedures have not been followed in taking statements.

5. As soon as possible after dealing with the incident, the prison officer first on the scene and other staff witnesses must make written notes. These will form the basis of both the witness statement to the police and form F254 in relation to internal proceedings. Each note should be recorded on form F2147, which should be available on every wing. The note must record details of:

how the officer became aware of the incident (was he or she present throughout? was it reported to him or her? who reported it? etc)

what the officer observed, for example injuries or damage potential exhibits left at the scene of the incident

what those involved said initially
the date and time the note is made.

6. The police should be contacted immediately on discovery of an alleged offence which may lead to a prosecution. Subject to their advice, after the prisoners concerned in the incident have been removed, the scene must be sealed and nothing disturbed, unless it is unavoidable, while awaiting the arrival of the police investigating officer. If exceptionally someone has to enter the sealed area, it is essential to inform the police investigating officer, if possible in advance.

7. Items at the scene must not be handled unless this is essential. In this event there must be minimum contact to reduce damage to marks or other evidence. Covering the hands before touching objects does not preserve such evidence.

8. The police may seize items of a prisoner's clothing which could be evidence if this is necessary to prevent concealment, loss or damage.

9. Guidance on giving evidence in court is contained in the card Prosecution Witnesses in the Crown Court and Magistrates' Courts (DOC 1 1991) and in Circular Instruction 7/1991

10. Charges should be laid in the normal way within 48 hours of the discovery of the alleged offence in case the referral does not result in a prosecution.

C. BREACHES OR ATTEMPTED BREACHES OF RESTRAINING ORDERS OR INJUNCTIONS (PROTECTION FROM HARASSMENT ACT 1997) REFER

Breach or attempted breach of restraining order or injunction
a) where the victim requests it governors must refer any breach of restraining order or an injunction to the police;

  Other cases

          in other cases governors have the discretion
    b)   whether to refer the matter to the police.

> Referral is most likely to be most appropriate where there have been previous attempted,
>
> or actual breaches of a restraining order or injunction.

Note

Where breaches or attempted breaches are referred to the police, governors must ensure that all relevant information is forwarded to them, including details of any previous breaches or attempted breaches that may have been dealt with under the prison discipline system.

APPENDIX 4. ADJUDICATIONS AND THE LAW: CASE LAW AND DEFINITIONS

A4.1 A prisoner may challenge the results of an adjudication, at law, in two ways.

A4.2 First a prisoner may seek leave to apply for judicial review of a hearing. This must generally be done within three months of a prisoner's grievance arising, though the Divisional Court has shown itself willing to extend this time if there are exceptional circumstances and if to refuse to do so would be manifestly unfair. Judicial review is the process by which the Queen's Bench Division of the High Court exercises control over decisions affecting the public law rights and liberties of the subject including adjudications. It does so under Order 53 of the Rules of the Supreme Court. An applicant for judicial review will apply to the court for an order, usually that of certiorari, which, if granted, allows the Divisional Court to review the decision. This, in turn, may lead to the decision being quashed. Proceedings are conducted by way of sworn written statements (affidavits) and generally the Divisional Court will be concerned with the manner in which the decision was made rather than the decision itself. Judicial review is effectively the prisoner's only avenue for redress within the British courts.

A4.3 Secondly a prisoner may apply to the European Court of Human Rights if he or she believes that there has been a breach of the European Convention on Human Rights. Should the Court find the application admissible its aim will be to achieve a friendly settlement between parties. If that is not possible it will refer the matter to the European Court of Human Rights for judgement. Before the Court will accept an application it must be satisfied that all domestic avenues for redress have been exhausted.

A4.4 The following judgements have influenced the procedure at adjudication over recent years. The list is not exhaustive and the summary given should not be taken as a substitute for reading the report of each case. Abbreviations used in the citation of cases are explained at the end of this Appendix. Judges are referred to by their seniority at the time of their judgement. Much of the litigation reviewed below relates to hearings before boards of visitors which, until a 1992 amendment to Prison Rules, had an adjudicatory role. The principles laid down by the courts relate equally to hearings before a governor or controller.

THE MAJOR JUDGEMENTS

A4.5 R v Board of Visitors of Hull Prison ex parte St Germain. (1978 2 All ER 198 QBD; 1979 1 All ER 701 CA) R v Board of Visitors of Hull Prison ex parte St Germain (No. 2) (1979 3 All ER 545)

These cases arose out of the Hull prison riot of 1976 and the subsequent adjudications. After the riot 235 prisoners were transferred to 13 different prisons. Over 500 disciplinary charges were brought against 185 of them. These were heard by itinerant adjudicators and thus the logistics of mounting the hearings were complicated. Despite these acknowledged difficulties the Divisional Court eventually held that there had been substantial breach of the rules of natural justice in the manner in which some adjudications had been conducted. The court laid down a number of principles to guide adjudicators in hearing charges in a fair manner.

i) Adjudicators must reach decisions solely on the evidence presented and thus must come to the hearing de novo.

ii) The accused has a right to a fair hearing. The court will not be concerned with a mere technical breach of a procedural rule. It will only interfere where this has amounted to a failure to act fairly.

iii) An adjudicator may take account of hearsay evidence provided that the accused does not dispute it. If he or she does, then the accused must be allowed to cross examine the witness whose evidence first appeared as hearsay. If calling the witness is impossible, the hearsay evidence must be dismissed.

iv) An accused must be allowed to call witnesses if this is necessary in order to establish a defence or mitigation. The adjudicator has a discretion to refuse to hear a witness but in doing so he or she must exercise discretion reasonably, in good faith and on proper grounds. Mere administrative inconvenience is not sufficient grounds upon which to refuse to call a witness.

A4.6 R v Secretary of State for the Home Department ex parte Tarrant (1984 1 All ER 799)

Following a riot and rooftop demonstration at Albany prison and a later violent confrontation at Wormwood Scrubs a number of prisoners faced serious charges at adjudication. They asked for and were denied either legal representation or the assistance of a friend at the hearings. They sought leave to apply for judicial review on this basis. The Divisional Court held that it was bound by the earlier decision in Fraser v Mudge (1975 3 All ER 78) that there is no right to legal representation at an adjudication. However, adjudicators are masters of their own procedure and the decision did not affect their discretion to allow it. The same applied to the assistance of a McKenzie friend (see below). Mr Justice Webster said that amongst those things adjudicators should take into account are:

i) the seriousness of the charge and of the potential penalty
ii) whether points of law are likely to arise
iii) the capacity of the prisoner to present his or her own case
iv) whether or not there are likely to be procedural difficulties
v) the need for reasonable speed
vi) the need for fairness as between prisoners and between prisoners and prison staff.

He confirmed that the accused must be allowed to ask questions of his or her witnesses and that such questions may be put direct. Only if the accused in some way abuses that facility should it be insisted that questions be put through the adjudicator. The Court indicated that the standard of proof applying in prison disciplinary proceedings is the criminal law standard namely that of proof beyond reasonable doubt.

A4.7 Leech v Deputy Governor of Parkhurst Prison/Prevot v Long Lartin Deputy Governor (1988 1 All ER 485)

The House of Lords resolved a conflict between irreconcilable decisions of the Court of Appeal in this jurisdiction and in Northern Ireland. In R v Board of Visitors of Camp Hill Prison ex parte King (1984 3 All ER 897) the court held that a governor's adjudication was not subject, directly, to judicial review though the Secretary of State's decision on any 'appeal' would be. In R v Governor of the Maze Prison ex parte McKiernan (1985 6 NIJB 6) the court held that a governor's adjudication could be directly reviewed. The House of Lords confirmed in Leech that the latter is a correct statement of law. Over the years the courts have regarded the position of the adjudicating governor as being similar to that of the commanding officer, the sea captain, the schoolmaster or the manager. None of these analogies can now be regarded as correct. Lord Bridge explained the position of adjudicating governor as follows:

ENGLISH PRISON LAW

"A prison governor may, in general terms, be described as a servant of the Secretary of State but he is not acting as such when adjudicating on a charge of a disciplinary offence. He is then exercising the independent power conferred upon him by the Rules. The Secretary of State has no authority to direct the governor ...

as to how to adjudicate on a particular charge or what punishment should be

awarded".

OTHER JUDGEMENTS AFFECTING PRACTICE

A4.8 R v Board of Visitors of Gartree Prison ex parte Mealy (1981 The Times, 14 November)

After riots at Gartree prison in 1978 Mr Mealy was punished at adjudication. He had faced charges which were heard in a different sequence from their numerical order. He equivocated over a plea and the hearing continued on the assumption that he had pleaded guilty. He was not allowed to put his own questions to one of his witnesses. He asked that the record of the preliminary hearing should be produced as evidence that a witness had changed his story and this was denied him. Mr Justice Hodgson acknowledged that adjudicators are masters of this own procedure. Nevertheless, the procedure having been explained to the prisoner by way of form F1145, there should be no departure from that procedure unless reasons for doing so are given. He added that "the prisoner could not be expected to have the flexibility of the trained legal mind and was likely to be confused if changes were made". The adjudications were quashed. The court held that:

i) an adjudicator must show that he or she will hear the evidence of every witness with an open mind

ii) if an accused's plea is equivocal a plea of not guilty should be entered.

A4.9 R v Blundeston Board of Visitors ex parte Fox-Taylor (1982 1 All ER 646)

Mr Fox-Taylor had been found guilty of fighting with another prisoner. Unknown to him and to the adjudicators there had been a prisoner witness. The witness had told staff what he had seen but this information was passed neither to the accused nor to the adjudicators. The Divisional Court ordered that the decision at the adjudication be quashed and held that where the authorities know the identity of a witness who may assist the accused make out his or her defence there is a duty to disclose that information. If they do not the adjudication is likely to be overturned for want of fairness even though the failure to call the witness is not the fault of the adjudicator. The applicant had suffered "a real detriment" by being deprived of the opportunity to call the witness.

A4.10 R v Liverpool Prisons Board of Visitors ex parte Davies (1982 The Times 16 October)

Mr Davies had been charged with being in possession of cannabis. In his defence he said that the jacket in which it had been found belonged to another prisoner but he refused to name him or call him as a defence witness. The Divisional Court held that the accused's reluctance to name a witness the identity of whom he or she knows does not place a duty on the authorities to investigate who that person may be.

A4.11 Rv Board of Visitors of Dartmoor Prison ex parte Smith (1986 2 All ER 651)

Mr Smith had been involved in an incident at Dartmoor prison and had been charged with an offence which was at that time prohibited under Rule 47 namely "does gross personal violence to an officer". The officer had suffered only a small cut over an eyebrow. The adjudicators accepted that gross personal violence had not been proved and ordered that a charge of assault be preferred. This was in accordance with Home Office advice then given to adjudicators to the effect that if the facts constituted a similar but less serious offence the charge could be reduced during the hearing. The Court of Appeal held that no such authority was given by the Rules, not was it possible at that stage to lay a less serious charge of assault because that would offend the requirement of Rule 48(1) that disciplinary charges should be laid "as soon as possible". That requirement is mandatory.

A4.12 Omitted

A4.13   R v Board of Visitors of Camp Hill Prison ex parte King (1984 3 All ER 897)
Prison officers had found a hypodermic needle wrapped in tissue paper hidden in an electrical conduit box in the ceiling of a cell. The four occupants of the cell all denied knowledge of the needle. They were each charged with being in possession of an unauthorised article. The deputy governor found the charge proved against the applicant on the basis that he had been in the cell knowing that the unauthorised article was there. The applicant argued that he could only be said to have had the needle in his cell if he had some control over it either by himself or jointly with others. The Court of Appeal held that the offence of having an unauthorised article in a prison cell could only be proved if it was shown that the accused not only knew of the article's presence but also that he or she had some control over it. (An appeal to the House of Lords was later successful, but on other grounds: see Leech above).

A4.14   R v Secretary of State for the Home Department ex parte Lee (1987 QBD 19 February (unreported) (Lexis CO/1644/86)).
Mr Lee was alleged to have assaulted prison officers and was granted legal representation at adjudication. His lawyers attended to interview him but found him in a disturbed state and unable to offer coherent instructions. Nevertheless he was declared fit to face the hearing. The Home Secretary had declined to allow an independent psychiatrist to interview the accused but later agreed to this. The Divisional Court made two declarations:

i)   an adjudicator is entitled to decide after considering expert evidence whether or not the accused is fit for adjudication

ii)   the adjudicator should dismiss a charge if, having heard the evidence, he or she is satisfied
that at the time of the alleged offence the accused could not, on medical grounds, be held
responsible for his or her actions.

A4.15   R v Board of Visitors of HMP Walton ex parte Weldon (1985 Crim LR 514)

Mr Weldon had been found guilty of assaulting prison officers on consecutive days. He had asked that each charge should be heard separately by different adjudicators each of whom would have been ignorant of the other charge. This was refused as being a departure from usual practice. In quashing the adjudicators' decisions the Divisional Court held:

i)   an adjudicator has a discretion whether or not to hear different charges against the same prisoner together, or to hear a charge knowing of the existence of another.

ii)   the adjudicator must exercise his or her discretion by deciding whether to proceed would give rise to apparent bias. The test laid down in R v Gough (see below) should be applied.

SOME DEFINITIONS

A4.16   Irrationality ('Wednesbury unreasonableness')

In Associated Picture Houses Ltd v Wednesbury Corporation (1948 1KB 223) Lord Greene stated that "A person entrusted with a discretion must ... direct himself properly in law. He must call his own attention to the matters he is bound to consider. He must exclude from his consideration matters which are irrelevant to what he has to consider. If he does not obey those rules he may truly be said ... to be acting unreasonably". Even where a person exercises a discretion for a proper purpose and disregards irrelevant considerations the court may still intervene if that person has "come to a conclusion so unreasonable that no reasonable authority could ever have come to it".

A4.17 Intentionally or recklessly

To be satisfied of mens rea (a guilty mind) it will be necessary to establish intention or recklessness on the part of the accused. To say that an accused intended something to happen means that he or she must have acted either with the purpose of making it happen, or in the knowledge that it was virtually certain to happen as a result of his or her act (oblique intention). To say that an accused was reckless as to whether something would happen means that he or she must have foreseen that it might happen and yet have gone on to take the risk of it. However, if the reason the accused did not foresee the risk of harm was that he was intoxicated through use of alcohol or drugs, then that will not afford him a defence if the risk would have been obvious to him had he been sober: R v Majewski (1977 AC 443). The only situation where an accused may rely on intoxication to show that he was not reckless is where the condition was involuntary e.g because a drink has been laced.

A4.18 Proof beyond reasonable doubt

This is the standard of proof necessary before an adjudicator can be satisfied that an accused is guilty of the conduct alleged against him or her. The phrase does not imply that the adjudicator has to be absolutely certain of guilt. Rather, as Mr Justice Denning explained in Miller v Minister of Pensions, (1947 2 All ER 372):

"If the evidence is so strong against a man so as to leave only a remote possibility in his favour which can be dismissed with the sentence: 'of course it is possible but not in the least probable', the case is proved beyond a reasonable doubt but nothing short of that will suffice".

Lord Chief Justice Goddard explained in R v Summers (1952 1 All ER 1059) that those deciding cases must be "satisfied so that they feel sure" of guilt before reaching such a finding.

A4.19 Bias

In ex parte Weldon (above) an adjudication was quashed since the adjudicators had not applied the proper test in assessing whether or not there was an appearance of bias. The authority on this is now R v Gough (1993 2 All ER 724). An appellant argued that there was an irregularity at his trial since it later emerged that a juror was his brother's next door neighbour. The brother was named at the trial, his address was mentioned and his photograph was shown to the jury. Despite this the juror did not connect the two. She had not seen the appellant before the trial and did not know that he was related to her neighbour whom she did not recognise from the photograph. The House of Lords dismissed the appeal. Except where a person acting in a judicial capacity has a direct pecuniary interest in the outcome, where bias can be assumed, the test to be applied whether at court or at an inferior tribunal, is whether or not, having regard to all relevant circumstances, there is a real danger of bias. In the context of an adjudication, is there a real danger that the adjudicator might unfairly regard the accused's case with favour or disfavour having regard to all relevant circumstances.

A4.20

It is unlikely that an adjudicator would be seen as biased simply because of distant previous knowledge of a prisoner's behaviour. In R v Board of Visitors of Frankland Prison ex parte Lewis (1986 1 All ER 272) the applicant had been found guilty of possession of a controlled drug. Later he discovered that the chairman of the adjudicating panel had been a member of the local review committee which had previously considered his application for parole and thus would have known that he was serving a sentence for drug related offences. The chairman agreed that he had recognized the applicant but said that he had forgotten details of his criminal record. Mr Justice Woolf dismissed the application for judicial review of the proceedings saying, in part, that adjudicators "must inevitably and frequently have a considerable knowledge of the background of a particular prisoner". Later in his judgement he said that adjudicators:

"should not be too ready to regard a general background knowledge of a particular prisoner as being something which makes it desirable for (them) not to continue with the adjudication on a particular charge. In deciding whether or not it is possible for a particular member of a board to adjudicate fairly ... the reasonable and fair-minded bystander would have to take into account the nature of the proceedings and the nature of the duties which the board has to perform."

A4.21 A mere technical breach

It is noted in the account of ex parte St Germain (above) that the Divisional Court will exercise its jurisdiction where there has been a failure to act fairly. It is not concerned with "a mere technical breach of a procedural rule". What constitutes this may vary from time to time according to the facts of each case. Examples from adjudication cases are as follows.

i) R v Board of Visitors of Pentonville Prison ex parte Rutherford (1985 The Times 21 February)

An application for judicial review was refused where a prisoner had been required to stand to present his case and had been denied writing materials. Mr. Justice Hodgson said that "there might be cases where it would be a breach of natural justice ... however it is not part of the High Court's job to lay down the precise procedure a board should adopt". (Good practice and guidance in this Manual require that the accused should be allowed to sit and be offered writing materials).

ii) R v Board of Visitors of Swansea Prison ex parte Scales (1984 The Times 21 February)

Form F1127 carried only details of the Prison Rule alleged to have been broken and omitted brief particulars of the offence. Mr Justice Hodgson said this would have been desirable but constituted insufficient grounds to order judicial review. (Good practice and guidance in this Manual require that brief particulars of the offence alleged should be included in F1127).

iii) R v Board of Visitors of Wandsworth Prison ex parte Raymond (1985 The Times 17 June)

The accused had not had sight of a welfare report prepared on him for presentation at the adjudication. Mr Justice Webster refused the prisoner's application for judicial review saying that "If there was a breach in this case it was a technical and marginal one and the applicant had not been prejudiced thereby".

A4.22 The McKenzie Friend

This person is a lay adviser who may, with the agreement of the adjudicator, assist the accused before and during the hearing. The term originates from McKenzie v McKenzie (1971 P33) where a judge in a divorce hearing had refused to allow a friend of the husband (an unpaid Australian barrister on placement with the husband's former solicitor) to sit at his side prompting him. In granting an appeal Lord Justice Davies cited the words of Lord Tenterden in the earlier case of Collier v Hicks (1831 109 ER 1290) as follows:

"Any person ... may attend as a friend of either party, may take notes, may quietly make suggestions and give advice; but no one can demand to take part in the proceedings as an advocate."

In ex parte Tarrant (above) Mr Justice Webster made it clear that an adjudicator had the discretion to allow a McKenzie friend at an internal disciplinary hearing. R v Leicester City Justices ex parte Barrow (1991 3 All ER 935 C.A) is a judgement which cannot be applied to prison circumstances since it specifically addressed hearings to which the public, and hence the McKenzie friend, has access. (Mr Justice Webster had drawn the same distinction in Tarrant). Nevertheless the judgement gives a helpful indication of the circumstances in which a McKenzie friend may be excluded from a hearing. Lord Donaldson explained that this could occur if:

"the use of his assistance ... is clearly unreasonable in nature or degree or if it becomes apparent that the assistance is not being applied bona fide but for an improper purpose or is being provided in a way which is inimical to the proper and efficient administration of justice by, for example, causing a party to waste time, advising the introduction of irrelevant issues or the asking of irrelevant or repetitious questions".

The status of a McKenzie friend does not extend the right to be heard to that person. It appears however, subject to the Court of Appeal view expressed above, that there is still a discretion left with those hearing charges as to whether or not to allow the McKenzie friend to speak on behalf of the accused. In Wood v Law Society (1993 The Times 30 July) a McKenzie friend (who happened to be a solicitor) was allowed to speak on behalf of an elderly and frail plaintiff.

RECENT JUDGEMENTS

Rv Secretary of State for the Home Department ex parte Wynter (1998 the Times 2 June)

Mr Wynter was charged with two disciplinary offences following a positive test under the mandatory testing procedures (MDT). At the adjudication Mr Wynter pleaded not guilty, and requested legal representation and the attendance of the forensic scientist. The adjudications were adjourned for a confirmation test. The confirmation test certified that there were traces of opiates and cannabinoids in his sample consistent with the abuse of controlled drugs. Mr Wynter again requested the presence of the forensic scientist which was refused and he was found guilty on both charges. Mr Wynter sought judicial review on the grounds that the confirmation test was hearsay evidence and therefore the forensic scientist should attend as a witness. Both adjudications were quashed on other grounds, but the court's guidance was sought on the circumstances in which an adjudicator could refuse a request for the attendance of the relevant laboratory scientist. The court held that:

(a) the confirmation test certificate is hearsay evidence, but that such scientific evidence may be dealt with differently from other types of evidence without compromising the over-riding requirement for fairness. The confirmation test certificate can therefore be admitted in evidence even where the prisoner disputes the evidence and the adjudicator exercises his discretion not to call the relevant laboratory scientist as a witness..

(b) prisoners should, in future, be given more information about MDT procedures and the checks carried out. If this were done it would rarely be appropriate for the adjudicator to call the relevant laboratory scientist to attend as a witness. Nonetheless there may be circumstances when it would be necessary to call the laboratory scientist as a witness.

Keenan v UK   (ECHR 3 April 2001)
Mark Keenan's medical history included paranoia, aggression, violence and self-harm. A diagnosis of borderline personality disorder and paranoid schizophrenia was made. Whilst in prison following an assault on his girlfriend he barricaded himself in a health care centre protesting against a transfer to another prison. Following an adjudication hearing on 15th April 1993 a suspended punishment of 14 additional days was imposed. On 30th April he assaulted two prison officers, one seriously. On 1st May 1993 he was assessed by a medical officer, with 6 months psychiatric training as an SHO, as being fit for segregation in the punishment block under Prison Rule 43. He was assessed by the medical officer as fit for adjudication which took place on 14th May 1993 and he was awarded 28 additional days plus 7 days loss of association and exclusion from work. This had the effect of delaying his release date from 23rd May 1993 to 20th June 1993. Issues arose over the lack of medical notes concerning his mental state, recognition as an identifiable suicide risk and the lack of attendances/references to a psychiatrist whilst in segregation. Mark Keenan killed himself whilst in custody on 14th May 1993.

The Court held 'the lack of effective monitoring of Mark Keenan's condition and the lack of informed psychiatric input into his assessment and treatment disclosed significant defects in the medical care for a mentally ill person known to be a suicide risk. The belated imposition on him in those circumstances of a serious disciplinary punishment – 7 days segregation in the punishment block and an additional 28 days to his sentence imposed 2 weeks after the event and only 9 days before his expected date of release – which may well have threatened his physical and moral resistance, is not compatible with the standard of treatment required in respect of a mentally ill person. It must be regarded as constituting inhuman and degrading treatment and punishment with the meaning of Artlcle 3 of the Convention. Accordingly the Court finds a violation of this provision.' There was also a breach of Article 13.

. Law Report abbreviations used:
AC: Law Reports: Appeal Cases All ER: All England Law Reports Crim LR: Criminal Law Review EHRR: European Human Rights Reports ER English Reports KB: Law Reports: Kings Bench Division Lexis: Legal database NIJB: Northern Ireland Judicial Bulletin

P: Law Reports: Probate Division QB: Law Reports: Queen's Bench Division

APPENDIX 5. ADJUDICATIONS AND THE LAW: EXTRACTS FROM STATUTES AND RULES THE PRISON ACT 1952 as amended

s.47 (1) The Secretary of State may make Rules for the regulation and management of prisons, remand centre, and young offender institutions respectively, and for the classification, treatment, employment, discipline and control of persons required to be detained therein.

(2) Rules made under this section shall make provision that a person who is charged with any offence under the Rules shall be given a proper opportunity of presenting his case.

THE CRIMINAL JUSTICE ACT 1961 as amended

s.23 (1) For the purposes of rules under section forty-seven of the Prison Act 1952 (which authorises the making of rules for the regulation and management of prisons and the discipline and control of persons required to be detained therein) any offence against the rules committed by a prisoner may be treated as committed in the prison in which he is for the time being confined.

(4) In this section the reference to prisons and prisoners respectively include references to Young Offender Institutions and persons detained in them.

THE PRISON RULES 1999 Offences against discipline

51. A prisoner is guilty of an offence against discipline if he —

(1) commits any assault;
(2) detains any person against his will;
(3) denies access to any part of the prison to any officer or any person (other than a prisoner) who is at the prison for the purpose of working there;
(4) fights with any person;
(5) intentionally endangers the health or personal safety of others or, by his conduct, is reckless whether such health or personal safety is endangered;
(6) intentionally obstructs an officer in the execution of his duty, or any person (other than a prisoner) who is at the prison for the purpose of working there, in the performance of his work;
(7) escapes or absconds from prison or from legal custody;
(8) fails to comply with any condition upon which he is temporarily released under Rule 9;
(9) administers a controlled drug to himself or fails to prevent the administration of a controlled drug to him by another person (but subject to Rule 52;)
(10) is intoxicated as a consequence of knowingly consuming any alcoholic beverage;
(11) knowingly consumes any alcoholic beverage, other than provided to him
pursuant to a written order under Rule 25(1);

(12) has in his possession-
(a) any unauthorised article, or
(b) a greater quantity of any article than he is authorised to have;
(13) sells or delivers to any person any unauthorised article;
(14) sells or, without permission, delivers to any person any article which he is allowed to have only for his own use;

(15) takes improperly any article belonging to another person or to a prison;

(16) intentionally or recklessly sets fire to any part of a prison or any other property, whether or not his own;

(17) destroys or damages any part of a prison or any other property, other than his own;

(18) absents himself from any place he is required to be or is present at any place where he is not authorised to be;

(19) is disrespectful to any officer, or any person (other than a prisoner) who is at the prison for the purpose of working there, or any person visiting a prison;

(20) uses threatening, abusive or insulting words or behaviour;

(21) intentionally fails to work properly or, being required to work, refuses to do so;

(22) disobeys any lawful order;

(23) disobeys or fails to comply with any rule or regulation applying to him;

(24) receives any controlled drug, or, without the consent of an officer, any other article, during the course of a visit (not being an interview such as is mentioned in rule 38);

(25) in any way offends against good order and discipline;

(a) attempts to commit,

(b) incites another prisoner to commit, or

(c) assists another prisoner to commit or to attempt to commit, any of the forgoing offences.

51A. Interpretation of rule 51

(2) For the purposes of rule 51 words, behaviour or material are racist if they demonstrate, or are motivated (wholly or partly) by, hostility to members of a racial group (whether identifiable or not) based on their membership (or presumed membership) of a racial group, and "membership", "presumed", "racial group" and "racially aggravated" shall have the meanings assigned to them by section 28 of the Crime and Disorder Act 1998(a).

Defences to rule 51(9)

52 It shall be a defence for a prisoner charged with an offence under rule 51(9) to show that:

(a) the controlled drug had been, prior to its administration, lawfully in his possession for his use or was administered to him in the course of a lawful supply of the drug to him by another person;

(b) the controlled drug was administered by or to him in circumstances in which he did not know and had no reason to suspect that such a drug was being administered; or

(c) the controlled drug was administered by or to him under duress or to him without his consent in circumstances where it was not reasonable for him to have resisted.

Disciplinary charges

53. -(1) Where a prisoner is to be charged with an offence against discipline, the charge shall be laid as soon as possible and, save in exceptional circumstances, within 48 hours of the discovery of the offence.

(2) Every charge shall be inquired into by the governor or, as the case may be, the adjudicator.

(3) Every charge shall be first inquired into not later, save in exceptional circumstances or in accordance with rule 55A(5), than:

(a) where it is inquired into by the governor, the next day, not being a Sunday or public holiday, after it is laid;

(b) where it is referred to the adjudicator under rule 53A(2), 28 days after it is so referred.

(4) A prisoner who is to be charged with an offence against discipline may be kept apart from other prisoners pending the governor's first inquiry or determination under rule 53A.

Determination of mode of inquiry

53A - (1) Before inquiring into a charge the governor shall determine whether it is so serious that additional days should be awarded for the offence, if the prisoner is found guilty.

(2) Where the governor determines:
(a) that it is so serious, he shall:
(i) refer the charge to the adjudicator forthwith for him to inquire
into it;

(ii) refer any other charge arising out of the same incident to the
 adjudicator forthwith for him to inquire into it; and

(iii) inform the prisoner who has been charged that he has done so;
(b) that it is not so serious, he shall proceed to inquire into the charge.
(3) If:
(a) at any time during an inquiry into a charge by the governor; or
(b) following such an inquiry, after the governor has found the prisoner guilty of an offence but before he has imposed a punishment for that offence,

it appears to the governor that the charge is so serious that additional
days should be awarded for the offence if (where sub-paragraph (a)
applies) the prisoner is found guilty, the governor shall act in accordance with paragraph (2)(a)(i) to (iii) and the adjudicator shall
first inquire into any charge referred to him under this paragraph not
later than, save in exceptional circumstances, 28 days after the charge
was referred.".

Rights of prisoners charged

54. - (1) Where a prisoner is charged with an offence against discipline, he shall be informed of the charge as soon as possible and, in any case, before the time when it is inquired into by the governor or, as the case may be, the adjudicator.

(2) At an inquiry into a charge against a prisoner he shall be given a full opportunity of hearing what is alleged against him and of presenting his own case.

(3) At an inquiry into a charge which has been referred to the adjudicator, the prisoner who has been charged shall be given the opportunity to be legally represented.

Governor's punishments

55. -(1) If he finds a prisoner guilty of an offence against discipline the governor may, subject to paragraph (2) and to rule 57, impose one or more of the following punishments:
(a) caution;
(b) forfeiture for a period not exceeding 42 days of any of the privileges under rule 8;
(c) exclusion from associated work for a period not exceeding 21 days;
(d) stoppage of or deduction from earnings for a period not exceeding 84 days;
(e) cellular confinement for a period not exceeding 21 days;
(f) [revoked by 2002 and]
(g) inthe case of a prisoner otherwise entitled to them, forfeiture for any period of the right, under rule 43(1), to have the articles there mentioned.
(h) removal from his wing or living unit for a period of 28 days.

(2) A caution shall not be combined with any other punishment for the same charge.

(3) If a prisoner is found guilty of more than one charge arising out of an incident, punishments under this rule may be ordered to run consecutively but, in the case of a punishment of cellular confinement, the total period shall not exceed 21 days.

(4) In imposing a punishment under this rule, the governor shall take into account any guidelines that the Secretary of State may from time to time issue as to the level of punishment that should normally be imposed for a particular offence against discipline.

Adjudicator's punishments

55A. - (1) If he finds a prisoner guilty of an offence against discipline the adjudicator may, subject to paragraph (2) and to rule 57, impose one or more of the following punishments:
(a) any of the punishments mentioned in rule 55(1);
(b) in the case of a short-term prisoner or long-term prisoner, an award of additional days not exceeding 42 days.

(2) A caution shall not be combined with any other punishment for the same charge.

(3) If a prisoner is found guilty of more than one charge arising out of an incident, punishments under this rule may be ordered to run consecutively but, in the case of an award of additional days, the total period added shall not exceed 42 days and, in the case of a punishment of cellular confinement, the total period shall not exceed 21 days.

(4) This rule applies to a prisoner who has been charged with having committed an offence against discipline before the date on which the rule came into force, in the same way as it applies to a prisoner who has been charged with having committed an offence against discipline on or after that date, provided the charge is referred to the adjudicator no later than 60 days after that date.

(5) Rule 53(3) shall not apply to a charge where, by virtue of paragraph (4), this rule applies to the prisoner who has been charged..

Forfeiture of remission to be treated as an award of additional days

56. -(1) In this rule, "existing prisoner" and "existing licensee" have the meanings assigned to them by paragraph 8(1) of Schedule 12 to the Criminal Justice Act 1991[12].

(2) In relation to any existing prisoner or existing licensee who has forfeited any remission of his sentence, the provisions of Part II of the Criminal Justice Act 1991 shall apply as if he had been awarded such number of additional days as equals the numbers of days of remission which he has forfeited.

Offences committed by young persons

57. - (1) In the case of an offence against discipline committed by an inmate who was under the age of 21 when the offence was committed (other than an offender in relation to whom the Secretary of State has given a direction under section 13(1) of the Criminal Justice Act 1982[13] that he shall be treated as if he had been sentenced to imprisonment) rule 55 or, as the case may be, rule 55A shall have effect, but -

(a) the maximum period of forfeiture of privileges under rule 8 shall be 21 days;

(b) the maximum period of stoppage of or deduction from earnings shall be 42 days;

(c) the maximum period of cellular confinement shall be ten days.

(d) the maximum period of removal from his cell or living unit shall be 21 days.

(2) In the case of an inmate who has been sentenced to a term of youth custody or detention in a young offender institution, and by virtue of a direction of the Secretary of State under section 99 of the Powers of Criminal Courts (Sentencing) Act 2000, is treated as if he had been sentenced to imprisonment for that term, any punishment imposed on him for an offence against discipline before the said direction was given shall, if it has not been exhausted or remitted, continue to have effect:

(a) if imposed by a governor, as if made pursuant to rule 55;

(b) if imposed by an adjudicator, as if made pursuant to rule 55A".

Cellular confinement

58. When it is proposed to impose a punishment of cellular confinement, the medical officer, or a medical practitioner such as is mentioned in rule 20(3), shall inform the governor whether there are any medical reasons why the prisoner should not be so dealt with. The governor shall give effect to any recommendation which may be made under this rule.

Prospective award of additional days

59. -(1) Subject to paragraph (2), where an offence against discipline is committed by a prisoner who is detained only on remand, additional days may be awarded by the adjudicator notwithstanding that the prisoner has not (or had not at the time of the offence) been sentenced.

(2) An award of additional days under paragraph (1) shall have effect only if the prisoner in question subsequently becomes a short-term or long-term prisoner whose sentence is reduced, under section 67 of the Criminal Justice Act 1967[14], by a period which includes the time when the offence against discipline was committed.

Removal from a cell or living unit

59A. Following the imposition of a punishment of removal from his cell or living unit, a prisoner shall be accommodated in a separate part of the prison under such restrictions of earnings and activities as the Secretary of State may direct..

Suspended punishments

60. - (1) Subject to any directions given by the Secretary of State, the power to impose a disciplinary punishment (other than a caution) shall include power to direct that the punishment is not to take effect unless, during a period specified in the direction (not being more than six months from the date of the direction), the prisoner
commits another offence against discipline and a direction is given under paragraph (2).

(2) Where a prisoner commits an offence against discipline during the period specified in a direction given under paragraph (1) the person dealing with that offence may -

(a) direct that the suspended punishment shall take effect;

(b) reduce the period or amount of the suspended punishment and direct that it shall take effect as so reduced;
(c) vary the original direction by substituting for the period specified a period expiring not later than six months from the date of variation;
or
(d) give no direction with respect to the suspended punishment.
(3) Where an award of additional days has been suspended under paragraph (1) and a prisoner is charged with committing an offence against discipline during the period specified in a direction given under that paragraph, the governor shall either:
(a) inquire into the charge and give no direction with respect to the suspended award; or
(b) refer the charge to the adjudicator for him to inquire into it

Remission and mitigation of punishments and quashing of findings of guilt

61. (1) The Secretary of State may quash any finding of guilt and may remit any punishment or mitigate it either by reducing it or by substituting another award which is, in his opinion, less severe.
(2) Subject to any directions given by the Secretary of State, the governor may remit or mitigate any punishment imposed by a governor or the Board of Visitors.*

* Boards of visitors no longer exercise disciplinary powers. This paragraph refers to punishment imposed before 1st April 1992.

Contracted out prisons

82. (1) Where the Secretary of State has entered into a contract for the running of a prison under section 84 of the Criminal Justice Act 1991 [16] ("the 1991 Act") these rules shall have effect in relation to that prison with the following modifications -

(a) references to an officer in the Rules shall include references to a prison custody officer certified as such under section 89(1) of the 1991 Act and performing custodial duties;

(b) references to a governor in the Rules shall be construed as references to a director approved by the Secretary of State for the purposes of section 85(1) (a) of the 1991 Act except -

(i) in rules 45, 48, 49, 53, 55, 61 and 81 where references to a governor shall be construed as references to a controller appointed by the Secretary of State under section 85(1) (b) of the 1991 Act, and

(ii) in rules 62(1), 66 and 77 where references to a governor shall be construed as references to the director and the controller;

(c) rule 68 shall not apply in relation to a prisoner custody officer certified as such under section 89(1) of the 1991 Act and performing custodial duties.

(2) Where a director exercises the powers set out in section 85(3) (b) of the 1991 Act (removal from association, temporary confinement and restraints) in cases of urgency, he shall notify the controller of that fact forthwith.

Contracted out parts of prisons

83. Where the Secretary of State has entered into a contract for the running of part of a prison under section 84(1) of the Criminal Justice Act 1991 that part and the remaining part shall each be treated for the purposes of Parts II to IV and Part VI of these Rules as if they were separate prisons.

Contracted out functions at directly managed prisons

84. (1) Where the Secretary of State has entered into a contract under Section 88A(1) of the

Criminal Justice Act 1991 ("the 1991 Act") for any functions at a directly managed prison to

be performed by prisoner custody officers who are authorised to perform custodial duties under section 89(1) of the 1991 Act, references to an officer in these Rules shall, subject to

paragraph (2) include references to a prisoner custody officer who is so authorised and

who is performing contracted out functions for the purposes of, or for purposes connected

with, the prison.

(2) Paragraph (1) shall not apply to references to an officer in rule 68.

(3) In this rule, "directly managed prison" has the meaning assigned to it by section 88A(5) of

the 1991 Act.

THE YOUNG OFFENDER INSTITUTION RULES 2000 AS AMENDED (EXTRACT)
OFFENCES AGAINST DISCIPLINE

55. An inmate is guilty of an offence against discipline if he

(1) commits any assault;

(2) commits any racially aggravated assault;

(3) detains any person against his will;

(4) denies access to any part of the young offender institution to any officer or any person (other than an inmate) who is at the young offender institution for the purpose of working there;

(5) fights with any person;

(6) intentionally endangers the health or personal safety of others or, by his conduct, is reckless whether such health or personal safety is endangered;

(7) intentionally obstructs an officer in the execution of his duty, or any person (other than an inmate) who is at the young offender institution for the purpose of working there, in the performance of his work;

(8) escapes or absconds from a young offender institution or from legal custody;

(9) fails to comply with any condition upon which he was temporarily released under rule 5 of these rules;

(10) administers a controlled drug to himself or fails to prevent the administration of a controlled drug to him by another person (but subject to rule 56 below);

(11) isintoxicated as a consequence of knowingly consuming any alcoholic beverage;

(12) knowingly consumes any alcoholic beverage, other than any provided to him pursuant to a written order of the medical officer under rule 21(1);

(13) has in his possession -

(a) any unauthorised article, or

(b) a greater quantity of any article than he is authorised to have;

(14) sells or delivers to any person any unauthorised article;
(15) sells or, without permission, delivers to any person any article which he is allowed to have only for his own use;
(16) takes improperly any article belonging to another person or to a young offender institution;
(17) intentionally or recklessly sets fire to any part of a young offender institution or any other property, whether or not his own;
(18) destroys or damages any part of a young offender institution or any other property other than his own;
(19) causes racially aggravated damage to, or destruction of, any part of a young offender institution or any other property, other than his own;
(20) absents himself from any place where he is required to be or is present at any place where he is not authorised to be;
(21) isdisrespectful to any officer, or any person (other than an inmate) who is at the young offender institution for the purpose of working there, or any person visiting a young offender institution;
(22) uses threatening, abusive or insulting words or behaviour;
(23) uses threatening, abusive or insulting racist words or behaviour;
(24) intentionally fails to work properly or, being required to work, refuses to do so;
(25) disobeys any lawful order;
(26) disobeys or fails to comply with any rule or regulation applying
to him;

(27) receives any controlled drug or, without the consent of an
officer, any other article, during the course of a visit (not being an
interview such as is mentioned in rule 16);

(28) displays, attaches or draws on any part of a young offender
institution, or on any other property, threatening, abusive, or insulting
racist words, drawings, symbols or other material;

(29) (a) attempts to commit,
 (b) incites another inmate to commit, or
 (c) assists another inmate to commit or to attempt to commit,
any of the foregoing offences.

Defences to rule 55(10)
56. It shall be a defence for an inmate charged with an offence under rule 55(10) to show that
(a) the controlled drug had been, prior to its administration, lawfully in his possession for his use or was administered to him in the course of a lawful supply of the drug to him by another person;
(b) the controlled drug was administered by or to him in circumstances in which he did not know and had no reason to suspect that such a drug was being administered; or
(c) the controlled drug was administered by or to him under duress or to him without his consent in circumstances where it was not reasonable for him to have resisted.

Interpretation of rule 55
57. For the purposes of rule 55 words, behaviour or material shall be racist if they demonstrate or are motivated (wholly or partly) by hostility to members of a racial group (whether identifiable or not) based on their membership (or presumed membership) of a racial group, and "membership", "presumed", "racial group" and "racially aggravated", shall

have the meanings assigned to them by section 28 of the Crime and Disorder Act 1998[9]

Disciplinary charges

58. - (1) Where an inmate is to be charged with an offence against discipline, the charge shall be laid as soon as possible and, save in exceptional circumstances, within 48 hours of the discovery of the
offence.

(2) Every charge shall be inquired into by the governor or, as the case may be, the adjudicator.

(3) Every charge shall be first inquired into not later, save in exceptional circumstances or in accordance with rule 60A(5) or rule 65(4), than:

(a) where it is inquired into by the governor, the next day, not being a Sunday or public holiday, after it is laid;
(b) where it is referred to the adjudicator under rule 58A(2), 28 days after it is so referred.

(4) An inmate who is to be charged with an offence against discipline
may be kept apart from other inmates pending the governor's first inquiry or determination under rule 58A.

Determination of mode of inquiry 58A. - (1) Before inquiring into a charge the governor shall determine whether it is so serious that additional days should be awarded for the offence, if the inmate is found guilty.

(2) Where the governor determines:
(a) that it is so serious, he shall:
(i) refer the charge to the adjudicator forthwith for him to inquire into it;
(ii) refer any other charge arising out of the same incident to the adjudicator forthwith for him to inquire into it; and

(iii) inform the inmate who has been charged that he has done so;

(b) that it is not so serious, he shall proceed to inquire into the charge.

(3) If:

(a) at any time during an inquiry into a charge by the governor; or

(b) following such an inquiry, after the governor has found the inmate guilty of an offence but before he has imposed a punishment for that offence,

it appears to the governor that the charge is so serious that additional days should be awarded for the offence if (where sub-paragraph (a) applies) the inmate is found guilty, the governor shall act in accordance with paragraph (2)(a)(i) to (iii) and the adjudicator shall first inquire into any charge referred to him under this paragraph not later than, save in exceptional circumstances, 28 days after the charge was referred.

Rights of inmates charged

59. -(1) Where an inmate is charged with an offence against discipline, he shall be informed of the charge as soon as possible and, in any case, before the time when it is inquired into by the governor or, as the case may be, the adjudicator.

(2) At an inquiry into charge against an inmate he shall be given a

opportunity of hearing what is alleged against him and of presenting his

own case.

(3) At an inquiry into a charge which has been referred to the adjudicator, the inmate who has been charged shall be given the opportunity to be legally represented.

Governor's punishments

60. -(1) If he finds an inmate guilty of an offence against discipline the governor may, subject to paragraph (3) and rule 65 impose

one or more of the following punishments:

(a) caution;

(b) forfeiture for a period not exceeding 21 days of any of the
  privileges under rule 6;

(c) removal for a period not exceeding 21 days from any particular
  activity or activities of the young offender institution, other than
  education, training courses, work and physical education in accordance
  with rules 37, 38, 39, 40 and 41;

(d) extra work outside the normal working week for a period not
  exceeding 21 days and for not more than two hours on any day;

(e) stoppage of or deduction from earnings for a period not exceeding 42
  days;

(f) in the case of an offence against discipline committed by an inmate
  who was aged 18 or over at the time of commission of the offence, other
  than an inmate who is serving the period of detention and training under
  a detention and training order pursuant to section 100 of the Powers of
  Criminal Courts (Sentencing) Act 2000, confinement to a cell or room for
  a period not exceeding ten days;

(g) removal from his wing or living unit for a period not exceeding 21
  days;

(2) If an inmate is found guilty of more than one charge arising out
of an incident punishments under this rule may be ordered to run
consecutively, but, in the case of a punishment of cellular
confinement the total period shall not exceed ten days.

(3) A caution shall not be combined with any other
punishment for the same charge.

(4) In imposing a punishment under this rule, the governor shall take
into account any guidelines that the Secretary of State may from time to
time issue as to the level of punishment that should normally be imposed
for a particular offence against discipline.

Adjudicator's punishments
60A. -(1) If he finds a inmate guilty of an offence against discipline the adjudicator may, subject to paragraph (2) and to rule 65, impose one or more of the following punishments:
  (a) any of the punishments mentioned in rule 60(1);
  (b) in the case of an inmate who is a short-term prisoner or long-term prisoner, an award of additional days not exceeding 42 days.
(2) A caution shall not be combined with any other punishment for the same charge.
(3) If an inmate is found guilty of more than one charge arising out of an incident, punishments under this rule may be ordered to run consecutively but, in the case of an award

of additional days, the total period added shall not exceed 42 days and, in the case of a punishment of cellular confinement, the total period shall not exceed ten days.

(4) This rule applies to an inmate who has been charged with having committed an offence against discipline before the date on which the rule came into force, in the same way as it applies to an inmate who has been charged with having committed an offence against discipline on or after that date, provided the charge is referred to the adjudicator no later than 60 days after that date.

(5) Rule 58(3) shall not apply to a charge where, by virtue of paragraph (4), this rule applies to the inmate who has been charged.".

Confinement to a cell or room
61. - (1) When it is proposed to impose a punishment of confinement in a cell or room, the medical officer, or a medical practitioner such as is mentioned in rule 27(3), shall inform the governor whether there are any medical reasons why the inmate should not be so dealt with. The governor shall give effect to any recommendation which may be made under this paragraph.

(2) No cell or room shall be used as a detention cell or room for the purpose of a punishment of confinement to a cell or room unless it has been certified by an officer of the Secretary of State (not being an officer of a young offender institution) that it is suitable for the purpose; that its size, lighting, heating, ventilation and fittings are adequate for health; and that it allows the inmate to communicate at any time with an officer.

Removal from wing or living unit
62. Following the imposition of a punishment of removal from his wing or living unit, an inmate shall be accommodated in a separate part of the young offender institution under such restrictions of earnings and activities as the Secretary of State may direct.

Suspended punishments

63. -(1) Subject to any directions of the Secretary of State, the power to impose a disciplinary punishment (other than a caution) shall include a power to direct that the punishment is not to take effect unless, during a period specified in the direction (not being more than six months from the date of the direction), the inmate commits another offence against discipline and a direction is given under paragraph (2).

(2) Where an inmate commits an offence against discipline during the period specified in a direction given under paragraph (1), the person dealing with that offence may -

(a) direct that the suspended punishment shall take effect; or
(b) reduce the period or amount of the suspended punishment and direct   that it shall take effect as so reduced; or
(c) vary the original direction by substituting for the period specified
  therein a period expiring not later than six months from the date of
   variation; or

(d) give no direction with respect to the suspended punishment.

(3) Where an award of additional days has been suspended under
  paragraph (1) and an inmate is charged with committing an offence

against discipline during the period specified in a direction given
under that paragraph, the governor shall either:

(a) inquire into the charge and give no direction with respect to the suspended award; or
(b) refer the charge to the adjudicator for him to inquire into it

Remission and mitigation of punishments and quashing of findings of guilt
64. - (1) The Secretary of State may quash any findings of guilt and
may remit a disciplinary punishment or mitigate it either by reducing it
or by substituting a punishment which is, in his opinion, less severe.

(2) Subject to any directions of the Secretary of State, the governor
may remit or mitigate any punishment imposed by a governor.

Adult female inmates: disciplinary punishments
65. -(1) In the case of a female inmate aged 21 years or over, rule
60 shall not apply, but the governor may, if he finds the inmate guilty of
an offence against discipline, impose one or more of the following
punishments:

(a) caution;
(b) forfeiture for a period not exceeding 42 days of any of the
  privileges under rule 6;

(c) removal for a period not exceeding 21 days from any particular activity or activities of the young offender institution, other than education, training courses, work and physical education in accordance with rules 37, 38, 39, 40 and 41;

(d) stoppage of or deduction from earnings for a period not exceeding 84 days;

(e) confinement to a cell or room for a period not exceeding 21 days;

(1A) In the case of a female inmate aged 21 years or over, where a charge has been referred to the adjudicator, rule 60A shall not apply, but the adjudicator may if he finds the inmate guilty of an offence against discipline, impose one or more of the following punishments:

(a) any of the punishments mentioned in paragraph (1);

(b) in the case of an inmate who is a short-term or long-term prisoner, an award of additional days not exceeding 42 days.

(2) If an inmate is found guilty of more than one charge arising out
of an incident, punishments under this rule may be ordered to run
consecutively, but in the case of an award of additional days, the total
period added shall not exceed 42 days.

(3) Paragraph (1A) applies to an inmate who has been charged with having committed an offence against discipline before the date on which that paragraph came into force, in the same was as it applies to an inmate who has been charged with having committed an offence against discipline on or after that date, provided the charge is referred to the adjudicator no later than 60 days after that date.

(4) Rule 58(3) shall not apply to a charge where, by virtue of paragraph (3), paragraph (1A) applies to the inmate who has been charged

Forfeiture of remission to be treated as an award of additional days

66. - (1) In this rule, "existing prisoner" and "existing licensee" have the meanings assigned to them by paragraph 8(1) of Schedule 12 to the Criminal Justice Act 1991.

(2) In relation to any existing prisoner or existing licensee who has forfeited any remission of his sentence, the provisions of Part II of the Criminal Justice Act 1991 shall apply as if he had been awarded such number of additional days as equals the number of days of remission which he has forfeited.

Delegation by governor

85. The governor of a young offender institution may, with the leave of the Secretary of State, delegate any of his powers and duties under these Rules to another officer of that institution.

Contracted out young offender institutions

86. - (1) Where the Secretary of State has entered into a contract for the running of a young offender institution under section 84 of the Criminal Justice Act 1991[10] (in this rule "the 1991 Act") these Rules shall have effect in relation to that young offender institution with the following modifications

(a) references to an officer shall include references to a prisoner

custody officer certified as such under section 89(1) of the 1991 Act;

(b) references to a governor shall include references to a director

approved by the Secretary of State for the purposes of section 85(1)(a)

of the 1991 Act except -

(i) in rules 49, 51, 52, 58, 58A, 60, 63, 64, 65 and 85 where references to a governor shall include references to a controller

appointed by the Secretary of State under section 85(1)(b) of the 1991 Act; and
(ii) in rules 67(1), 71 and 81 where references to a governor shall
include references to a director and a controller;

(c) rule 73 shall not apply in relation to a prisoner custody officer
certified as such under section 89(1) of the 1991 Act and performing
custodial duties.

(2) Where a director exercises the powers set out in section 85(3)(b) of the 1991 Act (removal from association, temporary confinement and restraints) in cases of urgency, he shall notify the controller of that fact forthwith.

Contracted out parts of young offender institutions
87. Where the Secretary of State has entered into a contract for the running of part of a young offender institution under section 84(1) of the Criminal Justice Act 1991, that part and the remaining part shall each be treated for the purposes of Parts I to IV and Part VI of these Rules as if they were separate young offender institutions.

Contracted out functions at directly managed young offender institutions
88. - (1) Where the Secretary of State has entered into a contract under section 88A(1) of the Criminal Justice Act 1991[11] for any functions at a directly managed young offender institution too be performed by prisoner custody officers who are authorised to perform custodial duties under section 89(1) of that Act, references to an officer in these Rules shall, subject to paragraph (2), include references to a prisoner custody officer who is so authorised and who is performing contracted out functions for the purposes of, or for purposes connected with, the young offender institution.

(2) Paragraph (1) shall not apply to references to an officer in rule
73.
(3) In this rule "directly managed young offender institution" means a
young offender institution which is not a contracted out young offender
institution.

Further information relating to the prison disciplinary system may be found in the European Convention for the Protection of Human Rights and Fundamental Freedoms and in the European Prison Rules, copies of which are available in the prison or young offender institution library.

APPENDIX 6. ADJUDICATION DOCUMENTATION: THE PRINCIPAL FORMS

The forms listed below are not available on the web-site.
Minor Report Book: Extract
F254 : Report to the Governor of alleged offence
F1127 : Notice of report
F1145 : Explanation of procedure
F256 : Record of hearing and adjudication
F256A : Continuation sheet

APPENDIX 7 OMITTED

APPENDIX 8. MANDATORY DRUG TESTING. TABLE OF MINIMUM WAITING PERIODS REQUIRED BEFORE A PRISONER MAY BE CHARGED AFTER FIRST RECEPTION INTO PRISON (OR CHARGED AGAIN)

Drug	Comment	Minimum Waiting Period
Amphetamines	including methamphetamines	4 days

Barbiturates	except phenobarbital phenobarbital	5 days 30 days
Benzodiazepines		30 days
Buprenorphine	Temgesic	14 days
Cannabis		30 days
Cocaine		4 days
Methadone		5 days
LSD		3 days
Opiates	including and morphinecodeine 6 monocetyl morphine	5 days 3 days

These time periods represent the minimum waiting periods, after a prisoner first entered the prison, before it would be safe to charge him or her under paragraph 9/10 and also the minimum period between samples upon which successive disciplinary actions for the same drug should be based. A sample taken within this minimum waiting period could, however, be used as evidence to support a charge of misuse of a different drug.

APPENDIX 9. MDT ADJUDICATIONS – FURTHER GUIDANCE

This appendix must be read in conjunction with paragraphs 5.7, 5.8 – 5.21 and 6.99

A9.1 This appendix provides further guidance on the evidential status of confirmation test certificates and how requests for the laboratory scientist to attend as a witness should be considered by the adjudicator.

Confirmation tests

A9.2 The confirmation test certificate is hearsay evidence. However, notwithstanding the restrictions on the admission and use of hearsay evidence set out at paragraph 5.7, and subject to the over-riding need for fairness, the confirmation test certificate can be admitted in evidence where the prisoner disputes the result of the test. The confirmation test certificate can be treated as an exception to the normal restrictions on the use of hearsay evidence because the quality of the evidence, and therefore, the reliability of the evidence provided by the certificate means that its admission is much less likely to result in unfairness to the accused than is the case with hearsay evidence on other issues.

Requests for the laboratory scientist to attend as a witness
A9.3 A prisoner can request that the relevant laboratory scientist attends as a witness: it is then for the adjudicator to decide whether or not he or she should be called. Such requests must be carefully considered on an individual basis in accordance with the guidance at paragraphs 5.8 – 5.21

A9.4 Where such a request is made the adjudicator should ask the prisoner why he or she wishes the witness to be called and should seek to establish what relevant evidence the prisoner believes the witness could give beyond that contained in the confirmation test certificate. Care should be taken to ensure that any issues raised by the prisoner, orally or in writing, are fully explained, understood and considered before making any decision to refuse or grant the request. Adjudicators should bear in mind the difficulties faced by prisoners in seeking to express and explain, unaided, challenges to scientific evidence. Where, however, the prisoner has only general queries (such as the effects of passive smoking or possible contamination of the sample), the adjudicator should be able to deal with these issues by reference to the appropriate section of the MDT manual and the supplementary guidance issued in this area and without the witness being called.

A9.5 A refusal to call the witness must be made on proper grounds (see paragraphs 5.8 – 5.21). Inconvenience is not a proper ground to refuse. If the adjudicator refuses any request for the relevant laboratory scientist to attend as a witness, the reasons for the refusal must be clearly stated and recorded on the F256 in case of any subsequent appeal.

A9.6 If the adjudicator decides to call the relevant laboratory scientist the adjudication should be adjourned. The laboratory carrying out urine analysis on behalf of the Prison Service will make the relevant laboratory scientist available at the request of the headquarters Drug Strategy Team. All requests for expert witnesses should be made through headquarters, not to the laboratory.

April 1998

APPENDIX 6 - LIST OF UNITED KINGDOM PRISONS

PRISON	ADDRESS
HMP ACKLINGTON	MORPETH, Northumberland NE65 9XF
HMP ALTCOURSE *	Higher Lane, Fazakerley, LIVERPOOL L9 7LH
HMP/YOI ASHFIELD*	Shortwood Road, Pucklechurch BRISTOL BS16 9QJ
HMP ASHWELL	OAKHAM, Rutland LE15 7LF
HMP/YOI ASKHAM GRANGE	Askham Richard, YORK YO23 3FT
HMYOI AYLESBURY	Bierton Road, AYLESBURY, Buckinghamshire HP20 1EH

Sally Ramage

PRISON	ADDRESS
HMP BEDFORD	St. Loyes Street, BEDFORD MK40 1HG
HMP BELMARSH	Western Way, Thamesmead, LONDON SE28 0EB
HMP BIRMINGHAM	Winson Green Road, BIRMINGHAM B18 4AS
HMP BLANTYRE HOUSE	Goudhurst, CRANBROOK, Kent TN17 2NH
HMP BLUNDESTON	LOWESTOFT, Suffolk NR32 5BG
HMP/YOI BRINSFORD	New Road, Featherstone, WOLVERHAMPTON WV10 7PY
HMP BRISTOL	19 Cambridge Road, Horfield, BRISTOL BS7 8PS
HMP BRIXTON	P O Box 369, Jebb Avenue, LONDON SW2 5XF
HMP BRONZEFIELD *	Woodthorpe Road, Ashford, Middlesex TW15 3JZ
HMP BUCKLEY HALL	Buckley Road, ROCHDALE, Lancashire OL12 9DP
HMP BULLINGDON	P O Box 50, BICESTER, Oxfordshire OX25 1PZ
HMP/YOI BULLWOOD HALL	High Road, HOCKLEY, Essex SS5 4TE
HMP CANTERBURY	46 Longport, CANTERBURY, Kent CT1 1PJ
HMP/RC CARDIFF	Knox Road, CARDIFF CF24 0UG

ENGLISH PRISON LAW

PRISON	ADDRESS
HMP/YOI CASTINGTON	MORPETH, Northumberland NE65 9XG
HMP CHANNINGS WOOD	Denbury, NEWTON ABBOTT, Devon TQ12 6DW
HMP/YOI CHELMSFORD	200 Springfield Road, CHELMSFORD Essex CM2 6LQ
HMP COLDINGLEY	Bisley, WOKING, Surrey GU24 9EX
HMP COOKHAM WOOD	ROCHESTER, Kent ME1 3LU
HMP DARTMOOR	Princetown, YELVERTON, Devon PL20 6RR
HMYOI DEERBOLT	Bowes Road, BARNARD CASTLE, County Durham DL12 9BG
HMP/YOI DONCASTER *	Off North Bridge, Marshgate, DONCASTER, South Yorkshire DN5 8UX
HMP DORCHESTER	North Square, DORCHESTER, Dorset DT1 1JD
HMP DOVEGATE*	Uttoxeter, Staffordshire ST14 8XR
IRC DOVER	The Citadel, Western Heights, DOVER, Kent CT17 9DR
HMP DOWNVIEW	Sutton Lane, SUTTON, Surrey SM2 5PD

PRISON	ADDRESS
HMP/YOI DRAKE HALL	ECCLESHALL, Staffordshire ST21 6LQ
HMP DURHAM	Old Elvet, DURHAM DH1 3HU
HMP/YOI EAST SUTTON PARK	Sutton Valence, MAIDSTONE, Kent ME17 3DF
HMP/YOI EASTWOOD PARK	Falfield, WOTTON-UNDER-EDGE, Gloucestershire GL12 8DB
HMP EDMUNDS HILL	Stradishall, Newmarket, Suffolk CB8 9YN
HMP ELMLEY (Sheppey Cluster)	Church Road, EASTCHURCH, Sheerness, Kent ME12 4DZ
HMP ERLESTOKE	DEVIZES, Wiltshire SN10 5TU
HMP EVERTHORPE	BROUGH, East Yorkshire, HU15 1RB
HMP/YOI EXETER	New North Road, EXETER, Devon EX4 4EX
HMP FEATHERSTONE	New Road, Wolverhampton, Staffordshire WV10 7PU
HMP/YOI FELTHAM	Bedfont Road, FELTHAM, Middlesex TW13 4ND
HMP FORD	ARUNDEL, West Sussex BN18 0BX
HMP/YOI FOREST BANK*	Agecroft Road, Pendlebury, MANCHESTER M27 8FB

ENGLISH PRISON LAW

PRISON	ADDRESS
HMP FOSTON HALL	Foston, DERBY, Derbyshire DE65 5DN
HMP FRANKLAND	Brasside, DURHAM DH1 5YD
HMP FULL SUTTON	Full Sutton, YORK YO41 1PS
HMP GARTH	Ulnes Walton Lane, Leyland, PRESTON, Lancashire PR26 8NE
HMP GARTREE	Gallow Field Road, MARKET HARBOROUGH, Leicestershire LE16 7RP
HMYOI/RC GLEN PARVA	Tigers Road, Wigston, LEICESTER LE8 4TN
HMP/YOI GLOUCESTER	Barrack Square, GLOUCESTER GL1 2JN
HMP GRENDON	Grendon Underwood, AYLESBURY, Buckinghamshire HP18 0TL
HMP/YOI GUYS MARSH	SHAFTESBURY, Dorset SP7 0AH
IRC HASLAR (Immigration Removal Centre)	2 Dolphin Way, GOSPORT, Hampshire PO12 2AW
HMP HAVERIGG	MILLOM, Cumbria LA18 4NA
HMP HEWELL	Hewell Lane, REDDITCH, Worcestershire, B97 6QQ
HMP HIGH DOWN	Sutton Lane, SUTTON, Surrey SM2 5PJ

PRISON	ADDRESS
HMP HIGHPOINT	Stradishall, NEWMARKET, Suffolk, CB8 9YG
HMYOI HINDLEY	Gibson Street, Bickershaw, WIGAN, Lancashire WN2 5TH
HMP HOLLESLEY BAY	WOODBRIDGE, Suffolk IP12 3JW
HMP/YOI HOLLOWAY	Parkhurst Road, LONDON N7 0NU
HMP HOLME HOUSE	Holme House Road, STOCKTON-ON-TEES, Cleveland TS18 2QU
HMP HULL	Hedon Road, HULL HU9 5LS
HMYOI HUNTERCOMBE	Huntercombe Place, Nuffield, HENLEY-ON-THAMES, Oxfordshire RG9 5SB
HMP ISLE OF WIGHT	Clissold Road Newport Isle of Wight PO30 5RS
HMP KENNET	HM Prison Kennet Parkbourn, Maghull LIVERPOOL, Merseyside L31 1HX
HMP KINGSTON	122 Milton Road Portsmouth PO3 6AS

ENGLISH PRISON LAW

PRISON	ADDRESS
HMP KIRKHAM	Freckleton Road, PRESTON, Lancashire PR4 2RN
HMP KIRKLEVINGTON GRANGE	YARM, Cleveland TS15 9PA
HMP LANCASTER CASTLE	The Castle, LANCASTER, Lancashire LA1 1YL
HMP/YOI LANCASTER FARMS	Far Moor Lane, Stone Row Head, Quernmore Road, LANCASTER LA1 3QZ
HMP LATCHMERE HOUSE	Church Road, Ham Common, RICHMOND, Surrey TW10 5HH
HMP LEEDS	Armley, LEEDS, West Yorkshire LS12 2TJ
HMP LEICESTER	Welford Road, LEICESTER LE2 7AJ
HMP/YOI LEWES	Brighton Road, LEWES, East Sussex BN7 1EA
HMP LEYHILL	WOTTON-UNDER-EDGE, Gloucestershire GL12 8BT
HMP LINCOLN	Greetwell Road, LINCOLN LN2 4BD
HMP IRC LINDHOLME	Bawtry Road, Hatfield Woodhouse, DONCASTER DN7 6EE
HMP LITTLEHEY	Perry, HUNTINGDON, Cambridgeshire PE28 0SR
HMP LIVERPOOL	68 Hornby Road, LIVERPOOL L9 3DF

PRISON	ADDRESS
HMP LONG LARTIN	South Littleton, EVESHAM, Worcestershire WR11 8TZ
HMP LOWDHAM GRANGE*	LOWDHAM Nottinghamshire NG14 7DA
HMYOI LOW NEWTON	Brasside, DURHAM DH1 5YA
HMP MAIDSTONE	36 County Road, MAIDSTONE, Kent ME14 1UZ
HMP MANCHESTER	Southall Street, MANCHESTER M60 9AH
HMP/YOI MOORLAND OPEN	Thorne Road, Hatfield, DONCASTER, South Yorkshire DN7 6EL
HMP/YOI MOORLAND CLOSED	Bawtry Road, Hatfield Woodhouse, DONCASTER, South Yorkshire DN7 6BW
HMP MORTON HALL	Swinderby, LINCOLN LN6 9PT
HMP THE MOUNT	Molyneaux Avenue, Bovingdon, HEMEL HEMPSTEAD, Hertforshire HP3 0NZ
HMP/YOI NEW HALL	Dial Wood, Flockton, WAKEFIELD, West Yorkshire WF4 4XX
HMYOI NORTHALLERTON	15A East Road, NORTHALLERTON, North Yorkshire DL6 1NW

ENGLISH PRISON LAW

PRISON	ADDRESS
HMP NORTH SEA CAMP	Freiston, BOSTON, Lincolnshire PE22 0QX
HMP/YOI NORWICH	Knox Road, NORWICH, Norfolk NR1 4LU
HMP NOTTINGHAM	Perry Road, Sherwood, NOTTINGHAM NG5 3AG
HMYOI ONLEY	Willoughby, RUGBY, Warwickshire CV23 8AP
HMP/YOI PARC *	Heol Hopcyn John, BRIDGEND, Mid-Glamorgan CF35 6AP
HMP PENTONVILLE	Caledonian Road, LONDON N7 8TT
HMP PETERBOROUGH*	HM Peterborough Saville Road PETERBOROUGH PE3 7PD
HMYOI PORTLAND	The Grove, PORTLAND, Dorset DT5 1DL
HMP/YOI PRESCOED	Coed-y-Paen, Pontypool, Gwent NP4 0TB
HMP PRESTON	2 Ribbleton Lane, PRESTON, Lancashire PR1 5AB
HMP RANBY	RETFORD, Nottinghamshire DN22 8EU
HMP/YOI READING	Forbury Road, READING, Berkshire RG1 3HY
HMP RISLEY	Risley, WARRINGTON, Cheshire WA3 6BP

PRISON	ADDRESS
HMP ROCHESTER	1 Fort Road, ROCHESTER, Kent ME1 3QS
HMP RYE HILL*	Willoughby, RUGBY Warwickshire CV23 8SZ
HMP SEND	Ripley Road, Send, WOKING, Surrey GU23 7LJ
HMP SHEPTON MALLET	Cornhill, SHEPTON MALLET, Somerset BA4 5LU
HMP SHREWSBURY	The Dana, SHREWSBURY, Shropshire SY1 2HR
HMP SPRING HILL,	Grendon Underwood, AYLESBURY, Buckinghamshire HP18 0TL
HMP STAFFORD	54 Gaol Road, STAFFORD ST16 3AW
HMP STANDFORD HILL (**Sheppey Cluster**)	Church Road, EASTCHURCH, Sheerness, Kent ME12 4AA
HMP STOCKEN	Stocken Hall Road, STRETTON, Oakham, Rutland LE15 7RD
HMYOI STOKE HEATH	Stoke Heath, MARKET DRAYTON, Shropshire TF9 2JL
HMP/YOI STYAL	Styal, WILMSLOW, Cheshire SK9 4HR
HMP SUDBURY	Ashbourne, DERBYSHIRE DE6 5HW

ENGLISH PRISON LAW

PRISON	ADDRESS
HMP SWALESIDE (Sheppey Cluster)	Brabazon Road, EASTCHURCH, Isle of Sheppey, Kent ME12 4AX
HMP SWANSEA	200 Oystermouth Road, SWANSEA, West Glamorgan SA1 3SR
HMYOI SWINFEN HALL	Swinfen, LICHFIELD, Staffordshire WS14 9QS
HMYOI THORN CROSS	Arley Road, Appleton Thorn, WARRINGTON, Cheshire WA4 4RL
HMP USK	47 Maryport Street, USK, Gwent NP15 1XP
HMP THE VERNE	The Verne, PORTLAND, Dorset DT5 1EQ
HMP WAKEFIELD	5 Love Lane, WAKEFIELD, West Yorkshire WF2 9AG
HMP WANDSWORTH	PO Box 757, Heathfield Road, LONDON SW18 3HS
HMYOI WARREN HILL	WOODBRIDGE, Suffolk IP12 3JW
HMP WAYLAND	Griston, THETFORD, Norfolk IP25 6RL
HMP WEALSTUN	WETHERBY, West Yorkshire LS23 7AZ
HMP WELLINGBOROUGH	Millers Park, Doddington Road, WELLINGBOROUGH, Northamptonshire NN8 2NH

Sally Ramage

PRISON	ADDRESS
HMYOI WERRINGTON	Werrington, STOKE-ON-TRENT, Staffordshire ST9 0DX
HMYOI WETHERBY	York Road, WETHERBY, West Yorkshire LS22 5ED
HMP WHATTON	14 Cromwell Road, NOTTINGHAM NG13 9FQ
HMP WHITEMOOR	Longhill Road, MARCH, Cambridgeshire PE15 0PR
HMP WINCHESTER	Romsey Road, WINCHESTER, Hampshire SO22 5DF
HMP WOLDS *	Everthorpe, BROUGH, East Yorkshire HU15 2JZ
HMP WOODHILL	Tattenhoe Street, MILTON KEYNES, Buckinghamshire MK4 4DA
HMP WORMWOOD SCRUBS	PO Box 757, Du Cane Road, LONDON W12 0AE
HMP WYMOTT	Ulnes Walton Lane, Leyland, PRESTON PR26 8LW

Source: HM Prison Service at http://www.hmprisonservice.gov.uk/prisoninformation/locateaprison/

INDEX – ENGLISH PRISON LAW

Abscond	82, 126, 131, 140, 154, 242, 252-253, 258 338, 455, 466, 487, 489, 503, 537, 558, 569
absolute	24, 36, 47, 59, 116, 157, 188, 216, 518, 551
access	4, 11, 13, 16-17, 25-26, 56-57, 60, 63, 67, 76, 88, 116, 125, 134, 157, 158, 161-162, 164, 171, 174-176, 189-190, 205-208, 210-211, 215, 224-226, 228, 233-234, 236-238, 243, 249, 251, 266, 272, 277, 287, 338, 351, 358, 370, 381, 436-437, 443, 447, 450, 462-463, 507, 521, 535, 554, 558, 569
adult	46-47, 54, 59, 60,.73-74, 77, 84, 89, 92-93, 95, 97, 102, 109-112, 115, 124, 128, 139, 164, 200, 210, 255, 265-268, 335-337, 423, 505-506, 510, 513, 578

allocation	6, 76-77, 80-81, 89, 112, 117-118, 123-124, 127-130, 133-134, 139, 140-141, 143, 229, 231, 272, 274, 277, 404
bar	187, 190
behaviour	15, 73-74, 80, 82-83, 95-98, 102, 110-111, 113-114, 128, 131, 140-142, 151, 167, 171, 173, 198, 201, 210, 212-213, 215, 243, 252, 256, 259, 263, 265-266, 268-269, 270-273, 275, 277, 292, 309, 339-340, 349, 425, 431, 435, 442, 446, 461, 468, 470-472, 480-481, 495-496, 498-503, 507, 533, 552, 559, 570-571
black	74, 90, 113, 149, 496, 500
boy	31-32, 103, 105-106, 108, 112-115, 117-118
breach	9, 35-36, 38-39, 59, 67, 76, 82, 84-85, 115, 134, 137, 142, 148, 155, 161-162, 164-165, 171, 175, 178, 186-187, 189, 191, 194, 196, 197, 201-202, 216, 271, 220, 244, 248, 254, 261, 269, 273, 279, 282, 295, 296, 428, 542-545, 553, 557
bully	132, 234
career	74
category	26, 32, 40, 67, 77-79, 81-82, 84-86, 91-92, 101-102, 124-141, 176-177, 183, 185-186, 190, 193, 199, 202, 206, 210, 217-219, 229, 272, 274, 286, 294, 536-537

carter   12, 13, 51

cell   21, 37, 39, 46-47, 50-51, 76-77, 79, 82,
                  85, 93, 99, 123, 125, 136, 161-162, 166,
                  210-211, 266-267, 271, 273, 278, 281,
                  287, 289-290, 308-309, 313, 318, 320,
                  323, 333, 336, 343-344, 346-347, 365,
                  377-378, 435, 449, 462, 478, 483-485,
                  491, 506-508, 510, 522, 526, 531, 538,
                  549 562-565, 574-576, 579

challenge   3, 6, 15-17, 39, 59, 70, 109, 112, 120, 132-
                  133, 136-138, 159, 161, 169, 173, 175,
                  177-178, 183-184, 188-189, 207-208, 215-
                  216, 219, 221, 293, 454, 458, 502, 515,
                  518, 519, 522, 543, 584

charge   2, 4, 5, 7, 8, 12, 16, 37-38, 60, 79, 82-83,
                  95-96, 144, 164, 172, 189, 195, 202-203,
                  215-216, 220-221, 241-242, 244-268, 273,
                  279-281, 285, 291-292, 299, 305-306,
                  340-348, 351, 363, 404, 422, 424, 427,
                  429-450, 452-454, 457, 458-501, 503,
                  508, 510-511, 515-516, 518-530, 532-534,
                  539-542, 544-550, 552, 555, 557-563,
                  566, 571-573, 575-580, 582-583

child   31-32, 54-62, 83, 87-88, 91, 96, 98, 100,
                  110-111, 115, 118, 141-143, 148, 151,
                  171-173, 175, 182, 185, 190-191, 218,
                  231,

civil	9, 27, 34, 43-44, 49, 63-64, 69, 71, 127, 155, 157, 159, 166, 199, 213, 217-219, 295, 328-329
claim	22, 64, 66, 91-92, 132, 202, 219, 238
client	22-24, 66, 68, 70, 178, 284, 444, 531-532
community	13, 32, 50, 57, 63, 66, 82-83, 91, 96-98, 109, 111, 119-120, 153, 199-201, 210-211, 231, 268, 286, 308, 503, 513
conduct	30, 37-38, 79, 88-89, 134, 155, 165, 183, 228, 230, 232, 242, 252, 260, 264, 268, 282, 292, 314, 338, 354-355, 364, 368, 384, 429, 433, 441, 453, 460, 464-466, 501, 503, 514, 520-521, 526, 529, 532, 541, 551, 558, 569
confidential	28, 228
conjugal	35-36, 75, 174-175
consent	81, 144, 147, 149, 159, 176, 237, 243, 255, 261, 292, 318, 326, 339-341, 367, 369, 378, 386, 388, 416, 424, 462, 470, 472, 486, 494, 559,-560, 570-571
conviction	30-31, 77, 85, 128, 130, 141, 144, 146-147, 151, 154,157, 159, 166, 172, 174, 179-183, 285, 294, 296, 311, 391, 393, 395-396, 404, 535
corporate	163-166, 281-282

course	19, 48, 69, 74, 90, 176, 236-237, 243, 245, 249, 261-262, 281, 286-290, 324, 339-340, 350, 372, 432-433, 436, 454, 456, 469, 477, 479, 483, 486-487, 490-492, 494, 502, 509, 519, 523, 529, 531, 537, 551, 559-560, 570-571
criteria	16, 18, 27, 32, 70, 81, 88,-89, 124, 126-130, 133, 138-142, 154, 212-214, 275, 441, 464, 496-497, 499-500, 539
damages	44, 64, 66, 85, 91-92, 166, 202, 243, 258, 339, 477-478, 501, 559, 570
dangerous	29, 45, 80, 89, 100-101, 124, 127, 149-150, 275, 371
data	13, 138
death	59, 64, 66, 85, 93, 118-119, 149-150, 163,-165, 282, 290, 299, 316, 365, 412
default	155, 217, 327, 331, 400, 404, 408
document	23, 38, 127, 132, 172, 211, 271, 275, 396-398, 413-414, 418, 450, 460, 532
drugs	7, 10, 23, 58, 73, 88, 102, 108, 112, 114, 126, 142, 150, 171, 254, 257, 276, 280, 297, 306, 335, 365, 379, 391, 473-474, 486, 489-492, 538, 551, 555

duty	2-3, 6, 8-9, 36, 45, 64, 85, 98, 110, 118, 120, 125, 149-150, 156, 163-164, 195-196, 201,-202, 220-221, 223-224, 233, 242, 252, 270, 282, 286, 338, 349-350, 369, 457, 465-466, 494, 507, 520, 531, 535, 540, 548, 558, 569
education	10, 57-58, 76, 81, 111, 116, 137, 158, 266, 318-320, 364, 400, 414,-415, 417, 476, 505, 510, 514-515, 574, 579
ecstasy	102-106, 108
emergency	25, 37, 189, 289, 351
escape	7, 50-51, 78-79, 86, 124-126, 130-132, 135-137, 176, 182, 184-185, 190-191, 217, 252-253, 267, 276, 280-281, 293, 295-296, 316, 390-391, 466-467, 487-489, 510, 536-537
fact	4-6, 9, 13-14, 24, 30, 47, 78, 132, 137, 166-167, 216, 239, 264, 294-294, 361, 479, 488, 496, 502, 538, 567, 581
family	35, 54, 59, 71-72, 75, 57, 90-91, 97, 114, 129, 135, 140-141, 143-144, 149, 156, 161-164, 166, 171-175, 180-181, 183, 188, 190, 196, 199, 201, 213, 215, 232, 307, 310, 323, 375, 298, 441
fatal	14, 163, 166
father	91

foreign	146-147, 154, 163-164, 190, 434
health	7. 20, 28-29, 34, 50, 57, 59, 61, 67, 72, 79, 81, 82, 85, 88, 90, 92-94, 142, 165, 169-170, 208, 213, 242, 252, 282, 315-318, 325, 336, 338, 358, 377, 384, 414-415, 417, 419, 432, 435-436, 449, 464-465, 467-468, 507-508, 511, 556, 558, 569, 576
heroin	84, 102, 105-108
history	32, 81, 84, 118, 126, 131, 135, 152, 182, 275, 288, 442, 451, 514, 519, 556
howard	46, 49, 117
immigration	39-40, 72, 99, 119, 162, 164, 184, 230-231, 237, 369-370, 402, 413, 591
immunity	398
illicit	102, 178, 186-188, 192, 236, 328
independent	3-4, 6, 18, 40, 45, 49, 51-53, 65, 88, 113, 142, 158, 163, 166, 170, 220, 223-224, 228, 246-248, 265, 267, 279, 292, 302-303, 370-371, 381, 404, 429-430, 437, 445-446, 454, 493, 504, 508-511, 517, 547, 549

information	1, 13,16, 24, 27-29, 33, 55-57, 60, 69, 87-88, 91-92, 98, 125, 129-132, 136, 138-139, 147, 150, 153, 172, 185, 192-194, 198, 208, 214, 226-227, 235-238, 244, 252, 268, 276,-278, 284, 289, 297, 301-302, 312, 326, 330, 368, 392, 396-398, 422, 431, 434, 436, 439, 442, 448, 454, 456-458, 465, 514-515, 521, 523, 529, 540, 543, 548, 555, 582
inhuman	59, 84, 137, 160, 557
inquiry	61, 93, 113, 119, 124, 146, 161-162, 218, 236, 238, 310, 341-343, 429, 450, 532, 560-562, 572-573
interest	26, 53, 67, 69-70, 80, 142, 175, 204, 285-286, 294, 355, 365, 395-396, 438, 517, 519, 533, 541, 552
isolation	137
jurisdiction	3, 24, 144-145, 147, 154, 232, 238, 283, 316, 367-368, 383, 387, 520, 546, 553
knives	100-101, 537
lawyer	22, 24, 60, 178-179, 186
licence	14, 35, 41, 46, 65, 82, 110, 126, 145, 153-155, 194-203, 230, 248, 253-254, 311-312, 323, 374, 382-383, 406, 467-469, 492, 540
limitation	160

location	6, 80, 83, 129, 212, 266, 269, 270, 272-274, 432, 449, 455, 505
lsd	103-105, 583
management	1-2, 8, 10, 12-13, 15, 25-26, 39-40, 48-49, 51, 80, 83, 143, 165, 189, 197, 224, 226-227 , 232-233, 272-275, 298, 303, 364, 368, 370-373, 380-381, 385, 388, 391,-393, 395-396, 398-399, 403-404, 408-409, 411, 427, 430, 444, 557
merit	129
mother	87-88, 141-143, 231
offender	12, 116, 476-477, 497, 569
organisation	53, 143, 162, 164, 182, 190, 230, 182, 307, 415-416
overcrowded	47, 76
parent	54-55, 90, 171, 273-274
parkhurst	3, 5, 17, 21, 44-45, 81, 546, 592
parole	14, 32, 44-46, 64-68, 74, 109-110, 120, 126, 135-138, 158-159, 196-197, 200-203, 229-230, 248, 267, 277, 251, 509, 513, 552
partner	69-70, 172

people	13, 16, 39, 44, 48-49, 51, 53-60, 62-63, 68-69, 74, 93, 96-101, 113-116, 118-120, 167, 181, 193, 216, 259, 429, 437, 457, 476
photograph	329, 353, 392, 395, 397, 398, 422, 551-512
police	15, 23, 26-28, 33, 46-47, 49, 64, 67, 70, 83, 86, 91, 96-101, 120, 124, 138, 150, 162, 146, 150, 162, 164, 176, 184-185, 192, 195, 198, 203, 233, 268, 279-293, 296, 300, 310, 317, 327, 329, 370, 379, 391, 411, 413, 419, 428, 448, 469, 489-491, 513, 523, 526-528, 532-537, 540-543
policy	1-2, 7, 9, 11, 13, 15-18, 24, 38, 40, 45, 49, 51-52, 87, 98, 112-113, 117, 124, 130, 133-134, 138, 141-142, 153, 160-161, 172-175, 178-179, 194, 201, 215, 218, 225, 233, 247, 286, 428, 520
population	46, 76, 78, 83, 90, 93, 99, 130
pregnant	36, 112, 435, 504
premises	45, 101, 163, 292, 357
privilege	20-25, 27, 166, 167, 169, 179, 186, 212-214, 284, 309-310, 317-318, 321, 323, 502, 505
probation	12-13, 46, 49, 74, 88, 114, 139, 142, 146, 159, 162, 167, 180, 186, 195, 198, 202-203, 235, 237, 414-415. 417-419, 507

proceedings	22-23, 27, 34, 64, 66, 70-71, 79, 144, 177, 180, 186-187, 190, 195, 203, 220, 233, 245-249, 264, 283, 288, 290-291, 310, 315, 328, 335, 337, 356-357, 363, 382, 384, 394, 396, 423, 438, 440, 443-444, 446, 450, 459-460, 468, 491, 511, 518-519, 521, 528, 533-535, 541, 543, 546, 552-554
procedure	12, 15, 17-18, 26, 129-130, 132, 147, 176, 185, 187, 192, 223, 225, 228, 237, 265, 267, 283, 351, 429, 433, 441-442, 450, 492, 513, 517, 521-524, 530, 544-545, 547, 553, 582
protection	11, 20, 29, 31, 56, 61, 83, 96-97, 118, 138, 149, 169-170, 172, 185, 190, 192, 201, 209, 211, 269, 280, 322, 325, 372, 383, 389, 542, 582
psychological	80, 137
public	9, 19, 26, 29-33, 35-39, 41, 43-45, 47, 49, 52-53, 55, 61, 63-64, 67-68, 70, 74-75, 86, 91-92, 100, 102, 111, 119, 124, 131-132, 140, 149, 161, 162, 164, 169-170, 172, 175-176, 179-180, 184, 190, 196-197, 201, 204, 217-219, 224, 231, 246, 248, 254, 284-286, 292, 296, 311, 317, 321, 325, 329, 341, 351, 373, 379. 387-388, 390, 395-396, 402-403, 405, 413-414, 417-419, 430-431, 436, 441, 507, 533, 539, 541, 543, 554, 560, 572

liability	6, 39, 282
limitation	160
medical	5, 10, 29, 30, 36, 39, 45, 79, 82, 84-85, 88, 128, 135, 140, 142, 146, 175, 195, 198-199, 228, 253, 256-257, 266, 288, 310, 315-320, 332-334, 347, 382, 435-437, 449, 453, 458, 463, 468, 471-472, 506, 508, 511-512, 522, 526, 549, 556, 565, 569, 576
remand	6, 8, 13, 21, 32, 76-77, 79, 85, 125, 135, 153-155, 167, 186, 199, 217, 267, 347, 376, 389-390, 399-405, 407, 409, 412, 432, 452, 513, 557, 565
repatriation	145-147, 232
report	3-4, 12-13, 36, 39, 49, 51-52, 62, 76-77, 83, 86, 88, 92-93, 97, 99, 112-113, 118, 124, 160, 177, 205, 216, 224, 234-235, 237, 239, 244, 268, 277, 288, 297, 316-317, 357-359, 368-370, 427-429, 431, 434, 436, 452-454, 491, 493, 501-502, 512, 514-515, 522, 526, 544, 553, 557, 582
research	52, 73-74, 79, 90, 93, 97
resettlement	69, 82-83, 129, 141, 197, 199-202, 330, 331, 535
resource	117, 434

review	3, 5, 9, 11-12, 17, 34, 39, 41, 44, 64, 66-68, 70, 79, 89, 109-110, 132, 134, 141, 159, 161-162, 183, 186, 196-197, 202-203, 212, 214, 218-219, 229-230, 248, 270-272, 327, 345, 424, 446, 449-450, 512, 517-518, 534, 543, 545-546, 552-553, 555, 557
risk	30, 32, 34, 36, 41, 52, 75, 77, 79-80, 88, 97-98, 118, 120, 125, 128, 130-133, 135-136, 140, 141, 144, 149, 164-165, 172-173, 177, 182-183, 190-191, 193, 196-197, 199, 202, 206, 208, 210, 217, 219, 252, 275, 277-281, 310, 316, 429, 435-436, 445, 448, 465, 514, 531, 538, 551, 556
routine	26, 137, 184-186, 188, 192
safeguard	8
scheme	64-65, 70-72, 78, 143, 148, 158, 160, 176, 209-211, 213, 216, 246, 250, 277, 454
school	48, 57, 74, 96-98, 100-101, 105, 112, 114, 300, 320
security	19, 21, 25-27, 35-36, 41, 44, 50, 77-79, 81-83, 86, 88, 93, 123-141, 143-144, 146, 157, 168-171, 176-178, 181-182, 184-185, 187-188, 190-193, 205, 207-208, 219, 229-230, 232-233, 267-268, 274, 276-277, 286-288, 292, 294, 296, 317, 321-322, 325, 328, 331, 336, 395, 397, 427, 436, 442-443, 457, 488, 514-515, 538-539

sex offender	81, 83-84, 192, 215, 269
standards	6, 12, 38-39, 110, 171, 210, 212-213, 282, 309
statutory	5, 8-9, 12, 16-17, 23, 25, 31, 36-37, 39-40, 43, 45, 145, 149, 151, 161, 166-167, 179, 202, 211, 224, 235, 237-238, 246, 255, 264, 305, 395-396, 410-411, 421, 505, 520
sue	299
suicide	39, 86, 93, 118, 163, 165, 270, 556
telephone	27, 137, 167, 169, 173-174, 188-194, 229, 266, 271-272, 289, 391, 454, 506-507
transfer	41, 78-79, 91-92, 132-135, 144-145, 147-148, 168, 180, 183, 195, 212, 232, 234, 273-277, 310, 333, 387, , 399, 433, 449, 556
transport	75, 96, 99, 169, 220, 283
treatment	3, 8, 13, 36, 39, 45, 48, , 50, 59, 66-67, 81, 84, 85, 93, 119, 123, 137, 146, 157, 160, 175, 183, 186, 195, 199, 215, 217, 228, 231, 287, 297, 307308, 310, 357, 364, 36-369, 375, 381-382, 404, 472, 556-557
unit	79, 81, 88, 116, 127-128, 142, 185, 197, 201, 230-233, 267, 270, 272-273, 275, 279, 343, 346-347, 432, 435, 449, 485, 504, 509, 510, 513, 527, 562, 564-565, 575-576

visit	4, 113, 166-169, 173-174, 177, 194, 196, 199, 202, 237, 243, 261-262, 287, 290, 310, 313-314, 322-324, 326, 339, 353, 358, 365, 368, 374, 380-381, 404, 442, 449, 455, 486-487, 502, 508, 515, 559, 570
wandsworth	76-77, 553, 597
warrant	27-28, 127, 155, 245, 283, 375-376, 385, 407, 466, 533
website	241, 532, 582
welfare	10, 87, 111, 141-142, 166, 172, 180, 182, 191, 230, 316, 323, 553
whitemoor	21, 77, 79, 117, 205, 207, 598
women	10, 36, 46, 75, 84-87, 89, 124, 140-141, 211, 313, 371
worker	96
wounding	151

Lightning Source UK Ltd.
Milton Keynes UK
UKOW041945040712

195483UK00009B/1/P